The surrounding countryside and the Chianti region

Touring Club of Italy

Touring Club of Italy
Chairman: *Giancarlo Lunati*
Chief Executive Officer: *Armando A. Peres*

Editorial Director: *Marco Ausenda*

Managing Editor: *Ada Mascheroni*

Senior Editor: *Anna Ferrari - Bravo*

General Consultant: *Gianni Bagioli*

Jacket Layout: *Federica Neeff*

Map Design: *Cartographic Division - Touring Club of Italy*

Authors: *Paolo De Simonis* (The Development of Florence and its
Surrounding Territory); *Maria Monica Donato* (Artistic and Cultural Development);
Stefano Miliani (Florence: Instructions for Use); *Martino Sacchi
and Giorgio Filippi / Ready-made, Milano* (from chapter 1 to chapter 10);
Bruna Buldrini and Maria Cecilia Picchi / K&B News Foto, Firenze
(Information for Travellers).

Translation and adaptation: *Antony Shugaar*

Copy Editor: *Derek Allen*

Drawings: *Antonello and Chiara Vincenti*

Layout: *Studio Tragni*

Production: *Stefano Bagnoli*

Picture credits: *Action Press: G.B. Gardin* 143;
Archivi Alinari: 19, 21 40, 56, 59, 60; *Archivi Alinari/Giraudon:* 17, 55, 57, 98, 100;
Archivio T.C.I./Gieffe: 13; *G. Arici:* 33; *Image Bank: L. Castañeda* 48, 75,
G. Colliva 90, *S. Dee* 50, *M.E. Newman* 71, *G.A. Rossi* 114, 126; *M. Mencarini:* 148;
G. Veggi 3; *G. Neri: G. Veggi/White Star* 10; *G. Neri: G. Veggi* 25, 85, 86, 102;
E. Papetti: 14, 109; *Polis: P. Ongaro* 83; *Stradella: D. Ceresa* 140,
M. Pacifico 9, 66, 79, 95, 112, 137, *A. Vergani* 23, 28.

Cover: *Image Bank: S. Allen*; *Archivi Alinari*; *Stradella: M. Pacifico*.

Foreword

Florence has been the cradle of many civilizations – that of the ancient Etruscans, the civilization of the Renaissance, the modern civilization of banking and trade, and the Victorian rediscovery of the pleasures of the Mediterranean. So, for any citizen of the modern world, a trip to Florence is, in some deeper sense, a voyage home, a journey to one's birthplace.
Florence is one of Italy's greatest cities, and one of the world's finest treasuries of art. It is every year the destination of millions of tourists.

To make your way through the madding crowd to the true pearls that Florence can offer to those who know how to find them, this book offers vital information.
There are two introductory chapters, which recount the history of Florence, along with its artistic and cultural development.
A third introductory chapter offers all of the suggestions you will need to tour Florence at its best. The central well of the book is broken down into 10 chapters, 6 of which are devoted to the city, the discovery of the historical and medieval center, such great museums as the Uffizi, great building complexes  as Palazzo Pitti and the Boboli Gardens, and the surrounding hills. The other four chapters feature tours in the surrounding areas, of Fiesole, the Mugello, the Valdarno, and in Florentine Chianti. In all, there are a total of 26 routes to explore, many of them walking tours, to discover everything in the city and the surrounding area that is worthy of note.
A final chapter contains all the addresses that may prove useful, with listings of museums, cultural institutions, famous stores, and the finest restaurants and hotels.
The iconographic apparatus, as it were, is particularly rich: there are numerous photographs and drawings, specially made, roughly 40 maps and plans of museums and monuments, city plans showing the routes to follow, and a detailed 27-page city atlas.

Contents

Maps and Plans

How to Use this Guidebook

■ We have attempted to use the original Italian names of all places, monuments, buildings, and other references where possible. This is for a number of reasons: the traveller is thus made more comfortable with the names as he or she is likely to encounter them in Italy, on signs and printed matter. Note also that maps in this book for the most part carry the Italian version of all names. Thus, we refer to Battistero and Chiostro degli Aranci rather than to Baptistery and Orange Cloister. On first mention, we have tried to indicate both the Italian and the

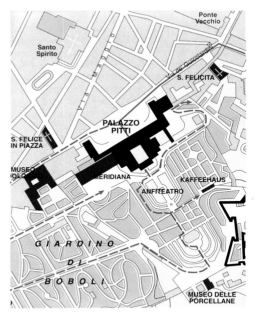

English equivalent; we have renewed this dual citation when it is the first mention in a specific section of text. In Italian names, one of the most common abbreviations found is "S." for "saint" (and "Ss." for "saints"). Note that "S." may actually be an abbreviation for four different forms of the word "saint" – "San", "Sant'", "Santo", and "Santa". Many other terms, while generally explained, should be familiar: "chiesa" is a church, "cappella" is a chapel, "borgo" and "via" are a street, "ponte" is a bridge, "museo" is a museum, "biblioteca" is a library, "torre" is a tower, "campanile" is a bell tower, "giardino" is a garden, "parco" is a park, "pinacoteca" is an art gallery,

The 15th-c. facade of the Church of S. Maria Novella, by Leon Battista Alberti

"teatro" is a theatre, "piazza" is a square, "ospedale" is a hospital, "porta" is either a door either a city gate.

Introductory Chapters. This guidebook opens with two chapters on the history of the city and its artistic development. Another chapter, "Florence: Instruction for Use", contains all the information you will need to organize your tour – from the addresses of Italian language schools to tips on how to use public transportation, from shopping suggestions to descriptions of the cuisine, from hints on the best times of year to visit to the most noteworthy cultural and folk events.

The Places to Visit. This section comprises 10 chapters, and is broken down into two parts. The first part – from chapter 1 to chapter 6 – is devoted to touring the city of Florence; the second part – from chapter 7 to chapter 10 – is dedicated to the countryside surrounding the city. Each chapter contains a number of routes – walking tours in the city, driving tours in the countryside – all accompanied by special maps.

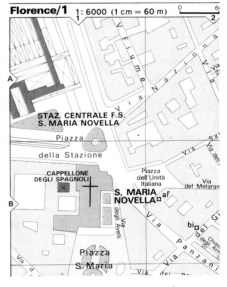

In all descriptions of monuments or landmarks differences in typography (names shown in **bold** or in *italics*) larger or smaller type size, and one asterisk (*) indicate the importance of each monument, museum, or other site. Written descriptions are accompanied by drawings and photos that help the reader to visualize works of art or architecture which he or she should not miss.

Information for travellers. A compendium of useful addresses, hotels and restaurants which suggests a selection of the finest hospitality facilities. Specific criteria are described on page 149. We provide information which is up-to-date as of the writing of this book. The reader should be aware that some subsequent changes may have occurred in hours or schedules.

Maps and plans. Monuments, hotels, restaurants, and other public facilities are marked on the Florence city atlas maps that appears at the end of this guidebook. Throughout this volume numeral in parentheses (5) indicate the map in question, while a letter and a number in parentheses (E2) refer to the sector of the map.
The notation *off map* indicates that the specific monument or location is not shown on the map.

Conventional Signs Used in the Maps

City maps

▭	Throughfares	⊞	Churches
▱	Main roads	▦	Gardens and parks
▱	Other roads	◻	Hotels
▭	Pedestrian ramps	•	Restaurants
▬■	Railroad lines and stations	✚	Hospitals
→	Walking tours	𝒊	Tourist information offices
▬	Particularly interesting monuments and buildings	⌒50	Contour map showing elevation and grade
◢	Interesting monuments and buildings	+++	Cemeteries

Excursion maps

⟹	Excursion, with direction followed	▨	Parks
▬	Highway	-----	Borders of countries
▬	Main roads	🏛	Villas
▬	Other roads	◩	Churches
▬	Stretch of scenic road	◪	Castles
⊙ **Certaldo**	Major places to see along the excursion	∴	Ruins
⊙ S.Lazzaro	Minor places to see along the excursion	▮	Monuments
○ Brozzi	Other places	✈	Airports
◹	Urban area		

8

The Development of Florence and its Surrounding Territory

Florence, enclosed within its walls

Ponte Vecchio was the strategic point around which the history of Florence and its surrounding territory developed. At first, there was just a ford; later, there was a ferry; finally there was a bridge. This area was chosen because there the Arno flowed at its narrowest, as it still does today. A second reason was the confluence with the river Mugnone, which created on the right bank an area protected by two watercourses. That was why Ligurian tribes settled here during the Neolithic; toward the end of the 10th c. B.C., Italic tribes, originating in the Tuscan-Emilian Apennines, followed the Ligurians. The Etr-

Panoramic view of the city with the Arno and Ponte Vecchio

uscans only passed through, establishing a ferry-crossing, where a barge shuttled back and forth; some slight distance away, and on higher ground, the Etruscans founded Fièsole, which, from the 6th c. to the 2nd c. B.C., ensured them strategic control over both the river passage and the road that ran along the valley of the Mugnone, and up toward the Apennine passes.

Florence was finally established as a Roman "colonia" in 59 B.C., during the springtime, the season of the "ludi florales" (hence, perhaps, the name "Florentia"). It was only a few years later that the first bridge was built across the Arno, slightly upstream from the site of the Ponte Vecchio. The plan of the new city was rectangular, with a perimeter of about 1,800 meters. It was protected by brick walls and round towers. There were two main thoroughfares, the "cardo" (running north-south) and the decumanus (east-west). The excellent location (the Arno was navigable, the Via Cassia ran nearby) encouraged the development of "Florentia," which, between the 2nd and 3rd c. A.D., boasted a population of over 10,000, had a river port, a theater and an amphitheater.

Following the collapse of the Roman Empire, the Byzantine walled perimeter (A.D. 541-544) contained fewer than 1,000 inhabitants; that perimeter was much smaller than the original one had been. Florence remained a marginal settelement under the Longobards, as well. It was not until the Carolingian era that signs of recovery began to appear: 2,000 inhabitants at the end of the 8th c. and nearly 5,000 inhabitants one hundred years later. The walled perimeter regained its Roman boundaries, save for on the north side.

After A.D. 1000, the city was profoundly caught up in the ecclesiastical reform movement; it became a major religious center, and a political force as well. By the middle of the 11th

c. the population had risen to 20,000. In part due to her fear of a military response on the part of the Holy Roman Emperor Henry IV, the countess Matilda of Tuscany decided (1078) to erect a new walled perimeter around Florence. This was the "cerchia antica," or ancient walls, described by Dante, equivalent in size to the Roman city and homogeneous in terms of layout and functions. In other words, the city had not yet assigned specific locations to various trades and activities, communities and organizations. There were no squares; only the courtyards of the many Romanesque churches (Santi Apostoli, S. Stefano al Ponte, S. Margherita). The first towers were being built, and the only true central structures were the baptistery, or Battistero di S. Giovanni, and S. Lorenzo, the first cathedral of Florence. At the turn of the 12th c., it could be said that Florentine society had already begun to take on the organizational structure of a Commune – a form of government typical of medieval Italy – even though recognition from the Holy Roman Emperor was not to come until 1183. Trade and crafts production – organized by the Arti, or Guilds – was growing considerably, both cause and effect of the rapidly swelling population: the new inhabitants took up residence in the *borghi* or suburban villages, that sprang up along the main thoroughfares radiating out from the chief city gates. Their names survive: Borgo S. Lorenzo, Borgo degli Albizi, Borgo de' Greci, Borgo S. Jacopo. When the population rose to 30,000, it became necessary, in 1172, to build a larger walled perimeter. This ring of walls extended across the Arno to the left bank, to protect the new settlements. Inside those walls, the urban structure remained by and large undifferentiated, studded with dozens of towers: these structures were the property of noble families and served as fortifications, much more than as residences (among the towers that still survive, let us mention the tower of the Visdomini, in Via delle Oche, and the tower of the Baldovinetti, in Borgo Santi Apostoli). The century that followed, however, more than any other period before it, was to determine the identity of Florence. Having regained its own surrounding countryside, the Commune, or city government, was to become the arena of a number of different struggles for power (amidst nobility, bourgeoisie, commoners, Guelphs, and Ghibellines), culminating de facto with the rise of the business and manufacturing class. Construction began on the Palazzo del Capitano del Popolo (literally, captain of the people; an office that was later called the "Bargello") in 1255. The unstoppable rise of trade – both domestic and foreign– made the city a major economic and financial player. The population swelled from 50,000 inhabitants in 1200 to 75,000 inhabitants in 1260, and to 100,000 inhabitants in 1300 (London had half that; Paris had twice that). Florence was not to attain these numbers again for another five centuries. Overall development continued despite the serious defeat in the battle of Montaperti (1260) at the hands of the Ghibellines; this loss was followed by the destruction of towers, houses, and palazzi. The Ponte Vecchio, which spanned the Arno, was soon joined by the Ponte alla Carraia (1218-20), the Ponte alle Grazie (1237), and the Ponte a S. Trìnita (1252). The rising "new" families began to build themselves residences that fit the typology of the *palazzo* (Palazzo dei Mozzi, Palazzo dei Peruzzi, Palazzo dei Frescobaldi), while the homes of commoners tended to comply with a standard layout – a few meters' frontage on the street, extending back into the center of the block. This layout can still be seen in many streets of historical central Florence.

The tower of Palazzo Vecchio

At the same time, to the east and the west of the city, in the heart of populous new "rioni," or quarters, the Dominican (1221) and Franciscan orders (1226) built convents; around them were built the basilicas of S. Maria Novella and S. Croce.

The level of construction that went on in the last twenty years of the century was remarkable, both in quantity and quality; the figure of Arnolfo di Cambio loomed over everything. In 1298 Arnolfo began work on the Palazzo dei Priori (later Palazzo della Signoria). As early as 1284 he began work on his most prestigious project, which was not completed until 1333: the new walled perimeter, 6 meters tall, with a tower punctuating the walls every 120 meters (in the Via del Baluardo, behind the Istituto d'Arte, you can see the best preserved section of wall). This walled perimeter enclosed a total of 430 hectares, and ran around a circumference of almost 9 kilometers. The walls enclosed not only the areas of new construction, but also broad areas of greenery, in anticipation of further developments. Such developments were not to occur for half a millennium.

Indeed, from this summit of achievements and expectations, Florence began to nose downwards, due to a series of disasters: the fire of 1306, the famine of 1315-17, the flood of 1333, and the plague of 1348. By the middle of the century the population had halved, and economic conditions were grim. In terms of urban development, there were no new projects. There was only completion of major public works already under way, especially along the central section lying between the Duomo and the Palazzo dei Priori: Campanile di Giotto (1334-59), Loggia del Bigallo (1352-58), Loggia della Signoria (1374-81), and Orsanmichele (1337-1404). Other projects – expansion, improvement, paving – were designed primarily to bring some order to the hodge-podge of new suburban villages, or "borghi," sadly in contrast with the regularity of Roman Florence. All this further solidified a basic urban layout that was to remain inviolable as long as the surrounding walls remained standing. All later projects – even the greatest works of genius – complied with this structure, tending to fit into it. Even the brilliant lifework of Brunelleschi – from the dome of the cathedral to the basilica of S. Lorenzo – tended to fit into existing projects and spaces.

While the economy was declining, the political structure was clearly tending toward autocratic rule, though not without opposition. From Cosimo the Elder (1389-1464) to Cosimo I the power of the Medici family progressed from fairly indirect to increasingly explicit; the Medici's power became fully institutional in 1570. In the earliest phase, the architectural influence of the Medici resulted mainly in efforts to display their prestige: the first Palazzo Medici (1444-64) stands in what was Via Larga (now Via Cavour), a northern extension of the Roman "cardo." Via Larga was the central axis of political and religious power, exemplified by the Palazzo dei Priori and the Duomo. Private construction tended to outweigh public works in volume, especially given the definitive triumph of the palazzo as the residential module of choice for the well-to-do mercantile bourgeoisie, situated especially at the fringes of the old city center (Palazzo Strozzi, Palazzo Rucellai, Palazzo Guicciardini): these are entirely independent buildings, which did not engender new complexes of construction; on the contrary, they tended to absorb the smaller existing buildings.

The rise of the Medici was met with numerous hindrances, including the check constituted by the siege of 1529-30 (with almost total destruction of all buildings neighboring the walls). The Medici however completed their rise to power with the return to Florence of Alessandro de' Medici: the Fortezza da Basso (1534), a fortress in which to take refuge and combat new revolts and uprisings, is a clear indication of the need of those holding absolute power to protect themselves *also* from internal threats. Cosimo I inherited a city of 60,000; he undertook a number of projects designed to bring order and uniformity to the city, fundamental steps in projecting an image and idea of a central State: Uffizi, Ponte S. Trìnita, garden or Giardino di Bòboli, reconstruction of Palazzo Vecchio (where Cosimo moved in 1540, transforming it into the residence of the sovereign of Florence).

Even under Cosimo's successors, the construction projects undertaken did little to modify the well-established urban layout, and in many cases constituted little more than adornments or theatrical touches. Following the brief reign of Gian Gastone, Tuscany passed into the hands of the House of Lorraine (or Lorena; 1734). Under Pietro Leopoldo (1765-92) came the suppression of many convents, which were then used as hospitals, hospices, and schools. The main focus of work was on the interiors of the palazzi and on the facades: the most extreme case came in 1792, with the plastering of the tower, or Torre di Arnolfo. There were no immediate major overhauls of the urban structure, neither under Ferdinando III nor during French rule. These governments, however, did slowly foster a cultural climate that encouraged planning and design. In that way, a consensus was finally reached concerning the most important points in the urban layout of Florence; specific agencies and institutions were selected to solve the issues in question. Florence had a population of 73,000 in 1810, which rose to 94,000 in 1851. The French Séguin company was given a contract in 1835 to build two iron suspension bridges (corresponding to what are now Ponte S. Niccolò and Ponte alla Vittoria), the Via dei Calzaiuoli was widened (1841), a new quarter was built around the Piazza dell'Indipendenza (1844-55) and another was built across from the Cascine (1850-55). Behind the church of S. Maria Novella rose (1848) the new railroad station, called the "Maria Antonia." A company called the Società Anonima Edificatrice built the first "working-class housing" (1849), taking inspiration from Belgian and French models. These "case per lavoratori" still stand on the Viale Strozzi.

Florence: from capital of Italy to capital of tourism

In the first census of the population of a unified Italy, Florence was shown to have 114,568 inhabitants as of 31 December 1861. That number had already risen to 146,441 when the city became Italy's new capital, from 1865 to 1870, resulting in the arrival of 20,000 new inhabitants. That was a large and sudden increase, and it came in an economic and urbanistic context that was wholly inadequate to the challenge.

The urgent demands of the new capital of Italy found improvised solutions, with ministeries being set up in the monumental buildings obtained through the suppression and expropriation of ecclesiastical institutions: the Ministry of Public Education was set up in the convent of S. Firenze, the Ministry of the Treasury in the Badia, the Ministry of the Navy in the convent of the Padri delle Missioni.

The need for change was felt generally, and it led to an incessant "construction-yard" atmosphere in Florence, over which towered the figure of Giuseppe Poggi (1811-1901), executor and strategic planner of these projects: his "overall plan for expansion" was developed to satisfy a forecast population increase of 50,000 inhabitants. The idea was to reshape Florence, moulding it into a European capital through a series of major public works projects. The first and most significant of these projects involved the demolition of the 14th-c. walls; in their place the "viali di circonvallazione," or ring roads, were built: a complete subversion of meaning which transformed a centuries-old barrier into a modern artery of communication. Only the city gates were spared: they too were transformed, however, from centuries-old nodes of transportation into new monumental urban furnishings, at the center of broad squares.

This busy pursuit of renovation and expansion came to a sudden halt after 1870, when the capital was moved to Rome. The most daunting project of those years was the "renewal" of the historical center, a project which required the demolition of the Mercato Vecchio and the Ghetto Ebraico. This project had long been the subject of furious debate, because this area – corresponding to the Florentia built by the ancient Romans – was particularly rich in architectural relics and reminiscences, but appeared badly neglected and rundown. Conditions of health and sanitation were unfit for a city that hoped to become a part of modern Europe.

It is well known, on the other hand, that "urban renewal" was prompted as much by motives of greed as by ambitions to improve the life of the city. In concrete terms, the great renewal program that was launched in 1885 meant the almost wholesale destruction of landmark buildings. In their place rose constructions that may have been debatable esthetically, but which were in fact intended for the benefit of the upper classes, in terms of costs and end-use: the new structures were certainly not built for the working-class inhabitants of the previous buildings. These people, along with those made homeless by the major demolition done to build the three new markets, crowded into the already over-burdened quarters of S. Croce and S. Frediano.

Beginning in the 1880s, however, the economic crisis began to ameliorate, particularly with the consolidation of the chemical and steel industries. Tourism played a decisive role. Following the 19th-c. phase of elite visitors – who often resided more than toured (especially the English "colony") – Florence moved toward mass tourism: 105,914 visitors in 1929, 160,221 in 1933. Overall, the economy experienced periods of crisis that coincided with wars, even though a number of companies profited over the short term, and on a "special" basis. The economy was particularly bad during the 1930s. Urban expansion, during this same period, was not the result of any coherent plan, nor was it "guided" by the force of attraction of any major structural identity: it was an uncontrolled growth, spreading out like oil over the countryside, along the grid of the old road system and along the railroad tracks.

WW II of course put an end to the growth of the city, but only for a short while, not for good. In 1945 Florence had: 16,400 rooms destroyed; 24,000 damaged; primary infrastructures, communications, and health care facilities almost annihilated; and 150,000 out of work. In 1946 the population had risen to 390,972, and the Fifties and Sixties produced major changes in the city. The manufacturing sector grew by 58 percent – one of the highest rates in all Italy – largely due to the flow of population out of the countryside, marking the end of "mezzadria," or sharecropping. The population had risen to 436,516 by 1961. Tourism then took off as a true industry, attracting as many as 2 million visitors each year.

Sadly, Florence – like many other cities – was unable to match its economic growth with high-quality architecture and urban planning (the excellent Urban Regulatory Plan of 1962 was betrayed, or in any case it remained on paper).

The various processes that have brought about the modern-day appearance of Florence have been less intense and focused than was the case during the great postwar *boom*: migration from the countryside reached its limit, the number of inhabitants attained a plateau and then began to decline: 457,803 in 1971, 403,294 in 1991. Many industries, especially after the flood of 1966, moved to outlying villages and towns; employment in the service industries rose to 70 percent; the tourist trade rose to peaks of as many as 6 million visitors a year. The risks of slipping into "service-industry ghet-

The refectory of S. Croce immediately following the floods of 1966

toization," then, are counterweighed by the condition of an urban center plagued by traffic, both of cars and pedestrians. On the ring roads, cars have erected – in a post-modern twist – a wall of metal and plastic that is as effective a barrier as the city walls once presented. And it is not uncommon to find your way barred by walls of human beings, in the little streets of the historic center, in front of the Uffizi, on the Ponte Vecchio.

Dialogue between environment and cultures

The province of Florence has a total surface area of 3,537.26 square kilometers, chiefly hilly, with a few high peaks and even fewer level plains.

The overall orographic system comprises three mountain ranges running from NW to SE: the Apennines, the range consisting of Monte Morello-Monte Senario-Monte Giovi, and the massif of Monte Albano. The Apennines have the highest peaks in the province: many tower above 1,000 m., and the highest altitude is 1,654 m. at the peak of the Monte Falterona. The hydrographic system is quite simple, on the other hand, and is based on the river Arno, which runs through the entire territory: major tributaries along the right bank are the Sieve, the Bisenzio, and the Ombrone; among those flowing into the left bank are the Greve, the Pesa, and the Elsa.

This is the natural and morphological terrain with which human cultures have interacted for so many millennia, shaping it in diverse fashions. The Apennine massif, in this sense, has played diametrically opposing roles at different times: the massif greatly hindered communications until a series of high passes were discovered and improved the situation. The Arno, an obstacle to communications until it was spanned by bridges, was for centuries a veritable fluvial roadway. The Vikings are thought to have sailed up it all the way to Florence; as recently as the turn of the 20th c., great rafts of newly felled trees were floated down the Arno to Pisa. These huge logs came from the forests on the slopes of the Apennines and the Pratomagno. Similarly, the medieval wool trade flourished up and down the course of the Arno. During the 16th c., the river was subjected to massive works of embankment; its course was straightened, so that it no longer looped and wandered through the flatlands upstream and downstream of Florence. The threat of flooding, of course, remains notoriously ever-present. The great and disastrous flood of 1966 was the last in a long series. There have been more than 50 floods since 1177. Note the numerous plaques on the walls of the historical center of Florence marking the high-water mark; the oldest dates from 4 November 1333, in Via di S. Remigio, at the corner of Via dei Neri.

Partly as a result of the interaction of cultural history and the environment, the boundaries

A "villa-fattoria" or farmhouse-villa on the hills of the Chianti area

of the province of Florence are not the same as the natural borders: mountain ranges and rivers tend to cross the province rather than to border it. Even the natural barrier of the Apennines, in part reinforced by various cultural aspects (from language to food), is politically meaningless. The border, for military and historical reasons, runs past the Apennine watershed, cutting crosswise across the valleys of the Santerno, the Senio, and the Lamone.

From the "centuria" to the "provincia"

The word *Arno* is derived from the root *arna*, literally, "deep river-bed," found also in France and Switzerland; likewise, *Monte Albano* is linked to a cognate root, *alba/alpa*, "rock," a derivation that explains both *Alba Longa* and *Alps*. These are both etymologies that date back before Latin, and may be traced to the Ligurian tribes, whose territory extended in fact to the hills and marshland of the Arno valley to the east of Monte Albano: an area that also marked the point of contact – and friction – with the southward-thrusting Etruscans. This is attested by the archeological remains of Fièsole and by the tombs of Quinto, Comeana, and Artimino.

The mark left by the Roman conquest that ensued can still be seen in old place names (the towns and villages of *Quarto, Quinto, Sesto,* and *Settimello,* were named for their respective distances from Florence along the Via Cassia) but especially in the context of the system of centuriation: this was the subdivision of the territory into square lots called "centuriae," or hundreds, as they were made up of 100 lots of lands comprising two "jugera" each, an ancient Roman land measurement equivalent roughly to 5,000 sq. m. These lots were assigned by lot to the "coloni." The land was thus divided into a regular grid, made up of trails, ditches, and embankments; it can still be seen in the plain to the west of Florence, between Castello and Prato.

In the high Middle Ages, the Longobard "judicaria" and the Frankish "county" substantially coincided with the Roman municipal partitions: in the context of a continuity that experienced some interruption in feudal times but returned when the Commune of Florence, consolidated internally, began the *reconquest* of the countryside in the 12th c.

The heritage of the late-Roman territorial organization, based on the country "villa," fell to the "curtis" of the high Middle Ages, which was later to become – in the functional context of feudal politics and economy, structurally modified by the addition of a walled perimeter and tower – the "castrum," or castle: between 1100 and 1300 there were more than 200 new towns in the territory (particularly well preserved are Sezzate, Nipozzano, and San Donato in Poggio).

In the general context of economic development from the year 1000 on, another major factor was the reorganization and redistribution of agricultural activity practiced by the monastic orders (Cluniac, Vallombrosan, Camaldolese, and – later – Cistercians) spread throughout the territory (abbey, or Abbazia di Vallombrosa; charter house, or Certosa del Galluzzo; abbey, or Abbazia di Montescalari; abbey, or Badia di S. Salvatore a Settimo; abbey, or Badia di Passignano; and convent, or Convento di Monte Senario).

The reappropriation of the countryside meant that the city of Florence came to blows with the various feudal alliances; this conflict ended in the triumph of Florence in the 13th c. Set as a seal of Florence's victory were the "terre nuove," or new towns, that were founded only a short while later, serving to unify and control these areas: thus, in the Mugello, Scarperia was founded in 1306 and Firenzuola in 1332. Both stood as bastions against the feudal clan of the Ubaldini. This political process went on simulatenously with an economic process that brought capital from the city to be invested in farmland through a type of contract called "mezzadria," or sharecropping: this peculiar institution was responsible for shaping both the human and physical landscape in a way that remained impressed upon central Tuscany right up until the 1960s, although with considerable variation over the years, of course. The landowner broke his property up into lots, or "poderi," and on each lot a family of "coloni," or settlers, lived and worked, giving up half of the yield of the lands to the landowner, and eking out a living on the other half. There was also a major architectural aspect to the "contratto mezzadrile," or sharecropper's contract: the landowner lived part of the year on his lands in buildings that ranged from the "casa-torre," or tower-house (which again mirrored an urban residential type shifted to the countryside) all the way to the "villa-fattoria," or farmhouse/villa; the "colono" lived in the center of the lot, or "podere," in a set of buildings that eventually developed into the typology known as the "casa colonica," especially from the second half of the 18th c. on.

Historically speaking, the towns which developed during the Middle Ages remained fairly stagnant (except Prato) for many centuries. The towns that have developed most solidly in the recent past are Empoli and especially Sesto, Scandicci, Bagno a Rìpoli, and Pontassieve: the result has been a true greater metropolitan area, with notable shifts in patterns of working and residence. A centuries-old tradition of agricultural production – based on sharecropping – developed into industrial activities fairly late, without any particular ties to previous crafts traditions (such as cutlery at Scarperìa or ceramics at Montelupo). A more profound sense of continuity may be found in those attitudes (familiarity with the market, multi-professional training, family-based organization) which seem to have been handed down from the sharecropping tradition to the small-business approach common to companies in this region.

Currently, the economic situation is quite differentiated. The strongest areas are those around Florence and the lower Valdelsana, respectively for machine tools and local manufacturing. Emerging industrial areas are the Valdarno and Chianti (due to the strong ties with the primary sector). In the Mugello-Val di Sieve, alongside the strong surviving primary sector, one must distinguish between the booming companies (in all categories) in the lower valley, and the poor performance of the geographically isolated Apennine areas. Tourism seems to be concentrated in elite resorts in the Chianti area, sharply differing from the mass tourism of Florence proper.

Artistic and Cultural Development

The origins and the Duecento, or 13th c.

Dante, in his *Paradiso*, evokes the austere Florence of his forebears, enclosed within the "cerchia antica," or ancient walled perimeter, built by the countess Matilda of Canossa (1078). The earliest major Florentine monuments date from that period, the time of the city's first moves toward independence: the basilica of S. Miniato al Monte and the Battistero, or baptistery. The two-color geometric patterns, which emphasize the interior structures on the exterior marble facings (classical influence, unique in European Romanesque), were to become, in the centuries that followed, a model of architectural clarity and rigor. Here too a tradition was born of creating beautiful public buildings without regard for expense: consider the mosaics of the Battistero; the project was begun in 1225, and was completed a century later.

The truly impressive burgeoning of monuments and culture – which was soon to set Florence apart, unrivalled – began during the decades of economic expansion that marked the construction of the outermost, immense walled perimeter (1284-1333). As early as the mid-13th c., when the florin was first coined, the Commune took up offices in the massive building that is now the Palazzo del Bargello (1255), the first of the many civil and sacred buildings that over the course of the next few decades were to constitute a new urban layout. Giovanni Villani, the 14th-c. chronicler, wrote that Brunetto Latini was the "beginner... of the refinement of the Florentines... in fine speech and in... leading the Republic." At the end of the century, Florence was a giant construction yard, a hotbed of culture and fine art. The transformation of traditional approaches, the growing awareness of a larger culture, extending beyond the city walls, and a newly rigorous style linked art and architecture with the blossoming of poetry of the "Dolce Stil Novo."

The leading figure in the city's new structure was Arnolfo di Cambio, architect and sculptor: his buildings – the Franciscan church of S. Croce (S. Maria Novella, a Dominican church, was already under construction), the new city hall (now Palazzo Vecchio), and the cathedral or Duomo (later enlarged) – are expansive, majestic, and beautifully structured; they feature pointed arches and cross-vaults, in contrast with the vertical soaring thrust and decorative approach of the Gothic style. The facing of the Duomo borrowed from the sober geometric decoration of the Battistero, or baptistery. The same "classical" proportion and measure, inherited from Nicola Pisano (from the middle of the 13th c. on, Pisa had been a major center of artistic innovation) and long practice in Rome, can be seen in his sculptures – solid and square-hewn – for the unfinished facade of the Duomo (1296-1302; now in the Museo dell'Opera).

The Trecento, or 14th c.: from the age of Dante and Giotto to the late Gothic

In painting, such solid figures can only be seen in the work of Giotto. Cimabue, who was Giotto's teacher (who had also been powerfully influenced by the Pisan and Roman styles), began to push the boundaries of the immutable and abstract formulas of Byzantine art, which till then had been the rule; Giotto completely discarded those formulas, in part under the influence of new ideas in sculpture. In the frescoes of Assisi (the 1290s), painting grasped and portrayed the depth of space for the first time, along with the volume of bodies and objects, the gestures and emotions of human beings, the settings in which people move and operate. It was a true revolution – to see its true dimensions, compare Cimabue's Crucifix in the church of S. Croce (badly damaged by the flood of 1966), nuanced by chiaroscuro but still heavily stylized, with the Crucifix by Giotto in the church of S. Maria Novella, ponderous and heavy like a real human body; or compare the Madonna di S. Trìnita by Cimabue with the Madonna di Ognissanti by Giotto (ca. 1310), a solid and human figure, set in a three-dimensional space (both are in the Uffizi). Giotto was sought after by the most illustrious clients in Italy. Around 1320 Giotto frescoed the chapels of the two wealthy banking families – the Bardi and the Peruzzi – in the church of S. Croce; here he attained a solemn majesty, in the wake of the stark drama he had portrayed in his frescoes in Padua. This work was to serve as inspiration to both Masaccio and Michelangelo. In 1334 Giotto was named Capomastro del Duomo, or head architect of the cathedral, on account of his great "scienza e dottrina," or learning and doctrine; he designed the Campanile or bell tower. His plans were partly modified after his death (1337). In terms of his historic stature, Giotto can be compared with Dante, his contemporary and fellow citizen (in Dante's *Divina Commedia*, written in exile, Florence is a constant presence). Both Dante and Giotto were great artists who enormously expanded the realm of reality which could be portrayed, respectively in painting and in verse. Both of them incorporated and outdid all prior experience, creating a new language, a decisive foundation for Italian art and literature. Until the middle of the century, Giotto's workshop propagated his new styles. Between 1330 and 1340, three pupils of Giotto worked in the church of S. Croce, where other leading members of the ruling Florentine bourgeoisie had their family chapels frescoed: Bernardo Daddi (who was perhaps more active in the production of panel paintings), Taddeo Gaddi, who created daring painted architecture, and Maso di Banco, who painted vast scenes, with pure and luminous colors. Giotto served as an inspiration to the sculptor Andrea Pisano, as well; from 1330 and 1342 Andrea executed major public projects: the first bronze door of the Battistero – here the solidity of the new style of painting was blended with an elegance worthy of French Gothic – and the first marble reliefs for the Campanile, or bell tower, possibly to designs by Giotto.

In the middle of the 14th c., an economic crisis and the outbreak of the plague (1348) marked a profound rupture in progress. Set against this backdrop, Boccaccio's *Decameron* staged a "human comedy" of penetrating psychological and social realism; in painting, on the other hand, realism lost ground, as many of Giotto's followers disappeared from the scene. In the 1350s and 1360s, the most influential artist working in Florence was Andrea Orcagna, who was also a noted architect and sculptor (he designed the Loggia della Signoria and built the tabernacle, or Tabernacolo di Orsanmichele); his habit of "casting" the great figures of Giotto in static poses, enclosed in narrow spaces (for instance, note the Pala Strozzi, an altarpiece, S. Maria Novella), was continued by many schools until the turn of the

"Madonna and Child" by Giotto (Uffizi Gallery)

15th c. Some artists worked against this trend, however: Giottino (Deposition from the Cross, Uffizi) and Giovanni da Milano (Cappella Rinuccini, S. Croce, 1365) added to the "structural" realism of Giotto a new attention to the more nuanced and subtle aspects of life: the texture of flesh, the qualities of cloth. This was practically a prelude to the late-Gothic style – elegant, spectacular, often steeped in a fairy-tale atmosphere, yet rich in vivid details – that was to dominate in late-14th-c. painting, until around 1420. Let us mention some of the various interpretations: the unreal, mystical Adoration of the Magi, by Lorenzo Monaco, with its undulating forms and its enameled hues (1422), hangs in the Uffizi, directly opposite from the crowded, sumptous, teeming naturalistic curiosity of Italy's most important late-Gothic artist, Gentile da Fabriano, in Florence from 1423 until 1425.

The Quattrocento, or 15th c.: from the Renaissance to the end of the "golden age"
Beginning in 1390, the economy recovered, and commissions began to be assigned for major sculptures once again, for buildings of great civic importance. Among those buildings were: the cathedral, or Duomo, the baptistery, or Battistero, the bell tower, or Cam-

panile, and the newly finished church of Orsanmichele, which the Arti (the professional guilds, major forces in Florentine political life) adorned with statues of their patron saints. Artists with great futures did their first projects: Lorenzo Ghiberti was victorious in the competition for the commission to do the second set of doors of the Battistero (1401). Ghiberti's submission was a piece of exceedingly late-Gothic naturalism (now in the Bargello, along with the competing work by Filippo Brunelleschi). Around 1415 however, the statues done by Nanni di Banco and Donatello for the Duomo (St. Luke and St. John, Museo dell'Opera) and for Orsanmichele (the Santi Quattro Coronati, or Four Crowned Saints; St. George, in the Museo del Bargello) marked a watershed. Gothic elegance gave way to a solid anatomical construction, a fierce and monumental stance that was clearly an emulation of ancient art (Donatello had already been to Rome, with Brunelleschi). These were the first sculptures of the Renaissance, civic and classical, like the culture of the period. Literature in the vernacular was in decline, humanists such as Coluccio Salutati and Leonardo Bruni rediscovered Greek and Latin literature, influenced by Petrarch (Florentine by descent), and emulated it in their civic involvement and dedication.

Roman architecture was the source of the techniques that Brunelleschi employed in designing and building the immense cupola of the Duomo, or catheral – this was a remarkable self-supporting structure, and it made Brunelleschi's reputation as an architect (1418). Antiquity and the Florentine Middle Ages – both Romanesque and the style of Arnolfo – remained sources of inspiration for Brunelleschi's buildings, from the Ospedale degli Innocenti (or foundling hospital, 1419) to the church of S. Spirito (ca. 1436). Their inimitable rigor – enhanced by the stone cornicework against white plaster – was the result of carefully calculated proportionate relationships and elegant geometric patterns. In the church of S. Lorenzo, built from 1420 on with the support and patronage of the increasingly powerful Medici family, the plan was based on a square module, while the funerary chapel (Sagrestia Vecchia) was a cubic room with a hemispheric vault. Brunelleschi's studies of the optical effects of geometric volumes led to the discovery of perspective, which Giotto had already grasped, empirically; Masaccio consacrated the used of perspective in painting, and brought Florentine art firmly into the Renaissance, in the same years during which Gentile da Fabriano was working in Florence. In the Cappella Brancacci al Carmine (stories of St. Peter, 1424-27) solid and stern figures – similar to the Prophets carried out by Donatello for the Campanile, or bell tower – stand solidly among rough urban or rural landscapes, rigorously portrayed in perspective. Thus, the moderate late-Gothic manner of the older Masolino, who worked on the project with Masaccio, appears dreamy and evanescent. In Masaccio's Holy Trinity (S. Maria Novella) the painted architecture was clearly Roman and influenced by Brunelleschi, while the Crucifix imitates the wooden Crucifixes that had recently been carved by both Brunelleschi and Donatello. Among these pioneers of the Renaissance, there was a full harmony and understanding. Leon Battista Alberti, the architect and humanist, came to Florence from Rome in 1434, and sang the praises – in his work *Della Pittura* – of the concerted rebirth of the arts.

In the same year, Cosimo the Elder extended the rule of the Medici over the city. Private patrons of the arts and building became pre-eminent: Cosimo had Michelozzo build the con-

The Church of S. Spirito

vent of S. Marco, as well as what is now called Palazzo Medici-Riccardi (from 1444 on); in a competition, Leon Battista Alberti designed – for the Rucellai family – the facade of S. Maria Novella and a majestic palazzo. Collections of books and art were formed; there was growing demand for domestic objects (like bridal chests). With the growing personalization of power and the Humanist cult of the individual, the portrait – in paint or stone – became increasingly popular. A new type of tomb that exalted the dignity of the dead therein laid (Bruni tomb, by Bernardo Rossellino in the church of S. Croce, 1450) developed as well. The classicism of Michelozzo, tempered by sober medieval details (rusticated facing), had more imitators than the rigorous architecture of Alberti; sculpture and painting also tended to wander from the radical approaches of the early pioneers. With the death of Masaccio at 27 (1428), a rough and severe style gave way to a more decorative approach: Filippo Lippi, who studied Masaccio's style, "pure without adornment," developed a more "graceful and ornate and mannered" style (Cristoforo Landino). Still, Masaccio's perspective found followers: the Dominican monk, Fra Angelico, was the first to copy it, though not its earthly realism so much as the evocation of a limpid and luminous space, worthy of divine perfection (frescoes of the Convent of S. Marco, 1438-46, and adjoining Museum). In the altar piece of S. Lucia de' Magnoli, by Domenico Veneziano (ca. 1445, Uffizi), the clear perspectival layout is immersed in springlike sharpness and clarity, embellished with minute descriptions, worthy of Flemish art; Andrea del Castagno concentrated on monumental portrayals of the human figure, set in ornate perspectival surroundings (Famous Men, ca. 1450, Uffizi; from Villa Carducci-Pandolfini); with Paolo Uccello, the passion for perspective went so far as to subvert its role in realistic portrayal, so that even the most riveting subjects were translated into abstract geometric research (Battle of San Romano, from Palazzo Medici; Uffizi).

Donatello (the longest-lived of the fathers of the Renaissance) never stopped experimenting with new techniques and forms; for Cosimo he created the bronze David, the first modern monumental nude (Bargello), as well as the stuccoes and bronze doors of the Sagrestia Vecchia in the church of S. Lorenzo. The solemnity of his earliest work gave way to a busy, unsettled manner (choir chancel of the Duomo, 1433-39, Museo dell'Opera); in his late years, the style turned tragic and tense (pulpits of S. Lorenzo, ca. 1460). Donatello worked alone: the twin chancel, by Luca della Robbia, has the same clean and composed grace as his work in glazed terracotta; Ghiberti, in the third door of the Battistero (1425-52), poured exquisite descriptive finesse into a new art of monumental sweep; and in the

Cameo portrait of Lorenzo the Magnificent

middle of the century, Desiderio da Settignano, an artist of "enormous grace and loveliness" (Vasari), established his reputation with the Marsuppini tomb in the church of S. Croce. The vibrant elegance of Desiderio and Lippi resulted, during the lifetime of Lorenzo the Magnificent, in a new artistic style of great refinement and skill. Andrea del Verrocchio created sculptures that were chiseled like so many jewels; for example, the monument to Piero and Giovanni de' Medici (Sagrestia Vecchia, 1472). The point of the needle of Italian political equilibrium, Lorenzo promoted a culture that was also an instrument of his own power and prestige: he worked to impose the Florentine vernacular – which flourished in poetry by Pulci, Poliziano (Politian), and Lorenzo himself – as the learned Italian language. Lorenzo sent artists – ambassadors of his style and taste – to work throughout Italy. Art, a new emanation of his court, was "private" and "elite" as never before: Lorenzo commissioned only one building, the Villa di Poggio at Caiano by Giuliano da Sangallo, a new type of suburban "palace."

One particularly interesting mirror of this culture can be seen in the work of Sandro Botticelli: in his Primavera (early 1480s, Uffizi) a classical myth is evoked with the idyllic elegance of the *Stanze* by Poliziano (the poet Politian), while the allegorical theme takes its inspiration from the doctrine of Marsilio Ficino and his Accademia Platonica, which met in the Villa di Careggi; this academy sought individual perfection in the synthesis between ancient knowledge and divine revelation.

The workshop of Verrocchio produced artists of a different nature and success: Ghirlandaio, who turned his brilliant flair for decoration to the celebration of the Medici milieu (Cappella Tornabuoni and Cappella Sassetti, in the churches of S. Maria Novella and S. Trìnita, 1485-90); Perugino, who was to be enormously successful with his sweetly solemn religious art (Lament Over the Dead Body of Christ, Galleria Palatina); and above all, Leonardo da Vinci, who was to extend the versatile approach of his master in the context of a universal scientific curiosity. In his Adoration of the Magi (Uffizi; left unfinished when Leonardo left Florence for Milan, 1482) he explored with the same subtlety human psychology and the nuance of forms in light; the composition, monumental and enveloping, inaugurated a new type of altar piece.

Michelangelo was educated and trained in the milieu of Lorenzo the Magnificent, in the school that sprang up around his collection of antiquities: this was the root of the constant reference to ancient times, and the love for poetry and Platonic thought, that we find in the artist. As early as the age of 15, Michelangelo revealed a monumental style taken from Masaccio and Donatello (Battle of the Centaurs and Madonna della Scala, 1490-92, Casa Buonarroti). In 1494, this "golden age" came to an end. Florence opened its gates to Charles VIII of France and expelled the heir of Lorenzo; the new Florentine Republic was led by the Dominican monk Savonarola, who inveighed against the luxury and indulgence of Lorenzo's reign. Michelangelo fled the city; Botticelli, converted to Savonarola's mysticism, rejected the Humanist tradition, and his work was filled with dramatic overtones (Calumny, 1495, Uffizi); Filippino Lippi (Cappella Strozzi, S. Maria Novella) and Piero di Cosimo (Liberation of Andromeda, Uffizi) produced a bizarre and biting art, which gives an unsettling and disturbing image of classicism itself.

The 16th c., or Cinquecento: later Renaissance, Mannerism, and courtly culture

The short-lived Republic was a period populated with great names. The chancellor was Niccolò Machiavelli; he retired to a life of study upon the return of the Medici (1512). He was to found, with the razor-sharp historical and political ideas of his book, *The Prince*, the theory of the modern state. Leonardo da Vinci and Michelangelo, who returned to Florence (1500-1501), were given major commissions, both public and private. In 1504 the young Raphael arrived; for the last time, Florence was an artistic capital. The David (1504, Accademia), established Michelangelo as an emulator of the ancients; although it had been intended for the Duomo, it was placed – as a symbol of the reborn republic – before the Palazzo Vecchio. Here, in the new Salone dei Cinquecento, Leonardo and Michelangelo were summoned to evoke the victories of Anghiari and Càscina; they completed only the preparatory cartoons, but they were so sensational that, from being copied so frequently, they were destroyed. Yet the duo went on to work in the same milieu, concentrating on religious painting: the Tondo Doni by Michelangelo (Uffizi), a powerful knot of brilliantly colored figures, is clearly a response to the soft chiaroscuro and the fluid compositions of Leonardo. The work of Leonardo was emulated instead by Fra Bartolomeo, an artist who painted spacious, solemn devotional images (Vision of St. Bernard, Uffizi), and by Raphel, who, in a variation on the theme of the sacred group, sought an increasingly natural compositional harmony. In his portraits, Raphael imitated the Mona Lisa, or La Gioconda (Madonna del Cardellino, Uffizi; Madonna del Granduca, portraits of the Doni, a couple, Galleria Palatina).

In 1506 Leonardo da Vinci returned to Milan; in 1508 Michelangelo and Raphael began working for Pope Julius II in Rome. In Florence, Andrea del Sarto remained faithful to a harmonious and monumental style of painting (frescoes in the cloister, or Chiostro dello Scalzo, 1507-26). Toward 1520, however, with his pupils Pontormo and Rosso Fiorentino, the equilibrium teetered. The period of Mannerism, fervid and brilliant, began: the style was marked by precarious compositions, irrational perspective, contrived poses; vivid colors, as in the Wedding of the Virgin Mary, by Rosso Fiorentino (S. Lorenzo) or diaphanous hues, as in the Deposition by Pontormo (S. Felicita). Perhaps this unsettling style was an indicator of the religious anxiety of the period; certainly this style of art was forced to deal with Michelangelo. Michelangelo, who returned after 1515 to work – as an architect as well as a sculptor – on the projects undertaken by Pope Leo X, and then by Pope Clement VII (two Medici popes), in the complex of S. Lorenzo, "did work that was quite different from that which men usually did" (Vasari). The vertical thrust, the plastic relief of the walls of the new funerary chapel (Sagrestia Nuova) unhinged the geometry of Brunelleschi's model of architecture and sculpture; in the vestibule of the Biblioteca Laurenziana, the unprecedented curving stairway was only a forerunner of all manners of Mannerist license. In the superhuman tension of the allegorical nudes for the Medici tombs, and in the Prisoners for the unfinished tomb of Pope Julius II (ca. 1530, Accademia), the conflict between spirit and matter took dramatic form, in a Platonic theme that was particularly congenial to Michelangelo as a poet, as well. These were the last masterpieces of an era in decline; in 1534 the artist returned to Rome, for good. The armies of the Holy Roman Empire had restored the Medici, who had been expelled once again in 1527. From 1537 on Cosimo I was securely in power under Spanish protection (he was to rule as grand duke from 1569). Guicciardini, the second great political writer of the 16th c., began his *Storia d'Italia*, a history of Italy, covering the previous forty years, years that had witnessed seemingly endless incursions of foreign armies across the Italian peninsula.

With the advent of absolutism, cultural life reorganized itself, re-forming around the new courts. While Florence lost its centuries-old primacy, the Accademia Fiorentina promoted the cult of Dante, Petrarch, and Boccaccio, while the Accademia della Crusca consecrated those authors as models of the Italian language; Giorgio Vasari, founder and sponsor of the Accademia delle Arti del Disegno ("disegno," or drawing, the "father" of the arts, is the pride of the Tuscan tradition), wrote a famous work entitled *Vite degli artisti* , or Lives of the Artists (1550-68) in which he defended and theorized the primacy of Florence, from Giotto to Michelangelo.

"Moses and the Daughters of Jethro" by Rosso Fiorentino (Uffizi Gallery)

Vasari was the architect and urban planner of the Uffizi, founded to contain the administrative offices of government; he was the creator of the daring "Corridoio Vasariano," which links the offices with Palazzo Pitti, the new Medici residence (1565). Francesco I preferred the multi-faceted Bernardo Buontalenti, who created in the Uffizi the Galleria and the exquisite Tribuna. Here, the treasures of the Medici family could be placed on exhibit (this is the oldest museum in Europe, therefore). Vasari also designed and built the first theater in Florence (1581-86); it was he who designed and decorated many of the villas and gardens of the first grand dukes: the grotto, or Grotta di Bòboli, is the fruit of his capricious fancy. Dominating the arts was a form of Mannerism, conceived as a quest for uncommon and exquisite elegance. Manufactories of precious products – such as tapestries – sprang up; there were plentiful productions of paintings and bronze figurines, intended for collectors. The developments in painting are nicely illustrated by the artists who worked in Palazzo Vecchio, from 1540 on: the impeccable Bronzino, who also did a series of superb, polished portraits of the members of the ruling family (Uffizi), and the exceedingly elegant Cecchino Salviati; Vasari led the team that, in dozens of allegorical, historical, and mythologic frescoes, exalted the Medici family as "dèi terrestri," or earthly gods (1556-72).

The new layout of Piazza della Signoria took into account new developments in sculpture, increasingly refined, and at the service of the powerful. The loggia contains two miracles of technical skill: the Perseus (1554) – upon which Benvenuto Cellini labored for decades, as he recounts in his fascinating *Vita* – and the Rape of the Sabines, by the court sculptor Giambologna, as a pure demonstration of virtuosity in composition (1583). The Fountain of Neptune, by Bartolomeo Ammannati (1575), celebrated the maritime ambitions of Cosimo I; the equestrian monument to Cosimo (1598), by Giambologna, crowned the new layout of the square.

The 17th c., or Seicento, and Florentine Baroque

From 1589 on the Uffizi housed scientific collections as well; in the 17th c., the greatest cultural developments in Florence were of a scientific nature. In 1610 Galileo Galilei became a guest of the court, shortly after his radical discoveries concerning the structure of the solar system; the Accademia del Cimento, founded by Leopoldo de' Medici (1657), undertook to apply Galileo's new experimental method.

In contrast with Rome, Florence was not particularly transformed by Baroque, which became popular here late, and even then largely in interiors. The models of the 16th c. were popular for many years: for the church of S. Gaetano, the most noteworthy of the very few buildings erected from scratch, there was an older design by Buontalenti, adapted by his follower Matteo Nigetti and later by Gherardo and Pier Francesco Silvani. The Cappella dei Principi (Nigetti), or chapel of the princes, the last addition to S. Lorenzo, had been planned ever since the times of Cosimo I (for its cladding in semi-precious stones, a special manufactory had been set up).

The production of paintings and frescoes was copious, though the most notable contributions came from outside Florence. From 1612 until 1621, the court had a biting, whimsical chronicler in the engraver of the house of Lorraine, Jacques Callot; another eccentric, the Neapolitan artist Salvator Rosa, painted somber landscapes and scenes of magic (1640-49). The centuries-old history of the celebrative decorations of the Palazzo Pitti (enlarged, though much of the original 15th-c. decoration was maintained) began with the exaltation of Lorenzo the Magnificent, in the spacious frescoes by the best local painter, Giovanni da S. Giovanni, who was educated in Rome (1634-36); a short while later Pietro da Cortona arrived, also from Rome; in the Sala della Stufa (hall of the stove) and the Sala dei Pianeti (hall of the planets) this artist revealed the dizzying and dazzling effects of Baroque, effects of which he was the unrivalled master. It was around 1670, under the pious and spectacle-loving Cosimo III, that it became common and standard practice to adhere to Roman Baroque: the finest example is the Cappella Maggiore, or main chapel, of the church of S. Maria Maddalena de' Pazzi. Among others, the Neapolitan painter Luca Giordano worked here; his luminous and vibrant work attracted the newly emerging dynasties, clans, and families: he frescoed the vaults of the gallery of Palazzo Riccardi (formerly Palazzo Medici), and in the Cappella Corsini at the church of the Carmine (1682-85).

The 18th c. and the Enlightenment

The last great Medici patron of the arts was Ferdinando, the son of Cosimo III. Keenly interested in enlivening the atmosphere in the city, Ferdinando de' Medici held the first art shows; he summoned Sebastiano Ricci to Florence, the founder of the great Venetian decorative style, but he also summoned the Bolognese artist Giuseppe Maria Crespi and the Genoan artist Alessandro Magnasco, who were developing a new and pungent realism, as well as the composer, Alessandro Scarlatti. With the death of Ferdinando (1713), the sponsorship of the arts by the Tuscan court virtually died out; with the extinction of the Medici dynasty, the throne passed to the grand dukes of Lorraine (1737), and the first of them ruled Florence from Vienna. Private initiative became fundamental: when the grand ducal manufactories languished, the Ginori family founded a porcelain manufactory (perhaps the most characteristic product of the 18th c.) and prospered enormously. In the meantime, a beginning was made at studying and organizing the enormous collections of books and art: the first were the immense collections bequeathed to the city by Anna Maria Luisa, the last of the Medici.

Pietro Leopoldo, the enlightened "philosopher-sovereign," brought the court back into the city of Florence (1765) and he undertook a vast series of reforms. He was the first in all Europe to abolish the death penalty; in an attempt to bring about a new approach to agriculture, he encouraged the studies of the Accademia dei Georgofili, founded in 1753. He was a reformer in the field of art, as well: the moribund Accademia del Disegno was replaced by the Accademia di Belle Arti, which was for many years thereafter an up-to-date and efficient academy of the arts. New renovations and decoration – in Palazzo Pitti (Sala Bianca), in the Villa di Poggio Imperiale, at the Uffizi – were carried out by sophisticated artists, up on the new styles of French classicism: the architects Paoletti and Del Rosso, the sculptor Spinazzi (he did the tomb of Machiavelli in the church of S. Croce), the painter Traballesi, the stucco artists of the Albertolli family. At the Uffizi, once again opened to the public, the art collections were newly ordered with clear educational intent, by the abbot Lanzi.

The 19th c.: Neoclassicism, Romanticism, and Realism

Florence under the house of Lorraine was an open and tolerant city, and welcomed Italian and European writers and artists, from Vittorio Alfieri to the French Neoclassical painter F.-X. Fabre. Neoclassicism was particularly successful under Napoleon, at the court of Elisa Baciocchi (1809-14); two figures of the Neoclassical school, Pietro Benvenuti and Luigi Sabatelli, led a major decorative campaign in Palazzo Pitti. The project, approved by the most celebrated artist of the time, Canova – who did the tomb of Alfieri (S. Croce) and the Venere Italica (or Italic Venus, Palazzo Pitti), to replace the famous Medici Venus, which had been carried off to Paris – was implemented following the restoration of the house of Lorraine (1815-24).

In the meantime, the cultural climate was changing. The sculptor Lorenzo Bartolini undertook a search for formal rigor, hearkening back to 15th-c. models (Carità, Pitti). Instead of classical themes, painters began to seek out episodes from medieval and Renaissance history, with clear political references: the Entrance of Charles VIII in Florence – by Giuseppe Bezzuoli (1829, Galleria d'Arte Moderna) – is an allusion to Napoleon. The same historical taste was responsible for the "period" facades of S. Croce and the Duomo (second half of the 19th c.) and the honor paid to Manzoni, in Florence from 1827 on, to work on his already famous historical novel ("I Promessi Sposi," or "The Betrothed"). Manzoni was in contact with the liberal milieu of the Gabinetto Scientifico Letterario, founded by G.P. Vieusseux in 1819. Vieusseux published a magazine called *Antologia* which was a mouthpiece for the pro-reform movement, seeking to make political, economic, and cultural changes. In 1833 Leopoldo II, the last grand duke, closed the magazine; this was the sign of a downturn in official culture, which could be detected in the arts as well.

The Accademia, clinging to an outmoded classicism, had in fact lost its position of leadership. Lorenzo Bartolini was the first to point the way to a new devotion to the real, or "vero" (tomb of the Countess Zamoyska, S. Croce); he was followed in this direction by the painters who began to meet at the Caffè Michelangiolo from 1855 on. The cafe was a meeting spot for young Italian patriots: Fattori, Lega, Signorini, Borrani, Cecioni, and others. They took the name of Macchiaioli: their approach to grasping an "impression of the truth" (Fattori) was through the juxtaposition of patches ("macchie") of color, as far as could be from the artificial polish of academic art. The subjects, too, were "veri," or realistic: landscape of the Tuscan countryside and coast, intimate domestic scenes; scenes of military life, entirely antiheroic, were particularly dear to Fattori. Following the harmonious activity of the 1860s, the group split apart; Signorini and Cecioni (the champion of a radical realism in the field of sculpture, too) began to look outward toward Europe; while Lega, Fattori, and Borrani, remained in Florence.

The 20th c., or Novecento

In the early-20th c., Florence was the source of many calls for reform. Gabriele d'Annunzio lived there for many years, a model aesthete and individualist; avant-garde journals – *La Voce* published by Prezzolini and Papini (from 1908), the Futurist *Lacerba* published by Papini and Soffici (from 1913 on) – led a campaign to bring Italian culture into the present. Although this campaign took anti-democratic, pro-war positions, it did encourage new and vital work (Serra, Cecchi, Michelstaedter) and a renewed Italian interest in European culture: French symbolism found an Italian echo in the poetry of Dino Campana. Between the two worlds wars, Soffici, once a follower of impressionism and cubism, advocated a return to local roots, and the "primitive" art of Ottone Rosai took its inspiration from the working class sections, or "rioni" of Florence; the Stazione, by Giovanni Michelucci (1935), clearly the manifesto of architectural rationalism, was the most successful modern addition to the fabric of Florence. New literary journals were founded in Florence: Montale, Vittorini, and Gadda wrote for *Solaria*, and lived in Florence for many years; hermetic poetry was founded (Mario Luzi continues to write in this style), and Pratolini made his debut. In the postwar period, other journals were founded, to encourage democratic culture (*Il Ponte* by Calamandrei) or new humanistic studies (*Paragone* by

Workshop for the restoration of ceramics

Longhi). In the 1950s and 1960s, the contributions of the Catholic left marked a new phase of militant culture (the educational ideas of Don Milani).

Nowadays, Florence is a busy educational center: aside from the University and such historic institutions as the Accademia dei Georgofili or the Gabinetto Vieusseux, there are many schools, some of which are non-Italian. There is an excellent school for restoration, fine crafts and artisanry (though the service industries are undercutting those trades), some publishing, and a thriving trade in books and antiques.

Florence: Instructions for Use

The cupola by Brunelleschi, Michelangelo's David, and the Uffizi are considered to be symbols of Florence, and rightly so; still, Florence does not live on Renaissance art alone. There is more, for better and for worse. For better, because the capital of Tuscany has an enormous historical and artistic heritage, much more varied than is commonly thought. Florence is also the site of numerous world-class scientific institutes. For worse, because the inertia and dead-weight of the past tends to hinder the dynamic potential of the city of Florence. Moreover, although it is a city of human dimensions, living there is expensive and sometimes difficult. In fact, the population is declining: the census of 1981 showed a population of 448,331, the census of 1991, only 403,294.

If this, by and large, describes the city, you cannot really know Florence until you have met the Florentines. Disputatious by nature, quick to engage in salty humor, they are so accustomed to having tourists in their midst that at first they ignore them completely; in fact, they are proud to live in a city that attracts so many admirers.

Because it is increasingly filled with hasty and frantic tourists, those who visit the capital of Tuscany would do well to avoid or go beyond the beaten paths taken by most visitors, ranging from the Galleria dell'Accademia to Piazza del Duomo, from Piazza della Signoria to Palazzo Pitti, with stops in Piazza di S. Croce or even up to Piazzale Michelangelo. These are certainly worth seeing, but the more authentic parts of Florence can be seen in the Oltrarno, in the quarters of S. Spirito and S. Frediano (as described by Vasco Pratolini), where an atmosphere still survives that elsewhere has been lost.

Aside from being a source of revenue, the presence of non-Italians in Florence is an old tradition. English, German, American, and French tourists – as well as many other nationalities – come to the capital of Tuscany to learn Italian, study art history, and work. At the outskirts of town (in the Badia Fiesolana) is the prestigious Università Europea, while many American universities have branches here; there is also a very active French Institute, various German schools, a German institute of art history (the so-called "Kunst"), the British Institute, and a Dutch institute of art history – they all bear witness to an ongoing cultural exchange between Florence and the rest of the world.

There are many **italian language schools** for non-Italians, which will also procure lodging in private homes. The *Centro di Cultura per Stranieri* in Villa Fabbricotti (Via Vittorio Emanuele II 64, tel. 472139) is run by the Università di Firenze; aside from offering courses in Italian for foreigners, this school offers courses in literature, Italian history, art history, music, and film. Among the private schools, let us mention a few that are particularly respected: *Eurocentro*, Piazza S. Spirito 9, with branches outside of Italy; *Centro Linguistico Italiano Dante Alighieri*, Via dei Bardi 12; *Scuola d'Italiano Linguaviva*, Via Fiume 17 (also a publishing house); *Lorenzo de' Medici*, Via Faenza 43, which also offers courses in graphics, architecture, and poetry; *Koiné*, Via Pandolfini 27, which employs particularly innovative methods.

The best times to go. In terms of weather, the best period ranges from late-March to the first half of June, or from September to October. Excessively hot and muggy in July and August, it is also advisable to avoid Florence at Easter, when it teems with tourists. From November to February, on the other hand, there is room almost everywhere, and you can visit museums without standing in line.

Unfortunately, the worst times to come are those when the most appealing **traditional festivals** are held. The most popular event is the *Scoppio del Carro*, a large fireworks display; it is considered a good omen for the city, and it occurs on Easter morning, in the space between the Duomo and the Battistero. Beginning in mid-June, *Calcio Storico*, or historic soccer, is played, with two semifinal matches and a final match; there is always a game on 24 June, the feast day of Florence's patron saint, John the Baptist. The game, much more violent than modern soccer, is exceedingly old (the earliest references date back to January 1491). It is played by the teams of the four quarters of the historic center: the Rossi (red team) of S. Maria Novella, the Verdi (green team) of S. Giovanni, the Azzurri (blue team) of S. Croce, the Bianchi (white team) of S. Spirito. Matches are played in Piazza di S. Croce, while tickets can be purchased at the Chiosco degli Sportivi in Piazza Anselmi (near the Piazza della Repubblica).

From May to September the Florentine countryside teems with feasts, festivals, and country fairs, usually bound up with farming seaons. Among the many festivals, note the Mostra Mercato del Vino Chianti Classico Gallo Nero – a wine fair – in Greve in Chianti, in the first half of September. Note the Festa dei Coltelli e del Ferro Battuto (wrought iron and knives), in late-August/September in Scarperìa. The Azienda di Promozione Turistica, or chamber of tourism, periodically publishes a calendar of popular events.

From April to June, the *Maggio Musicale Fiorentino*, or Musical May in Florence, is held; this festival was inaugurated in 1933, and is the oldest festival of operatic and symphonic music in Italy, as well as one of the most prestigious. You normally must purchase tickets far ahead of time (Teatro Comunale, Corso Italia 10, tel. 27791).

Important economic fairs include: *Pitti Moda* (fashion; spring and fall), in various locations; the *Mostra Mercato Internazionale dell'Artigianato* (handicrafts; late April/early May), at the Fortezza da Basso; the *Mostra Internazionale dell'Antiquariato* (antiques; September-October, odd-numbered years), in Palazzo Strozzi. As for events in the city, you can find a monthly publication in newsstands and bookshops, the *Firenze Spettacolo,* with up-to-date listings.

How to get there. The main routes to Florence by **car** are the *Autostrada del Sole A1*, the *Firenze-Mare A11*, which runs to Lucca and the Versilia, the *Superstrada Firenze-Pisa-Livorno* and the *Superstrada Firenze-Siena*. In the city of Florence, a car is nothing more than a burden, since most of the historic center is a "zona blu," or "blue zone," off limits to unauthorized traffic (the signs marked "Z.T.L."). If by chance your car is towed, the Parco Auto Requisite in Via dell'Arcovata 6, tel. 308249, can tell you where to pick it up. Of course, you will often be forced to use paid parking areas and lots (and they are often full). Open parking, with a custodian (hours 8 am-8 pm, Saturday 8 am-2 pm) is available at Porta Romana, Lungarno Torrigiani, Piazza Poggi (in Oltrarno); Piazza Beccaria, Piazza Vittorio Veneto, Piazza della Libertà, Piazza d'Ognissanti, and Via Alamanni. The largest parking lot – open

Flag bearers during the "Scoppio del Carro" display

24 hours a day – is at the Fortezza da Basso, on the train station side; this parking facility tends to be filled to capacity during the trade fairs of Pitti Moda and the Mostra dell'Artigianato. The largest enclosed parking facility open round the clock is located beneath the Piazza della Stazione; also note the Garage La Stazione, Via Alamanni 3a.

For those who choose to take the **train,** the *station of S. Maria Novella* is in the heart of town, and is well served by public transportation. The other stations are *Rifredi* (bus 28 to the center) and *Campo di Marte* (bus 18 and bus 19). Florence is connected with other cities in Italy and Europe by **long-distance coaches**: Lazzi, Piazza Adua at the corner of the Piazza della Stazione, tel. 215155, and Sita, Via S. Caterina da Siena 17, adjoining the Piazza della Stazione, tel. 214721.

Lastly, **air travel**. The *Aeroporto "Amerigo Vespucci"* is located in Perétola, in Via Termine 11, tel. 30615; for flight information, tel. 3061700; these is a Sita shuttle bus to the center, and taxis. In Pisa there is the *Aeroporto "Galileo Galilei"*, in the village of S. Giusto, linked to Florence by train; the trains (you must change in Pisa, but you can check your luggage through) leave and arrive every hour at the station of S. Maria Novella, where you can check in at the terminal of Binario (track) 5 (tel. 216073).

Information. It is generally a wise idea, when beginning your stay in Florence, to get in touch with one of the following **tourist information services**; while these offices will not make hotel reservations, they are helpful in other fields. *Ufficio Informazioni APT di Firenze*, Via Cavour 1r, tel. 2760382, weekdays 8:30-7:15 pm, holidays 8:30-1:30. *Ufficio Informazioni Turistiche del Comune di Firenze*, with two offices: Piazza della Stazione, under the cantilevered shelter, tel. 212245, summer 8:15-7:15 pm, winter 8:15-1:45 (hours subject to change); Chiasso Baroncelli 17-19r, tel. 2302124-2302033, hours as above. *APT* in Fièsole, Piazza Mino da Fiesole 36, tel. 598720, 8:30-1:30 from November to March and in August, 8:30-1:30, 3-6 from April to October, excluding August.

Before your departure, we heartily recommend **making hotel reservations**; here are some useful addresses: there is an information service called *Consorzio Informazioni Turistiche Ita*, with various offices: Office of the S. Maria Novella rail station, tel. 282893; Office of the Autostrada del Sole A1, Chianti Est (east) service station, tel. 621349; Office of the Firenze-Mare A11, a highway, Agip Perétola service station, tel. 4211800. A number of cooperatives will make reservations in their member hotels and pensioni. Here are some useful addresses: *Coopal*, Via Il Prato 2r, tel. 219525; *Family Hotel*, Via Trieste 5, tel. 4620080; *Florence Promohotels*, Viale Volta 72, tel. 570481.

For **camping**: *Federazione Italiana del Campeggio e del Caravanning*, Autostrada del Sole, Prato-Calenzano exit, via V. Emanuele 11, tel. 882391. In the high tourist season, campgrounds are filled to capacity. The camping areas that serve the city are located: in Viale Michelangelo 80, tel. 6811977; in Fièsole, in Via Peramonda 1, tel. 599069; in Bottai, on the outskirts of Florence, tel. 2374704 (bad for buses). For areas outside of Florence, consult the chapter "Information for travellers".

There are three **hostels**. The Ostello della Gioventù "Villa Camerata" is a youth hostel set in a handsome 15th-c. building, with park and camping area, located in Viale Righi 2-4, tel. 601451; you must have a youth hostel card. The other hostels are located: in S. Frediano, Via S. Monaca 6, tel. 268338; and via Faenza 94r, tel. 290804. Another solution for limited budgets is the Casa dello Studente "Gaetano Salvemini," a student dormitory, in Piazza dell'Indipendenza 15, tel. 4389603, open in the summer.

There is a genuine boom in **agritourism** in the Florentine and Tuscan countryside. The associations which can provide further information are: *Agriturist*, regional, Piazza S. Firenze 3, tel. 287838; *Agriturist*, provincial, same address, tel. 2396362; *Turismo Verde Provinciale*, c/o Confederazione Italiana Agricoltore, Viale Lavagnini 4, tel. 489760; *Terranostra*, c/o Coldiretti, Via dei Magazzini 2, tel. 280539. (In the chapter "Information for travellers" there is a selection of agritourism agencies in the province of Florence.)

Guided Tours. The *A.G.T. Firenze*, via Calimala 2, tel. 2302283, is an association including most authorized tour guides. They will organize visits to museums, palazzi, and monuments, either on foot or by bus, and in the surrounding areas as well (including Fièsole and Chianti). The *Cooperativa Sigma*, Viale Gramsci 9a, tel. 2478436, leads tours with an educational and cultural approach, to and through artistic and historical sites. Tourists can join organized tours on scheduled days, in Florence and in the surrounding areas. The *Sita Autopullman*, Via S. Caterina da Siena 17, tel. 214721-284661, organizes day-long outings – from March to November – to Pisa, Siena, San Gimignano; and year-round in Florence, with departures at 9:30 and at 2:30 from the agency *Lazzi Express*, in Piazza della Stazione 47r.

Trasportation. Most of the tourist itineraries in Florence are concentrated within the city walls, so distances are short and eminently walkable. What's more, only on foot can you move around with sufficient freedom to discover the remarkable allure of the old city. The center has, in any case, a good network of **city buses**, though the network is less efficient in the suburbs. You can get information, maps, and tickets at the offices of the *ATAF (Azienda Trasporti Autolinee Fiorentine, or municipal public transportation)*, in the structure located to the side of the station of S. Maria Novella, tel. 5650222. The tickets are for sale in cafes, newsstands, and tobacconists; they can be purchased for 60 minutes or for 120 minutes, for 24 hours, or in sets (eight 60-minute tickets). You must validate them as soon as you board a bus. For those who are not residents of Tuscany, the "Carta Arancio," literally, Orange Card, can be used on trains and public buses of the Florentine province.

To summon a **taxi**: call Radio Taxi, tel. 4390, or else 4798-4242.

Bicycling is a handy way of getting around, though there are virtually no bicycle lanes. Addresses for bicycle rentals (unless otherwise indicated, the season is from spring to September/October): *Ciao e Basta*, Via Alamanni at the corner of Piazza della Stazione, open all year round; *Alinari*, Via Guelfa 85r; *Bici Firenze*, Via S. Gallo 68r; *Motorent*, Via S. Zanobi 9r; *Promoturist*, Via Baccio Bandinelli 43. For a romantic ride in a horse-drawn **carriage** – for those who want to play the tourist to the hilt – the last twelve "fiaccherai," or hansom cabs, await customers in Piazza della Signoria and in Piazza del Duomo.

Bus lines offer pretty complete service throughout the province and the region. Here is a brief list of bus companies, with selected destinations: *Sita*, Via S. Caterina da Siena, at the corner of the Piazza della Stazione, tel. 214721, with service to Siena, San Gimignano, the Chianti area, Empoli, Valdarno, Val di Sieve; *Lazzi*, Piazza della Stazione 4, tel. 215155, with service to Prato, Arezzo, Piombino-Elba, Versilia; *Cap* (and *Copit*), Largo Fratelli Alinari 9, tel. 214637, with service to Impruneta, Prato, Poggio a Caiano, Pistoia, and the Mugello area. The national train service has recently reduced its service to local destinations. **Trains** leave from the station of S. Maria Novella, with service – in the province of Florence – to Borgo San Lorenzo, Empoli, Prato, and the Valdarno.

Foods and wines. Among the various local specialities traditionally served in Florence, pride of place goes to the "bistecca alla fiorentina," or Florentine-style steak, a slab of beef a couple of inches thick, traditionally grilled over an open flame, and generally eaten blood-rare. Other traditional dishes are "panzanella" (vegetables and soaked bread), or else "ribollita" (vegetables and bread, sometimes with pork rind, boiled for a very long time). It must be eaten with an excellent extra-virgin olive oil. The "trippai" – shops scattered through the less elegant sections of town, such as the Via Palazzuolo or in the fruit and vegetable market, or Mercato Ortofrutticolo di Nòvoli, or its counterpart in the center, the Mercato di S. Lorenzo – serve hefty sandwiches made of tripe or "lampredotto," sections of bovine intestine. It is still possible in central Florence to happen across a "vinaino," or small wine tavern where – either standing at the bar or even in the street – you can drink good Chianti Gallo Nero or Chianti Putto wine (they must have the official seal on the neck of the bottle). A very seasonal sweet, or pastry – served in September and early October – is the "schiacciata con l'uva," made with "black" wine grapes (used to make a very dark red wine). You can find it in Florentine bakeries, as well as in the land of Chianti Classico, which includes Radda and Castellina (in the province of Siena), Greve and surrounding areas. You can enjoy other wine-tours in Impruneta, Tavarnelle, and San Casciano Val di Pesa, on the edges of the section of Chianti that is "a denominazione di origine controllata," where the finest, government-certified wine is produced. Many farms sell wine and oil retail. And, just to stay on the subject of alcohol, Vin Santo is a white dessert wine, made with dried grapes and then allowed to ferment for two or three years in small kegs made of durmast wood.

Shopping. Florence is a paradise for shoppers. Elegant and refined shops stand alongside little boutiques and street markets, offering a great array of products and objects, often linked to the traditional crafts production that has made the city famous over the centuries. In Borgo Ognissanti and in Via Maggio, you will find the best antique shops, where you can often find minor masterpieces, while Via Tornabuoni, Via Vigna Nuova, and Via della Spada are the realm of Italian fashion: all of the most prestigious names of Italian fashion are concentrated in this area, from the Florentines Gucci, Ferragamo, and Emilio Pucci, to names such as Valentino, Armani and Mila Shön. Part of the Florentine tradition are clothing and accessories made of leather, often of superlative workmanship, good design, and affordable prices, especially in the shops around S. Lorenzo.

Particular fame attaches to the production of jewelry and silvery: aside from the great names of jewelry and metalwork, such as Buccellati, there are many spectaculars little shops, concentrated on the Ponte Vecchio. Far less expensive, but always of high quality, is the costume jewelry, sold in many shops behind the Duomo.

Good workmanship can be found in the shops selling embroideries on linen, tablecloths, camisoles, and handkerciefs. Less famous than in the past, but still excellent as souvenirs are hats, bags, and chests made of straw, another traditional product of Florence.

It is easy to buy ceramics in Florence, even though production is concentrated around Calenzano and Sesto Fiorentino.

It is fun to shop in the many markets, like the flea market held every day in Piazza dei Ciompi (where, the last Sunday of every month, an antiques market is also held).

Emergency and health facilities. Services. The main Florentine **hospitals** are (for emergencies, tel. 118): *Ospedale S. Maria Nuova*, Piazza S. Maria Nuova 1, tel. 27851, in the heart of Florence, with an emergency room for tourists; *Ospedale Pediatrico Meyer*, Via L. Giordano 13, tel. 56621; *Ospedale di Careggi*, Viale Morgagni 85, tel. 4277111; *Centro Traumatologico Ortopedico (CTO)*, Largo Palagi 1, tel. 4277111; *Ospedale Nuovo S. Giovanni di Dio*, Via di Torregalli 3, tel. 71921; *SS. Annunziata*, Ponte a Nìccheri, tel. 64490.

Police (for emergencies, tel. 113). Main stations: Commissariato and Questura, Via Zara 2; Piazza Duomo 5; Piazza del Tiratoio 6. Single telephone number, 49771.

Carabinieri (for emergencies, tel. 112). Stations: Borgo Ognissanti 48; Via dei Pilastri 54. tel. 24811.

Vigili Urbani, or City Police, Piazzale di Porta al Prato 6, tel. 32831.

Fire department, tel. 115.

Automobile Club Roadside Assistance, or Soccorso Aci, tel. 116. Headquarters: Viale Amendola 36, tel. 24861.

Post Office. Information, tel. 160. Main Post Office, Via Pellicceria 3, tel. 21136, hours 8:15-6 pm (for money transfers, etc.), 8:15-7 pm (for registered mail). Poste Nuove, or new post office, Via Pietrapiana 53-55, tel. 27741, hours 8:15-1:30 pm, Saturday 8:15-12:30 pm. Express

Antique stalls

Mail CAI Post, Via Alamanni 20 (train station of S. Maria Novella), 8:15-1 pm, 1:15 pm-7:30 pm (registered mail 2 pm-7 pm; express registered mail, 7 pm-10 pm).

Public Telephone Offices: Telecom Italia, Via Cavour 21r, open round the clock. Offices for long-distance and international phone calls: Poste Centrali, Via Pellicceria 3; Poste Nuove, Via Pietrapiana 53-55; train station of S. Maria Novella.

Structures for the handicapped. Though a fair number of telephone booths have been equipped for use by the handicapped, there are many problems and obstacles in Florence. Nor is the situation much better in the museums. Among the state collections, the Galleria dell'Accademia is well equipped. At the Uffizi there is the problem of getting up the steps of the loggia, but once inside there is an elevator. There is an elevator at Palazzo Pitti as well, while the upper stories of the Bargello, S. Marco, and Palazzo Davanzati are all inaccessible. The Museo della Scienza, or museum of science, has an elevator designed to accommodate wheelchairs; there remains the problem of the front steps. Among the city museums: Palazzo Vecchio has an elevator, S. Maria Novella has ramps, at S. Spirito the larger wheelchairs cannot get in, and the Museo Bardini also presents problems. It is impossible for the handicapped to visit the Museo dell'Opera del Duomo, while Casa Buonarroti, with an elevator only for smaller wheelchairs, offers free entry to groups of the handicapped, by advance reservation (tel. 241752). The situation is fairly reasonable in monumental gardens and in the Medici villas; the Museo Archeologico is also satisfactory, and has an elevator, as is the archeological area of Fièsole, which has ramps and passageways.

Florence by night. Aside from clubs and discos, there is a particularly Florentine way of spending the evening: taking a tour of the "vinerie" and "cantinette," sampling wine. Usually the wine is good and the atmosphere is relaxed. Unfortunately, they tend to close early, around 1 a.m. Here are a few names: the Osteria Fuori Porta, the Antica Mescita, Pane e Vino (all in the area around S. Niccolò), the Cantinetta di Verrazzano. At Settignano, there is the Sosta del Rossellino. The "caffè concerto," or cafe-chantants, in Piazza della Repubblica, should be considered tourist traps, with very high prices.

Italy: Useful Addresses

Citizens of Australia, Canada, New Zealand, and the United States can enter Italy with a valid passport, and stay for a period of not more than 90 days; citizens of Great Britain and Ireland, as members of the European Union, can travel either with valid passport or with valid identification card.

Foreign embassies in Italy

Australia:
Via Alessandria 215, Rome, tel. (06) 852721

Canada:
Via G.B. de Rossi 27, Rome, tel. (06) 445981

New Zealand:
Via Zara 28, Rome, tel. (06) 4404035-4402928

United States of America:
Via Vittorio Veneto 119/A, Palazzo Margherita, Rome, tel. (06) 46741

Great Britain:
Via XX Settembre 80, Rome, tel. (06) 4825441

Ireland:
Largo Nazareno 3, Rome, tel. (06) 6782541

Foreign Consulates in Italy

Australia:
Via Borgogna 2, Milan, tel. (02) 76013330 - 76013852

Canada:
Via Vittor Pisani 19, Milan, tel. (02) 6758001

New Zealand:
Via F. Sforza 48, Milan, tel. (02) 58314443

United States of America:
– Lungarno A.Vespucci 38, Florence, tel. (055) 2398276
– Via Principe Amedeo 2/10, Milan, tel. (02) 290351
– Piazza Repubblica 2, Naples, tel. (081) 5838111
– Via Re Federico 18/bis, Palermo, (consular agency), tel. (091) 6110020

Great Britain:
– Via S. Paolo 7, Milano, tel. (02) 723001
– Dorsoduro 1051, Venezia, tel. (041) 5227207

Italian embassies and consulates around the world

Australia:
12 Grey Street - Deakin, Canberra, tel.(06) 273-3333
Consulates at: Adelaide, Brisbane, Melbourne, Perth, Sydney.

Canada:
275 Slater Street, 21st floor, Ottawa (Ontario), tel.(613) 2322401

Consulates at: Montreal, Toronto, Vancouver.

New Zealand:
34 Grant Road, Wellington, tel.(4) 4735339 - 4736667

United States of America:
1601 Fuller Street, N.W., Washington D.C., tel.(202) 328-5500
Consulates at: Boston, Chicago, Philadelphia, Houston, Los Angeles, Miami, New York, New Orleans, San Francisco.

Great Britain:
14, Three Kings Yard, London W.1, tel.(0171) 3122200
Consulates at: Edinburgh, Manchester.

Ireland:
63/65, Northumberland Road, Dublin 4, tel.(01) 6601744

ENIT
In order to have general information and documentation concerning the best known places in Italy, you can contact the offices of the Ente Nazionale Italiano per il Turismo (ENIT), run by the Italian government; they are open Mon.-Fri., from 9 to 5.

Canada:
Office National Italien du Tourisme/Italian Government, Travel Office, Montreal, Quebec H3B 3M9, 1 Place Ville Marie, Suite 1914, tel. (514) 866-7667/866-7669, fax 392-1429

United States of America:
– Italian Government Tourist Board c/o Italian Trade Commission, New York, N.Y. 10022, 499 Park Avenue, tel. (212) 843-6884/843-6885, fax 843-6886.
– Italian Government Travel Office, Chicago 1, Illinois 60611-401, North Michigan Avenue, Suite 3030, tel. (312) 644-0996, fax 644-3019
– Italian Government Travel Office, Los Angeles, CA 90025, 12400, Wilshire Blvd. Suite 550, tel. (310) 820-0098/820-1898, fax 820-6357

Great Britain:
Italian State Tourist Board, London W1R 6AY, 1 Princes Street, tel. (0171) 408-1254 fax 493-6695

The Places to Visit: Florence

The Florence that is particularly worthy of careful exploration, the "historical city," once locked within its walled perimeter, is an irregularly shaped hexagon, about 3 km. across on the diagonal. It is a fairly small urban structure that is singularly rich in remarkable sites. Here only a tenth of the 403,294 inhabitants of Florence proper live (data from the 1991 census). The elimination of the city walls, the construction of entire new quarters and major public infrastructure, the modernization of the historical center – all triggered a process of transformation whereby Florence, from the second half of the 19th c., became a modern and productive city, faithful to its past but firmly rooted in the present.

The routes recommended in the city itself are for the most part ideal walking tours: the five routes that make up the first two chapters are confined to the small square area of the medieval center; the other remain within the four historical quarters of Florence, with rare "raids" into the outskirts of Florence.

In the text of each route, the words and names in *italics* and **bold** indicate major monuments and places of note; an asterisk marks things and places* that are of interest or important in their category.

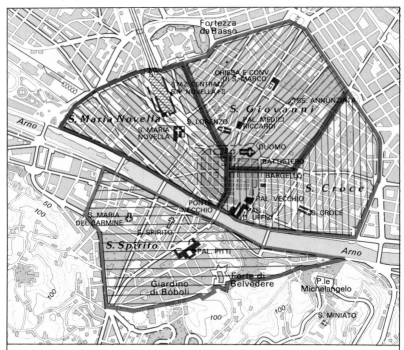

The historic quarters of Florence

Ancient core of the city, corresponding to the area later enclosed by the walls built in 1078.

The division of the city into four quarters dates from 1343.
There are three quarters "di qua d'Arno" literally, this side of the Arno:
S.Maria Novella, S.Giovanni, and S.Croce.
There is one quarter "oltr'Arno," literally across the Arno: S.Spirito.

0   400   800m

1 Piazza del Duomo and the Medieval Town

The layout and construction of the central area of Florence, bounded by the Duomo and Palazzo Vecchio to the north and south, and by Via del Procònsolo and Via de' Tornabuoni to the east and west, is still based – essentially – on the orderly layout of the ancient Roman city, with its decumanus maximus, corresponding to the modern Via del Corso. In the high Middle Ages, life in Florence revolved around the Battistero, one of the oldest religious structures in the city; by the end of the 13th c., however, its two fundamental aspects, religious and political, had been separated not only ideologically but physically as well, with the virtually simultaneous construction of the new cathedral (the modern-day Duomo or S. Maria del Fiore), beginning in 1296, and Palazzo Vecchio, begun three years later. These two buildings, then, represented the ideal fulcrum around which the entire city revolved (and still revolves). Sadly, the western section of Old Florence, lying to the west of Via dei Calzaiuoli, was entirely altered by the work done at the end of the 19th c. The urban structure was sharply simplified, while still maintaining the orthogonal layout. It is now marked by a fairly uniform and uninspiring array of buildings: it is no accident that the most notable feature is the great empty space of Piazza della Repubblica. The eastern area, bounded by the Duomo, Via del Procònsolo, and Piazza della Signoria, has on the other hand maintained much of its medieval character. You will recognize, for instance, a considerable array of civil typologies (such as the palazzi, towers, private loggias, and projecting wooden structures) and religious typologies (the Badia Fiorentina, the church of Orsanmichele) which give some sense of the ancient structure, with the crowded urban layout. The business, crafts, and trade of medieval Florence can still be seen in the street names: Via dei Calzaiuoli, Via dei Cimatori, Via degli Speziali, Via dei Magazzini – the streets of shoemakers, wool-clippers, chemists, and warehouses. Nowadays, the styles of the various streets are largely set by elegant shops, but this area too is beginning to suffer from an epidemic of pizza shops and fast-food outlets, which seem to be inevitable by – products of mass tourism.

The routes recommended run from the religious center of Florence, i.e., from Piazza del Duomo and Piazza di S. Giovanni, and explore the two different areas described above toward the Arno, omitting only the Palazzo Vecchio and Piazza della Signoria, to each of which a special chapter is devoted.

1.1 The Religious Center

At the center of the modern urban structure, the church of S. Maria del Fiore and the Battistero represent – along with the Piazza del Duomo and the Piazza di S. Giovanni – the spiritual heart of Florence. The most distinctive and fundamental characteristic of this profoundly urban space is its honeycomb configuration around the two monuments. The two structures stand alone, as if they had then been "wrapped" in the surrounding buildings. It is precisely because of this structure that the route recommended here actually coincides with the squares ("piazze") and tour of the monuments that stand in those squares. The present-day appearance of this space – relatively regular and homogeneous – was attained only after a long series of redesigns and construction projects. When construction began on the cathedral, or Duomo, a number of other urban projects were undertaken in order to accommodate the area

to its new uses: the Piazza del Battistero was paved and raised (1289), the hospital, or Ospedale di S. Giovanni was demolished (1296), the sarcophagi that surrounded the Battistero were removed, the Loggia del Bigallo was built (1352-58), and, lastly, it was prohibited for buildings to jut out and cover the square (1363). All the same it was not until the 19th c. that the architectural complex in question acquired its final, present appearance. Among the additions were: the construction of the "palazzi" on the south side of Piazza del Duomo (1826-30), the partial demolition of the Palazzo dell'Arcivescovado – pushing the facade back (1885-95) – the widening of the main streets that flow into the square (between 1841 and 1870), and lastly the installation of the cast-iron railing that surrounds the church. Nowadays the square – once a major focal point of civic events, such as knightings, popular assemblies, and decrees – enjoys

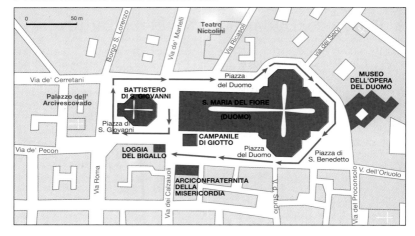

this role only on occasion of the Festa di S. Giovanni, or feast day of St. John, and the celebration of Easter, with the picturesque "scoppio del carro," or "explosion of the carriage," a pyrotechnical exhibition which is viewed as an omen of the future.

Basilica di S. Maria del Fiore* (1 C3-4; 2 F5-6; 3 F2). At the first, stunning glimpse, the massive structure of the Duomo, or cathedral of Florence, offers an apparently unified image; it is, however, actually the product of a number of different interventions over the centuries. The basilica was begun in 1296 by Arnolfo di Cambio to replace the old cathedral (S. Reparata), which the city had outgrown. Arnolfo had designed a building that extended lengthwise, with a nave and two aisles, which emerged into an ortogonal apse with apses on each side, like the petals of a flower sprouting out from the stem. Work came to a halt following the death of the architect (ca. 1310). It was not until more than forty years later that Francesco Talenti proposed a vigorous and definitive revision of the original plan. The apsidal section was completed, with the apses and the tambour of the dome, in 1421.

The construction of the cupola is a chapter all its own. After lengthy and passionate debates, the technical aspects of the project were entrusted to Filippo Brunelleschi. The knottiest detail in construction was the problem of scaffolding, considering the size of the cupola (diameter ca. 42 m.). The problem was brilliantly solved with the invention of an entirely new technique, which Brunelleschi had developed in his studies of ancient Roman domes. This innovative technique did not require the traditional wooden scaffolding. The dome was completed in

1436, but it was not until 1446 that the lantern, in the shape of a little temple, was added, completed in 1468 with a bronze orb and cross by Verrocchio.

S. Maria del Fiore is 153 m. in length, 38 m. in width at the nave and aisles, and 90 m. across at the transept; it is the fourth-largest church on earth, following St. Peter's in Rome, St. Paul's in London, and the Duomo of Milan. It can hold as many as 30,000 persons. These numbers help one to see just how the cathedral was essentially a building on a scale with the entire city – which is precisely as Arnolfo had originally conceived it. It had the strong support of the entire Florentine community: its interior is vast, rational, and beautifully lit. It is like an enclosed "piazza"; and by that is meant, first and foremost, a place in which to gather, a meeting place, an assembly site for the community – as well as a house of worship. Consider the public readings of Dante's "Divina Commedia" that were held here, with the enthusiastic support of the Commune, or city administration.

The **facade**, designed and partly built by Arnolfo, was destroyed in 1587 because it was "out of fashion": the facade you admire today was built at the end of the 19th c. by Emilio De Fabris, who took his inspiration from the ornamental motifs along the sides. The portals have bronze doors, also executed at the end of the 19th c., by Augusto Passaglia and Giuseppe Cassioli.

The **right side** features the oldest and most "Gothic" stretch of the church – the first two bays contain the *door* known as the *Porta del Campanile*. Not far from the apse – after the next two bays, which are marked by large twin-light mullioned windows and faced with marble in the Florentine Gothic style typical of the second half of the 14th c. – is the *Porta dei Canonici*, a door in full flamboyant Gothic (end of the 14th c.). In the lunette of this door it is possible to admire a *Virgin Mary with Christ Child*, attributed to Niccolò di Piero Lamberti or Lorenzo di Giovanni, and *angels* by Lamberti.

The **apsidal section** is a vast, lively assembly of apses and apsidioles covered by half-domes and shored up by flying buttresses: the best view – unforgettable – can be had from the corner of Via del Procònsolo and Via dell'Oriuolo. The high octagonal tambour is crowned in certain parts by a gallery, by Baccio d'Agnolo; construction was halted at the advice of Michelangelo who denounced it as a "cricket cage."

The grand ribbed octagonal **cupola** by Brunelleschi – the most challenging and daring architectural undertaking of the 15th c., or Quattrocento – constitutes the first great achievement of Renaissance architecture. It rises above the building in defiance of gravity, completing the physical structure of the cathedral, or Duomo.

If we continue our tour of the building by following the **left side**, we will encounter the handsome *Porta della Mandorla**, a door named after the mandorla motif contained in the Gothic cusp, framing the high relief of *Our Lady of the Assumption*, by Nanni di Banco (1414-21). In the lunette is a mosaic (*Annunciation*) executed to a cartoon by Domenico and Davide Ghirlandaio, which can be dated back to 1491. Before coming

back to the facade, a take a look at the late-14th-c. *Porta di Balla*. It takes its name ("balla," Italian for "bale," as in "bale of wool") from the nearby Via dei Servi, once known as the Borgo di Balla because of the presence of the manufactories of the Arte della Lana, or Guild of Wool Workers.

The **interior** of the Duomo, built to a Latin-cross plan – divided up into a long nave and two long aisles linked by series of broad arches, supported on massive piers – produces an effect of austere grandeur. Overhead, a long gallery runs the length of the nave and the cross apse. The floors are made of polychrome marble and reproduce the motif of the labyrinth; they were designed by Baccio d'Agnolo and were not completed until the middle of the 16th c. The Duomo of Florence is the church with the greatest number of pieces of old stained glass in all Italy, no fewer than 44 in its 55 windows. In the lunette over the central portal (1, in the plan on page 34), *Coronation of the Virgin Mary*, a mosaic attributed to Gaddo Gaddi; on the right (2), *tomb of Antonio Orso* bishop of Florence, by Tino di Camaino.

In the right aisle, under the 1st bay (3), note the *bust of Brunelleschi*, by Buggiano (1446), a *statue of a prophet* (Isaiah or Daniel) of uncertain attribution (either by Donatello or Nanni di Banco), and the *Tondo di Giotto*, by Benedetto da Maiano (1490); in the 3rd bay (4), *funerary monuments* frescoed by Bicci di Lorenzo, while in the 4th bay (5), note the *bust of the philosopher Marsilio Ficino*, by Andrea Ferrucci (1521). When you reach the cross-vault, you find

The Basilica of S. Maria del Fiore viewed from the Forte Belvedere

1 Piazza del Duomo and the Medieval Town

yourself beneath the enormous dome, entirely covered by a fresco of the *Last Judgement* (by Giorgio Vasari and Federico Zuccari, 1572-79). Lower down, note the eight 16th-c. statues of *apostles* (6-13). At the center, the octagonal enclosure of the choir (coro), in marble, is decorated with bas-reliefs by Baccio Bandinelli and Giovanni Bandini, and surrounds the main altar, also by

Bandinelli, surmounted by a *Crucifix*, by Benedetto da Maiano (1497).
Around the cross vault are the three apses of the transept and the presbytery (each with five chapels). Between the right apse and the central one is the Sagrestia Vecchia or Sagrestia dei Canonici, on the door of which it is possible to admire the glazed terracotta lunette by Luca della Robbia (*As-

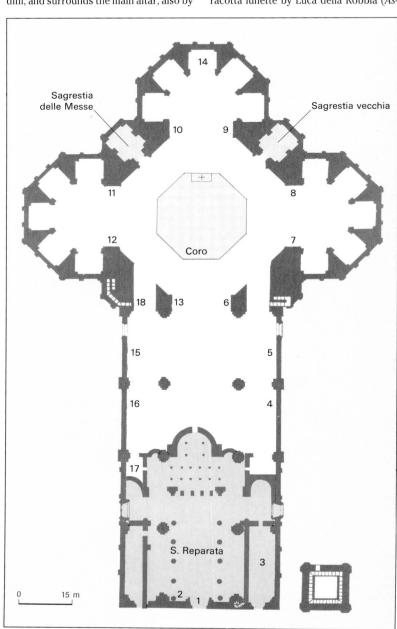

The Basilica of S. Maria del Fiore: plan

34

cension*; ca. 1450); inside are paintings by 15th- and 16th-c. artists. Beneath the altar of the central apse (14) stands the *Arca di S. Zanobi** (1432-42), a tomb with a bronze urn containing the relics of St. Zanobi; this is a masterpiece by Lorenzo Ghiberti. In the lunette of the Sagrestia delle Messe, or sacristy, is another terracotta (*Resurrection**; 1444) by Luca della Robbia, who also did the splendid bronze *door** (1445-69); note the important *intarsias* decorating the cabinets and walls, by Giuliano and Benedetto da Maiano. It was in this sacristy, on the morning of 26 April 1478, that Lorenzo the Magnificent managed to find shelter during the Conspiracy of the Pazzi, while his brother Giuliano de' Medici was being stabbed to death in another section of the same cathedral. In the left apse, on the floor, note the bronze *sundial* by Paolo dal Pozzo Toscanelli (ca. 1450). This sundial marks the summer solstice (21 June), by a ray of sunlight that passes through a hole in the cupola.

In the 4th bay of the left aisle (15) you may observe the famous panel by Domenico di Michelino (1465), a scene entitled *Dante and His Worlds*: the poet holds out an open copy of his "Divina Commedia," and from the book a ray of light shines down upon Florence. In the 3rd and 2nd bays (16 and 17) note the two immense frescoes, the so-called **equestrian monuments***, dedicated respectively to Giovanni Acuto and Niccolò da Tolentino, famous condottieri who fought with the Florentine army; they were painted, again respectively, by Paolo Uccello (1436) and Andrea del Castagno (1456); after them, note the *bust of the organist Antonio Squarcialupi* by Benedetto da Maiano (1490).

From the 2nd bay of the right aisle you can climb down to the remaining fragments of the ancient cathedral of **S. Reparata**, which dates from the 4th/5th c.; this is sometimes improperly referred to as a "crypt."

From a little door at the end of the left aisle (18) you can climb up to the cupola: the first part of the climb up leads to the gallery on the interior of the tambour. From here, you enjoy a remarkable view of the interior of the church; the second part of the climb is quite demanding (463 steps in the narrow space between the inner shell and the outer shell of the cupola). From the gallery that runs around the lantern, at an altitude of 91 m. from earth, there is a splendid panoramic view* of the city.

Campanile di Giotto* (1 C3). This bell tower takes its name from the fact that it was designed by the great artist Giotto. It rises,

slender and sheer, to the right of the cathedral. It is clad in polychrome marble; its plan is square, and it is reinforced at the corners by octagonal buttresses. It stands 84.7 m. tall, and is 14.45 m. in width. Much as was the case with the Duomo, or cathedral, construction was interrupted and resumed a number of times. Work was first begun by Giotto in 1334; by the time the artist died, he had completed only the lower order, with its distinctive reliefs set in hexagonal panels. Work continued under the supervision of Andrea Pisano. Andrea Pisano borrowed the diamond motif in the second zone, and installed niches for statues on the next two floors. Work was completed in 1359 under Francesco Talenti who was responsible for the top three floors, which are marked by broad gabled twin- and three-light mullioned windows; these lighten the massive structure, which terminates in a high crowning cornice, an emulation of the cornice that runs along the top of all the facades of the Duomo. The sculptures, reliefs, and statues are an integral part of the structure, and not mere decorative elements; the originals are now preserved in the Museo dell'Opera del Duomo, and copies stand in their place.

The panels on the base illustrate: in the first register, the *activities of humanity* (originals by Andrea Pisano and, on the side facing the church, by Luca della Robbia), and in the second register, the *Planets* (which influence the lives of men), the *Virtues* (which determine men's behavior), the *Liberal Arts* (which shape men's spirits; originals by Andrea Pisano), and the *Sacraments* (which sanctify the existence of men; attributed to Alberto Arnoldi). In the niches on the story above, statues of the *Patriarchs*, *Kings*, *Prophets*, and *Sibyls* (the originals, all by Andrea Pisano, were in time replaced with works by Donatello and Nanni di Bartolo).

A spiral staircase with 414 steps leads up to the terrace on the crown of the Campanile; from here it is possible to admire a handsome panoramic view* of the nearby Duomo and the rest of the city.

Battistero di S. Giovanni* (1 C3). This, literally, the baptistery of St. John, is probably the oldest religious building in Florence; it faces the Duomo. The existing structure dates from the 11th c.; the traditional belief that it was originally a Roman temple is now discounted. The building has an octagonal plan; the exterior facing is decorated with geometric motifs in marble from Luni (white) and Prato (green). It is surrounded by a continuous trabeation that separates the lower level, formed of pilaster strips and columns – from the upper level, with octagonal semi-columns supporting three round arches. There is a third order, added later, that is then surmounted by a pyramidal roof, which conceals the cupola within. In 1202 the rectangular apse was added; it is commonly called the "scarsella."

The Arte dei Mercanti, or merchants' guild, patron of the Battistero, embellished it with a great number of remarkable artworks; especially noteworthy are the three bronze *doors* *, which serve as a sort of giant illustrated Bible.

The **south door** (which originally faced the Duomo), by Andrea Pisano, is the oldest

The Battistero of S. Giovanni

door (1330); it is subdivided into twenty-eight panels: the upper twenty panels illustrate *scenes from the life of St. John the Baptist* (the patron saint of Florence), while the eight lower panels depict *Humility* and the *Cardinal and Theological Virtues*. The rich bronze Renaissance *frieze* (1452-62) that frames the door was the work of Vittorio Ghiberti, the son of Lorenzo. Above the portal, note the bronze group by Vincenzo Danti (*John the Baptist*, his *executioner* and *Salomè*, 1571).

The **north door** is the first of the two doors designed and executed by Lorenzo Ghiberti (1403-24). The breakdown is similar to the south door: the upper twenty panels depict *scenes from the New Testament* while the eight lower panels show the four *Evangelists* and the four *Fathers of the Church*. The style, while still late-Gothic, stands out for its flexible lines and realistic portraiture (in the left impost it is possible to make out a self-portrait of Ghiberti himself). Above

the portal, *John the Baptist Preaching*, a bronze group by Giovanni Francesco Rustici.

The **east door**, named the **Porta del Paradiso** by Michelangelo – there is now a copy in its place, while the original is preserved in the Museo dell'Opera del Duomo, and is undergoing restoration – was commissioned in 1425, and was designed and executed by Ghiberti. This door is a clear example of the mastery and independence of style attained by the artist. The masterpiece illustrates, in ten panels (instead of the usual twenty-eight; also, square instead of diamond-shaped), *scenes from the Old Testament*. In the cornice there are 24 niches with *Bibilical figures*, alternating with 24 tondos with *heads of artists* who were contemporaries of Ghiberti (there is another self-portrait of Ghiberti in this door). Above the portal, note the marble group, *Jesus and John the Baptist* by Andrea Sansovino (1502) and an *angel* by Innocenzo Spinazzi (now being restored).

The **interior** has an octagonal plan (diameter, 25.6 m.), while the arrangement of the columns is reminiscent of the Roman temple of the Pantheon. The eight sections are faced with two-tone marble, embellished above the mullioned windows with geometric motifs. The floor, similar to that in S. Miniato al Monte, in inlaid marble, presents an interesting design, facing the Porta del Paradiso, with the *Sun* and the *signs of the Zodiac*. In the middle of the central octagon stood the ancient baptismal font; it was removed in 1576 and replaced with another *font*, decorated with six bas-reliefs of the Pisan school (1371); it stands along the second wall. To the right of the apse is the *tomb of Baldassarre Cossa*, who was antipope as John XXIII. This remarkable tomb was built by Donatello in collaboration with Michelozzo (1421-27); the structure is adorned by a false drapery that links the monument to the columns, as if it were a baldachin. The decoration of the Baptistery is completed with the splendid tiles of the *mosaics* *, in the Byzantine style, in the apse (begun in 1225 by Jacopo da Torrita) and the mosaics in the cupola, with their distinctive concentric arrangement, culminating in the figure of Christ Enthroned. This second series of mosaics, which required more than thirty years to complete (1270-1302), involved the labor of Venetian masters, working to cartoons by Tuscan artists. Among those artists was, in all likelihood, Cimabue. The subjects illustrated include the *Last Judgment, stories from Gene-*

sis, stories of Joseph, stories of Mary and Christ, and *stories of John the Baptist.*

Museo dell'Opera di S. Maria del Fiore (1 C4). Located at n. 9 in Piazza del Duomo, this museum was opened in 1891, but as far back as the 15th c. it had been used as a storehouse for artworks not in use; it contains major sculptures from the Battistero, and from the facade and interior of the Duomo, as well as the panels that originally decorated the Campanile.

On the ground floor, just past the courtyard and the vestibule (ticket window) – above the doors of which are two *lunettes* by Andrea della Robbia – you enter the large hall of the ancient facade of the Duomo, containing all the sculptures from the facade built by Arnolfo di Cambio (depicted in a drawing from that period). That facade was demolished in 1588. Note the remarkable *statue of Boniface VIII* *, by Arnolfo di Cambio; a *St. Luke* by Nanni di Banco and a *St. John* by Donatello. From the entrance you enter two small rooms dedicated to Brunelleschi, containing his funerary mask, wooden models of the cupola and lantern, and tools from the construction yard. In the adjacent halls: illuminated codices, liturgical goldwork, wooden models of the facade of the Duomo that were never built, and a *Virgin Mary with Christ Child, saints, and donors*, by Bernardo Daddi (1334).

If you climb up to the floor above, at the mezzanine you will find the little hall containing the unfinished marble group of a later *Pietà* * by Michelangelo (1550-53), intended by the artist (who portrayed himself in the figure of Nicodemus) as an adornment to his own funerary monument.

On the upper floor you will find the Sala delle Cantorie, or hall of choir chancels, so-called because of the two splendid **marble chancels** * by Luca della Robbia (1431-38) and Donatello (1433-39); these were removed from the sacristy doors of the Duomo in 1688. Each of the two features a joyous depiction of children singing, dancing, and making music, yet they differ in style and conception of space: the first one is pervaded by a classical serenity, while the second is looser in approach, and is shot through with a Dionysian vitality. In the same hall you will find the 16 statues that once stood in the niches of the bell tower, or Campanile; they include four *Prophets* (ca. 1348-50) and two *Sibyls* (1342-48) attributed to Andrea Pisano, as well as the *Sacrifice of Isaac*, a joint effort by Nanni di Bartolo and Donatello (1421), and *Habakkuk*, commonly known as the "Zuccone," or

Pumpkin-Head, by Donatello, who also carved the **Penitent Mary Magdalene** *, an emotionally powerful wooden statue belonging to Donatello's later years (1453-55). The hall on the left displays the *panels* * from the Campanile, or bell tower, transferred here between 1965 and 1967. They are arrayed as they were originally installed. Note the hexagonal panels of the lower order, all carried out – save for the last five, which are by Luca della Robbia (1437-39) – by Andrea Pisano (almost certainly to cartoons by Giotto; ca. 1348-50), including the *Creation of Adam*, the *Creation of Eve*, *Working the Earth, Music, Astronomy, Hunting, Weaving, Navigation, Farming, Architecture*; these are followed by the rhomboidal panels of the upper order: the *Planets*, the *Virtues*, the *Liberal Arts* (school of Andrea Pisano) and the *Sacraments* (Alberto Arnoldi); it is interesting to note that, for the first time, alongside the "artes liberales," the "artes minores" were also depicted.

Beyond the Sala delle Cantorie, you will enter the Sala dell'Altare, dominated by the *silver altar frontal* * from the Battistero, a masterpiece of the goldsmith's art, begun in 1366 and completed only in 1477-80. We should point out the central statuette of *John the Baptist* by Michelozzo, the *Birth of Jesus* by Antonio Pollaiolo (left side), the *Decapitation* by Andrea del Verrocchio (right side), the silver *Cross* by Betto Betti (above the altar) and the enameled *predella* by Antonio Pollaiolo and Miliano Dei. In the hall, moreover, are numerous notable art works, including: *panels* * from the Porta del Paradiso by Ghiberti; *St. Zanobi* and *scenes from the life of St. Zanobi*, an altar frontal by the Maestro del Bigallo (13th c.); Byzantine *mosaics* on panel (14th c.); *embroidered wall hangings* executed to cartoons by Antonio Pollaiolo with *stories of John the Baptist and Jesus* (1480); two small sculptures by Andrea Pisano (*St. Reparata* and *Christ Giving a Benediction*); *bust of a woman with a cornucopia* by Tino di Camaino.

Loggia del Bigallo (1 C3). Set directly across from the south door of the Battistero, at the right corner of Via dei Calzaiuoli, this small palazzo (mid-14th c.) is attributed to Alberto Arnoldi, the "capomastro," or foreman, of the Duomo. The Compagnia del Bigallo was an organization founded in 1244 to assist the elderly, orphans, and the poor. In the elegant marble *loggia*, with its broad round arches – surmounted at the floor above by handsome trilobate mullioned windows – lost or abandoned children were placed.

In the Sala dei Capitani, inside (currently closed), note the *Madonna della Misericordia*, a fresco dating from 1342; it features the earliest known view of the city of Florence. Inside the loggia, note the *tabernacle* by Noferi d'Antonio (1515), marble sculptures by Arnoldi (1359-64), *predella* by Ridolfo del Ghirlandaio, and *Crucifix* by the Maestro del Bigallo (ca. 1260), one of the earliest Florentine paintings on panel.

At n. 19 in Piazza del Duomo, facing the Campanile, is the headquarters of the *Arciconfraternita della Misericordia*, or brotherhood of mercy. This organization was also founded in 1244 by St. Peter Martyr to transport the sick to hospital and to bury the dead during outbreaks of the plague. This charitable association is greatly loved by the Florentines, and its members still perform their acts of mercy.

1.2 From the Duomo to the Bargello and on to Piazza de' Giudici

This route sets out from the area behind S. Maria del Fiore and leads toward the river Arno along the Via del Procònsolo, Via dei Leoni, and Via de' Castellani. The route follows the perimeter of the 11th-c. walls of Florence; it runs past several of the most important and notable buildings in the city: the Bargello, the Badia Fiorentina, and Palazzo Gondi. There are two "specialized" museums, so to speak (the Museo di Antropologia, or museum of anthropology, at the beginning of the route, and the Museo di Storia della Scienza, or museum of the history of science, at the end); in a sense they frame one of the most important art museums in Florence and in Italy, the Museo del Bargello.

From the Badia, a detour will take you into the heart of medieval Florence, with its narrow, picturesque streets; although the monuments are of minor importance, they are still worth visiting.

Palazzo Nonfinito (1 D4). Set at n. 12 in the Via del Procònsolo, this palazzo was begun in 1593 for Alessandro Strozzi, but it was left unfinished, as its name implies. The ground floor, attributed to Bernardo Buontalenti, is notable for the square-hewn blocks of the facing, the impressive portal, and the unusual windows, decorated by fanciful ornamental motifs.

This palazzo contains, on the ground floor and the second floor (starting point for visitors to the museum), the **Museo Nazionale di Antropologia ed Etnologia**, the first museum of anthropology and ethnology founded in Italy (in 1869, by Paolo Mantegazza). It boasts a major collection of objects and artifacts from all over the world. The first twelve halls (excepts halls VI, VII, and VIII) are devoted to Africa: note the wooden sculptures from central Africa. The halls running from XIV to XIX are devoted to the Americas: particularly rare is the feathered mantle made by natives of eastern Brazil (hall XV); also note the statue made of trachyte (a form of volcanic rock) from ancient Mexico and depicting the god of the sea (hall XVIII). The halls that follow are devoted to Asia (and especially to Malaysia) and Oceania: among the numerous objects, note the material from the third voyage of Captain Cook in the Pacific (1779), including human heads from the Solomon Islands, sterns and prows of Maori canoes, and a very rare specimen of the "Heva," a costume worn during funerals by Tahitian priests (hall XXV). Also note the magnificent war pirogue, encrusted with mother-of-pearl, from the Solomon Islands (hall XXV). Lastly, on the ground floor you will find material from the former Museo Indiano, or Indian Museum, which was incorporated into the Museo di Antropologia in 1913 (these halls are open only on the third Sunday of the month).

Palazzo Pazzi (1 D4). At n. 10 in the same street, this palazzo was built by Giuliano da Maiano (1458-69), and is also known as the "Palazzo della Congiura," in reference to the conspiracy carried out by the Pazzi family against the Medici in 1478. The contrast between the rustication of the ground floor and the smooth plaster of the two upper floors, embellished by elegant twin-light mullioned windows, is a significant piece of aristocratic domestic architecture of the 15th c. The courtyard in particular is exquisite.

With a short detour to the left along Via Ghibellina, you soon reach (at n. 110) the *Palazzo Borghese* (1 D5), built in 1821 by Gaetano Baccani for Camillo Borghese, the husband of Pauline Bonaparte; this is a rare example of Florentine Neoclassical architecture. Since 1844 it has housed the Circolo Borghese and the Circolo della Stampa, two clubs.

Palazzo del Bargello* (1 D4). This was the first public building in Florence under the Commune; it was built for the Capitano del Popolo. It took the name of Palazzo del

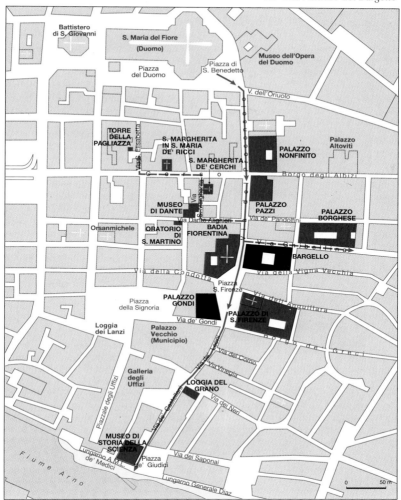

Bargello (slang, roughly equivalent to "cop" or "screw") when it became the residence of the Capitano di Giustizia, that is, chief of police, and therefore the site of the jails, in 1574. Built in two stages, in the 13th and 14th c., the earlier section incorporated an existing *tower*, known as the *Torre Volognana*, set at the corner of what is now the Via Ghibellina. It was only in the second phase that the building was raised and enlarged, extending to what is now the Via dell'Acqua. The stern palazzo, restored in the 19th c. (1858-65), now houses the **Museo Nazionale del Bargello***, one of the most notable collections of art in the world, especially for Renaissance sculpture, and in particular Tuscan Renaissance sculpture. In the wake of the flood of 1966 the museum was radically reinstalled, in accordance with new knowledge obtained through the restoration of the artworks.

Entering from the Torre Volognana, whose bell sounds only at the turn of the century, you enter the large, well proportioned medieval *courtyard** surrounded on three sides by a portico with broad arches, set on octagonal pillars; on the fourth side – the oldest one – rests the *staircase* built by Neri di Fioravante (1345-67). In the center of the courtyard, there is a handsome octagonal well; on the walls, note the heraldic crests of the "Podestà" and the "Giudici di Ruota," officers of Florence. Note the marble statuary (15th/17th c.): six allegorical statues by Bartolomeo Ammannati, *Ocean* by Giambologna, *Allegory of Fiesole* by Tribolo, and the *Cannon of St. Paul* (a head of St. Paul adorns the breech of the cannon) by Cosimo Cenni. On the east side of the courtyard, you can enter the Sala del Trecento, which contains, among other things, art works from Orsanmichele, a *Virgin Mary with Christ Child* by Tino di Camaino, and a group of three *acolytes* by Arnolfo di Cambio. Michelangelo is the predominant figure in the Sala del Cinquecento, a hall which you enter by passing under the stairway in the courtyard: the *Tondo Pitti** (ca. 1504), is an unfinished relief, and it stands next to the **Bacchus*** (1496-97), Michelangelo's first

The "Tondo Pitti" by Michelangelo

major classically inspired sculpture, and the *David-Apollo** (1530-32; a statue that is hard to interpret clearly) and the **Brutus*** (1539), the only bust ever carved by the artist, a portrait, according to Vasari, of the tyrant-killer, Lorenzino de' Medici. Surrounding these works are a number of smaller items, inspired by Michelangelo's work, by Tribolo, Ammanati, and Baccio Bandinelli. Of considerable interest are the refined sculptures by Benvenuto Cellini (especially the originally bronzes on the base of the Perseus, the marble works dedicated to *Ganymede* and *Narcissus*, and the *bust of Cosimo I**); by Giambologna (the agile and enchanting **Winged Mercury***, 1564); by Jacopo Sansovino (the *Bacchus* of 1510, clearly in contrast with the work of Michelangelo); and a bronze relief by Vincenzo Danti.

On the **second floor**, an interesting series of sculptures depicting *animals* (including the famous *turkey*) – done in bronze by Giambologna for the grotto of the Medici Villa of Castello – occupies the balcony that stands at the top of the 14th-c. staircase.
The other great figure in this museum is Donatello, whose works are on display in the splendid and majestic *Salone del Consiglio*

Generale*, built by Neri di Fioravante in 1340-45 when the original building was erected. Among these works, particular note should be given to the renowned **St. George*** (1416), from the tabernacle of Orsanmichele, along with the two *Davids**, one done in Donatello's youth, in marble (1408-9) and the other, world-famous, in bronze (ca. 1440), a harmonious composition of a figure devoid of all triumphant pride, the first nude produced by Humanist art. Among the other works by Donatello are the *bust of Niccolò da Uzzano*, a faithful portrait done in polychrome terracotta, the *marzocco* (1418-20), that is, a lion supporting a lily symbolizing Florence, l'*Atys-Amor*, a handsome bronze, and the dramatic *Crucifixion*, both works from Donatello's later years. Other renowned works surround this fundamental exhibition area: in particular note the two famed panels* depicting the *Sacrifice of Isaac*, one by Lorenzo Ghiberti and the other by Filippo Brunelleschi, carried out for the 1401 competition for the north door of the Battistero di S. Giovanni. These are considered to be two of the earliest pieces of Renaissance sculpture. Worthy of particular note – besides the work by Agostino di Duccio, Michelozzo, and Luca della Robbia (the *stories of St. Peter* and the *Madonna della Mela*) – are two lovely statues by a pupil of Donatello's, Desiderio da Settignano: the *Young St. John**, once attributed to Donatello, and the *Madonna Panciatichi*, a marble bas relief.
If you pass through the Sala Islamica (or Islamic hall; carpets, fabrics, bronze and ivory objects from Arab culture), you will reach the Sala Carrand, with objects of the applied arts, from the collection donated to Florence by a French antiquary of that name in 1888. Alongside is the Cappella di S. Maria Maddalena, or chapel of Mary Magdalene, frescoed around 1340 by the workshop of Giotto: on the far wall note the fresco of *Paradiso* with a *portrait of a young Dante* at bottom right; *choir stalls* and a *lectern* by Bernardo della Cecca (1483-88). The successive Sala degli Avori (hall of ivories) features 265 pieces of ivory, dating from the 5th to the 17th c.; in particular, note the *tip of a crosier* said to be by *Yves de Chartres* (12th c.). Adjacent to the Sala Bruzzichelli (16th-c. furniture and the *Virgin Mary with Christ Child* by Jacopo Sansovino) is the Sala delle Maioliche (hall of majolica), which features items ranging from the 15th to the 18th c., from every part of Italy.

On the **third floor**, pass through the halls of Giovanni della Robbia and Andrea della

Robbia (note the three glazed terracottas: *bust of a youth, Madonna degli Architetti,* and the *Madonna del Cuscino*), you will enter the Sala dei Bronzetti, which contains Italy's leading collection of bronze figurines: aside from the two masterpieces by Antonio Pollaiolo (*Hercules Crushing Antaeus*) and Benvenuto Cellini (*Ganymede*), there are works by Giambologna and the Riccio. In the same hall, note the *fireplace* by Benedetto da Rovezzano. If we retrace our steps we find the Sala del Verrocchio, whose famous bronze **David*** stands in the middle of this hall (ca. 1470), distinguished by a realism that is entirely different from Donatello's classicism; also by Verrocchio are the delicate *Lady with a Nosegay** and the *bust of Piero di Lorenzo de' Medici**. Among the many other sculptures dating from the late-15th c. we should point out the *bust of a young soldier** by Antonio Pollaiolo, the *bust of Battista Sforza** by Francesco Laurana, the *bust of Pietro Mellini* by Benedetto da Maiano, as well as a number of works by Mino da Fiesole and Antonio Rossellino.

Badia Fiorentina (1 D4). This building, literally the "Florentine Abbey," lies within a forbidding enclosure wall that rises directly across from the Bargello; it is an ancient Benedictine monastic complex, founded in 978 by Willa, the mother of the Marchese Ugo di Toscana ; in the church, which was dedicated to S. Maria Assunta della Badia Fiorentina (Our Lady of the Assumption of the Florentine Abbey), Dante writes that he saw Beatrice for the first time. The building underwent a first renovation in 1285; this renovation was overseen by Arnolfo di Cambio, who reoriented the church along an east-west axis, with the apse overlooking the Via del Procònsolo. At the end of the 15th c., the loggia in the atrium and the Chiostro degli Aranci (Cloister of Orange-Trees) were added, but it was not until the 17th c. that the church attained its present appearance and layout. Matteo Segaloni, in this period, renovated the church into a solemn Baroque style, built to a Greek-cross plan, oriented north and south. The entrance runs above a copy of the original splendid late-15th-c. portal by Benedetto da Rovezzano (in the pediment, note the terracotta by Benedetto Buglioni). From the courtyard, you can see the hexagonal *campanile*, one of the defining elements of the Florentine "skyline." The city of Florence partially demolished the abbey in 1307 as punishment of the abbey's monks, who refused to pay a tax; it was rebuilt in 1330 with the addition of two registers of Gothic mullioned windows and a cusped crown.

The interior of the church contains works from the late-15th c. (on the left wall, *Apparition of the Virgin Mary before St. Bernard**, an exquisite painting by Filippino Lippi, carried out ca. 1485, a masterpiece of Florentine art of the latter part of the Quattrocento), the 16th c. (in the left arm of the transept, altar piece by Vasari), and the 18th c. (in the presbytery and in the right arm of the transept). Under the chancel on the left arm of the cross vault, note the *tomb of the Marchese Ugo di Toscana**, or Hugo of Tuscany, by Mino da Fiesole (1469-81), who also carved the altar frontal with *the Virgin Mary and St. Leonard and St. Lawrence* (wall adjacent to the entrance wall) as well as the *tomb of Bernardo Giugni* (next wall). In the right arm of the transept, a noteworthy *organ* built by Onofrio Zeffirini da Cortona in 1558 and still working.

A door to the right of the presbytery leads into the marvellous *Chiostro degli Aranci* (Cloister of Orange Trees; closed during church services) built by Bernardo Rossellino in 1432-38. One of the most interesting architectural projects of the early Florentine Renaissance, the cloister is two stories tall. The top floor is decorated with a series of 15th-c. frescoes with *scenes from the life of St. Benedict.*

A slight detour along Via Dante Alighieri allows you to walk through one of the best preserved sections of medieval Florence. In a wide space in the road, not far away, stands the so-called home of Dante Alighieri, or *Casa di Dante*, a picturesque but fanciful reconstruction dating from the turn of the 20th c. The ground floor is used to hold temporary exhibitions; the upper floors house the *Museo Casa di Dante* (entrance in Via S. Margherita 1; 1 D4), a museum with archives of documents related to Florence in the time of Dante, and with a collection of editions of the "Divina Commedia," or Divine Comedy. Not far away stands the *Oratorio di S. Martino,* an oratory built directly behind the early church of S. Martino del Vescovo; this was the parish church of the Alighieri family. If you walk back to the Casa di Dante, you can take the Via S. Margherita, where you will see the little *church of S. Margherita de' Cerchi,* mentioned as early as 1032. This church contained the tombs of the Portinari family – the family of Beatrice – and it is possible that Dante himself was married to Gemma Donati here. At the end of Via S. Margherita you turn left into the Corso; you will then reach the *church of S. Margherita in S. Maria de' Ricci* (1 D4), which was built in 1508. The present-day facade was added in 1610; the interior, which was renovated in 1769 by Zanobi Del Rosso, is in solemn late-Baroque style. Continuing along in the same direction, you then turn right in the Via S. Elisabetta: in the Piazza S. Elisabetta, nearby, stands

The Complex of S. Firenze, which now houses the Courts Building

the *Torre della Pagliazza*, a tower with a remarkable semi-circular plan. The name dates back to the Middle Ages, when it was used as a prison; the foundation of the tower appears to date back to a complex of Roman baths.

Palazzo di S. Firenze (1 E4). Set in the Piazza di S. Firenze, this complex – dedicated to S. Fiorenzo – is one of the most interesting pieces of Florentine late-Baroque architecture to survive. Construction was drawn-out and trouble-ridden: in 1645 the Padri Filippini (Philippine Fathers) began work on a large church, designed by Pietro da Cortona; funds ran short, and it became necessary to reduce the scale of the project. The complex took on its definitive appearance in 1772-75, when Zanobi Del Rosso demolished the old church of S. Firenze and built the oratory of the congregation, giving it a facade that was symmetrical to the church's facade and then joining the two buildings. The interior of the church of S. Filippo Neri contains canvases and bas-reliefs dating from the 18th c. Of particular interest, because it is closely linked with St. Philip Neri's own religious conception, centered around the "canto delle laudi, (literally, the singing of praises), is the *oratory* by Zanobi Del Rosso. The light, refined, and elegant architecture is clear evidence of the growing importance of music, and the development of the oratory from a place of prayer and reflection into an auditorium. Since a considerable portion of the complex of S. Firenze now houses the Tribunale, or

courts building, the oratory is used for judicial hearings today, and is open during court (the entrance is directly to the right of the entry hall into the Tribunale).

Palazzo Gondi* (1 E4). Also standing in Piazza S. Firenze is one of the most emblematic Florentine palazzi of the 15th c. Construction was begun in 1490 by Giuliano da Sangallo, who took his inspiration from the great projects that had already been erected (Palazzo Medici, Palazzo Pitti, and Palazzo Rucellai), but which had been left unfinished. One typical feature of palazzi of the time that is found here is the use of three different types of ashlars, becoming smoother with each successive story – in Italian, "bugnato a scalare." Above the jutting bracket cornice, on the right, is a columned belvedere; at the bottom, between the portals, note the stone benches. In 1874 the original central structure was completed and enlarged in the direction of Palazzo Vecchio by Giuseppe Poggi, who added a seventh window and a third portal. The palazzo, still owned by the family, is not open to the public. When the palazzo was enlarged in the 19th c., a number of houses were torn down to make room; in one of them Leonardo da Vinci had once lived, and it is traditionally said that he painted "La Gioconda," or the Mona Lisa, here.

If you continue along Via dei Leoni and pass the rear facade of Palazzo Vecchio on your right, you will find yourself in a broad space, or plaza, overlooked, on the left, by the *Loggia del Grano*, the last in a series of loggias (Loggia del Pesce and Loggia del Mercato Nuovo) which were built to contain the various city markets (respectively: grain, fish, and the new market). This loggia was built in 1619 by Giulio Parigi and it has two levels. At the end of the 19th c., the building was raised and was adapted for use as a theater; over the years, it was converted into a movie theater.

Palazzo Castellani (1 F3-4). Overlooking Piazza de' Giudici is a building with a particularly stern appearance, dating from the 14th c.; between 1574 and 1841 this building held the offices and hearing rooms of the Giudici di Ruota, magistrates responsible for hearing civil suits. Until 1966 it held the offices of the Accademia della Crusca, Italy's national dictionary, perhaps the Italian equivalent of the OED.
Since 1930 this "palazzo" has housed the **Museo di Storia della Scienza**, a museum of the history of science organized around two main collections: the Medici collection of scientific instruments (16th and 17th c.) and the counterpart collections assembled by the house of Lorraine (18th c.). Alongside the numerous astrolabes, solar clocks, sun-dials, and "archipenzoli," or plumb-rules (rudimentary instruments for ensuring that a surface or a straight line is level), you may be particularly interested in seeing the original scientific instruments owned and used by Galileo Galilei (halls IV and V): note the *lens* of the telescope used by Galileo in 1610 to make his great astronomical discoveries (the moons of Jupiter, the craters of the Moon, the phases of Venus, sunspots, and the stars of the Milky Way), the only two original telescopes, built by Galileo in his own workshop, to survive. Of great interest is the material pertaining to early cartography and geography (hall VII): among the numerous items, we should point out a large *armillary sphere* * dating from the second half of the 16th c., built by Antonio Santucci delle Pomarance; a facsimile of the famous *globe* by Fra Mauro; and a splendid *planisphere* in parchment, by Lopo Homem (1554).
The third floor contains chiefly instruments and devices built in the 18th c. (aside from a really valuable *astronomic clock* from the sixteenth century, in hall XII). Note the virtuoso mechanical movements of the *writing hand* and the *clock of perpetual motion* (in hall XII).

1.3 The Area Around Piazza della Repubblica

This route can be broken up into three sections. The first section begins at Piazza del Duomo and then runs along the busy and exciting Via dei Calzaiuoli, with a distinctly 19th-c. appearance; from there you can tour Orsanmichele and the other monumental landmarks that stand around it. The second stretch of the route runs through the 19th-c. center of Florence, with the enormous Piazza della Repubblica, and then cuts through an area that abounds with Renaissance palazzi (among which Palazzo Strozzi) lining elegant streets; note the dignified and wealthy Via de' Tornabuoni. Finally, you will arrive in Piazza S. Trìnita; you now have two choices. A detour along Borgo Santi Apostoli will take you through one of the most "medieval" streets in Florence; the last part of the route takes you along Via Porta Rossa, past Palazzo Davanzati (Museo della Casa Fiorentina Antica, the Museum of the Early Florentine Home), and the Loggia del Mercato Nuovo. Here the route turns toward the river Arno and comes to an end at the Ponte Vecchio.

Orsanmichele * (1 D3). The finely decorated front of the church of S. Michele in Orto – better known as Orsanmichele – stands out unmistakably along the Via dei Calzaiuoli. The parallelepiped plan is due to the fact that the building, originally, was meant for an entirely different function. This in fact was originally a loggia, built in 1290 by Arnolfo di Cambio, in which the grain market was held; following the great fire of 1304, the structure was rebuilt and enlarged in 1337. Between 1367 and 1380 the arcades on the ground floor were closed up with three-light mullioned windows with exceedingly fine decorations; also two more floors were added – for use as storerooms – punctuated on all four sides by airy twin-light mullioned windows. The market was moved elsewhere at the end of the 14th c., and the loggia was transformed into the church of the Guilds (the "Arti," or Arts); the government of the Signoria, or Seigneury, ordered those Guilds to decorate the exterior, in the pillars set between the arches, with aedicules or **tabernacles** containing statues of the various patron saints, statues by the leading artists working in Florence in the 15th and 16th c.
In Via dei Calzaiuoli we find (from left to right): the Tabernacolo dell'Arte di Cali-

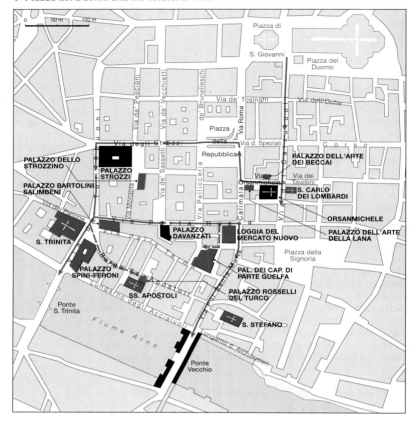

mala (or tabernacle of the cloth merchants), with a statue of *St. John the Baptist*, carved by Lorenzo Ghiberti in the years 1412-16, in what is still a Gothic style; the Tabernacolo del Tribunale di Mercatanzia (merchant's court), with the *Incredulity of St. Thomas*, a bronze group by Andrea del Verrocchio (1467-83); and the Tabernacolo dei Giudici e Notai (judges and notaries) with a bronze statue of *St. Luke* by Giambologna. If we turn into the Via Orsanmichele we find: the Tabernacolo dei Beccai (butchers) with a marble statue of *St. Peter* (1408-13), attributed to Brunelleschi; the Tabernacolo dei Conciapelli (tanners) with a marble statue of *St. Philip* by Nanni di Banco (ca. 1415). Nanni di Banco also did the later marble figures of the Tabernacolo dei Maestri di Pietra e Legname (stonecutters and carpenters): *Four Crowned Saints*, and a bas-relief with *architects and sculptors at work*; the Tabernacolo degli Armaiuoli (armorers), with a statue of *St. George*, a copy in bronze of the marble masterpiece by Donatello, and a bas-relief of *St. George Freeing the Daughter of the King* (the originals are preserved in the Museo del Bargello). In

the Via dell'Arte della Lana you will see: the Tabernacolo dell'Arte del Cambio (money changers), with a statue in bronze of *St. Matthew* by Ghiberti (1419-22), and, above it, two statuettes (*Archangel Gabriel* and *Our Lady of the Annunciation*) attributed to Piero di Niccolò Lamberti; the Tabernacolo dei Lanaiuoli (wool drapers) with a bronze statue of *St. Stephen* by Ghiberti (1428); and the Tabernacolo dei Maniscalchi (farriers) with a marble statue of *St. Eligio*, and a bas-relief with a *miracle of the saint*, both by Nanni di Banco. The circuit of the building is completed by following the Via de' Lamberti side, where you will find: the Tabernacolo dei Linaioli, Rigattieri e Sarti (linen drapers, old-clothes men, and tailors), with a statue of *St. Mark* (copy of an early work by Donatello, 1411-13); the Tabernacolo dei Pellicciai (furriers) with a statue of *St. James* and a bas-relief depicting the *Decapitation of St. James*, attributed to Niccolò di Piero Lamberti; the Tabernacolo dei Medici e Speziali (doctors and apothecaries) with the *Madonna della Rosa*, or Our Lady of the Rose, a marble sculptural group attributed to Pietro di Giovanni

Tedesco (1400); and the Tabernacolo dei Setaiuoli e degli Orafi (silk merchants and goldsmiths) with *St. John the Evangelist*, in bronze, by Baccio da Montelupo (1515).

The interior, with a rectangular plan, is broken up into two aisles by square pillars with round arches, surmounted by cross vaults, and decorated with frescoes (figures from the Old and New Testaments) that date from the late-14th c. The two pillars against the wall toward the Via Orsanmichele feature conduits for unloading grain from the upper floors (they were used as grain store rooms until the 16th c.). Note the stained-glass windows, with *stories and miracles of the Virgin Mary*. On the altar at the far end of the left aisle is a marble sculptural group depicting *St. Ann, the Virgin Mary, and the Christ Child*, by Francesco da Sangallo (ca. 1526). At the end of the right aisle is a *tabernacle* * by Andrea Orcagna (1355-59), a masterpiece of Florentine Gothic: an aedicule, richly decorated with marble inlay, set on four pillars embellished with slender tortile columns and tall pinnacles. The base is adorned with panels depicting the *virtues* and *stories of the Virgin Mary*, while the rear features a large high relief carving (*Transit and Assumption of the Virgin Mary*), also by Orcagna (1359). The altarpiece enshrined in the tabernacle is the *Madonna delle Grazie*, Our Lady of Grace, by Bernardo Daddi (1347).

Facing Orsanmichele is the *church of S. Carlo dei Lombardi* (1 D3), which was built between 1349 and 1404, as is evident from the gable-end facade with little hanging arches and a cusped portal. At the end of the 17th c. it was deeded to a company of Lombard brothers devoted to St. Charles Borromeo (in Italian, "S. Carlo dei Lombardi"). The interior features paintings from the 14th, 17th and 18th c.

As you walk along Via Orsanmichele you may note the 14th-c. *Palazzo dell'Arte dei Beccai*, at n. 4, and – nearly facing it – the *Palazzo dell'Arte della Lana* (the guild of the wool drapers), one of the wealthiest and most powerful guilds in medieval Florence. The building (which has been the headquarters of the Società Dantesca, an organization for the study of Dante, since the turn of the 20th c.) comprises a tower-house and another shorter building. A walkway built in 1569 connects the building with the upper-floor halls of Orsanmichele. Inside (not open to the public) are frescoes from the 14th c.

On the corner of Via Orsanmichele and Via dell'Arte della Lana stands the Gothic *Tabernacolo di S. Maria della Tromba* (14th c.), a tabernacle that was moved here at the turn of the 20th c., from its original location (Mercato Vecchio, or Old Market, the present-day Piazza della Repubblica); it contains a panel painted by Jacopo

del Casentino (*Virgin Mary Enthroned, with Angels and Saints*).

Piazza della Repubblica (1 D3; 4 A5; 5 A1). This is the showiest result of the new urban plan of the late-19th c.; the plan devastated for once and for all an area which had managed to preserve intact much of its medieval character. The present-day piazza, broad and rectangular, is surrounded by massive buildings that have little of the traditional Florentine discretion; it was built as an enlargement of the old Piazza di Mercato Vecchio, which in turn was built on the site of the ancient Roman Forum. Along the porticoes, crowned by the large arch that leads into the Via degli Strozzi, there are a number of cafes (including *Paszkowski* and *Giubbe Rosse*), two meeting spots for Florentines, frequented in the past by Italian artists and authors (Soffici, De Chirico, Papini, Gadda, Vittorini, Montale). In the Piazza della Repubblica stands the *Colonna dell'Abbondanza*, or Column of Abundance, topped by a copy of an original sculpture by Donatello (*Affluence*, or Plenty).

Palazzo Strozzi * (1 D2). Standing in the Piazza Strozzi, this is one of the loveliest Renaissance palazzi in Florence. The design, which was clearly influenced by Michelozzo's Palazzo Medici, was by Benedetto da Maiano, but Cronaca, who continued the work, modified it considerably by adding the distinctive jutting cornice, which was inspired in turn by classical models. Construction, which was begun on 6 August 1489 for specific astrological considerations, was halted in 1504, continued in 1523, and definitively suspended in 1538, upon the death of Filippo Strozzi the Younger: the southern side and half of the cornice remained unfinished. Exemplary in its proportions, the palazzo rises three floors; note the two orders of mullioned windows on the upper floors, and the single order of rectangular windows on the ground floor. Also note the immense portals with rusticated arches (one on each side), the lamps at the corners, the wrought-iron torch-holders (a rare example of surviving Renaissance wrought-iron work) and, lower down, rings for hitching horses.

Through the elegant interior courtyard, designed by Cronaca, you enter the halls of the palazzo, headquarters of numerous cultural institutes, including the *Gabinetto G. P. Vieusseux*.

At n. 2 in Piazza degli Strozzi stands the so-called *Palazzo dello Strozzino*, built in the middle of the 15th c. around an existing little square, which in time was incorporated as its courtyard. The palazzo was left unfinished; a fourth story was added in the 19th c.; the building was adapted for use as a movie theater in the 1920s by Marcello Piacentini. Today it is a movie house, the Cinema Teatro Odeon.

Via de' Tornabuoni (1 C-D-E2). Lined by refined shops and major 16th- and 17th-c. palazzi, this elegant street is to Florence what Via Monte Napoleone is to Milan and Via dei Condotti is to Rome. At the end of the Via degli Strozzi, you will find the *Palazzo del Duca di Nortumbria*, or Duke of Northumbria, dating from the end of the 16th c., rebuilt at the start of the 20th c. by Adolfo Coppedè. If you continue to the left, toward Piazza S. Trìnita, you will see, among other buildings, at n. 7 the *Palazzo del Circolo dell'Unione*, thought to have been designed by Vasari, and at n. 5 the *Palazzo Strozzi del Poeta*, in typical Baroque style.

Piazza S. Trìnita (1 D2). This major crossroads, for traffic in the distant past and the present day (at the center stands the *Colonna della Giustizia*, or Column of Justice, taken from the Roman Baths of Caracalla), offers passage across the Arno, over the Ponte di Santa Trìnita. On the right is the Basilica di S. Trìnita, on the left, at n. 1, Palazzo Bartolini Salimbeni (16th c.), and directly across, the impressive Palazzo Spini-Feroni.

S. Trìnita (1 D2). This is one of the oldest churches in Florence; the original Romaneseque building was erected in the second half of the 11th c. by the order of the Vallombrosani, and was then rebuilt in the Gothic style in the first half of the 14th c., probably under the supervision of Neri di Fioravante: construction continued until the turn of the 15th c., amidst halts and interruptions. The facade, made of "pietra forte," was rebuilt in 1593-94 by Bernardo Buontalenti in a serious Mannerist style.
The Gothic interior, built to an Egyptian cross – or tau cross – plan (a T-shape, in simpler language), is divided into a nave and two aisles by rectangular pillars with graceful pointed arches and cross vaults. On each of the side aisles, there are five chapels, as well as the four chapels of the transept, separate from the square apse. On the interior facade you can still make out the remains of the early Romanesque church. Almost all of the chapels were renovated in the 17th c. In the right-hand aisle, note in particular: the 3rd chapel (1, in the plan above), with *Virgin Mary Enthroned,*

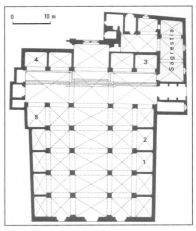

The Church of S. Trìnita

Christ Child, and Saints, a panel by Neri di Bicci, while on the wall is a fresco by Spinello Aretino; the 4th chapel (2), is the only one to maintain its original 15th-c. appearance (including the wrought-iron gate), with altar piece by Lorenzo Monaco (*Annunciation*) and a series of frescoes with *stories of the Virgin Mary* by the same artist (1420-25). From the right transept you can enter the sacristy, built by Lorenzo Ghiberti between 1418 and 1423 as the Cappella degli Strozzi, or family chapel. Also in the transept is the *Cappella Sassetti** (3), renowned for the major series of frescoes by Domenico Ghirlandaio (1483-86); the theme, commissioned by Francesco Sassetti, a friend of Lorenzo the Magnificent, was the *life of St. Francis,* but the scenes are set in 15th-c. Florence; you can see the Palazzo della Signoria and the Loggia dell'Orcagna, the facade – still Gothic – of the church of S. Trìnita and the bridge of the same name, in the version that stood here prior to 1557. On the altar is an *Adoration of the Shepherds,* also by Domenico Ghirlandaio (1485). In the 2nd chapel in the left transept (4), *tomb of Benozzo Federighi** , one of Luca della Robbia's masterpieces, in marble and polychrome majolica (1454). In the 5th chapel in the left aisle (5), note the wooden statue of *Mary Magdalene,* by Desiderio da Settignano, completed, according to Vasari, by Benedetto da Maiano (ca. 1455).

Palazzo Bartolini Salimbeni (1 D2). Designed and built by Baccio d'Agnolo (1520-23), this is one of the finest examples of a palazzo in full Renaissance style, "alla romana" (in the Roman manner): note the columns flanking the portal, the triangular pediments, and the niches); moreover, all three types of Florentine stone were used (pietra forte, pietra serena, and pietra bigia).

Palazzo Spini-Feroni (1 E2). This palazzo was built at the end of the 13th c. in a good strategic location: it guarded the Ponte di S. Trìnita. Over time it was repeatedly rebuilt; in 1824, the great tower and the Arco dei Pizzicotti, a large arch, were demolished, to facilitate traffic on the Lungarno (or, riverfront promenade). It served as the Florence town hall, or Municipio, during the years when Florence was capital of the new united kingdom of Italy (1865-71).

Ponte S. Trìnita (1 E1-2). Via de' Tornabuoni empties onto the Lungarno on a line with this light and airy bridge, one of the loveliest in Europe. It was built by Bartolomeo Ammannati as a replacement for an earlier bridge, which had collapsed following the flood of 1557. This bridge, whose value lies at least in part in its daring construction technique, spans the Arno with three elegant polycentric arches at the extremities of which stand four statues depicting the *Seasons*, placed there in 1608. The bridge was destroyed by the retreating German army on 4 August 1944; it was rebuilt in 1952, by workmen adhering scrupulously to the original plans, in part using original stone blocks recovered from the river.

After returning to Piazza S. Trìnita you enter the *Borgo Ss. Apostoli* (1 E2-3), a charming street that is still lined by buildings dating from the 13th and 14th c. Here you are immersed in a medieval atmosphere. Roughly halfway along this street, on the right, is Piazza del Limbo, with the **church of the Ss. Apostoli**, one of the most noteworthy Romanesque monuments in all Florence. Next door to the church, with an entrance at n. 19 in Borgo Santi Apostoli, stands the *Palazzo Rosselli del Turco*, built in 1507 by Baccio d'Agnolo for the Borgherini family.

Palazzo Davanzati* (1 D-E2). This austere aristocratic home dates from the 14th c. To reach it, you may take the Via Porta Rossa from Piazza S. Trìnita. Built around the middle of the 14th c. by the Davizzi family, this palazzo then became the property of the Bartolini family, and in 1578 of the Davanzati family (their large coat-of-arms stands out on the facade). The building is tall and narrow and comprises five separate levels: the ground floor with an enclosed loggia with three portals, three stories with depressed-arch windows and, above that, a large open loggia, added in the 16th c. The building still has the stern appearance of a fortified structure which, in case of need, could present

an armed defense (in fact, in the ceiling of the lower loggia there are are four "piombatoi di difesa," where molten metal could be poured onto attackers beneath).

The interior – restored to "period style" at the turn of the 20th c. by the antiquary Elia Volpi – allows the visitor to relive the atmosphere of everyday life in a Florentine palazzo of medieval times. Note in particular the Gothic *corte*, or courtyard, with a handsome stairway and a well.

Since 1956 the palazzo has been the site of the **Museo della Casa Fiorentina Antica**, or museum of the early Florentine home. The furniture (beds, chests, boxes, kneeling stools, and cabinets) and other objects (tapestries, paintings, pottery, dishes, and terracotta containers) in the house come from other museums, state collections and private donations. The original furnishings, which belonged to Elia Volpi, were sold by him at auction. Recently, a display area has been opened with exhibitions of European lace, from the 16th to the 20th c.

On the second floor, of particular note, are: the *Sala dei Pappagalli*, or hall of parrots, with painted walls, featuring geometric patterns in the lower section, and a frieze of trees on the upper section; the master bedroom, called the *Sala dei Pavoni* or hall of peacocks, is decorated with heraldic crests and with a faux wall paper with a geometric motif. On the third floor, only the bedroom still features frescoed walls, with depictions of an adventurous and sentimental medieval legend: The Chatelaine de Vergi.

Palazzo Davanzati

Mercato Nuovo (1 D-E3). This "new marketplace" was built by Cosimo I for the sale of valuable goods; the Loggia del Mercato Nuovo was built between 1547 and 1551 by Giovanni Battista del Tasso; nowadays it houses a lively market for Florentine crafts products (especially craft objects made of straw). At the center of the market lies a marble wheel, marking the point in which the "carroccio," a cermonial cart, was placed prior to battles; here, too, dishonest

the ancient former *church of S. Stefano al Ponte* (documented as early as 1116; plan, 1 E3). The central portal, with alternating white and green strips, is also Gothic. It actually serves as the home of the Orchestra Regionale Toscana, and is open during concerts. The interior was radically renovated in the Baroque style, affecting the altars and the decorations, around the middle of the 17th c. Of special note is the stairway to the presbytery, the fanciful Manneristic invention of Bernardo Buontalenti (1574), formerly in the church of S. Trìnita.

Ponte Vecchio, the most famous bridge in Florence

merchants were pilloried. On the southern side (toward the Palazzo della Borsa Merci) is the so-called *Fontana del Porcellino* (or fountain of the piglet; actually a statue of a wild boar, a bronze copy by Pietro Tacca (1612) of the Hellenistic original, in marble, now in the Uffizi. A tradition has it that if you toss a coin into the fountain and you rub the snout of the boar, you will return to Florence.

The **Palazzo dei Capitani di Parte Guelfa** (1 E3) rises directly behind the Loggia del Mercato Nuovo. Built at the turn of the 14th c., it was enlarged to the rear, overlooking Via di Capaccio, by Brunelleschi and again around 1589 by G. Vasari, who also built the graceful *loggetta* at the right corner. The building was restored during the Twenties, and the main facade once again featured large Gothic mullioned windows and crenelation; also, the open exterior staircase was rebuilt. Inside (currently being restored), note the *Salone di Brunelleschi*, a great hall with walls punctuated with fluted pilasters, terminating in capitals, with a caisson ceiling by Vasari; above one door, note the glazed terracotta by Luca della Robbia.

In a secluded "piazzetta" on the left side of Via Por S. Maria, looms the facade – Romanesque in the lower section and Gothic in the higher – of

Ponte Vecchio* (1 F2-3). At the end of Via Por S. Maria, the banks of the river Arno are linked by the most famous bridge in Florence, literally the "old bridge," which can fairly be described as unique. It was built in 1345 by Neri di Fioravante (or by Taddeo Gaddi, according to Vasari), at the Arno's narrowest neck, over three arches so solidly built that they have outlasted many centuries, unlike the earlier arches, which collapsed during floods. The new bridge was quickly lined with shops and ateliers, first made of wood and later built in masonry. Until the end of the 16th c., these shops belonged mostly to butchers and herbalists. The grand duke Ferdinando I had these shopkeepers replaced with shops run by goldsmiths and silversmiths. From that time on, the image of this bridge has been inextricably bound up with the "madielle" (little display windows with distinctive shuttered hatches) densely packed with objects made of gold. At the center of the bridge is a small plaza, free of shops, from which one can enjoy a lovely view of the river, in both directions. The Ponte Vecchio was the only bridge not destroyed by the Germans in their retreat from Florence in August of 1944.

2 Piazza della Signoria and the Uffizi

The area around Piazza della Signoria, one of the "beating hearts" of Florence, a must even for the hastiest of visitors, contains a number of the most universally renowned symbols of the city, such as the Palazzo Vecchio and the Galleria degli Uffizi. Recent archeological excavations have shown that this area was occupied by major buildings during Roman times, while in the Middle Ages it was dominated by the tower-houses of Ghibelline families. The area was transformed from the 14th c. onward into the political center of Florence, counterbalancing the religious center comprising the Duomo, or cathedral, and the Battistero, or baptistery, with the construction of Palazzo dei Priori (now Palazzo Vecchio) and the Loggia della Signoria.

The urban structure that surrounds the square – which survived intact, despite 19th-c. plans for radical renovation – has largely preserved its medieval characteristics, from the narrow dark lanes all the way to the warm hues of stones and plaster, so different from the marble used in churches and cathedrals. Looming over the entire square is the massive bulk of Palazzo Vecchio; the various additions and renovations of this palazzo offer documentation of great moments in the history of Florence, from the stern austerity of the medieval Commune to the sumptuous style of the Medici family. There is a perfect metaphor in the clash between the traditional and austere exterior and the spectacular interior, a glorification of absolutism. And it was the centralization of political power under the Medici that led to the remarkable urban structure of the Piazzale degli Uffizi and the Palazzo degli Uffizi, tangible signs of the concentration of administrative and bureaucratic power into the hands of the prince.

Even today Piazza della Signoria, despite the attacks leveled during various controversies, ranging from that over the souvenir stalls to the issue of repaving the square, still has the dignity and austerity of bygone times, and has withstood the assault of ambitious real estate developers. Its ancient allure has survived intact.

2.1 Piazza della Signoria

Rightly counted among the most splendid and famous squares in all Italy, Piazza della Signoria (1 E4; 4 B5; 5 B2) was built in the Middle Ages, and was originally much smaller than it is today. The original square at the northern facade of the Palazzo dei Priori (as Palazzo Vecchio was originally called) was enlarged, organized, and embellished over the course of centuries of history, without any single overarching plan; the extension westward gave the square its modern configuration with two orthogonal spaces, while maintaining the distinctive asymmetrical position of Palazzo Vecchio. On the south side, in the late-14th c., the Loggia della Signoria was built; roughly two centuries later, the spectacular complex of the Uffizi was added, with its "piazzale" conceived as an extension toward the Arno. On the west side, the medieval Loggia dei Pisani was demolished in 1871 to make way for the construction of the Palazzo Lavisan (now headquarters of Assicurazioni Generali), which profoundly altered the general volumetric layout of the piazza, while the area to the north still preserves medieval (Palazzo della Mercatanzia) and Renaissance

structures (Palazzo Uguccioni). It was not until the second half of the 16th c. that the various sculptural monuments were installed, giving the square its modern-day appearance, somewhere between stage setting and museum.

Monuments. Between Via delle Farine and the north side of Palazzo Vecchio stands the bronze *equestrian monument to Cosimo I de' Medici**, by Giambologna (1594-98). At the left corner of the facade of Palazzo Vecchio stands the large *Fonte di Piazza* or *Fonte del Nettuno**, a fountain built by Bartolomeo Ammannati and assistants, among them Giambologna (1563-75). The giant marble statue of Neptune, the god of the sea, is fairly awkward, and has suffered the withering sarcasm of the Florentines, who call it the "Biancone," roughly "white elephant"; the satyrs and sea deities, made of bronze, set at the edges of the basin, are clearly more graceful and lively in line.

In front of the fountain, an inscription on a round stone set into the pavement marks the spot of the execution of the monk Girolamo Savonarola and his two Dominican disciples (23 May 1498).

At the left corner of the stairs in front of Palazzo Vecchio stands the *Marzocco*, that is, the lion that symbolizes Florence; this is a copy (now undergoing restoration) of the original sculpture in "pietra serena" by Do-

The Fountain of Neptune

natello, now in the Museo del Bargello. A little to the right, atop a high pedestal, is a recent reproduction (1980) of the bronze group depicting *Judith and Holofernes*, by Donatello. The original is on display inside the palazzo, in the Sala dei Gigli, or hall of lilies. To the side of the main portal of the palazzo is the *David*, a marble copy of the original by Michelangelo, carved between 1501 and 1504 and moved to the Galleria dell'Accademia in 1910; the giant statue (4.34 m.) was set up as a symbol of the triumph of republican freedom over Medici tyranny, but it was preserved even after the Medici restoration, as a symbol of the political craft and wiles of the small Florentine state in its dealings with the brute force of its external enemies. Alessandro de' Medici, duke of Florence, commissioned Baccio Bandinelli to sculpt a marble group, *Hercules and Cacus* (1534), and had it placed across from the David, as a symbol of the victory of the Medici dynasty over their own enemies in Florence, to counterbalance the "republican" masterpiece by Michelangelo; from the very beginning this sculpture offended the esthetic sensibilities of the Florentines, and gave rise to much debate and talk.

Palazzo Vecchio* (1 E4). Symbolic monument of political power in Florence and, simultaneously, the most outstanding piece of civil architecture of the Florentine Trecento, or 14th c., this building was begun in 1299, to plans by Arnolfo di Cambio, as the *Palazzo dei Priori*. It served to house the Priori, the highest magistrates under the Commune, from the beginning of the 14th c. on. It became the *Palazzo della Signoria* in the 15th c., and then the residence of the Medici from 1540 to 1565, when its name was changed to "Palazzo Vecchio," the "old palace," after the grand duke shifted his residence to Palazzo Pitti. The Italian Parlamento met here in the years when Florence was capital of a newly united Italy (1865-71); it is now the Municipio, or Florence town hall.

The original core of the building had a compact parallelepiped shape, and was faced in rusticated ashlar, made of "pietra forte." It stood three stories tall, and had two registers of mullioned windows in the Gothic style. It is surmounted by a high parapet/gallery, jutting sharply out on corbels, with two stacked galleries: one with a roof and window openings, one open to the sky, with rectangular merlons (known as the Guelph style of merlons, or crenelation). Beneath the little hanging arches, between the corbels, are painted the heraldic crests of the Florentine Republic. The **tower**, dating from 1310 (94 m. tall), was largely built with the materials from the previous tower of the Foraboschi; toward the top this tower extends outward into a distaff shape, bearing the same crenelated motif as appears on the gallery of the palazzo, with a slight modification in the hanging arches (pointed arches instead of round arches) and in the crenelation (swallowtail); the tower is surmounted by a belfry shaped like an aedicule, with four stout columns, and yet more crenelation.

On the left side of the palazzo, it is possible to trace the successive enlargements: the enlargement of the 14th c., with the door known as the *Porta di Tramontana*, leading into the Camera dell'Arme (A, in the plan on page 51; the hall is open only for exhibits), the only room that preserves its medieval structure; the enlargement of 1495, which served to create the Salone dei Cinquecento; the enlargement of the second half of the 16th c., which extended the building all the way to the Via dei Leoni, behind.

In the second half of the 16th c. the interior of the palazzo was completely rebuilt by Vasari, at the wishes of the grand duke Cosimo I de' Medici; the new version became a model for all European palaces. You enter the **courtyard*** (B), around which stood the medieval building. The courtyard was rebuilt in 1453 by Michelozzo in the style of the high Renaissance, and it was decorated in 1565 – on the occasion of the wedding of Francesco de' Medici with Jane of Austria – under the supervision of Vasari, with grotesques and a series of *views of the cities of the Hapsburg empire*. On this occasion, a fountain was built at the center of the courtyard and, on the basin made of red porphyry, the graceful sculpture of a *Putto with a Dolphin* by Andrea del Verrocchio was placed (replaced in 1959 with a copy; the original is inside, on the Terrazzo di Giunone, or Terrace of Juno). In the passageway between this courtyard and the successive Cortile della Dogana, or Courtyard of Customs (C), a large two-flight staircase, designed by Vasari, leads up to the **second story**.

The **Salone dei Cinquecento*** (I, in the plan on page 52) an enormous room, 53 x 22 m., 18 m. tall, was built between 1495 and 1496 by Antonio da Sangallo, Cronaca, and Francesco di Domenico. It was built to house the Consiglio Generale del Popolo, the new assembly of the Republic (composed of 500 members, as the Italian name suggests), ordered by Savonarola after the expulsion of the Medici. When Cosimo I moved into the palazzo (1540), he made this "salone," or great hall, the symbol of his own absolute power, transforming it into an audience hall and creating a raised tribune,

known as the *Tribuna di Udienza*. Built by Baccio Bandinelli, it stood at the left end of the room, was meant to hold the ducal throne, and contained statues of members of the Medici family. Later, between 1563 and 1565, the coffer ceiling was raised about seven meters, and was later decorated with a series of paintings by Vasari and assistants (at the center is the *Apotheosis of Cosimo I*; around it are allegories and stories of Florence). By the same artist and assistants are the paintings on the entrance wall (depicting three episodes of the war with Pisa) and those on the facing walls (three episodes of the war with Siena). At the center of the latter wall note the *Genius of Victory** by Michelangelo, a marble group carved in 1533-34 for the tomb of Pope Julius II della Rovere; the group was not used and was therefore donated by the nephew of the artist to Cosimo I; facing it is a plaster model of *Florence Triumphing over Pisa* by Giambologna.

To the right of the entrance stands the *Studiolo di Francesco I de' Medici* (II), a princely study, and one of the most noteworthy creations of Florentine Mannerism. The room is quite small, windowless, and was built under the supervision of Vasari between 1570 and 1575; it contains numerous paintings reflecting the prince's interests in natural science. Around the center of the vault, which features frescoes depicting *Nature* and *Prometheus*, are arrayed the four *Elements* (water, air, fire, and earth) and, in the corners, the "complexions," which is to say, the various states of the human soul: *Phlegm*, *Blood*, *Choler*, and *Melancholy*.

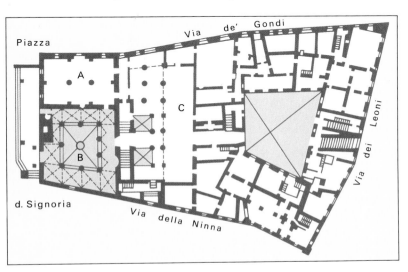

Palazzo Vecchio: first floor

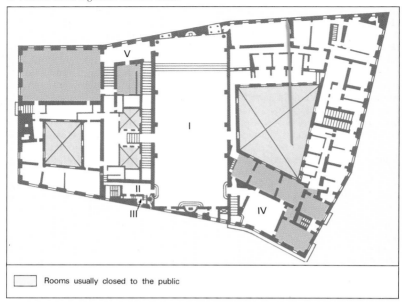

Rooms usually closed to the public

Palazzo Vecchio: second floor

Bronze statuettes of mythological deities are set in the eight gilt niches. Hidden by doorways, a stairway leads to the *Tesoretto* (III; usually closed to the public), a small richly decorated treasure chamber, where the most valuable objects were stored. From here a secret stairway led out of the palazzo.

Take the door opposite the "studiolo" to enter the *Quartiere di Leone X* (1555-62), begun by Giovanni Battista del Tasso and completed by Vasari; it is dedicated to the glorification of the Medici. The only hall that can be toured bears the name of Leo X (hall IV), first pope of the dynasty, whose secular name was Giovanni de' Medici; he was the son of Lorenzo the Magnificent, and was elected to the papal throne in 1513. The pictorial decoration of this and the other halls in the "quartiere" (not open to the public; used as offices by the city government) was carried out by Vasari and assistants.

On the **third floor**, above the Quartiere di Leone X, is the *Quartiere degli Elementi* (literally, quarter of the elements; 1555-58), comprising a series of halls, rooms, and terraces dedicated to the pagan deities, splendidly decorated with allegorical paintings, by Vasari and assistants. In the Terrazzo di Giunone, literally terrace of Juno, originally an open terrace that was enclosed by Bartolomeo Ammannati at the end of

the 16th c., note the *Putto with Dolphin* * by Verrocchio, a copy of which is found in the first courtyard of the palazzo.

A gallery overlooking the Salone dei Cinquecento leads to the *Quartiere di Eleonora* (the section of the house that belonged to the wife of the grand duke Cosimo I). The most interesting room in this section is the *Cappella di Eleonora* * (1, in the plan shown on the right), a chapel built by Giovanni Battista del Tasso and decorated (1540-45) by Bronzino, who certainly was at the height of his artistic powers at the time.

You continue, through more frescoed halls, until you reach the *Cappella dei Priori* or *Cappella della Signoria* (2), a chapel built between 1511 and 1514 by Baccio d'Agnolo and decorated by Ridolfo del Ghirlandaio. Next is the **Sala dell'Udienza*** (audience hall; 3), with a gilt coffered ceiling by Giuliano da Maiano and frescoed walls, by Francesco Salviati. After you pass through the marble *door* with a *statue of Justice*, by Benedetto and Giuliano da Maiano, you enter the **Sala dei Gigli*** (hall of lilies; 4; it takes its name from the decoration on the wooden ceiling – also by Giuliano da Maiano – that alludes to the symbol of the Anjou dynasty, protectors of the Guelph faction). Here too the two Da Maiano brothers built the marble *portal* leading into the next hall. The large *fresco* on the wall opposite the entrance, which depicts a series of Roman characters, is by Domenico Ghirlandaio (1482-85). The hall features the restored original bronze group of **Judith and Holofernes***, by Donatello.

Adjacent are two rooms: the Cancelleria della Repubblica Fiorentina (chancery of the Florentine Republic; 5), where Machiavelli worked, and the Sala delle Carte Geografiche (hall of maps; 6), with painted *Ptolemaic charts* and a large *globe*, executed by Egnazio Danti and Stefano Buonsignori.

At the exit of the Sala dei Gigli, you descend to the Quartiere del *Mezzanino* (normally closed to the public), built by Michelozzo by lowering a number of rooms on the second floor. Only three halls are open to the public, containing the "Donazione Loeser": a collection of sculptures and paintings of the Tuscan school, 14th/16th c. The adjoining halls contain a collection of antique musical instruments belonging to the Conservatorio Cherubini (open to scholars, with authorization from the Conservatorio, or conservatory).

After you return to the second floor, you will enter the "ricetto" (V), which leads into the Sala dei Dugento (hall of 200; generally closed to the public; it is used for meetings of the Consiglio Comunale, or town council), with a handsome lacunar ceiling by Benedetto and Giuliano da Maiano. From the "ricetto" you can also enter the Sala degli Otto (hall of 8; used as an office): note the carved wooden ceiling.

Loggia della Signoria (1 E3). Also improperly termed the "Loggia dell'Orcagna" (from the nickname of the artist, Andrea di Cione,

who supposedly designed the loggia) and also the *Loggia dei Lanzi* (because during the reign of the duke Alessandro I de' Medici, the German Lanzichenecchi, or Lansquenets, camped here), this loggia was built by Benci di Cione and Simone Talenti (1376-82) for the assemblies and public cerimonies of the Signoria.

This building offers mute testimony – with its three bays with large round arches, with the polylobate panels, the straight-line crown, and the silhouette of the cornicework – to the blend of late-Gothic style with classical style.

In the high panels, set between the arches, note the *Theological and Cardinal Virtues*, carved to models by Agnolo Gaddi in the second half of the 14th c.

Under the left arcade is the renowned **Perseus*** by Benvenuto Cellini, a large bronze statue (3.2 m. tall) depicting the hero raising high the head of the newly slain Medusa; it was completed after nearly ten years of failed efforts, due to technical problems involved in casting so large a work. In 1554 it was placed in the loggia, in explicit competition with the masterpieces of Michelangelo and Donatello, set before Palazzo Vecchio. Under the right arcade, note the **Rape of the Sabines***, a marble group by Giambologna (1583); it is thought to be the first sculpture created without one perspectival point of view being emphasized over all the others, so that it could

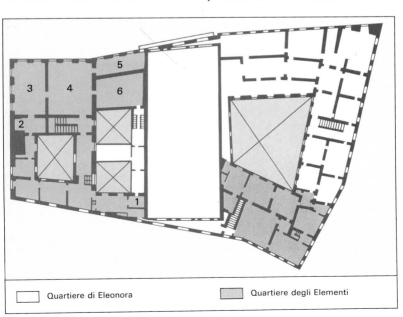

| Quartiere di Eleonora | Quartiere degli Elementi |

Palazzo Vecchio: third floor

be admired from all directions.

Inside the loggia: on the right is another marble group by Giambologna, *Hercules with the Centaur Nessus* (1599); at the center, an ancient copy of a Greek original from the 4th c. B.C., *Menelaus Holding up the Body of Patroclus*; on the left, *Abduction of Polyxena*, a 19th-c. Florentine sculpture by Pio Fedi. On the far wall, note six Roman statues of women.

Lastly, a curious note: on the right wall, a Latin inscription notes that the grand duchy did not adopt the common calendar until 1750 (before that, the Florentines celebrated the New Year from 25 March, i.e., from the Incarnation of Christ).

Also in the square. At n. 5, in the Palazzo della Cassa di Risparmio, is the provisional home of the *Raccolta d'Arte Contempo-* *ranea "Alberto della Ragione"* (1 D-E3): this collection of modern art, occupying 21 halls, features works of some of the most noteworthy Italian artists of the 20th c. (including Filippo de Pisis, Corrado Cagli, Franco Gentilini, Arturo Tosi, Ottone Rosai, Virgilio Guidi, Mino Maccari, Mario Sironi, Massimo Campigli, Giorgio de Chirico, Giorgio Morandi, Carlo Carrà, Mirko, and Marino Marini), and will someday be housed in the future Museum of Contemporary Art.

At n. 7 stands the *Palazzo Uguccioni*, an original late-Renaissance building erected by Mariotto di Zanobi Folfi (1549), and probably designed by Michelangelo or by Antonio da Sangallo.

At the corner of Via de' Gondi, at n. 10 stands the *Palazzo del Tribunale di Mercatanzia*, originally built in the 14th c., where merchants settled disputes.

2.2 The Uffizi

The focal point of this route is the tour of the renowned Galleria degli Uffizi, one of the most noteworthy Italian collections of art, and one of the largest collections on earth. It is housed in the Palazzo degli Uffizi, which you can reach from Piazza della Signoria, by heading toward the banks of the Arno between the Loggia dei Lanzi and Palazzo Vecchio. This building was erected at the behest of Cosimo I de' Medici, who at the time was at the apex of his power and wealth. The purpose of the building was to unite in one structure thirteen different magistracies (hence "Uffizi," or offices), that till then had been scattered in various buildings. With this action, reinforced by the 'physical' connection of the Uffizi with Palazzo Vecchio, on the one hand, and with Palazzo Pitti – via the Corridoio Vasariano – on the other, the grand duke officially sanctioned the centralization of all power and the entire apparatus of state into his own hands.

Piazzale degli Uffizi and Palazzo degli Uffizi (1 E3-4; 4 C5; 5 C1-2). Piazzale degli Uffizi is the handsome area enclosed by the three wings of the Palazzo degli Uffizi, a majestic building designed by Vasari, who undertook its construction in 1560; the building was completed, after Vasari's death, by Bernardo Buontalenti and Alfonso Parigi (1580). The palazzo, with an architraved loggia, in Doric style (a style that was "more solid and more certain, and which had always greatly pleased the Duke," as Vasari was to write), is made up of two long parallel wings, joined at one extremity by a short transverse wing. Vasari incorporated into the first stretch of the right wing (also called the west wing, or the "ala di ponente") the ancient Palazzo della Zecca, or Mint (you should also note the unusual *Porta delle Suppliche*, or door of supplications, by Buontalenti, while the church of S. Pier Scheraggio – which dated from the 11th c. and had already been partly demolished in order to make way for the widening of Via della Ninna – was incorporated into the left wing (or east wing, or "ala di levante"). The square, oriented in such a way as to frame in perspective the Palazzo Vecchio, is open at the far end over the Arno; from there one has a handsome view of Ponte Vecchio.

Galleria degli Uffizi* (1 E3-4). This gallery is located in the Palazzo degli Uffizi, and possesses one of the leading and best-known collections on earth of Italian and European art from the 12th to the 18th c.: Tuscan art up to the 16th c. is a fundamental part of the collection; Venetian art is an equally important component, along with Northern European art and the collection of self-portraits; there is a remarkable collection of antiquities.

Considered the first museum of modern Europe, the Uffizi has undergone extensive transformations and additions over the course of its four centuries of life. In 1581 Buontalenti, at the wishes of the grand duke Francesco I, enclosed the loggia on the third floor of the east wing, to accommodate a collection of statues and paintings. In 1584 the same architect built the octagonal gallery, also in the east wing, to contain the most precious objects in the Medici collections; two years after, he built a large theater, which was later destroyed. The original core of the gallery expanded, generation after generation, through the constant interest and encouragement of the Medici; the collections included not only works of art, but also weapons, naturalistic specimens, and objects of technical and scientific interest. The original criteria for the selection of paintings came from Vasari, and there was a special focus on the artists of the Cinquecento (the artists that Vasari, in his "Vite," or "Lives," had described as 'moderni'); it had been Vasari's idea to balance the statues of the great Florentine masters (Donatello, Michelangelo) against statues of the ancients, to show how the Florentines had been able to emulate the ancients.

In 1631, following the marriage of Ferdinando II to the daughter of the last duke of Urbino, the Uffizi received paintings by Piero della Francesca, Raphael, Titian, and Federico Barocci (the so-called "inheritance of Urbino"); the works of other Venetian painters were the contribution of the cardinal Leopoldo, brother of the grand duke; Leopoldo also began the collection of drawings, miniatures, and self-portraits. Between the end of the 17th c. and the beginning of the 18th c., Cosimo III enlarged the collection with Flemish paintings and with the purchase of exquisite statues in Rome, including the famed Medici Venus.

In 1737 Anna Maria Luisa, the last of the Medici, left the entire collection to the dukes of Lorraine, on the condition that it remain in Florence for all time, inalienable and open to the public. Between 1771 and 1772 the house of Lorraine began to reorganize the immense body of material, concentrating on the painting, sculpture, and applied arts, and spinning off the scientific collections and the arms and armor. The Uffizi began to acquire its modern-day constitution as a collection of paintings in the second half of the 19th c., but it was not until the beginning of the 20th c., especially following the expansion of the sections devoted to the Trecento and the Quattrocento, that the Uffizi began to be a chronologically complete exhibition of great Italian painting.

Currently, 2,000 works of art are on display, while another 1,800 pieces lie in storage. A major reorganization is planned; the exhibition area will extend to the second floor as well, to the rooms that until recently (1988) were occupied by the Archivio di Stato, or state archives. Following the damage caused by the terrorist attack of 27 May 1993, some halls in the third corridor are temporarily closed.

The entrance is located at the beginning of the east loggia (on your left if you are arriving from Piazza della Signoria). On the ground floor, in the rooms originally forming the *church of S. Pier Scheraggio*, which was incorporated into the palazzo by Vasari, is the series of frescoes of *Famous Men* * by Andrea del Castagno (ca. 1450), originally from the Villa Carducci-Pandolfini a Legnaia, as well as an *Annunciation* by Botticelli (1481), a fresco detached from the church of S. Martino alla Scala.

A large staircase, built by Vasari, leads to the second floor, where the Medici theater once stood. This area now contains the *Gabinetto dei Disegni e delle Stampe* *, or

Detail of the ceiling in the first corridor of the Uffizi

Cabinet of Drawings and Prints: an exceptional graphics collection comprising more than 100,000 sheets, from the 14th to the 20th c. (open only to scholars, for purposes of study).

If you continue along the large staircase you will reach the third floor, where there

are two vestibules, which lead into the gallery, and which contain a collection of busts of grand dukes and Roman statues.

Collection of sculpture. The visit begins with a walk through the corridors that correspond to the three wings of the building. In these corridors, with their richly decorated ceilings, there is a large collection of Roman sculptures and Roman copies of Greek originals. These works, retouched and in some cases partly redone during the Renaissance, constituted a fundamental part of the gallery until the 19th c. We should point out, in the first corridor (east): *Hercules and the Centaur*, a Roman sarcophagus with a depiction of the *Legend of Phaedra and Hippolytus*, and another *Hercules*; to the sides of the Tribuna entrance, *Hercules*, from an original statue by Lisippo, and *bust of Hadrian* (once belonging to Lawrence the Magnificent); in the second corridor (south): *head of a dying giant, Seated girl, ready to dance*, and an altar with the *Sacrifice of Iphigenia*; in the third corridor (west): two statues of *Marsyas*, a *Celestial Venus*, and a bust of a *boy*.

As we return to the beginning of the first corridor, we encounter Hall 1, devoted to Roman antiquities (sculptures, reliefs): note in particular three Roman copies of the *Doriforo* by Polyclitus, a *torso* in green basalt and a bust of *Cicero* made of onyx.

Collection of painting. The gallery proper begins with the large section devoted to Tuscan painting from the Duecento to the Quattrocento (13th to 15th c.; halls 2-15),

"Coronation of the Virgin Mary" by Lorenzo Monaco

arranged chronologically. Opening this section is a powerful and unforgettable comparison between three famous Madonnas 'in maestà,' meaning paintings of the Virgin Mary, enthroned, with a court of saints (Hall 2). The first, known as the **Madonna Rucellai***, was painted by the Siennese artist Duccio di Buoninsegna (1285); this work still reveals a certain influence of the Byzantine stylistic tradition. The second, known as the **Maestà di S. Trìnita***, was painted toward the end of the 13th c. by the Florentine artist Cimabue; here, we can already see a trend toward concrete portrayal, relief, and volume. It is not until we reach the **Madonna d'Ognissanti***, however, by Giotto (ca. 1310) – even more than in his *polyptych of Badia* (ca. 1301) – that we see decisive steps taken toward true realism, with chiaroscuro, a sense of depth, and the arrangement of the surrounding figures.

The work begun by the great forefathers of Italian art continues with the artists of the Siennese Trecento (14th c.; Hall 3): Simone Martini and the two Lorenzetti brothers, Ambrogio and Pietro. Simone Martini's **Annunciation*** (1333) – with a golden, abstract, highly Gothic atmosphere – does contain touches of realism (the lilies, the shadow in the book, the shyness or reluctance of the Virgin Mary); the Lorenzetti brothers, closer to the sensibility of Giotto, are present with the *stories of St. Nicholas* (ca. 1330), the *Virgin Mary with Saint Nicholas and Saint Procolo* (1332) and the *Presentation in the Temple* (1342), all works by Ambrogio; and the *Madonna in gloria* (ca. 1340) and the *Pala della Beata Umiltà* (ca. 1340), by Pietro.

The workshop of Giotto (Hall 4) dominated in Florence in the Trecento, although there was a certain creative aridity after the middle of the century: the most significant work on display here is the *Deposition from the Cross** by Giottino. It is surrounded by paintings by Bernardo Daddi (including the predella of the *polyptych of S. Pancrazio*), Taddeo Gaddi, the brothers Nardo, Andrea and Jacopo di Cione, and Giovanni da Milano (*polyptych of Ognissanti*).

The period of International Gothic (Halls 5-6), which flourished in Tuscany between the end of the 14th c, and the early-15th c., had its most elegant artist in Lorenzo Monaco; alongside his *Coronation of the Virgin Mary* (1414) hangs an *Adoration of the Magi* (1422); compare it with Gentile da Fabriano's treat-

Portraits of Battista Sforza and Federico da Montefeltro, by Piero della Francesca

ment of the same theme in an **Adoration of the Magi*** (1423) which is a triumph of profane and naturalistic Gothic. Note the *Thebaide* (by an unknown Florentine artist) with its remarkably vivid details, and the *Madonna dell'Umiltà* (attributed to Masolino) for its evanescent sweetness.

The next room (Hall 7) is full of masterpieces, and is dedicated to the early Tuscan Renaissance. It begins with Masaccio, who achieved the revolution in painting that Donatello and Brunelleschi brought about, respectively, in sculpture and architecture. In the *Virgin Mary with Christ Child and St. Ann**, which Masaccio painted around 1424 with Masolino, note the Virgin Mary, solemn and clearly corporeal (she was painted by Masaccio). Fra Angelico in his *Coronation of the Virgin Mary* (ca. 1435) – amidst a clearly Gothic profusion of gold – shows a new sensibility in his careful attention to perspective in the choirs of angels. One can hardly help but note the **Battle of San Romano***, painted by Paolo Uccello at the end of the 1430s for Cosimo the Elder; this panel is famous for its intricate perspective, which has lances, horses, and men all converging toward the central vanishing point, strangely frozen into a surreal motionlessness. Domenico Veneziano is present with his painting *Virgin Mary, Christ Child, and Saints* (ca. 1445), a sacred conversation that is given a realistic perspective and lit by sunlight pouring in from above. His pupil, Piero della Francesca, developed the description of details in his **portraits of the duke and duchess of Urbino*** (ca. 1465);

among the detailwork, note the jewelry, the wrinkles in the skin, and note the attention to landscape and the careful perspective.

The next two halls contain works by Filippo Lippi and Antonio Pollaiolo; these paintings show an increasingly refined elegance, a clear forerunner of the work of Botticelli (by him, in Hall 9: *Strength*, 1470, his earliest documented work, and the *Story of Judith*, from ca. 1472). In Hall 8, is the *Coronation of the Virgin Mary* by Lippi (1441-47); here the artist integrates the influence of sculpture of his time (Donatello, Luca della Robbia) with the virtuosity inspired by the Flemish; also by Lippi you can admire the elegance of the *Virgin Mary with Christ Child and angels* (ca. 1465) and two *Adorations of the Christ Child*; more traditional are the *Virgin Mary with Christ Child and saints* and the *Annunciation* by Alesso Baldovinetti. The distinctive subjects of Antonio Pollaiolo (Hall 9) are the human body in motion (as in the *Labors of Hercules*) or portraits (note the enchanting *portrait of a woman*).

In the large Hall 10-14 we see Hugo van der Goes (right wall) with his important **Portinari Triptych*** (ca. 1475), commissioned by Tommaso Portinari, agent of the Medici in Bruges. When this work arrived in Florence, it greatly reinforced the influence of Flemish art in Tuscany: its chief impact was due to its capacity for description (the background, the light, the flowers, the shepherds). Certainly it influenced, for instance, the *Adoration of the Shepherds* by Domenico Ghirlandaio, painted in 1487 (on the left).

But the star of the hall is Sandro Botticelli. If his youthful *Virgin Mary and Saints* reveals his dependence upon Lippi, the *portrait of a man with medal of Cosimo the Elder* (1475) unquestionably features a Flemish background. *Pallas and the Centaur* (the centaur clearly symbolizes man, torn between reason and instinct, who allows himself however to be guided by divine wisdom) is the first of the 'mythologies', i.e., the allegories of Neo-Platonic inspiration, which were painted in the early 1480s for Lorenzo de' Medici, cousin of Lorenzo the Magnificent; next comes the renowned **Primavera***, or Spring, which develops – with its solemn rhythm of a sacred conversation – the theme of divinity attained through love; while the **Birth of Venus*** may personify the birth of true beauty through the effects of the Spirit. After his spectacular *Madonna del Magnificat*, however, the tone became sterner (*Madonna della Melagrana*, altar piece of *St. Barnabas*). Botticelli studied Dante, and was inspired by his work for his *Coronation of the Virgin Mary* with its archaic gold background, while the preachings of Savonarola (1494) brought a new wave of pessimism and mysticism to his work: *Calumny* (ca. 1495) thus expressed the failure of Humanistic optimism, and proclaimed the baseness of man, forcing Truth to succumb.

The next room (Hall 15) has two masterpieces by Leonardo da Vinci, the early *Annunciation*, painted when the artist was only twenty, and the unfinished **Adoration of the Magi***, in which he eliminates the traditional components (the shed, St. Joseph, the festive procession of the Magi) and concentrates on the Virgin Mary and the Christ Child, isolated in the center. Surrounding these paintings are works by Verrocchio (*Baptism of Christ*, ca. 1475: the angel on the left is by Leonardo da Vinci), by Perugino (*Christ in the Garden, Pietà*), by Signorelli (*Crucifix with Mary Magdalene*), by Piero di Cosimo (*Incarnation*, ca. 1505), and by Lorenzo di Credi (*Adoration of the Shepherds*).

In the little adjoining room (Hall 16), once a loggia, is a *Deposition in the Tomb* by Rogier van der Weyden (ca. 1450), a temporary installation. Hall 17, known as the "Stanzino della Matematica," was built at the behest of Ferdinando I for scientific instruments, like the previous room, and it contains two of the best-known marble sculptures in the Uffizi, *Hermaphrodite* and *Amor and Psyche*, Roman copies from Hellenistic models; you enter this room from Hall 18.

The little octagonal room called the **Tribuna*** (Hall 18), the oldest in the gallery, was famous in centuries past because it held the most important, best-loved, and liveliest items in the Medici collections. This is the only room still to maintain the original basic theme of the Uffizi, i.e., the contrast between the ancients (the statues) and the moderns (the paintings). Around the exceedingly handsome *table*, inlaid with semi-precious stones (1649) stand a number of famous sculptures: *Dancing Faun* (Greek replica, 3rd c. B.C.), the vibrant *Wrestlers*, the much-admired *Medici Venus** (1st c. B.C.), copy of an original by Praxiteles, *Knife-Grinder* and *Young Apollo*. The painters belong to the Florentine Cinquecento. On the walls are works by: Vasari (*Lorenzo the Magnificent*), Pontormo (*Cosimo the Elder, Virgin Mary with Christ Child and Young St. John*), Bronzino (*Bartolomeo Panciatichi* and his wife *Lucrezia*, the *portraits of the little Medici princes*, the *Duchess Eleonora with Her Son Giovanni, Young Man with a Lute*), Rosso Fiorentino (*Putto Musician*), Andrea del Sarto (*Young Man with the 'Petrarchino'*, i.e., a copy of Petrarch's "Canzoniere") and others.

Hall 19 gravitates around the paintings by Luca Signorelli and Perugino: note, by Signorelli a *Virgin Mary with Christ Child* (ca. 1490) and a *Sacred Family*, which was to serve as inspiration for Michelangelo's Tondo Doni (Hall 25); there is an array of portraits by Perugino, particularly the *Monks* in profile (1500), the *portrait of Francesco delle Opere* (1494), and the *portrait of a young man*. Surroundings these works are paintings by Lorenzo di Credi (*Annunciation*) and Piero di Cosimo (*Liberation of Andromeda*).

In Hall 20 there are major examples of German painting between the 15th and 16th c.: most of the work is by Albrecht Dürer. You can clearly admire his skill in rendering concrete reality, of northern influence (*portrait of his father*, 1490); you can also note his debt to Italian art, chiefly in his mastery of perspective and use of color (*Adoration of the Magi*, 1504; *St. Philip and St. James*, 1516).

Hall 21 features Venetian painting from the second half of the 15th c., or Quattrocento; the protagonists here are Giovanni Bellini and Giorgione. By Bellini note the *Lament over the Dead Christ*, but especially the learned and arcane **Sacred Allegory***, intended for a learned and refined audience of Humanists. The mysterious characters, involved in a sacred conversation, stand out against a lake in the background, and are bathed in golden light. Giorgione, in his youthful works, *Judgement of Moses* and *Judgement of Solomon*, was clearly influenced by northern European naturalism; also by Giorgione is the melancholy and allusive portrait of a *Warrior with His Page*, which was inspired by a work by the Attic painter Apelles. Among the other painters whose work appears in this room: Bartolomeo Vivarini, Cosmè Tura, Cima da Conegliano (*Virgin Mary with Christ Child*), and Vittore Carpaccio.

In Hall 22 we return to northern and Flemish culture, with Albrecht Altdorfer (*stories of St. Florian*, ca. 1530) and portraits by Hans Holbein the Younger (*Sir Richard Southwell*, 1536, and *self-portrait*). Also note the presence of work by Hans Memling, among other Flemish artists (*Mater Dolorosa, Virgin Mary Enthroned, Benedetto Portinari,* and *St. Benedict*).

Hall 23 is devoted to Lombard and Emilian painting of the Quattrocento and Cinquecento. Andrea Mantegna, court painter in Mantua, is the patriarch of the Renaissance in Northern Italy. The *Madonna delle Cave* is emblematic of his work, epic and pristine; alongside it you may note the *Portrait of the Cardinal Carlo de' Medici* and a triptych (*Ascension, Adoration of the Magi,* and *Circumcision*) from the Palazzo Ducale in Mantua. While the style of Vincenzo Foppa (*Virgin Mary with Christ Child and an angel*, ca. 1480) can be traced back to Mantegna, Leonardo da Vinci was clearly the inspiration for Boltraffio (*Narcissus*), Bernardino Luini (*Herodiad*) and Sodoma (*Christ with His Jailers*). Correggio's style of painting is wholly different, and is almost entirely personal; consider his *Rest on the Flight into Egypt, with St. Francis* (ca. 1517), with its distinctive and innovative diagonal structure, and the *Virgin Mary in Adoration*. Hall 24 (closed to the public) contains a part of the exceptional Medici collection of miniatures.

After you have crossed the second corridor, the tour of the museum resumes in the third corridor, with a group of halls (25-27) dedicated to Florentine paintings in the first four decades of the 16th c. In Hall 25, we find two substantially traditional painters – Fra Bartolomeo (*Apparition of the Virgin Mary to St. Bernard*, 1504-7) and Mariotto Albertinelli (*Visitation*, 1503); therefore the contrast with a work that is clearly an ar-

chetype of Mannerism is particularly dramatic: the **Tondo Doni*** by Michelangelo (Michelangelo may also have created the *frame*). Painted in 1504 or shortly thereafter, this work depicts the sacred family (St. Joseph is shown handing the Christ Child to

The "Tondo Doni" by Michelangelo

the Virgin Mary) in an absolutely unconventional manner; the nudes seen in the background probably represent the pagan world, excluded from salvation (this could be the significance of the low wall directly behind the sacred family, in the foreground). Also note the unsettling *Salome* by the Spanish master, Alonso Berruguete (ca. 1515).

Almost contemporary with the Tondo Doni are the early works of Raphael on display in Hall 26: these are *portraits* of the duchess and duke of Urbino, *Elisabetta Gonzaga* and *Guidobaldo da Montefeltro* (this latter is the son of the duke and duchess painted by Piero della Francesca), and *Francesco Maria della Rovere*, their heir. Next is the famous **Madonna del Cardellino*** (1505-6), a harmonious and natural blend of different sources of inspiration (Leonardo, Michelangelo, Fra Bartolomeo). From Raphael's Roman period comes the important **portrait of Leo X***; here Raphael shows full mastery of his use of color (note the symphony of reds) and a great virtuosity in detail. Alongside these masterpieces hangs the *Madonna of the Harpies** (1517), by Andrea del Sarto: his sweet and solemn style of painting is also exemplified in the *Pala Vallombrosana*, an altar piece, and in his *St. James* (1528).

Works by two Mannerist artists, Pontormo and Rosso Fiorentino, hang in Hall 27: of special note, by Pontormo, the *Dinner in Emmaus** (1525), while by Rosso Fiorentino, note the *Virgin Mary with Christ Child and* saints (1518) and *Moses Defending the Daughters of Jethro* (ca. 1523). Also of interest are the works by Bronzino: (*Christ, Dead, with the Virgin Mary and Mary Magdalene* and the *Panciatichi Sacred Family*).

The next room (Hall 28) is dedicated to Titian. The Venetian artist is represented with a vast anthology of portraits, ranging from a *Knight of Malta* (ca. 1510), to portraits of *Francesco Maria della Rovere* and *Eleonora Gonzaga*, duke and duchess of Urbino, and the *portrait of Lodovico Beccadelli* (1552). Titian's celebrated **Venus of Urbino*** – here the artist makes full use of the lessons learned from the work of Giorgione, Bellini, and Carpaccio in a painting in which color shapes and embodies reality – is flanked by his *Flora* (ca. 1520), midway between myth and portraiture, and *Venus with Cupid* (ca. 1550). Note the *Sacred Family, with Young St. John and Mary Magdalene* by Palma the Elder (ca. 1515).

Halls 29-31 feature artists from central Italy and from the region of Emilia-Ferrara. Of special note, in the first room, are the works by Parmigianino, with his *Virgin Mary with Christ Child and saints* (1530) and especially the renowned **Madonna with Long Neck***, a painting that was left unfinished (note, to the right of the prophet in the background, the foot of a figure left unfinished). It appears with works by Luca Cambiaso (*Virgin Mary with Christ Child*, ca. 1570; Hall 29), by Mazzolino (*Virgin Mary with Christ Child and saints*, 1522-23; Hall 30), and by Dosso Dossi (*Virgin Mary in Glory, and Saints John the Baptist and John the Evangelist*; Hall 31).

Hall 32 continues the review of Venetian painting of the Cinquecento, or 16th c., which extends into part of Hall 35. The paintings hanging in this section are largely the work of Sebastiano del Piombo and Lorenzo Lotto (Hall 32), Paolo Veronese (Hall 34) and Tintoretto (Hall 35). Sebastiano painted the *portrait of a woman* and the *Death of Adonis* (ca. 1511), while Lotto did the *Susannah and the Elders* (1517). Following the interval of Hall 33 (also called the "Corridoio del Cinquecento"; this corridor contains a series of portraits by European artists, as well as a number of paintings from the second half of the Florentine Cinquecento, or 16th c.), we return to Venetian painting with Paolo Veronese (Hall 34): among the works by Veronese, you should note the Manneristic *Sacred Family* (ca. 1564); also note the *Transfiguration* by the

Portrait of Charles V by Van Dyck

Brescian painter Giovan Girolamo Savoldo and the portrait of *Anonymous with Book* by the Bergamasque artist G.B. Moroni. In Hall 35, alongside a number of paintings by Jacopo Bassano, we have numerous works by Tintoretto: *portraits*, mythological scenes (*Leda*) and religious subjects. And Tintoretto certainly influenced El Greco in his *St. John the Evangelist and St. Francis* (ca. 1600). In this same room, you can admire the works of the Urbino-born Federico Barocci: aside from the portrait of the last duke of Urbino, *Francesco Maria II della Rovere*, which should be compared with the portrait by Titian of his ducal ancestor with the same name (Hall 28), you should note the *Noli me tangere* (ca. 1590) and especially the large *Madonna del Popolo** (1579) – painted for the Confraternita della Misericordia of Arezzo. This painting gives shape to the more "human" aspects of the Counter Reformation (as does the *Stigmata of St. Francis* by Cigoli).

The tour of the museum continues, after the exit vestibule, with Italian and non-Italian artists of the 17th and 18th c. Hall 41 is devoted chiefly to Rubens, forerunner of the Baroque style. Rubens painted the great canvases of the *Battle of Ivry* and the *Entrance of Henry IV into Paris* (1627-30), episodes from French history transformed into epics and viewed in the light of the teachings of Mantegna, Leonardo da Vinci, Raphael, and Titian. Alongside these majestic and "important" paintings are a Rubens *self-portrait* (interesting to compare this one with the *self-portrait* by Velázquez), and a portrait of his wife, *Isabella Brandt** (1625-26). A pupil of Rubens, Antonie Van Dyck excelled in official portraits: *the equestrian portrait of Charles V* originated from the portrait by Titian, in Madrid; note also the *portrait of Jean de Montfort*. Justus Suttermans (*portrait of Galileo Galilei*, 1635) completes the hall.

The last "historic" room in the gallery, Hall 42, interrupts the chronological sequence of paintings: it contains the *Group of the Niobìdi**, Roman copies of Hellenistic originals. The statues were inspired by the myth of Niobe, who was so proud of her many children that she was punished by Apollo and Diana, who gained their revenge by murdering her children. The sculptures were unearthed in Rome in 1583: they were moved to the park of Villa Medici, and remained there until they were installed in this room, designed expressly to hold them (1781). Also note the *Vaso Medici*, actually a Neo-Attic krater from the 1st c. A.D.

Caravaggio is the central figure of hall 43, dedicated to early-17th-c. painting in Rome. His **Bacchus*** strives for descriptive accuracy, and concedes nothing to the myth; the same is true of his *Medusa**, in reality a tournament shield; note the raw violence of the depiction. Equally impressive is the *Sacrifice of Isaac*, for which Caravaggio used the same model he had used for the Medusa. It is interesting to compare these works with the classical *Venus* (or *Bacchante*, 1588) by Annibale Carracci. Also worthy of note are works by Guercino (*Summer Sports*, 1617), by Claude Lorrain (*Port, with Medici Villa*, 1637) and by Salvator Rosa (*Landscape with figures*).

More paintings from 17th-c. Holland are displayed in hall 44: the most noteworthy works are two *self-portraits** by Rembrandt, one from about 1634 and one from thirty years later; in them the artist strives to at-

tain psychological truth, as he does in the portrait of *An Old Man*. Other artists include: Jan Brueghel the Elder (*Landscape with Ford*, 1607), Hercules Seghers (*Mountainous Landscape*), Jacob van Ruysdael (*Landscapes*, 1660-70), Rachel Ruysch (*Fruit*, 1711), and Jan Steen (*Dinner*).

The painting of the 18th c. is the subject of the last room in the gallery (hall 45): the Italian artists Crespi (*Family of the Painter*, 1708), Piazzetta (*Susannah and the Elders*, 1720), Canaletto (*Views* of the Grand Canal and Palazzo Ducale), Guardi (*Capricci*), Rosalba Carriera (*Felicita Sartori*), Alessandro Longhi (*Venetian Noblewoman*) hang alongside work by the French artists Nattier, Liotard, and Chardin and the great Spanish painter Goya (*Countess de Chinchòn*).
From the terrace at the end of the west corridor, you enjoy a remarkable panoramic view* of Piazza della Signoria.

If you retrace your steps, between halls 25 and 34 you will find the passageway that leads to the *Corridoio Vasariano* (open by reservation). Built in 1565 by Vasari, for Cosimo de' Medici, this corridor basically constituted a handy, private, high-security road linking the Uffizi with Palazzo Pitti, over the Ponte Vecchio. In it there are roughly 700 works of art: in the section located inside the Uffizi are works by artists influenced by Caravaggio, artists of 17th-c. Bologna, Rome, Venetia, Genoa, Naples, and Lombardy, and artists of 18th-c. Italy and France. The section running over the Ponte Vecchio begins the celebrated *collection of self-portraits**. This collection opens with Italian artists up to the 18th c. (in particular, note the self-portraits of Vasari, Bernini, and Annibale Carracci), continues with non-Italians, also up to the 18th c. (among them: Rubens, Rembrandt, Velázquez, and an early copy of the self-portrait by Dürer) and then ends with artists of the 19th and 20th c. (among them: David, Canova, Hayez, Delacroix, and Ingres).

The exit vestibule, between halls 35 and 41, was originally the entrance to the gallery. Among other 17th-c. paintings it holds the *Madonna della Neve* by Guido Reni; note also the *torso of satyr* and the *Wild Boar**, copy of an original by Lysippus, in turn imitated by Pietro Tacca for the "Porcellino" of the fountain in the Mercato Nuovo.

3 The Quarter of S. Giovanni

Enclosed by Via Faenza to the west, Borgo Pinti to the east, and the walls of the outermost fortified perimeter, the quarter of S. Giovanni developed from the late Middle Ages onward into a fairly regular system of roads around a fundamental artery, the Via S. Gallo (a continuation of the Roman "cardo maximus"). This area saw a concentration of convents, hospitals, and hospices for pilgrims, alternating with residential lots with a distinctive structure – a narrow street front stretching back quite far into the interior of the block.

In the 15th and 16th c., this area was profoundly modified by the active presence of the Medici, who made it their "general headquarters": aside from the family residence (now Palazzo Medici-Riccardi), fundamental monuments of this cultural policy are the complex of S. Lorenzo and the convent of S. Marco (it was from here at the end of the 15th c. that Savonarola launched his ascetic revolution). Numerous other buildings contribute to the prevalently Renaissance flavor of the quarter. Of particular note is the harmonious group of structures (porticoes, hospital, church, and confraternity) assembled around Piazza della Santissima Annunziata. There are modern additions, as well, largely in the context of 19th-c. projects: the extension of Via Larga (now Via Cavour) out to the walls and the opening of what are now Via XXVII Aprile and Piazza della Indipendenza

3.1 From the Duomo to the Accademia

This route is quite intricate and complex; it begins near the Baptistery of S. Giovanni and continues along the axis of Via de' Martelli-Via Cavour, running deep into a part of the city that abounds in relics of the Renaissance and the Medici family: Palazzo Medici-Riccardi; the complex of S. Lorenzo, with its mausoleum-sacristies; the convent of S. Marco, cultural center of the city under the Medici; not to mention the other lesser landmarks. The first stretch of this route – extending as far as Piazza S. Marco – runs along "show-case streets," such as the present-day Via de' Martelli and Via Cavour, rich in noteworthy architecture. The detours reach, for example, into areas that developed in the 19th c. (Mercato Centrale di S. Lorenzo, a major market), or else run past green havens of peace (the two hectares of the Orto Botanico, or botanical garden), or, in one case, as far as the edges of Florence (Museo Stibbert). Among the other museums past which the route runs, we should point out the Museo S. Marco and the Galleria dell'Accademia.

Via de' Martelli (1 B3; 3 E2). To the left of the facade of the cathedral, or Duomo runs this very lively street, which takes its name from the houses and family of the Martelli, along the left side of the street. At the corner of Via de' Gori stands the *church of S. Giovanni Evangelista*, known as *S. Giovannino degli Scolopi*, begun by Bartolomeo Ammannati in 1579 and completed by Alfonso Parigi the Younger.

Palazzo Medici-Riccardi* (3 D-E2). This was the first, superb example of a noble home in Renaissance Florence. It was built between 1444 and 1462 by Michelozzo di Bartolomeo for the Medici family, who made it their chief residence until 1540. Note the distinctive graduation of the external facing, progressing from the high-relief rustication of the ground floor to the hewn ashlars of the second floor, and ending with the smooth surface of the third floor. The facades, with twin-light mullioned windows, are topped by a sharply jutting cornice, in the classical style. In 1517 the large "finestre inginocchiate" (windows set on volute

Palazzo Medici-Riccardi

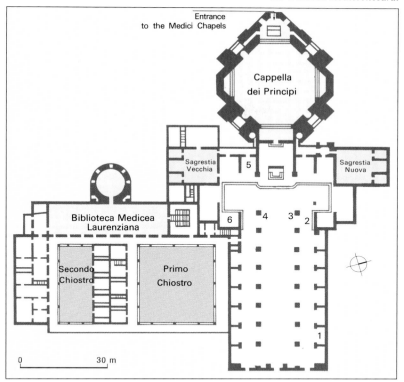

Entrance
to the Medici Chapels

Cappella
dei Principi

Sagrestia
Vecchia

Sagrestia
Nuova

5

Biblioteca Medicea
Laurenziana

6   4   3   2

Secondo
Chiostro

Primo
Chiostro

1

0   30 m

The Complex of S. Lorenzo

brackets) were installed. A "panca da via," or street-side bench, runs the entire length of the facade. The Riccardi family, who purchased the palazzo in 1659, added a wing with seven windows on the main facade. It now houses the Florence Prefecture.

You then enter the first *courtyard**, surrounded by a portico with Corinthian columns, topped by a high frieze, with twin-light mullioned windows on the second floor and a loggia on the third floor. Under the portico you can see much of the Collezione Riccardi, one of the richest private archeological collections in Florence . The first stairway on the right leads to the **Cappella dei Magi***, a masterpiece of the early Florentine Renaissance, by Michelozzo (the architecture) and Benozzo Gozzoli (the frescoes). The chapel – square, with a small apse for the altar – contains carved and inlaid wooden *stalls* along the walls; the *ceiling* is also made of carved, painted, and gilt wood, while the *floor* is decorated with inlaid marble and porphyry. On the walls, note the series of frescoes depicting the *Cavalcade of the Magi**, by Gozzoli (1459-60); the great descriptive and narrative talent of the artist, both in de-

picting landscape and characters (note the clothing of the figures, largely representing members of the Medici family), make this one of the best-known pictorial complexes of the Renaissance.

Piazza S. Lorenzo (3 E1). Behind the Palazzo Medici-Riccardi, this square is dominated by the facade of the Basilica di S. Lorenzo; in the background you can see the impressive dome of the Cappella dei Principi. The scene is made picturesque by the popular and lively marketplace. At the corner of the stairway leading up to the church stands the *monument to Giovanni dalle Bande Nere* (a mercenary commander and soldier of fortune, father of Cosimo I de' Medici), by Baccio Bandinelli (1540).

Basilica di S. Lorenzo* (3 E1). This basilica is considered to be one of the great architectural masterpieces of the early Florentine Renaissance. The facade is faced in simple rough-hewn stone, because the grandiose design by Michelangelo was never built. Counterbalancing this rough facade is the lively interior of the high 'tiburio', with the large dome of the Cappella dei

63

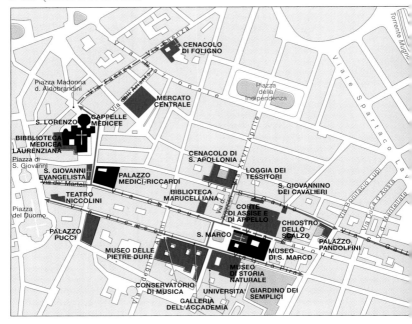

Principi, the smaller dome of the Sagrestia Nuova, and the 18th-c. campanile. According to tradition, an Ambrosian church was built in the 4th c., and then rebuilt in the Romanesque style in the 11th c. The present-day construction dates from the 15th c., when the Medici, wishing to make it their family church, decided to radically renovate it, entrusting the project to Brunelleschi. That architect presented his designs in 1421, and began work, but the church was not finished until after Brunelleschi's death (1446), and was completed in 1461 by Antonio Manetti.

Inside one is immediately impressed by the remarkable harmony of the proportions by Brunelleschi. The nave and the two side aisles are divided by two lines of columns with Corinthian capitals, topped by round arches. The nave is topped by a lacunar ceiling, while the side aisles have ribbed vaults. The internal facade is by Michelangelo. In the second chapel on the right (1, in the plan on page 63) is the *Wedding of the Virgin Mary*, by Rosso Fiorentino (1523). Between the last chapel and right transept, you will find the marble *altar of the Sacrament** (2) by Desiderio da Settignano (ca. 1460), a refined piece of artwork that served as a model for many subsequent similar works. Before it (3), one of the *bronze pulpits** (the other one is in the facing aisle), late and unfinished works (ca.

1460) by Donatello and assistants, completed in the first half of the 17th c. with wooden panels made to look as if they were made of bronze; in the right-hand pulpit, note the *Martyrdom of St. Lawrence* and the *Resurrection* (respectively the first and sixth, proceeding from the small aisle to the right); in the left-hand pulpit (4), note the dramatic *Deposition*, believed to be by Donatello. In the left arm of the transept, the first chapel on the right (5) contains a wooden sculpture of the *Virgin Mary with Christ Child*, attributed to Giovanni Fetti (late-14th c.); the Cappella Martelli (6), an altar piece by Filippo Lippi (*Annunciation*, ca. 1450). Also note, on the wall at the head of the left aisle, a large fresco by Agnolo Bronzino (*Martyrdom of St. Lawrence*, 1565-69).

At the end of the left transept, a door leads into the **Sagrestia Vecchia***, or old sacristy, built by Brunelleschi (1421-26): this stupendous Renaissance creation is the product of a perfect fusion between architectural structure and the plastic decoration by Donatello. The structure is basically a cube topped by a hemispherical dome, with spandrels split up by ribbing in grey stone ("pietra grigia"). The little apse reproduces the same structure. The following are by Donatello: the *frieze* of cherubim and seraphim, the large lunettes over the doors (with *St. Cosma* and *St. Damian* on the right, and *St. Lawrence* and *St Stephen* on the

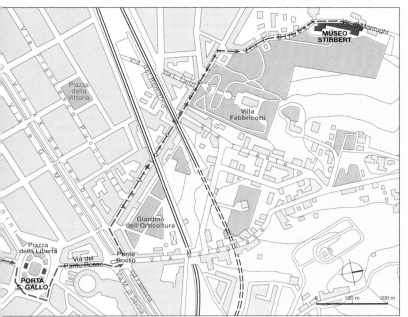

left), the tondoes in the walls (*Evangelists*) and in the spandrels (*stories of St. John the Evangelist*). The *bust of St. Lawrence* (on the right) is probably by Desiderio da Settignano, even though it has been attributed to Donatello, while Andrea Cavalcanti, known as the Buggiano, carried out the *tomb of Giovanni di Bicci de' Medici and his wife Piccarda Bueri* (at the center). The remarkable fresco in the vault of the apse depicts the appearance of the sky over Florence on the night of 4 July 1442. Donatello also did the bronze *doors*, with lively and expressive figures. On the left wall is the complex and refined *funerary monument to Piero and Giovanni de' Medici*, executed by Verrocchio in 1472, with a remarkable use of different materials (a source of inspiration for many decorative motifs used in the Renaissance).

Biblioteca Medicea Laurenziana* (3 E1). You enter this library by crossing the remarkable *first cloister* (entrance to the left of the facade of the basilica), executed in the style of Brunelleschi, with two registers of arches. At the far corner, note the *monument to Paolo Giovio*, bishop of Como, by Francesco da Sangallo (1560). This library is one of the most interesting architectural creations of the Florentine Cinquecento, a product of the great genius of Michelangelo; it possesses Italy's greatest collection of manuscripts. Michelangelo Buonarroti was

commissioned to create this structure by Pope Clement VII, specifically to house this collection, begun by Cosimo the Elder. Work began in 1524 under the personal supervision of Michelangelo, and was completed in 1568 by Bartolomeo Ammannati and Giorgio Vasari.

Cappelle Medicee* (3 E1). This name describes the complex of chapel/Mausoleum of the Princes, and the Sagrestia Nuova di S. Lorenzo, set within the vast dome of the basilica, its exterior similar to the apse of S. Maria del Fiore.
At number 6, Piazza Madonna degli Aldobrandini (plan page 63), you enter a crypt which leads onto the **Cappella dei Principi**, a splendid mausoleum of the Medici family. Devised by Cosimo I, it was built at the behest of Ferdinand I, according to plans laid down by M. Nigetti. Statues of each prince were to have been placed in the niches above the tombs, but only two - those of Ferdinand I (by P. Tacca, 1626-32) and Cosimo II (by Pietro and Ferdinando Tacca, 1626-1642) - were actually carried out.
From the corridor opposite the entrance, you can enter the **Sagrestia Nuova***, or New Sacristy, one of Michelangelo's masterpieces and a prototype for all Mannerist architecture. It is so-called in order to distinguish it from the Sagrestia Vecchia, or Old Sacristy, by Brunelleschi. In reality it is the funerary chapel of the family of Loren-

65

zo the Magnificent; the project was assigned to Michelangelo in 1520 by Pope Leo X and his cousin, Giulio Cardinal de' Medici. The artist worked on it, though with interruptions, until 1534, the year he left for Rome, leaving it unfinished; it was later completed by Vasari and Ammannati (1554-55). The architecture of the interior is inspired by that of the Sagrestia Vecchia, but expresses a greater vertical thrust, due to the inclusion of a pair of windows with pediments. The stone ribbing in "pietra serena" stands out against the white plaster, giving an impression of restless dynamism which is also transmitted to the sculptural **monuments*** by Michelangelo, set in the same space. To the right of the entrance is the *tomb of Lorenzo the Magnificent and his brother Giuliano*: a simple base upon which lies the sketchy but remarkable statue of the *Virgin Mary with Christ Child*, carved by the artist in 1521; on the sides, *St. Cosma* (on the left), by Giovanni Angelo Montorsoli, and *St. Damian* (on the right) by Raffaello da Montelupo, statues executed to designs by Michelangelo. On the right wall is the *monument to Giuliano, duke of Nemours*, the son of Lorenzo the Magnificent; he is depicted in soldier's garb, with a baton of command, and his face is idealized, quite unlike the actual appearance of the subject (to anyone who pointed out this discrepancy, Michelangelo replied that after ten centuries no one would notice anymore). On the sarcophagus lie the figures of *Day* (right), its face unfinished and shrouded in shadow, and *Night* (left), depicted as

a sleeping woman. Facing them is the *monument to Lorenzo, duke of Urbino*, depicted as a thoughtful condottiere (1533). Beneath him lie the statues of *Dawn* (1531) and *Dusk* (1531-32).

Piazza Madonna degli Aldobrandini marks the beginning of the long Via Faenza where the former *convent of the Monache di Foligno* (2 C4) stands at n. 40; this complex was built at the turn of the 14th c., and was completed in 1429. Inside, you can visit the large refectory, with a *Last Supper*, done by pupils of Perugino, among frescoes by Bicci di Lorenzo, detached from the original walls.
Take a short detour to the left in Via Nazionale (2 C4), and you can see the *Tabernacolo delle Fonticine*, a spectacular tabernacle built in 1522 by Giovanni della Robbia.
Another detour in Via dell'Ariento leads to the *Mercato Centrale di S. Lorenzo* (3 D1), a market which is the largest and most interesting piece of iron-and-glass architecture— designed by Giuseppe Mengoni – built in Florence in the second half of the 19th c.

Via Cavour (3 A-B-C-D 2-3-4). This continuation of Via de' Martelli is a thoroughfare lined with a profusion of noteworthy palazzi, chiefly from the 17th and 18th c. There is Palazzo Medici-Riccardi, and the older, 14th-c. *Palazzo di Bernardetto de' Medici* (n. 31), and the 16th-c. *Palazzo Dardinelli* (n. 37), by Santi di Tito.
At n. 43 is the site of the *Biblioteca Marucelliana*, a library created between the end of the 17th c. and the beginning of the 18th c. by the Florentine abbot Francesco Marucelli and opened to the public in 1752. It pos-

Interior of the Cappella dei Principi

sesses more than half-a-million volumes, manuscripts, letters, and documents (in particular, a series of texts by Ugo Foscolo and letters by Silvio Pellico).

Piazza S. Marco (3 C3). This broad, tree-lined square, with a bronze statue in its center, the *monument to General Manfredo Fanti* (1873), lies midway along the straight Via Cavour.

On the left side, at n. 51, is the so-called *Palazzina della Livia*, by Bernardo Fallani (1775-80), commissioned by the grand duke Pietro Leopoldo as a gift to a dancer named Livia Malfatti Raimondi. It now houses the Circolo Ufficiali, an officers' club. On the opposite side of the square is the main building of the Università and the Accademia di Belle Arti, or academy of fine arts; on the north side is the church of S. Marco with adjoining convent.

Università degli Studi (3 C3). The building that now houses the rectorate, the Aula Magna (or great hall) and university offices stands on the site of the old grand-ducal stables. The University of Florence was founded as the "Studium Generale" in 1321; law, literature, and medicine were the subjects taught. It was at the behest of Pope Clement VI that the first Italian Department of Theology was established. From the second half of the 15th c. on, there were transfers and breakaways in university teaching, alternating between Florence and Pisa; it was not until after 1859 that all subjects were taught together in the capital of Tuscany.

At the mouth of the Via Ricasoli, beneath the proto-Renaissance portico of the former Hospital of S. Matteo, is the entrance of the *Accademia di Belle Arti* (3 C3), a university institute for artistic education, established in 1784.

S. Marco (3 C3). Built originally in the 14th c., this church was thoroughly rebuilt and enlarged (apse and sacristy) by Michelozzo in the first half of the 15th c. The present-day facade is by Fra G.B. Paladini (1777-78). The interior, with a central nave, was further renovated in the last quarter of the 16th c. (side chapels) and in the late-17th c. (apse and gilt inlaid ceiling). On the counterfacade, above the portal, note the large 14th-c. *Crucifix*. In the first altar on the right, *St. Thomas Praying Before the Crucifix*, by Santi di Tito (1593); in the second altar, *Virgin Mary and Saints* by Fra Bartolomeo (1509). Through a vestibule at the end of the right side of the nave, you can enter the sacristy built by Michelozzo, where – aside from a

sarcophagus with a statue in bronze of *St. Antoninus*, or *S. Antonino*, attributed to Giambologna – there are exquisite sacred furnishings from the 15th to 18th c.

On the main altar note the *Crucifix* by Fra Angelico (ca. 1425-28). Along the left side of the nave note the Cappella Salviati, or Cappella di S. Antonino, a chapel built to plans by Giambologna; he and his school also did the bronze bas-reliefs.

Museo di S. Marco * (3 C3). Adjacent to the church, this museum is installed in a section of the handsome rooms of the convent, renovated – also by Michelozzo – in accordance with a simple and rigorous Renaissance style. Among those who once lived here are Fra Giovanni da Fiesole (known as Fra Angelico), who painted several masterpieces here, St. Antoninus, bishop of Florence, Savonarola, who was prior, and Fra Bartolomeo, another renowned painter. The most remarkable feature of the museum is the collection of paintings by Fra Angelico. Aside from the frescoes in the cells of the monks, in fact, from 1869 on, the halls on the ground floor were gradually filled with virtually all the paintings by Fra Angelico in Florence, alongside the masterpieces that were already present.

A tour of the museum begins with the *Chiostro di S. Antonino*, a cloister built by Michelozzo prior to 1440, with a portico set on slender columns, topped by a cross-vault. Among the numerous frescoes, note the well-preserved fresco by Fra Angelico depicting *St. Dominick Kneeling Before Jesus on the Cross*, at the end of the entrance wall (1, in the plan on page 68). Near the entrance of the Sala del Capitolo (Chapter Hall; 2) is the famous bell, known as the "Piagnona," that pealed on the night of 8 April 1498, when Savonarola was arrested.

The paintings by Fra Angelico that come from the Accademia and the Uffizi are displayed in the large *Sala dell'Ospizio* (A). The most notable paintings are: the **Deposition of Christ** * (also known as the *Pala di S. Trìnita*), commissioned by the Strozzi family for that church, and completed in 1432 by Fra Angelico, replacing Lorenzo Monaco who had begun the altar piece by paintings the cusps; the famous **Pala di S. Marco** *, an altar piece commissioned by the Medici in 1440 for the main altar of the church, devoted to the theme of the *Sacred Conversation* with St. Cosma and St. Damian, sadly ruined by an inept restoration in the 19th c.; and the **Tabernacolo dei Linaiuoli** * (ca. 1433-34), a tabernacle with a marble cornice designed by Ghiber-

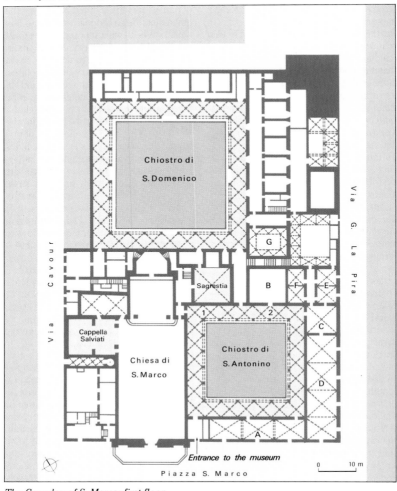

The Complex of S. Marco: first floor

ti, a work that is fundamental to an understanding of the painter, especially his study of perspective. Also observe: the *triptych of St. Peter Martyr* (prior to 1429), in which the influence of Masaccio is evident; the so-called *Pala d'Annalena* (after 1434), considered to be the first Renaissance altar piece; the *Last Judgement* (ca. 1431) and, alongside it, a small panel depicting the *The Naming of the Baptist* (prior to 1435); three small panels (possibly doors of reliquaries for the sacristy of S. Maria Novella) depicting the so-called *Madonna della Stella*, *Annunciation and Adoration of the Magi*, *Coronation of the Virgin Mary*; the so-called *Armadio degli Argenti* of the church of SS. Annunziata (after 1450), a complex of 35 panels, depicting *stories of Christ*, conceived and executed by Fra Angelico (except for three panels attributed to Alesso Bal-

dovinetti); the *Lamentation at the Death of Christ* (1440); another *Sacred Conversation* (1450-52).

A passageway to the left of the Sala del Capitolo takes you to the *Sala del Cenacolo* (hall of the Last Supper; G), where you can admire the fresco of the *Last Supper** by Domenico Ghirlandaio (ca. 1480), rich in symbols and allusions.

From the same passageway, you can climb up to the second floor of the convent, occupied by the sequence of cells of the monks, extending along three sides of the cloister, or Chiostro di S. Antonino. The rooms are decorated with the famous **series of frescoes***, designed by Fra Angelico as a guide in meditation for the monks. The preparatory drawings are probably all by Fra Angelico, but the frescoes themselves (ca. 1442-45) were done with the assistance of pupils, with uneven results.

On the wall facing the stairway is the renowned *Annunciation*, by Fra Angelico (ca. 1442): this masterpiece treats a theme that the artist has dealt with in other works; here the theme is treated with a great monumental approach and greater austerity. On the opposite wall is the *Crucifix with St. Dominick*, also by Fra Angelico; note the iconographic motif of Christ's blood spilled for humanity.

To the left of the Annunciation, the first corridor begins; in the cells along the left side of this corridor, Fra Angelico worked almost alone, painting a series of masterpieces, infused with a sublime mysticism: *Noli me tangere* (cell 1); *Lamentation over the Body of Christ* (cell 2); *Annunciation*, simple and rigorous (cell 3); *Crucifixion* (cell 4); *Nativity* (cell 5); *Transfiguration*, one of the most significant frescoes in the series (cell 6); *Christ Derided* (cell 7); and *Coronation of the Virgin Mary*, with its circular configuration, bound up with medieval conceptions of theology (cell 9). At the end of the second corridor, overlooking the square, is the Quartiere del Priore (quarter of the prior, comprising three cells). The cells that overlook the cloister were reserved for novices; for that reason the decoration in every cell offers a single "didactic" theme as a subject for meditation for the new monks: *St. Domenick in Adoration of the Crucifix*. If you return to the first corridor, you can visit the cells on the cloister side; these are decorated in accordance with a program which called for the presence of the Virgin Mary and St. Dominick in all the frescoes. On the right wall of cell 25 is the *Madonna delle Ombre*, or Our Lady of the Shadows, one of Fra Angelico's most famous works, executed around 1450. In the third corridor, a number of the frescoes in the cells on the left can probably be attributed to Benozzo Gozzoli (*Temptation of Christ*, 32, and *Christ Praying in the Garden*, 34); the same artist may have done the *Adoration of the Magi*, which decorates the second cell (39) in the Quartiere di Cosimo il Vecchio, or quarter of Cosimo the Elder, at the end of the right corridor.

On the same side, you will find the **Biblioteca***, or library, a refined creation by Michelozzo in the purest Renaissance style, divided by two tall colonnades with perfect proportions.

Museo di Storia Naturale (3 C3). This museum is the successor to the Imperial Regio Museo di Fisica e Storia Naturale, a museum of natural history founded in 1775 by the grand duke Pietro Leopoldo in Palazzo Torrigiani in Via Romana. It possesses the most important natural history collections in Italy. In this building (entrance at n. 4 di Via Giorgio La Pira) there are three sections: Mineralogy and Lithology, Geology and Paleontology, and Botany; not far away is the herb garden, or Giardino dei Semplici.

The **Museo di Mineralogia e Litologia** originated from the Medici collections of polished and carved stones. It now includes roughly 40,000 mineral samples, including: a transparent topaz weighing 151 kg. (the second-largest on earth), and an aquamarine weighing 98 kg. There is a noteworthy regional collection of Elban minerals.

The **Museo di Geologia e Paleontologia** possesses one of the largest collections of minerals and fossils in Italy (roughly 300,000 pieces).

The **Museo Botanico**, the largest botanical museum in Italy, has a number of herbaria (one dating from the 16th c.), collections of wax models, and a fine wood collection. The Erbario Tropicale possesses one of the world's best collections of samples from Ethiopia and Somalia.

The **Giardino dei Semplici** (literally, Garden of the Simples, or *Orto Botanico*, meaning Botanical Garden; entrance in Via P.A. Micheli n. 3; plan, 3 B-C4) was founded in 1550 by Cosimo I de' Medici. It is one of the oldest gardens of its sort in the world. Still, the original structure has been greatly modified, especially during the 19th c. It covers roughly two hectares, and there are about 6,000 plants, from all over. The oldest trees date from the turn of the 19th c., save for a yew tree planted in 1720.

From Piazza S. Marco, if you continue along the extension of Via Cavour for a way, you can see – at n. 57 – the *Casino Mediceo di S. Marco*, the modern Palazzo della Corte d'Appello (3 B3), or Appeals Courts, built by Bernardo Buontalenti between 1568 and 1574, as the den and study of the grand duke Francesco I.

A short distance further along, at n. 69, is the entrance to the **Chiostro dello Scalzo** (3 B3), a cloister which once belonged to a religious order known as the Scalzo, because the cross-bearer in their processions always went barefoot ("scalzo"). There is a series of frescoes by Andrea del Sarto with *stories of St. John the Baptist* (1507-26); two of the scenes are by Franciabigio.

Cenacolo di S. Apollonia (3 C2). This is the ancient refectory of the former Benedictine monastery (entrance at n. 1 in Via XXVII Aprile) that occupies the block between Via S. Gallo and Via XXVII Aprile. Andrea del

Castagno decorated the room with exquisite frescoes, after 1444: of particular note on the far wall is the *Last Supper* with scenes, above it, of the *Resurrection*, the *Crucifixion*, and the *Deposition*, all of them unified in perspective. Other works by the same master include *Cristo in pietà*, with preparatory drawing, which was painted for the monastery, and the *Christ Crucified, with Mourners, St. Benedict, and St. Romualdo*, originally taken from the cloister of the former convent of S. Maria degli Angioli.

Via S. Gallo (3 A-B-C 2-3). This street dates back to earliest Florence; it once led to the northern gate of the city. Along it, you will see a series of handsome buildings. If you follow this street away from the center, you will see, on your right, the 16th-c. *Loggia dei Tessitori* (3 B2), with five arcades, and then the *church of S. Giovannino dei Cavalieri*. The interior, with a nave and two aisles, and with a truss roof, is embellished with notable artwork from the 15th and 17th c. At n. 74 stands the **Palazzo Pandolfini** (3 A3), built to plans by Raphael, but after 1520; it comprises two main wings, with a portal made of rusticated ashlars.

At the end of the street lies *Piazza della Libertà*, one of the strategic points in the ring roads around Florence. Facing the mouth of the street stands the *Porta S. Gallo* (1285; 8 F1), adorned with groups of sculpture from the turn of the 14th c. (in the tabernacles) and a 16th-c. fresco (in the lunette). Beyond the fountain that stands at the center of the square is the *triumphal arch of Francesco Stefano di Lorena* built in 1739 by Jean-Nicolas Jadot to celebrate the entrance of the grand duke into Florence.

The long detour described below is worth taking, if only to see the **Museo Stibbert** (7 C5), which possesses one of the world's richest collections of old weapons and costumes, as well as collections of objects from the applied arts (furniture, sculpture, tapestries, porcelain, and so on). The route from Porta S. Gallo runs along Via del Ponte Rosso, a short stretch of Via XX Settembre, and then Via Vittorio Emanuele II, until it meets the Via Federico Stibbert, which leads to Villa Stibbert (n. 26).

The Museum, which constitutes an exceedingly rare example of 19th-c. museography, comprises the collection accumulated in his own home by Frederick Stibbert (1838-1906) – an exceedingly wealthy and eclectic Englishman with a Tuscan mother – not for the mere taste of collecting but with the intention of increasing the understanding of civil and military traditions of Europe and the Orient, in three main areas (costumes, arms, heraldry). Stibbert willed the museum to the English government, which donated it to the city of Florence, which in turn set up a foundation (1908).

The roughly 50,000 items in the museum (dating from the end of the 15th c. to the beginning of the 19th c.) were arranged according to the whims of Stibbert himself; he arranged entire rooms, with furniture and art. There are 60 rooms, occupied by the museum and by family apartments, transformed into a sort of museum-home.

There are a number of remarkable exhibits: *Procession of Italian and German Knights* * (16th/18th c.) and another Procession of Ottoman Knights (16th c.), in the Salone della Cavalcata (hall 9); *Indian arms and armor* * (16th/18th c.), in the last of the Eastern halls (8); *group of samurais* *, in the first of the Japanese halls (55). Particularly rich and noteworthy is the collection of costumes (16th/17th c.) in halls 38-41. Lastly, we should point out the museum also has a sizable collection of early paintings (14th/17th c.), including works by Luca Giordano, Cosimo Rosselli, Pieter Brueghel the Younger, Carlo Crivelli, Sano di Pietro, Neri di Bicci, and Pietro Lorenzetti.

Galleria dell'Accademia* (3 D3). Easily reached from Piazza S. Marco, at n. 60 in Via Bettino Ricasoli, this gallery is particularly famous for its collection of Michelangelo sculptures; it also has a major collection of Florentine paintings from the 14th to the 16th c.

The gallery was founded in 1784 by the grand duke Pietro Leopoldo for an avowedly educational purpose: it would serve to provide the students of the neighboring Accademia di Belle Arti, or Academy of Fine Arts, a series of illustrious examples against which to measure themselves; it was for this reason that he selected only Florentine works, considered unquestionable masterpieces. The gallery acquired a number of sculptures by Michelangelo Buonarroti during the course of the 19th c.; by the turn of the 20th c., it had become a full-fledged "Museo di Michelangelo" (aside from sculptures, it also has numerous casts of sculptures by Michelangelo held elsewhere). After the collection of paintings was broken up, during the Twenties and Thirties, the gallery was thoroughly renovated and reinstalled (though not until the Eighties); the purpose was to highlight the historic origins of the gallery, enriching it with other artwork that helped to understand the artistic culture of Florence during Michelangelo's lifetime.

The tour begins with the Sala del Colosso, so called because in the 19th c. it held a plaster copy of one of the Giant Dioscuri from Monte Cavallo in Rome. At the center is the original plaster model of the *Rape of the*

Sabines by Giambologna. The panels on the walls offer a sample of Florentine painting from the turn of the 16th c.; among other works, we should mention: *Mystical Wedding of St. Catherine* by Fra Bartolomeo (1512), *Deposition from the Cross*, begun by Filippino Lippi and completed by Perugino (possibly with help from Raphael).

In the next *gallery* you can see the four giant **Prigioni***, or Prisoners, by Michelangelo. These statues were executed around 1530, and were left unfinished; they were meant to form part of the great tomb of Pope Julius II. Because the project of the tomb was later drastically reconsidered, they were left in Florence, and were donated by the sculptor's nephew to the grand duke Cosimo I and placed in the Bòboli gardens; from there they were then moved to the Accademia (1909). Between the two Prigioni on the right is a statue of *St. Matthew** (also unfinished), executed between 1505 and 1506 for the Opera del Duomo, the organization responsible for the construction of the Florence cathedral. The statues were then abandoned in a storehouse of the cathedral. This group of works is particularly useful in understanding the "unfinished" quality of Michelangelo's work, a quality that was inspired by the Neoplatonic philosophy that was dominant in Florence at the time. Aside from the external vicissitudes, in fact, these and other statues – apparently left unfinished by Michelangelo – are actually quite complete in artistic terms. Leaving the visitor with the imaginary completion of the image – the task of giving them a definitive meaning – these sculptures are perennially vivid and alive.

On the far end, in the Neoclassical *apse*, stands the renowned statue of **David*** (4.1 m. tall), executed between 1502 and 1504 from a giant block of marble. A beginning had already been made on the statue by Agostino di Duccio and Antonio Rossellino, but the project had then been abandoned because of technical problems. The Biblical figure of David was often used by artists of the Florentine Renaissance, in that it represented cunning and intelligence defeating brute force; it was an allusion to Florence itself which, though not the strongest state in Italy, had for decades dominated the peninsula. A special committee of Florentine artists decided to place the David in front of Palazzo della Signoria, as a symbol of vigilance in the defense of liberty; for this reason, the statue was completed (so there would be no doubt as to its true meaning).

The "David" by Michelangelo

The apse wings contain works by Florentine contemporaries of Michelangelo. In the right wing, note the *Venus and Amor, or Cupid** by Pontormo (ca. 1532), painted to a cartoon by Michelangelo, and marked by a distinctive Mannerist atmosphere. In the left wing, you can see perfect examples of the two directions of Florentine painting in the late-16th c.: the late-Mannerist school, refined and intellectual (*Dispute Concerning the Immaculate Conception* by Carlo Portelli), and the reaction to that school, simple and naturalistic (*Entrance of Christ into Jerusalem* by Santi di Tito).

On the right side of the gallery is the entrance to the *Sale Fiorentine*, or Florentine Halls, which contain an anthology of Florentine painting of the Quattrocento; the exhibit shows clearly the development of that painting, under the influence of Masaccio, Fra Angelico, and Domenico Veneziano. In the first hall is the so-called *Cassone Adimari*, painted by Giovanni di Ser Giovanni, also known as the Scheggia, a half-brother of Masaccio; this work depicts, with great authenticity, a view of Florence in celebration. In the little hall in the corner, note: a small panel depicting the *Visitation*, one of the first paintings by Perugino in Florence (ca. 1470); the *Holy Trinity between St. Bene-*

71

dict and *St. Giovanni Gualberto* by Alesso Baldovinetti; the *Tebaide*, or Solitude attributed to Paolo Uccello. In the last hall, note the *Virgin Mary with the Christ Child, Youthful St. John, and Two Angels* by Sandro Botticelli (1470 c.); and a small panel depicting the *Madonna del Mare, or Virgin of the Sea*, probably a youthful work by Filippino Lippi.

To the left of the apse of the David is the entrance to the large hall of the **Gipsoteca Bartolini**, a sculpture gallery that opened in 1985. The plasters on display here by Lorenzo Bartolini (one of 19th-c. Italy's greatest sculptors) are not mere copies taken from completed works, but working models that were used for creating the marble sculptures; they are mostly portraits (268 busts).

On the left side of the same wing, you will find the *Sale Bizantine*, or Byzantine Halls, so-called because they contain a number of notable works of painting prior to Giotto, a period generally described as Byzantine. You then enter the central hall, with the famous panel of *Mary Magdalene and Stories from Her Life*; this work shows strong Byzantine influence, and was painted by an unknown artist described conventionally as the "Maestro della Maddalena." Other paintings – such as the *Virgin Mary Enthroned with the Christ Child and Four Saints* by the so-called Maestro di S. Gaggio, and the *Tree of Life* by Pacino di Bonaguida – indicate the progressive development of Giottoesque realism.
The small hall on the right is occupied by the work of artists who assimilated Giotto's lesson (22 *panels* by Taddeo Gaddi, ca. 1330; *Crucifix* by Bernardo Daddi, after 1340) and works of what is known as "giottismo di fronda," or, literally, "fringe Giotto-ism," a reference to the work of those painters who developed a special sensitivity to color (among these works, note the *Christ in Pietà between the Virgin Mary, Mary Magdalene and St. John the Baptist* by Giovanni da Milano, 1365). In the small hall on the left, note a number of paintings from the workshop of the three Orcagna brothers.

You can climb the stairs at the end of the hallway set in the outer courtyard up to the second floor; in the halls on this floor, opened in 1985, is a remarkably rich display of paintings from 14th- and 15th-c. Florence. In particular, note work by Lorenzo Monaco. Especially interesting, in the large hall following the first small hall (where there are two large *Crucifixes* by Lorenzo Monaco), is the collection of *polyptychs*. A number of these well preserved works can be seen as they were originally seen, complex hybrids of painting, sculpture, and architecture. In the third hall, aside from 14th-c. and late-Gothic panels, there is a collection of *Russian icons*, unrivalled anywhere in Italy today. They were collected by the house of Lorraine, and date from the 16th to 18th c. The last little hall abounds in Florentine late-Gothic masterpieces; among them are an *Annunciation* by Lorenzo Monaco, a work from his mature period, and the *predella* for the altar piece of S. Trìnita, which was later painted by Fra Angelico.

Conservatorio di Musica "Luigi Cherubini" (3 D3). In continuity with the Galleria dell'Accademia, the Conservatory (entrance at n. 2 in Piazza delle Belle Arti) was established in 1849 as an "Istituto Musicale," part of the Accademia di Belle Arti, becoming an independent body in 1860. It possesses a major musical library and an important *Museo degli Strumenti Musicali* (Museum of Musical Instruments; not open to the public), which among its items of great worth, includes a number of extremely valuable "Stradivari."

Opificio delle Pietre Dure (3 D3). With its entrance at n. 78 of the Via degli Alfani (a cross street of the Via Ricasoli), this is a state-run institution, internationally recognized, one of the leading schools in Italy in the field of art restoration. It was established in 1588 by the grand duke Ferdinando I de' Medici as a workshop for the processing of rare and semi-precious stones for the decoration of the Cappella dei Principi in the church of S. Lorenzo, and was originally housed in the Uffizi.
The interesting **Museo** adjoining contains works in stone and imitation marble, paintings on rock, and the Medici collection of rock materials.

If you return to Via Ricasoli and head toward the Duomo, you will see on the left, along Via de' Pucci, the immense complex of the *Palazzi Pucci* (3 E2), which extends as far as Via dei Servi; the central palazzo (n. 4) preserves the facade added by Ammannati, while the facade at n. 6 was rebuilt in the 17th c.
After you return to Via Ricasoli, on the right is the *Tabernacolo delle Cinque Lampade*, decorated with a fresco from the workshop of Cosimo Rosselli. Still further along is the *Teatro Niccolini* (3 E2), the oldest theater in Florence, built in 1652 as the "Teatro del Cocomero" and later named after the tragic playwright Giovanni Battista Niccolini (1782-1861).

3.2 From the Duomo to Borgo Pinti

Starting from the left apse of the Duomo, you can take the Via dei Servi; the first notable stop will be at the Piazza della SS. Annunziata, with its major Renaissance buildings (Ospedale degli Innocenti, Basilica della SS. Annunziata). Continue along the Via della Colonna to reach the Museo Archeologico, the largest archeological museum in Tuscany; of particular note are the Etruscan artifacts, while this is Italy's second-most-important museum in terms of Egyptian artifacts and art. You will then walk through the area of Borgo Pinti; many 16th-c. artists chose to live in this area (Antonio da Sangallo the Elder, Giuliano da Sangallo, Perugino, Pontormo, Giambologna, and Benvenuto Cellini, to name the best known). Then you wind up along the avenues, or "viali," that run along the early walls. Here, the surging traffic rushes past the charming "Isola dei Morti," or Island of the Dead, as the Cimitero degli Inglesi, or English Cemetery, has come to be called.

There are two detours from Via dei Servi, at the beginning of this route: the first detour leads to Piazza di S. Maria Nuova, with its late-Renaissance porticoes (a visit to the Museo di Preistoria, or museum of prehistory, and the Museo di Firenze Com'Era, or museum of old Florence is suggested); the second detour runs past the unfinished rotunda by Brunelleschi.

Via dei Servi (3 D-E 2-3). The early "Borgo di Balla" almost immediately spreads out into a "piazzetta" in which the *church of S. Michele Visdomini* stands; this 14th-c. structure was entirely rebuilt and endowed with chapels in the second half of the 16th c. Inside, on the second altar on the right, note the *Sacred Conversation*, a masterpiece by Pontormo (1518). Further along, at n. 12, *Palazzo Sforza Almeni*, attributed to Bartolomeo Ammannati and, at n. 15, *Palazzo Niccolini*, built to plans by Domenico di Baccio d'Agnolo (1548-50) and decorated with frescoes from the 17th and 18th c.

Arcispedale di S. Maria Nuova (3 E-F3). This hospital, with a three-wing loggia overlooking the Piazza di S. Maria Nuova (you can reach it by turning off onto the Via Bufalini), is the oldest in Florence: it was in fact founded in 1288 by Folco Portinari, father of Dante's Beatrice; nonetheless, the present external appearance is that of a building from the late-16th c.; that is when it was rebuilt, to plans by Bernardo Buontalenti. The construction of the cloisters and the enlargement of the *church of S. Egidio* date from the turn of the 15th c.; inside the church in question is a large marble *tabernacle* by Bernardo Rossellino (1450), with a door by Ghiberti; also there are paintings from the late-16th and the 17th c. On the right side of the church is the Chiostro delle Medicherie, a cloister, with glazed terracotta by Giovanni della Robbia; on the

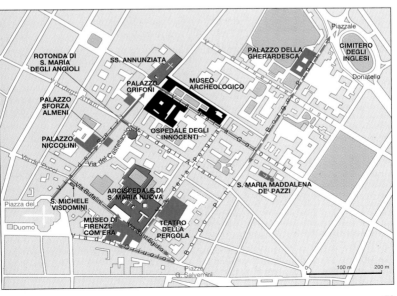

left side, after an atrium, is another cloister, the Chiostro delle Ossa.

Museo Fiorentino di Preistoria and Istituto Fiorentino di Preistoria (3 F3). This museum is located almost directly across from the Arcispedale, in the former convent of the Oblate (entrance in Via S. Egidio n. 21). It was founded in 1946 to contain the prehistoric collections present in Florence. The items are arranged on two floors, according to chronological and geographic criterion, beginning with the Florence region.

Museo di Firenze Com'Era (3 F3). Also set in the former convent of the Oblate, but with an entrance in Via dell'Oriuolo n. 24, this museum features documentary material (drawings, paintings, prints, etc.) that illustrates the development and transformation of the city over time. Once the plan to create a full-fledged museum of the city in the complex of the Oblate had come to naught, little material remained here: the most notable is surely the series of the twelve *Views of the Medici Villas*, painted in 1599 by the Flemish artist Justus Utens; the views depict the territorial system of the grand ducal villas, and were meant to adorn the Villa di Artimino, the ideal center of that system.

A short detour from Via S. Egidio leads you to Via della Pergola where, at numbers 12-30, the *Teatro della Pergola* (3 F4) stands, the most important theater in Florence. Built in wood by Ferdinando Tacca in 1656 and rebuilt in masonry a century later, it acquired its present appearance between 1828 and 1837 with the work of Bartolomeo Silvestri and Gaetano Baccani.

After you return to Via dei Servi, you continue toward the Piazza della SS. Annunziata; shortly thereafter, a detour to the right in Via degli Alfani leads to the so-called *Rotonda di S. Maria degli Angioli** (3 D-E3), the most notable of the ruins of an early Camaldolese convent. The building, with a central plan, was designed and partly built by Brunelleschi between 1433 and 1434: work was halted when the building had reached a height of about 7 m.; the unfortunate completion of the upper section dates from 1936.

Piazza della SS. Annunziata (3 D3). At the end of Via dei Servi, you will find one of the most harmonious and well-composed squares in Florence, of great interest in terms of urban planning and architecture. The square existed as early as the second half of the 13th c., and its balanced and regular appearance is an expression of the single overall plan by Filippo Brunelleschi

who, in the first half of the 15th c., designed the two opposed lateral porticoes, which converge perspectively toward the dome of the basilica, at the far end of the square. Brunelleschi actually built the right portico, the one extending before the facade of the Ospedale degli Innocenti, or foundling hospital, designed in 1419; the similar portico of the Confraternita dei Servi di Maria, on the left, was begun a century later by Antonio da Sangallo the Elder and Baccio d'Agnolo.

The original configuration of the square was partly modified in the first half of the 17th c. with the construction of the portico of the basilica (1601), and the addition of the large *equestrian statue of Ferdinando I*, by Giambologna (completed by Pietro Tacca in 1608), and the two *fountains*, also by Tacca (1629).

On the left-hand corner of Via dei Servi is the *Palazzo Grifoni* (now *Palazzo Budini Gattai*; 3 D3), built in brick by Bartolomeo Ammannati between 1563 and 1574; it is now the headquarters of the Provincial Government and the President of the Tuscan Region.

Ospedale degli Innocenti (3 D4). This foundling hospital is one of the earliest and most successful examples of civil architecture of the Renaissance; it is also a symbol of the city's Humanistic conscience. Florence built this specially-equipped structure to provide a decent solution to the social drama of abandoned children. The building, designed by Brunelleschi and built from 1419 on at the expense of the wealthy Corporazione della Seta, or silk-workers' guild, was completed by Francesco della Luna. In Brunelleschi's exquisite **portico***, which overlooks the square, we find innovative features, such as its size (equivalent to the length of the building), and the use of rigorously geometric proportions (the width of the arches is in fact the same as the height of the columns and the depth of the portico). In the webs of the ribbed arches are eight *tondoes* in glazed terracotta, by Andrea della Robbia.

You enter the Chiostro degli Uomini, a cloister begun by Francesco della Luna and completed by Stefano di Jacopo Rosselli; from here, two flights of stairs lead up to the hall of the **Pinacoteca**, or painting gallery, which contains a small number of works, of exceedingly high artistic caliber. Of special note: *Coronation of the Virgin Mary, between St. Michael and St. Mary Magdalene*, a late-Gothic painting by the Maestro della

The equestrian statue of Ferdinando I and the Ospedale degli Innocenti

Madonna Strauss; *Virgin Mary with Christ Child and an Angel* by Sandro Botticelli; *Virgin Mary with Christ Child*, glazed terracotta by Luca della Robbia; *Virgin Mary Enthroned, with Christ Child and Saints* by Piero di Cosimo; *Adoration of the Magi* by Domenico Ghirlandaio. In the gallery (open, with permission from the head office) there are detached frescoes, including works by Lorenzo Monaco and Alessandro Allori, taken from various buildings throughout Florence.

Basilica della SS. Annunziata (3 C-D4). Founded by the religious order of the Servi di Maria in 1250 as a small oratory, this church was later enlarged. It finally acquired its present structure with the construction of the large circular apse surrounded with chapels; work was begun in 1444 by Michelozzo and completed by Leon Battista Alberti (1477). At the turn of the 17th c. the portico was extended the length of the facade. The central portal gives access to the Chiostrino dei Voti; on the walls of this small cloister are several of the most important **frescoes*** of Florentine art of the late Quattrocento and early Cinquecento. Beginning from the right: *Assumption* by Rosso Fiorentino (1517) and *Visitation* by Jacopo Pontormo (1514-16), frescoes that clearly show the way in which the nascent Mannerist sensibility was moving away from the Renaissance sensibility, then in sharp decline; the latter school is represented here by the work of Franciabigio, who painted the *Wedding of the Virgin Mary* (1513), and by Andrea del Sarto, who painted one of his masterpieces, the *Birth of the*

Virgin Mary, dated 1514, and the *Arrival of the Magi* (1511). Following those are the *Nativity* by Alesso Baldovinetti (1460), and the series of the *stories of St. Philip Benizzi*: the first fresco is by Cosimo Rosselli (1476), the other five are by Andrea del Sarto (1509-10). On the right wall, a remarkable marble bas-relief by Michelozzo depicting the *Virgin Mary with the Christ Child*.

The **interior** of the basilica was extensively decorated – between the 17th and 18th c. – in sumptuous Baroque style. Immediately to the left is the *Cappella dell'Annunziata**, a temple-shaped chapel, comprising an exceedingly elaborate enclosure with marble columns and a bronze grating, by Maso di Bartolomeo (1447); a rococo baldachin was added to it. On the altar, behind a protective grate, is a 14th-c. fresco of the *Annunciation*, particularly venerated by the Florentines. In the interior chapel is a painting of the *head of Christ** by Andrea del Sarto (ca. 1514). On the altars of the second and third chapels, on the left, are major frescoes by Andrea del Castagno, depicting respectively *St. Julian* (1455-56) and the *Holy Trinity with St. Jerome* (1454), where psychological realism and a profound sense of depth and texture mingle with a dynamic tension. In the fifth chapel, note the *Assumption of the Virgin* by Pietro Perugino (1506). At the end of the left wing of the cross vault, in the Cappella del Santissimo Crocifisso, is a terracotta statue of *John the Baptist*, by Michelozzo.
The presbytery comprises a large circular *apse*, surrounded by nine chapels, designed

by Michelozzo and completed by Alberti. The Baroque decorations were added at the turn of the 18th c.; particularly noteworthy, on the main altar, is a 17th-c. silver *ciborium*. Among the paintings that adorn the chapels, we should mention a panel by Perugino depicting the *Virgin Mary with Christ Child and Saints* (third chapel from the left) and a *Resurrection* by Bronzino (fourth chapel). Note the fifth chapel, the Cappella della Madonna del Soccorso, renovated by Giambologna as his own funerary chapel, and decorated largely with work by Giambologna himself and by his pupils.

In the right wing of the cross vault, the side chapel on the left features a large marble group by Baccio Bandinelli, depicting the *Pietà*; the central chapel (designed by Ferdinando Fuga) has a handsome silhouetted *Crucifix*, of uncertain attribution (Andrea del Castagno or Alesso Baldovinetti).

From the left transept, you can enter the *Chiostro dei Morti** (cloister of the dead; open by request, contact the sacristan), which dates from the time of the 15th-c. renovation; it was later frescoed with a series of *stories of the Servi di Maria*; note in particular the painting above the entrance to the church, the so-called *Madonna del Sacco**, a masterpiece by Andrea del Sarto (1525). Lastly, worthy of note, in the Cappella della Compagnia di S. Luca, is a fresco of the *Virgin Mary, Christ Child, and Saints* by Pontormo.

Museo Archeologico* (3 D4). Housed in the Palazzo della Crocetta (Via della Colonna n. 38), this archeological museum is a landmark in any understanding of Etruscan civilization and art; there is also a section devoted to Ancient Egypt, the second most important in Italy, following the Museo Egizio in Turin. As of this writing, only a part of the vast collection is on display: restoration is still underway on much of the collection, damaged by the flood of 1966; moreover, the museum as a whole is being reinstalled.

The Museo Archeologico developed out of the Etruscan collections of the houses of Medici and Lorraine, originally held in the Uffizi; while the ancient Egyptian section was established in the first half of the 19th c. by Leopoldo II through the acquisition of existing collections and through "field expeditions." In 1880, all of the collections were moved to the present location; in 1898 the section called the "Museo Topografico dell'Etruria" was opened, designed to present a chronological and geographic view of

Etruscan culture. This cluster of exhibits, devastated by the flood of 1966, is still being restored.

The complex operation of the reinstallation of the Museo Archeologico will take a number of years before the final version is attained. Therefore, in reading the following description, consider that moves and changes – even substantial ones – may be made, affecting large collections and individual works.

On the second floor, part of the halls are occupied by the **Antiquarium Etrusco-Greco-Romano.** The first two halls contain Etruscan funerary sculptures, especially cinerary urns; we should mention in particular the marble *sarcophagus of the Amazons**, found in Tarquinia (hall IX) and the *sarcophagus of the fat man**, in alabaster, from Chiusi (hall X). The tour continues in hall XII, where bronze tools from Roman times, Etruscan mirrors, and Greek and Roman bronze figurines are on exhibit. The adjoining hall XIII contains the so-called *Idolino**, a statue of a young man found in Pesaro in 1530, originally thought to be a Greek original but recently identified as a copy of a statue of an athlete made during the reign of Augustus, dating from the 5th c. B.C. Also note the *torso of a statue of a man* (480-470 B.C.) and *head of a horse*, an original from Greek late-classical period or from Hellenistic times, or possibly a Roman copy made during the reign of Augustus. The long hall XIV contains several of the most notable items in the museum: the *statue of Minerva*, probably an Etrusco-Roman copy of an original by Praxiteles; the *Speechmaker**, an Etruscan work from the 1st c. B.C., discovered in 1566 at Sanguineto (Perugia); the *Chimera**, a mythical creature with three heads, found in Arezzo in 1553, and dating from the 5th to 4th c. B.C.; note the legend TINSCVIL on the right fore-paw, which is the dedicatory formula for votive offerings to the god Tin (the Etruscan counterpart of Roman Jove).

Past hall XV (objects in bronze from various periods), the Antiquarium continues on the third floor with a major *collection of Attic and imitation ceramics*. Standing out in particular is the so-called *François Vase**, an Attic krater with black figures, dating from 570-560 B.C.; also worthy of note are two Attic "*hydrie*" with red figures, by the painter of Meidias, dating from the end of the 5th c. B.C. Also on the third floor are two "kouroi" (funerary or votive sculptures, depicting young men) dating from the 6th c. B.C.; these are known as the *Apollo Milani** and the *Apollino Milani**, from the name of the donor.

Of the collections not open to the public, let us point out a group of funerary sculptures from the area around Chiusi: among the most interesting items: *Mater Matuta** (the early Italic goddess of fertility and motherhood), an urn dating from 460-450 B.C.; another *cinerary urn*, in polychrome alabaster; the cover of a *statue-cinerary urn*; the clay *sarcophagus of Larthia Seianti**, dating from the first half of the 2nd c. B.C. The glyptics collection (engraved precious stones) is also off limits to the public.

Also on the second floor is the **Museo Egizio** (currently, access from the hall XI, the last hall in the museum). The exhibits are being reinstalled in accordance with chronological and topographic criteria: so far eight exhibit areas have been readied, covering Egyptian civilization from prehistory to the end of the New Kingdom, but as of this writing, only the halls I-VIII, and XI are open to the public. Among the material of the earliest period, note a false-door stela from a tomb in Saqqara, depicting *Shery and his wife seated at a banquet table* (hall I). A number of statues and portraits date from the XVIII dynasty and the New Kingdom (*head of the queen Tiy*; *Thutmosis III*; *funerary portrait of a woman*, temporarily installed) are on exhibit in hall III, along with a nearly intact *wooden cart*. The three successive halls contain various material dating from the New Kingdom: particularly noteworthy are *Hathor nursing the Pharaoh Horemhab* (hall IV) and the papyri preserved in hall VI. In hall VII, note elements of the *funerary furnishings of Amenhotep* (stelae, vases, statues, and fragments of walls); in the last room (hall XI), devoted to the Ptolemaic era, note the two *stelae* upon which the deed to the tomb is inscribed, and bas-reliefs depicting *hunting scenes* and *craftsmen at work*.

S. Maria Maddalena de' Pazzi (3 E5). The church, which stands at n. 58 in Borgo Pinti, a cross-street of Via della Colonna, was founded together with the adjoining Benedictine convent in 1257, and was rebuilt by Giuliano da Sangallo at the end of the 15th c. Note the *cloister* standing before it, with an Ionic quadriporticus, which Vasari says was the first project undertaken by Sangallo as an architect.

The interior is a single hall, with six chapels on either side. At the end of the 15th c. and the turn of the 16th c., the church was embellished with paintings by Botticelli, Perugino, Ghirlandaio, and others; those works are now in Florentine and foreign museums. Most of the artwork is now made up of items from the 17th and 18th c. The main chapel, built in the second half of the 17th c. as a mausoleum for the saint, is the finest example of Roman Baroque in Florence.

From the sacristy you enter the monastery's former chapter hall ("sala capitolare"), where there is a notable *Crucifixion**, frescoed by Perugino (1493-96), which covers the entire far wall of the hall; the scene is depicted as if it were viewed through the arches that divide up the walls.

If you follow the outermost section of Borgo Pinti, on the left side you will find, at n. 99 – set in a garden (3 C5) that abounds with exotic plants – the *Palazzo Della Gherardesca* (not open to the public), originally a notable creation of Giuliano da Sangallo; all that survives of the original is the courtyard with handsome bas-reliefs. At the end of the road lies Piazzale Donatello, at the center of which is the *Cimitero dei Protestanti*, also known as the *Cimitero degli Inglesi* (Protestant or English cemetery; 3 C6); this cemetery dates from the first half of the 19th c.

4 The Quarter of S. Maria Novella

The western section of Florence, lying between the Via Faenza and the Arno, revolved around a fulcrum that was at once religious, political, cultural, and artistic: the Dominican religious settlement of S. Maria Novella, established in the 13th c. in a symmetrical position to its Franciscan counterpart of S. Croce with respect to the medieval town center. Both orders attempted to introduce a new religious spirit into lay culture, but the Dominicans, with a better cultural grounding, supported religious orthodoxy with greater intransigence. Near the banks of the Arno was the Borgo Ognissanti, a neighborhood that revolved around the church of Ognissanti and the convent of the Umiliati, a Lombard religious order that specialized in the spinning and weaving of wool. Beginning in the mid-13th c., they had developed a prosperous wool industry in this area.

In this quarter, you will find other areas that are sharply distinct in terms of history and setting: the area between S. Maria Novella and Ognissanti, which has a distinctly medieval atmosphere, though clearly reshaped during the Renaissance; the area of S. Pancrazio, distinguished by the work carried out by Leon Battista Alberti for the wealthy and powerful Rucellai family; the southern side of the Prato, with a compact row of 16th-c. houses for the workers in the wool industry.

If we move toward the outer ring roads (or, "viali di circonvallazione"), the urban layout is marked – in the roughly triangular area set between the Prato, the Arno, and the Cascine – by 19th-c. residential quarters, largely filled with middle-class villas and homes. Twentieth-century architecture, finally, is represented by a single major project: the train station of S. Maria Novella, built in the 1930s not far from the convent complex of S. Maria Novella.

Outside of the quarter is the Parco delle Cascine, the great green park of Florence, popular with Florentines on holidays, especially on the Feast of the Ascension, when the "Festa del Grillo" is held. Long ago, there was a great grasshopper hunt on that occasion; it was customary to bring the little insects in wicker cages back to town to listen to their song.

From S. Maria Novella to the Parco delle Cascine

The tour suggested here sets off from S. Maria Novella, but it is articulated thereafter like spokes of a wheel, according to routes suggested by the dense network of streets converging on the Dominican complex. A first route runs through an area plagued by heavy traffic, extending along the side of the railroad station, to the menacing, unsettling, looming bulk of the Fortezza da Basso; another one runs toward the center (Via de' Tornabuoni and Via della Vigna Nuova), but then veers off along the Arno, where a long walk will take you to the green Parco delle Cascine.

A brief detour at the beginning of this second route allows you to tour one of the lesser-known collections of art (Galleria Corsini); a longer detour (Via Palazzuolo and Via della Scala) runs by an odd curiosity (the pharmacy of the convent of S. Maria Novella) and comes to an end at the "Prato," along the avenues of the old walls

Piazza S. Maria Novella* (2 E-F3). This is one of the loveliest squares in Florence; it was created between 1287 and about 1325 by demolishing existing houses in order to create a space before the Dominican church of S. Maria Novella, for religious preaching. In later times non-religious events were held here as well, such as the Palio dei Cocchi (a horse race established by Cosimo I in 1563). In its present incarnation, the square is dominated on the north side by the majestic facade of the church; in the central area stand two marble *obelisks* (1608), supported by bronze turtles, executed by Giambologna; these marked the finish lines in the Palio dei Cocchi.

On the southern side, facing the church, is the *Loggia dell'Ospedale di S. Paolo*, the only part to survive intact from a charitable institution dating back to the 13th c. Amidst the arches and at the extremities, note eleven medallions of glazed terracotta by Andrea della Robbia; above the door in the right side, note a lunette, also by Andrea della Robbia, depicting the *Embrace of St. Domenick and St. Francis.*

S. Maria Novella* (2 E3). This is one of the best-known and most interesting churches

The Piazza and the Church of S. Maria Novella

in Florence; it was begun in 1278 for the Dominican order. The church was nearly completed, including the campanile, by the middle of the 14th c., but the **facade***, which had never been finished, was reconfigured, from about 1458 on, to designs by Leon Battista Alberti, at the behest of Giovanni Rucellai (whose name is engraved on the triangular pediment). Alberti, while preserving some features of the original Gothic facade, set against them elements taken from classical culture: the resulting facade is a splendid and harmonious composition, with very precise proportional relations and a homogeneous encrustation of white and green-black marble, a typically Tuscan architectural decoration. The remarkable invention of Alberti is the upper section of the facade: the tall horizontal partition and the entire upper order, crowned by a triangular pediment, and joined to the lower order by two large and minutely inlaid volutes. Alberti preserved the circular Gothic window, setting it in a tripartite array of two-tone pilaster strips. In the upper pediment, note the shining sun, symbol of the Dominican order; other emblems to be seen here include that of the Rucellai family (feathers in a ring) and the personal emblem of Giovanni Rucellai (a sail bellying in the wind).

The **interior**, built to a Latin-cross plan, is divided into a nave and two aisles by piers made of "pietra forte," with pointed arches and cross-vaults.

In the lunette of the portal is the *Nativity*, a detached fresco, clearly inspired by Botti-celli. In the right aisle, in the 2nd bay (1, in the plan on page 80), note the *tomb of the Blessed Villana*, by Rossellino and Desiderio da Settignano (1451); in the 6th bay is the entrance to the 15th-c. Cappella della Pura (2), which contains an image of the *Virgin Mary* that is said to be miraculous. At the end of the right arm of the transept, a set of steps leads up to the 14th-c. Cappella Rucellai (3), on the altar of which stands a *Virgin Mary with Christ Child*, marble statue by Nino Pisano (mid-14th c.); the center of the floor is occupied by the *tomb stone of Fra Leonardo Dati*, a bronze bas-relief by Lorenzo Ghiberti (1425-26).

In the transept, note the Cappella di Filippo Strozzi (4), a chapel decorated with *frescoes* by Filippino Lippi, who also designed the stained glass (*Virgin Mary with Christ Child, two angels, and St. John and St. Philip*); on the far wall is the *tomb of Filippo Strozzi*, by Benedetto da Maiano (1491-95). The main chapel, known as the Cappella Tornabuoni (5), contains a renowned **series of frescoes** by Domenico Ghirlandaio and assistants (1485-90), depicting: in the vault, the *Evangelists*; on the left wall, *scenes from the life of the Virgin Mary*; on the right wall, *stories of St. John the Baptist*; and on the far wall, *Coronation of the Virgin Mary and Saints* and *Stories of Saints*. These splendid paintings also have great value as documents; among the sacred scenes, there are portraits of artists, thinkers, and celebrities of high Florentine society. The wooden choir, beneath the frescoes, is by Baccio d'Agnolo (ca. 1485-90), and was greatly renovated by Vasari in 1566. In the successive chapel,

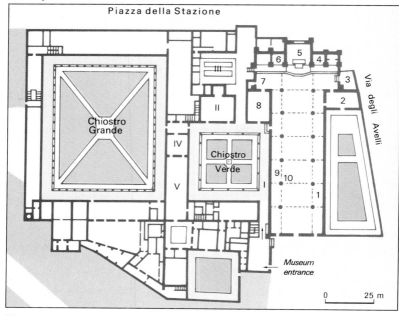

The Church and the Cloisters of S. Maria Novella: plan

or Cappella Gondi (6), note the architecture made of white and black marble and red porphyry, by Giuliano da Sangallo (1503), which serves as a sober frame to the *Crucifix** by Brunelleschi, the only wooden sculpture that the artist is known to have made.

At the head of the left arm of the transept is the raised Cappella Strozzi (7), a chapel that was completed around 1335. The walls are covered with vast *frescoes** by Nardo di Cione, brother of Orcagna (ca. 1350-57): on the left is the *Paradiso*, on the far wall is the *Last Judgement*, and on the right is the *Inferno*. On the altar, a panel by Orcagna depicts *Christ, Risen, Presents the Keys to St. Peter and a Book to St. Thomas, the Virgin Mary, St. John the Baptist, and Other Saints* (1357).

In the left wall of the transept is the entrance to the *sacristy* (8), a 14th-c. room rebuilt in the 17th/18th c. Inside, to the right of the entrance, is a *marble lavabo* in a glazed-terracotta niche by Giovanni della Robbia (1498); higher up is the *Crucifix*, a panel painted by a youthful Giotto (prior to 1312); at the far end, an enormous 16th-c. *cabinet*.

In the left aisle, in the 3rd bay (9), is a famous fresco by Masaccio (ca. 1427), depicting the **Holy Trinity*** with the Virgin Mary, St. John, and the Lenzi family, kneeling (in the lower register, a reclining skeleton): this intense and highly expressive

work is one of the most important creations of the Florentine Quattrocento. It was probably done with the collaboration of Brunelleschi, who worked on the deep triumphal arch painted in perspective in the background. On the penultimate pillar in the aisle (10), note a marble *pulpit* executed by Buggiano, to a design by Brunelleschi.

Museo di S. Maria Novella (2 E3). This museum comprises part of the cloisters of the convent and a number of adjoining rooms, with several exceedingly interesting series of frescoes.

From the entrance portal, to the left of the facade of S. Maria Novella, you can enter an atrium, and from there, you can reach the *Chiostro Verde*, or Green Cloister, which was built by Fra Jacopo Talenti (1332-50 and after). The cloister is distinguished by large depressed arches on massive octagonal pillars. On three sides of the portico the walls were frescoed with "terra verde" (hence the name of the cloister) with *stories from Genesis*; these frescoes were begun around 1425-30 by Paolo Uccello and others artists, and were completed in the first half of the 15th c. The most important episodes, painted by Paolo Uccello, are found on the wall of the entrance: among them, note *The Universal Deluge** and *The Drunkenness of Noah** (I, in the plan above), masterpieces that are particularly distinctive for their unnatural use of perspective and color.

On the side of the cloister opposite to the entrance, you can go into the **Cappellone degli Spagnoli** (II), former chapter hall of the convent, built by Fra Jacopo Talenti (ca. 1343-55); this large chapel was used in the 16th c. for religious services by the Spaniards who formed the entourage of Eleonora of Toledo, wife of Cosimo I. The large rectangular hall, with pointed-arch cross-vault, was entirely frescoed by Andrea di Buonaiuto and assistants (ca. 1367-69) with a large *series of paintings** that highlight the role played by the Dominican order in the struggle against heresy. In the webs of the ribbed vaults: *The Navigation of St. Peter*, the *Resurrection*, *Ascension*, and *Pentecost*; wall facing the entrance: there are three *episodes from the Passion*; entrance wall: *stories of St. Peter Martyr*; right wall: *The Church Militant and Triumphant**; left wall: *Triumph of St. Thomas Aquinas*. In the far "scarsella," or central-plan apse, note a canvas depicting *St. James, Being Led to His Martyrdom, Cures a Paralytic*, by Alessandro Allori (1592). The adjoining Chiostro dei Morti (or Cloister of the Dead; III), which existed even before the arrival of the Dominican order, was rebuilt around the middle of the 14th c.

From the Chiostro Verde, on the corner opposite to the entrance, you enter a vestibule which contains the entrance of the museum's exhibition halls: two of those halls (IV V; once an ante-refectory and a refectory) in which paintings, reliquaries, holy furnishings, and other material are on display.

In the same vestibule is the old entrance to the Chiostro Grande, or large cloister; this structure lies in the center of the part of the convent that now houses the Scuola Allievi Sottufficiali Carabinieri (a police academy; open only with permission from head office). This is the largest cloister in Florence, with 14th-c. porticoes and a 15th-c. loggia on the upper floor on the north side. The nearby medieval buildings contain, among other things, the *Cappella dei Papi*, or Chapel of Popes, with 16th-c. decorations.

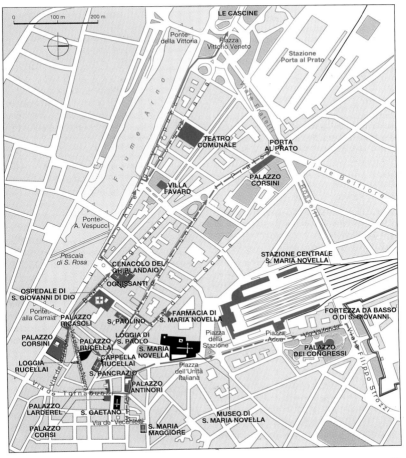

Stazione Ferroviaria di S. Maria Novella (2 C-D2). This railroad station was built between 1933 and 1935 in the area behind the church of S. Maria Novella; it is one of the most interesting pieces of Rationalist architecture ever built in Italy. It was designed by the Gruppo Toscano, under the direction of Giovanni Michelucci. The facade, made of "pietra forte," features a single great wall of glass, which extends to the ticket window area and the main gallery, 106 m. in length. The interior is organized in an extremely functional manner, and features some exceedingly elegant details.

Running along the right side of the station, take Via Valfonda to reach Viale Filippo Strozzi, which is overlooked by the great bulk of the *Fortezza di S. Giovanni** (2 A2-3), also known as the *Fortezza da Basso* to distinguish this "lower" fortress from the Forte di Belvedere, high on the hill of Bòboli. The enormous fortress (ca. 10 hectares in area) with a pentagonal plan, was built at the command of Duke Alessandro de' Medici. It was meant more as protection against civil uprisings and tumults than against attacks on Florence from without (note that the donjon faces the city), and it was built to plans by Antonio da Sangallo the Younger, in 1534. The external walls, which were originally 12 m. tall, still have their original appearance only on the side facing the tracks and in the area around the *keep*, which is faced with "pietra forte" ashlars. Inside, note the enormous *guard room*, an octagonal hall roofed over with a dome made of herringbone brickwork.
On the opposite side of the Viale Filippo Strozzi, facing the fortress, is the *Palazzo dei Congressi* (Pierluigi Spadolini, 1964-69; 2 B3), built by closely merging new architecture and an existing 19th-c. villa.

Piazza degli Antinori (2 F4). A labyrinth of narrow lanes (Via delle Belle Donne, Via del Trebbio) links Piazza S. Maria Novella with this small and alluring open area, located at the NW corner of the Roman walls, which once ran along what is now Via de' Tornabuoni. The name of the square comes from the **Palazzo Antinori** (n. 3), a fine example of a 15th-c. Florentine home, built by Giuliano da Maiano (1461-69). Note the elegant porticoed courtyard.

S. Gaetano (2 F4). This church, mentioned in documents dating from as early as the mid-11th c., faces Palazzo Antinori; it was entirely rebuilt in the Baroque style after 1604. The facade features two orders of fluted pilaster strips, and is richly decorated. Above the central portal you can see the insignia of the Theatine order, set between two allegorical figures; atop the side portals are statues of Theatine saints; in the upper

order, between the large corniced window and the upper pediment, note the Medici coat-of-arms.
The **interior***, one of the few surviving examples of Florentine Baroque, has a single nave and is built to a Latin-cross plan, with side chapels. In the upper sections of the church you can see one of the most significant series of 17th-c. Florentine sculpture to survive (by Antonio Novelli and others), with marble statues depicting the *Apostles* and the *Evangelists*, and bas-reliefs. The canvases and frescoes which decorate the chapels and the transept date from the 17th c., save for a few exceptions ; of particular note, on the altar of the 2nd chapel on the left, is the *Martyrdom of St. Lawrence*, an altar piece by Pietro da Cortona, completed in 1637.

A fairly short walk (Via degli Agli, Via de' Vecchietti) leads from Piazza degli Antinori to the **church of S. Maria Maggiore** (2 F4). Founded in early times (prior to the 11th c.), the church was rebuilt in the Gothic style in the second half of the 13th c. High up on the Romanesque campanile, on the side overlooking the Via de' Cerretani, is a late-Roman bust of a woman (the so-called "Berta"). The interior is typical of the Cistercian typology, with a nave and two aisles, divided by pointed arches set on square pillars, and terminating in three chapels. In the side chapels, note the frescoed vaults and a variety of artwork, largely dating from the 17th c.; in the main chapel in the presbytery, note the detached frescoes, attributed to Jacopo di Cione, depicting *Herod Ordering the Slaughter* and the *Slaughter of the Innocents* (1395-1400); in the chapel to the left of the main chapel, note the polychrome wooden bas-relief, with the *Virgin Mary Enthroned with the Christ Child* and, surrounding it, paintings on panel (13th c.).
From the sacristy you can enter the 16th-c. cloister of the old convent, with frescoes dating from the turn of the 17th c.

Palazzo Corsi (4 A4). At n. 16 in Via de' Tornabuoni stands this palazzo, once Palazzo Tornabuoni, built by Michelozzo in the mid-15th c. and renovated by Ferdinando Ruggieri (1736); in the end it was rebuilt by Telemaco Bonaiuti (1862-64). Note the *loggia* that runs along beside the church of S. Gaetano. Inside, all that survives of the original building is a part of the 15th-c. courtyard, a large staircase, and several frescoed vaults.
At n. 19 is the entrance to the late-Renaissance *Palazzo Larderel* (4 A3), built in 1580, to plans by Giovanni Antonio Dosio.

Piazza de' Rucellai (4 B3). This route is crowded with luxury shops and boutiques – Via de' Tornabuoni, Via della Vigna Nuova – and runs to a triangular square, Piazza de' Rucellai, designed by Leon Battista Alberti. One of the sides is faced by the Renaissance **Palazzo Rucellai** (4 A3), built in successive phases, in the second half of the 15th c., by Bernardo Rossellino, to plans by Alberti. The facade, which was left unfinished on the right side, features the classical stacking of orders, for the first time in the Renaissance; on the three floors – made of smooth ashlars, separated by string-course cornicework and punctuated by pilaster strips – there are small square windows on the lower floor, and mullioned windows on the upper floors. This building houses the Archivi Fotografici Alinari, an historic photographic archive, and, on the ground floor, a related museum of photography, the *Museo di Storia della Fotografia Fratelli Alinari*.

Perpendicular to the palazzo is the **Loggia Rucellai** (1463-66; 4 A-B3), with three arcades with fluted cornices; now protected by plate glass.

S. Pancrazio (4 A3). This building, a former church, is located not far from Piazza de' Rucellai: Via de' Palchetti and Via dei Federighi lead directly to it. As a church, it

most significant pieces: *Gentleman on Horseback*, polychrome gesso, 1937 (ground-floor hall); *Swimmer*, wood, 1932 (mezzanine); *Dancers* in the round (upper floor).

Cappella Rucellai (4 A3). Once linked with the left side of the church of S. Pancrazio (present-day entrance from Via della Spada), this was the family chapel of the powerful Florentine family, and was rebuilt at the behest of Giovanni Rucellai. The prior 14th-c. structure was rebuilt by Leon Battista Alberti in accordance with the nascent Renaissance sensibility; it has a rectangular plan and barrel-vault ceiling, and it contains the *Tempietto del S. Sepolcro* * – also designed by Alberti and completed in 1467 – a scale reproduction of the Holy Sepulcher in Jerusalem. Classically elegant, this little temple has walls punctuated with Corinthian pilaster strips, and faced with ornamental panels; the trabeation is crowned by a lily-shaped crenelation.

After walking through the left-hand stretch of Via della Spada, you will continue along the Via Palazzuolo, where you will see, in a small square off on the left (4 A2), the *church of S. Paolino*, dat-

The interior of the Apothecary and Perfumery of S. Maria Novella

was one of Florence's oldest (documents mentioning it date back to the 9th c.); it was rebuilt between the 14th and 15th c., then completely transformed again in the 18th c., and deconsecrated in 1808.

After a long period of neglect, the church was recently restored. Since 1988 it has been the site of the **Museo Marino Marini**, with a noteworthy collection of work by the Pistoia-born 20th-c. painter and sculptor. Among the

ing from the 10th c. but rebuilt at the end of the 17th c. The facade, in rusticated ashlars, is decorated with heraldic crests. The interior has a single nave, with a vaulted ceiling and side chapels; particularly noteworthy are the altars and the polychrome marble dating from the 17th and 18th c.

Take a jog to the right, cross the Via del Porcellana, and you will reach the Via della Scala (2 D-E1-2); follow this street away from the center, and you will see, at n. 16, the famous *Officina Profu-*

The Lungarno Corsini from the Ponte alla Carraia

mo-*Farmaceutica di S. Maria Novella* (historic apothecary and perfumery; workshop and retail outlet). The frescoed halls contain 17th-c. pharmacist's vases, alambics, thermometers, and other instruments.

Via Palazzuolo opens out into the elongated triangular area, known as the *Prato* (or "Meadow"; 9 B6), where a market was held as long ago as the 13th c., and where races were once run with Barbary horses.

At the end of the Prato, on the right (n. 58), stands the *Palazzo Corsini*, begun in 1591 to plans by Bernardo Buontalenti. Note the interesting Italian-style garden, with terracotta furnishings and statues.

At the intersection of the Prato with the surrounding ring roads, which follow the ring of the old walls, lies Piazzale di Porta al Prato. The *Porta al Prato* (9 A-B6), a gate that is quite similar to the Porta S. Gallo and Porta alla Croce, was built in 1285; inside is a 16th-c. fresco.

Piazza Goldoni (4 B2). Overlooking the river Arno (Ponte alla Carraia), at the end of Via della Vigna Nuova and at the mouth of Borgo Ognissanti, this square, at the corner of Lungarno Corsini, features the *Palazzo Ricasoli*, attributed to Michelozzo, though actual construction was begun (1480) after his death.

Palazzo Corsini (4 B3). Overlooking the Lungarno Corsini (though the entrance is at n. 11 in Via del Parione), this is an unusually large building for Florence; it is made up of three wings which wrap around a courtyard. The courtyard is closed toward the Lungarno by a fourth, lower wing of the building. Atop this fourth wing is a terrace which extends out to the side wings. Pier Francesco Silvani drew up the plans and began construction (1648-56); it was continued by Alfonso Parigi, Pietro Tacca, and Antonio Maria Ferri. Silvani also designed the spiral staircase inside.

On the second floor, you can visit the **Galleria Corsini**, one of the leading private art collections in Florence (founded in 1765). Part of the allure of this collection is the fact that it still has the feel of a private art gallery set amongst the lavish furnishings of an aristocratic villa (note the Roman *krater* in hall I). The collection of paintings is centered around Florentine, Italian, and European painting of the 17th and 18th c., with a few remarkable pieces of Renaissance art. One should note in particular: *Apollo and the Muses*, panels begun by Giovanni Santi and Evangelista di Piandimeleto, and completed by Timoteo Viti (hall III); *portrait of Julius II*, which is attributed with some uncertainty to Raphael; five *allegorical figures* by Filippino Lippi; and a *Crucifixion*, attributed to Antonello da Messina (hall IV).

Borgo Ognissanti (4 A-B 1-2). This street dates back to early Florence, and it takes its name from a religious complex founded by the order of the Umiliati; the street in fact runs toward this complex. We should point out the *Ospedale di S. Giovanni di Dio* (n. 20), a hospital founded in 1380, and the *Casa-Galleria* (n. 26), an Art-Nouveau (in Italian, 'Liberty') building by Giovanni Michelazzi (1911).

Church of Ognissanti (4 A2). Founded in 1251 by the order of the Umiliati, this church has a handsome Baroque facade (Matteo Nigetti, 1637) with two orders divided in three by pilaster strips, with fanciful niches and windows; it is crowned by a great escutcheon of Florence; on the portal, note the glazed-terracotta lunette attributed to Giovanni della Robbia or Benedetto Buglioni. On the right rises the slender *campanile*, dating from the 13th or 14th c.

The interior, with its single nave and deep transept, abounds in Baroque decorations of the 17th and 18th-c.

Cenacolo del Ghirlandaio (2 F2). From the cloister adjoining the church of Ognissanti (entrance at n. 42) you can go into the former refectory of the convent, which contains in the far wall a frescoed *Last Supper**, by Domenico Ghirlandaio; this fresco is admirable in particular for its descriptive style and serene setting; on the left wall is the preparatory design. All around, other frescoes and preparatory designs.

If you follow the Lungarno Amerigo Vespucci (4 A-B 1-2) away from the center, you can look out over the river and see the *Pescaia di S. Rosa*, a weir, as well as all that remains of the locks on the Canale Macinante and the waterwheels. The next wide area in the Lungarno is dominated by the *Villa Favard* (9 C6), by Giuseppe Poggi (1847); it now houses the Economics Department of the University of Florence. From here, you will turn into Corso Italia; in that street, at n. 12, is the Neoclassical facade of the *Teatro Comunale* (9 B5), an opera house and concert hall designed by Telemaco Bonaiuti (1862)

Parco delle Cascine (plans 6 and 9). At the end of the Lungarno Vespucci and beyond Piazza Vittorio Veneto, lies this large park (total surface area of about 118 hectares; 3 km. in overall length) which takes its name ("Cascine," or farmhouses) from the farms of the Medici estate; here, in the 16th c., cattle were raised. The park was not opened to the public until the turn of the 19th c., and since then it has been a favorite destination for Florentines. Circulation of automobiles is limited to the main thoroughfare, and even there only as far as Viale del Pegaso.

Thus, if you are interested in touring the entire park, we recommend cycling. Along the right side of Viale degli Olmi are athletic facilities (Sferisterio, or handball court; Velodromo, or bicycle-racing track; Tennis Club; and Ippodromo, or horse track). After you cross the Piazzale delle Cascine, you continue along the Viale dell'Aeronautica, with the large field, or Prato del Quercione, on your left; past the intersection with Viale del Pegaso, the trees grow thick and very tall, and then thin out as you approach another field, the Prato delle Mulina. At the park's westernmost extremity, where the river Mugnone flows into the Arno, stands the striking *Monumento Funebre dell'Indiano*, or funerary monument of

Characteristic cages during the Crickets' feast at the Cascine

the Indian; here, in 1870, the Maharaja of Kohlepur lies buried; he died, quite young, here in Florence. The riverfront is marked by the *Ponte-Viadotto all'Indiano* (1969-76), an innovative structure, 210 m. in length; it has two levels, for cars and for pedestrians.

5 The Quarter of S. Croce

This quarter, symmetrical with the quarter of S. Maria Novella, includes nearly all of the eastern section of the historical center. The area, once marshy and subject to flooding, was given a boost in importance by the construction, between the 13th and 14th c., of the Franciscan settlement of S. Croce. The church, built with the funds of the leading families in this quarter (Bardi, Peruzzi, Cerchi, Alberti, Baroncelli), was conceived as a particularly vast structure. Besides serving as a house of worship, it also became a gathering place for the populace of the quarter, with whom – it should be noted – the Franciscans had established a close and fruitful relationship.

The square lying before it, one of the largest and most geometric in the city, has been one of the town's gathering places for centuries: here competitions, festivals, and performances were held, like those described in the "Stanze" by Politian (or Poliziano). In the elliptical route of Via Torta, Via de' Bentaccordi, and Piazza de' Peruzzi – to the west of the square – you can easily make out the perimeter of the Roman amphitheater.

The costume display which takes place before the Florentine soccer match in Piazza S. Croce

S. Croce was for centuries the most populous and working-class of Florence's quarters, with a major wool industry; often the palazzi of the merchants (like the palazzo of the Corsi family, now the site of the Museo Horne) contained great vats in their basements for the dyeing of fabrics.

Another characteristic of this area was that the structures of the administration of justice were located here (first the Bargello, then Palazzo Castellani and, from the 19th c. on, the complex of S. Firenze: these sites are all described in route 1.2, page 38) as was the prison (Isolato delle Stinche). Even the various street names reflect the curious origins of the place: Via dei Neri takes its name from the dark-clad medieval brotherhood ("neri" means "black ones") who accompanied those about to be executed on their last walk to their place of execution.

The urban structure and layout of this quarter clearly shows signs – it is quite common to see Renaissance buildings overlapping with medieval edifices, for example – of the stratification that has been produced over the last few centuries. The quarter was modified especially during the 19th and 20th c. Among the major projects dating from the 19th c. we should cite the middle-class residential quarter of the Mattonaia (1864-66), which sprang up around the immense Piazza d'Azeglio, as well as the construction of the Lungarno della Zecca Vecchia (1870), a riverfront promenade where the bourgeoisie built little villas and palazzi overlooking the river, replacing the more traditional buildings, set against the town walls. The most disastrous demolition took place under Fascism, with the construction of the buildings of the Ufficio Tecnico Erariale, or land office (Via dell'Agnolo) and the new Post Office building (Via Pietrapiana, Via Verdi).

5.1 From S. Croce to the Lungarno della Zecca Vecchia

Setting out from Piazza di S. Croce – after a tour of the Franciscan complex (basilica, cloisters, the Cappella Pazzi, the Museo dell'Opera) – this route at first runs close to the center of the city, along the main thoroughfare of Borgo S. Croce, which is lined with major palazzi. As you follow the route, you will then go on to explore the area adjoining the line of Via de' Benci and Via Verdi. The winding route and the various detours allow you to reach the major architectural sites (such as the Palazzo Peruzzi, the church of Santi Simone e Giuda, and the church of S. Remigio), as well as to venture deeper into the heart of the quarter, which preserves a particularly interesting urban stratification.

The second part of the route leads to the Arno on a line with the Ponte alle Grazie; then a pleasant stroll with a fine view takes you along the Arno to Piazza Piave and to the fish pond, or Pescaia di S. Niccolò, along the Lungarno della Zecca Vecchia.

Piazza di S. Croce (1 E5-6; 5 C4). This vast, regularly proportioned square was built in the Middle Ages, and lay immediately behind the walls of Communal Florence (those in turn ran the length of what are now Via de' Benci and Via Verdi), in close context with the complex of Franciscan architecture which stands on the eastern side of the square. The southern elevation of the square (to the right of the church) features a number of distinctive buildings jutting out on brackets, or corbels, including the Palazzo dell'Antella; facing it across the square are buildings that are simpler in style. Among these, it is possible to recognize the original medieval structures, narrow and tall. The square, which was essentially designed to accommodate great crowds of the faithful, has been used for more secular pursuits as well: as early as the 14th c., and especially during the Renaissance, feasts, jousts, and matches of "Calcio Fiorentino," or Florentine Soccer were held here; soccer matches still take place in the space bounded by slender pillars and benches, all made of "pietra serena."

On the side of the square opposite to the basilica, at n. 1, stands the *Palazzo Cocchi-Serristori*, believed to be the work of Giuliano da Sangallo (1469-74) who, influenced by his previous experience in Rome, designed the unusual facade with the two upper registers punctuated by pilaster strips framing arches and windows. Note how the facade extends laterally.

Palazzo dell'Antella (5 C4). The broad facade – jutting forth on brackets – of this building (numbers 20-22) was executed by Giulio Parigi, who combined two existing homes. It features a large fresco decoration, with *Virtues* and *Divinities*, completed in 20 days, between 1619 and 1620, by a dozen artists working under the supervision of Giovanni da S. Giovanni. A round slab of marble (dated 1565), set beneath the third window from the left, marked the center line for the great game of football. There is a corresponding slab on the opposite side of the square.

Basilica di S. Croce* (1 E6; 5 C4). This is one of the most famous churches in Florence; it is well known for its beauty and for the concentration of fine art (including celebrated series of frescoes), as well as for the great number of "illustrious Italians" buried within its walls.

This building, traditionally said to have been built by Arnolfo di Cambio, was begun in 1295, to replace an existing church somewhat smaller in size. It was completed around 1385; still the church was not consecrated until 1443. The facade, by Nicolò Matas, is a later addition done in the Neo-Gothic style (1853-63), as is the bell tower (Gaetano Baccani, 1847). To the left of the church courtyard is the 19th-c. *monument to Dante*. The sides of the church are particularly distinctive in the "skyline" of Florence, because of the notable bare triangular pediments of the side aisles, which frame large Gothic mullioned windows. Along the sides there are also two 14th-c. porticoes.

The **interior**, broad and majestic, follows the same T-plan layout (a tau cross) found in many large convent churches, with a long transept and a polygonal apse. The nave and two aisles are divided by two rows of large pillars with octagonal cross-sections, supporting great pointed arches; the broad nave has a truss roof. As was the case in S. Maria Novella, there was originally a partition running across the church; it divided the section reserved for monks from the area reserved for the faithful. This partition was torn down in 1566 by order of Cosimo I, in accordance with the dictates of the Counter Reformation. Note the re-

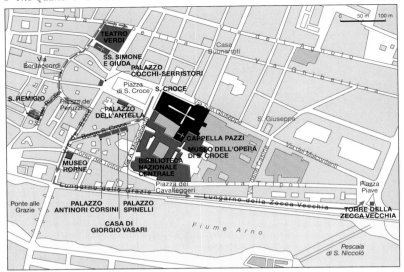

markable stained-glass windows, dating from the 14th and 15th c.

In the right aisle, between the 1st and the 2nd altar (1, in the plan on page 89), stands the 16th-c. *tomb of Michelangelo*; on the pillar opposite, set in a marble mandorla, the *Madonna del Latte* by Antonio Rossellino (1478); between the 2nd and the 3rd altar (2), *cenotaph of Dante Alighieri* (1829); following (3) is the *monument to Vittorio Alfieri* (an 18th-c. Italian author) by Antonio Canova (1810); on the 3rd pillar, toward the nave (4), is a *pulpit** by Benedetto da Maiano, a refined and solid structure, with five panels depicting *stories of St. Francis*; after the 4th altar (5), *tomb of Niccolò Machiavelli* (1787), with a famous inscription – "Tanto nomini nullum par elogium" (No praise can be high enough for so great a name). Then, after the 5th altar (6), an aedicule made of "pietra serena," with a splendid *Annunciation** by Donatello (1435 c.), a high relief in which a decided anti-classicism can be detected in the contrast between the humble material used ("pietra serena") and the precious decoration. Immediately following a side-door (7) is the *monument to Leonardo Bruni**, a Humanist, the first illustrious personage to be buried in S. Croce; this monument was built by Bernardo Rossellino (1444-45), clearly following the teachings of Leon Battista Alberti. This monument was a model much emulated during the Renaissance. Alongside is the *tomb of Gioacchino Rossini* (1900) and, following the last altar (8), is the *tomb of Ugo Foscolo*, another Italian man of letters (1939).

In the right arm of the transept is the large Cappella Castellani (A), a chapel with a series of frescoes by Agnolo Gaddi and assistants (*stories of St. Anthony Abbot, St. John the Baptist, St. John the Evangelist, and St. Nicholas of Bari*); the handsome *tabernacle* is by Mino da Fiesole, while the painted *Cross* is by Niccolò Gerini. At the end of the transept is the Cappella Baroncelli (B), a chapel frescoed with *stories of the Virgin Mary* by Taddeo Gaddi (1332-38), who also did the stained glass, the four *Prophets* high on the exterior, and perhaps the *polyptych* on the altar (though many attribute it to Giotto).

A portal, the work of Michelozzo, leads into the corridor of the Sagrestia del Noviziato or Androne del Noviziato (C), a vesibule which was also built by Michelozzo, in about 1445. This vesibule in turn leads into the **sacristy**, a large and particularly handsome 14th-c. room. On the right wall, among the large frescoes by Niccolò Gerini and Spinello Aretino, you should note the fresco by Taddeo Gaddi (*Crucifixion*); on the left, note the *bust of the Savior*, an enameled polychrome terracotta by Giovanni della Robbia. The inlaid cabinetry (15th c.) is by Giovanni di Michele. At the end of the sacristy is the Cappella Rinuccini (D), closed off by the original gratework (1371) and frescoed by Giovanni da Milano, between 1363 and 1366 with *stories of Mary Magdalene* (on the right) and *stories of the Virgin Mary* (on the left); on the altar, *polyptych* by Giovanni del Biondo.

At the end of the corridor of the sacristy, you enter the Cappella Medici (E), a chapel with simple, spare lines, designed by Michelozzo; on the altar, note the *Virgin Mary with Christ Child, amidst angels and saints*, an altar piece, in enameled terracotta, by Andrea della Robbia (ca. 1480).

After you return to the church, you can tour the far chapels, five on either side, divided by the main chapel. Particularly noteworthy are the *Cappella Peruzzi* and the *Cappella Bardi* (F and G), which contain the last two **series of frescoes *** done by Giotto, work produced at the height of his powers (1320-25), with a vast sweeping sense of space and composition. Sadly, only fragments now survive. In the Cappella Peruzzi, note the series with the *stories of St. John Evangelist* (right wall) and *stories of St. John the Baptist* (left wall). In the Cappella Bardi is the series with the *stories of St. Francis*, which alternates chronologically from one wall to the other. A number of scenes on the left wall (*Francis removes his clothing, in the presence of the bishop Guido and his own father, Bernardone, The saint appears in the church of Arles before St. Anthony as he preaches*) develop in a more mature and panoramic style the episodes depicted in the upper church of Assisi; on the altar, note the 13th-c. panel with *S. Francis and stories from his life.*

The particularly lovely **main chapel** (H) shows clear signs of influence by the Gothic style from across the Alps, with its vertical thrust, the umbrella-ribbing of the vault, and the three, exceedingly tall twin-light mullioned windows. The series of frescoes that decorates the chapel – the *story of the discovery of the True Cross*, taken from the "Legenda Aurea" by Jacopo da Varagine – is linked to the name of the church (S. Croce means, of course, Holy Cross); the frescoes are by Agnolo Gaddi (ca. 1380 c.), who also did nearly all the stained glass.

Among the chapels to the left of the main chapel, we should point out the last two in particular: the Cappella Pulci-Berardi (I), which features 14th-c. frescoes by Bernar-

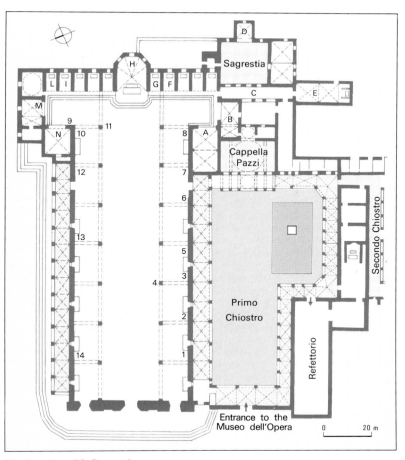

The Complex of S. Croce: plan

The polyptych on the altar of the Cappella Baroncelli: detail

do Daddi and an altar piece in glazed terracotta by Giovanni della Robbia; and the Cappella Bardi di Vernio (L), which is frescoed with *stories of St. Sylvester* by Maso di Banco (ca. 1340).

At the leftmost extremity of the transept, there is another Cappella Bardi di Vernio (M), enclosed by a grate (1335). In this chapel, above the altar, stands a wooden *Crucifix* by Donatello, criticized as excessively rough by Brunelleschi. According to Vasari, Brunelleschi then carved his great Crucifix for S. Maria Novella, to express his point. Next comes (last chapel in the transept) the Cappella Machiavelli or Cappella Salviati (N), with *tombs*.

As you enter the left aisle, you will see the 19th-c. *monuments to the composer and musician Luigi Cherubini* (9) and the *engraver Raffaello Morghen* (10); in front of the pillar is a monument to *Leon Battista Alberti* (11), by Lorenzo Bartolini; after the 6th altar is the *monument to Carlo Marsuppini* * (12), a successor of Leonardo Bruni (interred opposite) as Segretario della Repubblica Fiorentina: built by Desiderio da Settignano and inspired by Rossellino, this is one of the finest examples of a 15th-c. sepulcher; between the 5th and the 4th altars (13), note the *Pietà* by Agnolo Bronzino and, on the floor, the *tomb stone of Lorenzo Ghiberti, with his son Vittorio*; lastly, between the 2nd and the 1st altars (14), note the 18th-c. *tomb of Galileo and his pupil Vincenzo Viviani.*

Museo dell'Opera di S. Croce (5 C4). This museum of the construction of the church of S. Croce occupies a number of rooms in the convent to the right of the church. In it is the Cappella Pazzi, a chapel by Brunelleschi, considered a masterpiece. The museum features primarily architectural fragments and elements dating from the 14th and 15th c., originally from the Franciscan complex itself.

You will enter the handsome *first cloister*, which still preserves a 14th-c. style; at the center are a *warrior*, a bronze by Henry Moore, and *God the Father, Seated* by Baccio Bandinelli.

In the background, note the **Cappella Pazzi***, a perfect example of Renaissance architecture. Work on this chapel was begun by Brunelleschi between 1429 and 1430, but construction proceeded slowly until 1470. The portico extending before the chapel has six Corinthian columns made of "pietra serena." These columns support a tall attic broken by an arch; in the trabeation, note the *frieze* with cherubs' heads, by Desiderio da Settignano. A low cylindrical dome, surmounted by a conical roof, looms over the building. In the barrel vault of the portico there is a small cupola with tondoes and rosettes made of glazed terracotta, by Luca della Robbia; he also did the tondo with *St. Andrew*, set above the doorway, with stupendous carved doors, by Giuliano da Maiano (1472).

The interior has a structure quite similar to that of the Sagrestia Vecchia, or old sacristy, of S. Lorenzo: there are two rooms, surmounted by cupolas, but the larger room has a rectangular plan instead of a square one, because of the obstacles presented by existing structures. Along the walls runs a bench, made of "pietra serena" – used during the meetings of the Capitolo del Convento, or ruling body of the convent – upon which are based the Corinthian pilaster strips that punctuate the walls. The decoration is closely bound up with the architectural structure: in the 12 tondoes, note the *Apostles* in glazed ceramics, one of Luca della Robbia's masterpieces; in the polychrome medallions in the spandrels of the cupola, note the four *Evangelists*, possibly by Brunelleschi himself.

After you return to the cloister, you will enter the former 14th-c. refectory (first hall of the Museum), which contains major art works. Among them, on the immediate right, note the large **Crucifix*** by Cimabue, the masterpiece that was most severely damaged by the flood of 1966. On the far wall, note the fresco by Taddeo Gaddi (1333), consisting of the *Tree of the True Cross*, four *sacred stories* and a *Last Supper* (in the lower register), which served as a model for later decorations of convent refectories. On the side walls, note six fragments of a large fresco by Andrea Orcagna (*Triumph of Death*, *Last Judgment*, and *Inferno*), one of the most dramatic and powerful documents of 14th-c. Florentine art, along with other frescoes from the 14th and 15th c. On the left side stands the *statue of St. Louis of Toulouse* * by Donatello (1424) made of gilt bronze, originally set in one of the exterior tabernacles of Orsanmichele (the tabernacle in which it now stands is a copy), and transferred to the facade of S. Croce in 1460. On the same wall, near the door, is a detached fresco depicting *St. John the Baptist and St. Francis*, by Domenico Veneziano. The other five halls feature lunettes, detached frescoes, preparatory drawings, fragments of stained glass, various Della Robbia artworks and sculptures, mostly from the 14th and 15th c.

You will then return to the first cloister, and

The Cappella Pazzi

through a handsome *portal* by Benedetto da Maiano you will enter the elegant *second cloister**, with broad arcades on the ground floor and a loggia on the upper floor, probably the work of Bernardo Rossellino (1453).

Borgo S. Croce (5 C3-4). This ancient road runs at an angle to the normal street grid, and is lined by a remarkable number of historical buildings.

Museo Horne (5 D3). This museum is set in the *Palazzo Horne* (entrance at n. 6 in Via

de' Benci, at the end of the Borgo S. Croce), built at the end of the 15th c. for the Corsi family and attributed to Cronaca. It contains a major collection of paintings, sculpture, majolica, glass, coins, and plate, dating back to the 14th/16th c. Both the building and the collection once belonged to the eclectic English collector, Herbert Percy Horne, a scholar of Florentine art of the 15th and 16th c. At the turn of the 20th c., Horne purchased this building and restored it in order to recreate a refined Renaissance home.

Palazzo Peruzzi (5 C3). If you climb a short distance along the Via de' Benci toward Piazza di S. Croce, you will note, at the corner of Piazza de' Peruzzi, the vast complex of Palazzo Peruzzi, extending as far as the Borgo de' Greci. This composite structure was built at the end of the 13th c. by combining a number of existing, separate buildings into a single building. Note the remarkable curving elevation, which overlooks the oddly shaped Piazza de' Peruzzi.

Take a detour along Via de' Bentaccordi and Via Isola delle Stinche from Piazza de' Peruzzi, and you will reach a little square with the ancient **church of Ss. Simone e Giuda** (12th/13th c.; 5 B3). The next block is occupied by the *Teatro Verdi* (entrance further along, in Via Ghibellina 99-101; 5 B3-4), the second-largest theater in Florence (seats 1,500).

Another detour from Piazza de' Peruzzi: take Via de' Rustici and Via Vinegia to the **church of S. Remigio** (5 C3). Founded in the 11th c., this church was rebuilt in the Gothic style between the end of the 13th and the turn of the 14th c. The gable-pitch facade has, as its sole decoration, a series of hanging arches under the eaves. The interior has a nave and two aisles, all equal in height, divided by large octagonal pillars with a cross vault. The restoration (not a very successful one) that followed the flood of 1966 has uncovered on the walls fragments of 14th-c. frescoes.

Ponte alle Grazie (5 D3). This bridge, set at the southern extremity of Via de' Benci, gives its name to the Lungarno alle Grazie. It is a descendent of the bridge built in 1237, and destroyed by the Germans in 1944; it was built in 1957. The original bridge, with nine arches, withstood all the Arno's floods, and featured tabernacles, which were in turn replaced by oratories, hermitages, and shops. These, in turn, were destroyed in 1876, in order to expand the width of the bridge to the requirements of trolley transport.

Biblioteca Nazionale Centrale (5 D4). This is one of the most important libraries in

Italy; it occupies a large eclectic-style building that overlooks the Piazza dei Cavalleggeri (between the Lungarno delle Grazie and the Lungarno della Zecca Vecchia) and was built between 1911 and 1935. A law dating from 1885 requires that a copy of every book and publication printed in Italy be deposited here. It currently holds – on 85 km. of shelves – 24,721 manuscripts, 3,780 incunabula, about 5 million books and a million letters. Among the most notable and rarest works are: a *Missal* used by the Tyrolean Church, a 10th-c. codex; the *Codex of the Commedia*, perhaps the oldest edition of the Divine Comedy in existence (first half of the 14th c.); the *Maguntina Bible*, an incunabulum dating from 1462; a *Divina Commedia*, or Divine Comedy, published in Florence in 1481, with commentary by Cristoforo Landino and engravings attributed to Botticelli.

If you continue along the Lungarno della Zecca Vecchia you will reach – in the middle of Piazza Piave – a tower, the *Torre della Zecca Vecchia* (5 D6), one of the surviving fragments of the outermost walled perimeter.

5.2 From S. Croce to S. Salvi and on to the Campo di Marte

From Piazza di S. Croce, the route penetrates into the heart of the quarter of S. Croce, following Via delle Pinzochere (the name comes from a tertiary order of Franciscan nuns), one of the streets that has best preserved its original working-class culture. After you cross the Via Ghibellina, where the Casa Buonarroti is located (notable museum), the route continues to the corner of Via Pietrapiana. You may take a couple of detours (along the medieval Borgo degli Albizi and across the 19th-c. Piazza d'Azeglio), and then you will head away from the center: from here on we recommend making use of a car. Once you reach Piazza L.B. Alberti by following Via Vincenzo Gioberti, you will turn into the Via Lungo l'Affrico; the first cross street on the right, Via Tito Speri, leads to the complex of the old Vallombrosan monastery of S. Salvi (Museo del Cenacolo di Andrea del Sarto, featuring a Last Supper by that artist).

This itinerary ends in the area of the major athletic complexes in the Campo di Marte.

Casa Buonarroti* (5 B5). With an entrance

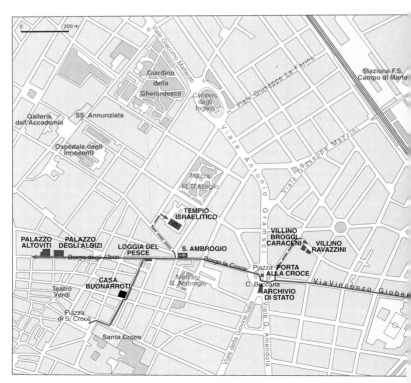

at n. 70 in Via Ghibellina, this home of the Buonarroti family stands on the site of three houses, purchased by Michelangelo between 1516 and 1525; the artist lived in them. The palazzo, built at the wishes of the great grand-nephew of the artist, Michelangelo the Younger (1568-1647), was bequeathed by the last surviving descendant (Cosimo, who died in 1858) to the city of Florence. In 1859, it was opened to the public as a museum, hosting the collections of art and archeology of the Buonarroti family.

On the ground floor (Hall 1) note the *bust of Michelangelo** by Daniele da Volterra. Halls 2-5 are used for exhibit space. In Hall 6, *portraits of Michelangelo* (16th/19th c.); in the next halls are the art collections – paintings, terracotta, etc. – of the Buonarroti family (Halls 7 and 8) and the archeological collections (Hall 9).

On the second floor, among the most notable works are two renowned reliefs by Michelangelo (hall 11): the *Battle of the Centaurs** (prior to 1492), a marble relief that is clearly linked to 15th-c. culture by the mythological subject, but quite innovative in its experimentation with the "unfinished" and in terms of its formal approach; the *Madonna della Scala** (Virgin of the Stairway; 1490-92), Michelangelo's first work,

remarkably original though clearly inspired in technique by the work of Donatello, as well as in the background and in the depiction of the Virgin Mary. In hall 12, note the *model for the facade of S. Lorenzo*, executed in wood and designed by Michelangelo, and the *model for a river god*, possibly a preparatory study for a statue in the Sagrestia Nuova, or new sacristy, of the church of S. Lorenzo. Note the *Gallery** (hall 18), built by Michelangelo the Younger to commemorate his illustrious grand-uncle; this is one of the most notable complexes of the Florentine 17th c. (1612-28): the floor is covered with polychrome majolica tiles and the doors have wooden inlays; on the walls and ceiling, note major frescoes by the leading Florentine painters of the time – depicting the glories of Michelangelo. In the following room (hall 19), inside one wall, is the *Studiolo di Michelangelo il Giovane**, the study of Michelangelo the Younger. Lastly, in the Biblioteca, or library (hall 21) a number of *sketches* by Michelangelo are on display.

Piazza dei Ciompi (5 A-B5). At the end of Via Buonarroti, there is a daily antiques market here, offering relative bargains. Toward the Via Pietrapiana is the *Loggia del Pesce*, built by Vasari (1567) for the Mercato Vecchio, or old market; the loggia was dismantled when the Piazza della Repubblica was built, and then rebuilt here in 1951; it is decorated with tondoes in polychrome terracotta (depicting marine creatures) and grand-ducal heraldic crests.

Borgo degli Albizi (5 A3-4). This street follows the course of the Roman "decumanus maximus" (the modern-day Corso). At n. 12 is the *Palazzo degli Albizi*, with a plaster facade, rebuilt at the turn of the 16th c. Facing it (at n. 15) stands the *Palazzo degli Alessandri*, another residence of the powerful Albizi family; burnt and badly damaged during the revolt of the Ciompi (1378), it was rebuilt and, at the turn of the 15th c., it was one of the largest in Florence. At n. 18 stands the *Palazzo Altoviti*, known as the "Palazzo dei Visacci," built by joining together three existing buildings (ca. 1600); the facade, built by Giovanni Battista Caccini, was adorned by fifteen marble herms (1600-1604), or statues in the form of a square pillar, surmounted by a bust or a head; these fifteen herms feature *portraits of Florentines* "di mirabil dottrina," i.e., of great genius (Dante, Petrarch, Boccaccio, Marsilio Ficino, and others). Further along (n. 26) is the *Palazzo Ramirez de Montalvo*, built by

The Borgo degli Albizi

Bartolomeo Ammannati (1568) on behalf of a noble Castilian of the Medici court; note the heraldic crest at the center of the facade. There is also an interesting "graffito" decoration designed by Vasari, depicting the virtues of the courtier.

S. Ambrogio (5 A6). At the end of the external section of Via Pietrapiana stands one of the oldest churches in Florence (10th c.), rebuilt in the 15th c., with the construction of the Cappella del Miracolo and the side altars.

Inside the church, the Renaissance side-altars are decorated with paintings from the 14th-16th c. Among them note, in the 1st altar on the left, a panel by Alesso Baldovinetti depicting *Saints and Angels*. In the Cappella del Miracolo (chapel of the miracle, to the left of the main chapel) is the marble *tabernacle* built by Mino da Fiesole (1481-83), with a chalice said to have played a part in a miracle; the episode is described in a lively pictorial narrative, in the adjoining *fresco* by Cosimo Rosselli (ca. 1486).

A detour along the Via de' Pilastri and then to the right along Via L.C. Farini leads to the *Tempio Israelitico* (or synagogue; 1874-82; 3 F6), an eclectic construction with Moorish and Byzantine motifs; adjoining is the *Museo Ebraico di Firenze*, or Jewish Museum of Florence, which features objects of Hebrew ceremonial and a number of ancient codices.

If you continue along the Via Farini you will reach the **Piazza Massimo d'Azeglio** (3 E6): this broad and geometric space is the heart of the Quartiere della Mattonaia, and was built in the second half of the 19th c. in one of the areas still undeveloped inside the outermost walled perimeter.

Piazza Cesare Beccaria (10 C1). You can take Borgo la Croce, along the line of Via Pietrapiana, to reach this square. It is a "theatrical" creation of the late-19th c., built after the demolition of the outermost walled perimeter of Florence, when the great "viali di circonvallazione," or ring roads, were built. In the center, standing alone, is a gate of the old walls, the *Porta alla Croce* (in the lunette, note the 16th-c. fresco, attributed to Michele di Ridolfo del Ghirlandaio). To the south of the square, between Viale della Giovine Italia and Viale Giovanni Amendola, is the new location of the *Archivio di Stato* (or state archive, 1978-86; 10 D1), one of the richest collections of documents in all Europe.

Not far away, in Via Scipione Ammirato, we should point out two small villas, *Villino Broggi-Caraceni* and *Villino Ravazzini* (numbers 99 and 101; 10 C2), fanciful Art-Nouveau creations by Giovanni Michelazzi.

S. Michele a S. Salvi (10 C4). Beyond Piazza Beccaria, if you continue on a straight line along Via Vincenzo Gioberti you will reach Piazza L.B. Alberti; from here, a long viaduct over the railroad and Via Tito Speri lead to the church of the old Vallombrosan convent of S. Salvi, in the 16th-c. style. The interior, built to a Latin-cross plan, with a truss roof, is enriched with artworks, mostly from the 14th/16th c.

Museo del Cenacolo di Andrea del Sarto (10 C4). This museum, set in a number of rooms in the former Vallombrosan monastery of S. Salvi (entrance in the Via di S. Salvi, n. 16). You enter a long gallery, containing paintings from early-16th-c. Florence. All the way back, a room contains fragments of the *funerary monument of St. Giovanni Gualberto*, by Benedetto da Rovezzano (1507-13). After the Sala del Lavabo and the kitchen, you will reach the convent's refectory. Here you can admire the enormous fresco of the **Cenacolo***, or Last Supper, by Andrea del Sarto (1526-27). So handsome is this work that the Imperial troops did not dare to destroy it when they occupied the convent, during the siege of Florence in 1530.

Campo di Marte (10 A3-4). This is the name of the largest athletic area in all Florence, crisscrossed and surrounded by broad drives and promenades. Among the athletic facilities, note the *Stadio Comunale* (city stadium; Pier Luigi Nervi, 1931), a remarkable piece of architecture.

6 Oltrarno

The entire sector of Florence across the Arno is occupied by the quarter of S. Spirito, once called the Sestiere d'Oltrarno.

During the Middle Ages this area was specialized – as was the quarter of S. Croce – in manufacturing activities connected with the wool industry. Indeed, by the second half of the 15th c., the major annual woolens fair (which was traditionally held on St. Martin's Day in Piazza della Signoria) had been moved to Piazza S. Spirito. The working-class character of this quarter – described and celebrated by the Italian authors Aldo Palazzeschi and Vasco Pratolini in some of their best-known works – was later reinforced by the concentration of crafts workshops. Though those workshops are now dwindling, they are still a fundamental part of life in Oltrarno.

The Oltrarno is distinguished by a number of monumental "focal points": the convent complexes of S. Spirito and the Carmine, the two religious structures around which life in this quarter revolved for many centuries; Palazzo Pitti (where the Medici court was moved in the mid-16th) with the adjoining Giardino di Bòboli, both palazzo and gardens much larger than was customary in Florence; the complex of S. Miniato, a stupendous Romanesque addition to the green hillside.

In the eastern section of the quarter is a network of distinctive streets called "coste" (Costa di S. Giorgio, Costa de' Magnoli, Costa Scarpuccia), which preserves the somewhat countryfied atmosphere of old Florence, running steeply up to the Collina di Bòboli, on the summit of which stands the Forte di Belvedere: this is one of the most charming sites in Florence.

6.1 The Area Around Palazzo Pitti

The first section of the route is focused on the tour of the Pitti complex, for three centuries a ducal and then royal residence, and now the site of some of the most important Florentine art museums.

Via de' Bardi and Via di S. Niccolò constitute the backbone, or chief thoroughfare, of the historical eastern section of the quarter. Branching off from this axis run the various roads that climb the hill, or Collina di Bòboli, culminating in the massive bulk of the fortress, or Forte di Belvedere: we recommend climbing up along the Costa di S. Giorgio, though the Via di Belvedere and Costa Scarpuccia are equally lovely.

Leaving aside its remarkable views and architectural monuments, Via de' Bardi is the best way to reach the notable Museo Bardini. An entirely different landscape is offered by the parallel Lungarni: the regular breadth of these riverfront promenades, lined by handsome palazzi and pleasant views of the river, offer a relaxing way back to the center.

A hall of the Palatine Gallery in Palazzo Pitti

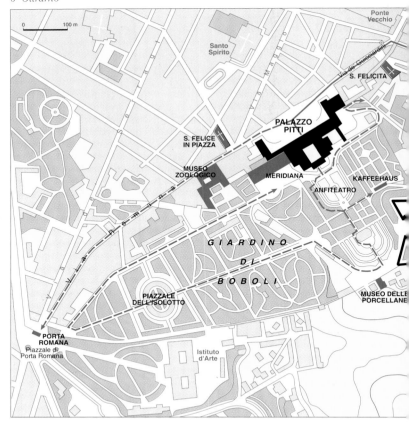

Piazza Pitti and Palazzo Pitti* (4 D-E3).
Piazza de' Pitti – set at an unusual angle on
a slope at the base of the hill of Bòboli – is
dominated by the immense facade of Palazzo Pitti, which thrusts forward with two
porticoed structures. This palazzo is the
largest one in all Florence (the facade is 205
m. long), and is faced with large stone ashlars. The original building, begun around
1458 for the merchant and banker Luca Pitti, is believed to have been designed by Luca Fancelli. Construction, which was halted
in the wake of the banker's financial collapse, resumed just one century later, when
the palazzo was purchased by Cosimo I
and Eleonora of Toledo; it became the new
site of the Medici court. In 1558 Bartolomeo
Ammannati began work on enlarging the
building, and replaced the two side portals with massive windows with scrollwork
("finestre inginocchiate"). Despite the fact
that the work to enlarge the facade continued for well over two centuries (the two
lower wings built in the 17th c. and two
further wings added in the 18th-19th c.), it is
noteworthy that, in all this work, the mod-

ular sequence of the original construction
was unfailingly respected and reproduced,
resulting finally in the great and spectacular creation that we can see today. The
palazzo – which for three centuries was
the residence of the Medici and of the Lorena (Lorraine) – housed the court of Savoy in
the period when Florence was capital of
Italy (1865-71).

The central portal leads to the porticoed
courtyard, built by Ammannati (1558-70)
along with the two lateral wings, perpendicular to the main wing. This is a grand assembly of porticoes, windows, and loggias
supported by three registers of rusticated
pilasters. The fourth side is open, above, toward the terrace with the Fontana del Carciofo (or Fountain of the Antichoke); below,
there are two niches with antique groups of
statuary and a 17th-c. *Grotta di Mosè*, or
grotto of Moses, an elliptical pool behind
which stand five statues, each set in a niche.
Palazzo Pitti is a major museum site: the Galleria Palatina and the Appartamenti Reali
(royal apartments; both are located on the

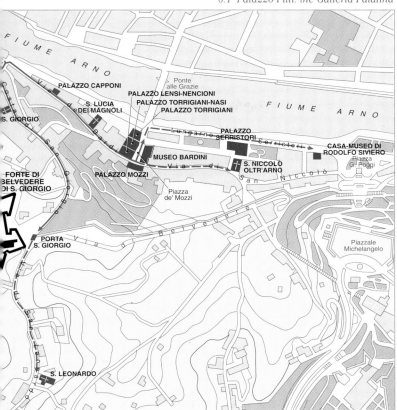

second floor), the Galleria d'Arte Moderna (gallery of modern art; on the third floor), the Museo degli Argenti (museum of silver; in rooms on the ground floor and the mezzanine), the Museo delle Carrozze (museum of carriages; in the roundabout on the left). Other buildings, set in the adjoining Giardino di Bòboli (Boboli gardens), contain interesting collections: the Palazzina della Meridiana, or palace of the sundial (Galleria del Costume and Donazione Contini Bonacossi, respectively a museum of clothing and fashion, and a private bequest), the Casino del Cavaliere (Museo delle Porcellane, or museum of porcelain).

Galleria Palatina*. This "palatine gallery" is the best surviving example of the collections of paintings created by the princes of the Baroque era and the Enlightenment. The Galleria Palatina was created between the end of the 18th c. and the first few decades of the 19th c. It was then that the portion of the immense body of art belonging to the Medici that simply could not fit into the Uffizi – with the addition of even further acquisitions – was transferred here so as to become available to the public at large. The current installation, which dates from the first half of the 19th c., follows no systematic criteria. It is organized strictly according to decorative considerations: the paintings are hung in cunning patterns, chiefly meant to enhance the lovely carved gilt frames; the halls are embellished with splendid tables – Baroque, Neoclassical, and 19th-c. bases support table surfaces inlaid with semi-precious stones and stone chips.

The 500 paintings that comprise the original core collection of the Galleria Palatina came from the personal collections of the various members of the Medici family, and were donated in 1743 – in accordance to the will of the last of the Medici, Anna Maria Luisa de' Medici – to the city of Florence. The collection is made up of masterpieces of Italian and European art, in particular of the 16th and 17th c. There is a remarkable core collection of works by Raphael, Andrea del Sarto, and Titian, featuring all of the great artists of the Florentine school and some

97

major figures from the Venetian school of the 16th c. There are also renowned paintings by Caravaggio, Rubens, Van Dyck, and works from the 17th-c. Dutch school.

After you pass through the vestibule, you will walk, in succession, through the Sala degli Staffieri, or hall of the footmen, the Galleria delle Statue, or gallery of statues, and the Sala di Castagnoli; from there, on the left, you enter the gallery proper. The halls all take their names from the frescoes that decorate the vaults; the first five halls were painted by Pietro da Cortona (1641-47), in accordance with a complex program exalting the dynasty of the Medici; the other halls were painted by artists in the first half of the 19th c.

The first room, the Sala di Venere, or hall of Venus, features the statue of the *Venere Italica*, or Italian Venus, by Antonio Canova, originally commissioned to take the place of the Medici Venus in the Uffizi, and four masterpieces by Titian: *The Concert**, a painting done in his youth (ca. 1510-12); a **portrait of Pope Julius II*** (1545), copied from the portrait by Raphael (now in the National Gallery in London), though the work proved to be much more than a copy; *La Bella* (ca. 1536), painted for the duke of Urbino; a **portrait of Pietro Aretino*** (1545), whose rich palette of colors (especially the reds) renders a masterfully complex and unsettling depiction of this remarkable character. Alongside these paintings note the two vast and majestic landscapes by Rubens, and two sea paintings by Salvator Rosa (1640-49).

In the Sala di Apollo, or hall of Apollo, there is a large altar piece with a *Sacred Conversation** by Rosso Fiorentino (1522); it was enlarged in the 17th c. to fit a Baroque frame. Its precocious Mannerist style appears directly across from two works, dating from only slightly later, by Andrea del Sarto: the rigorous and balanced *Pietà* (1523-24), and the peaceful Medici *Sacred Family*, one of the artist's last creations. Two famous paintings by Titian stand out in this room: the **Young Englishman*** (ca. 1540); **Mary Magdalene*** (prior to 1548), a much-copied work. From the Venetian school, note: the subtle and nuanced *portrait of Vincenzo Zeno* by Tintoretto; known as *The Nymph and the Satyr*, although it actually describes an episode from Ariosto's "Orlando Furioso"; the *Hospitality of St. Julian*, a large canvas by Cristofano Allori (ca. 1612-18). The *Resurrection of Tabitha*, a youthful work by Guercino, and *Cleopatra*,

a late work by Guido Reni, are two paintings central to the Bolognese school of art of the 17th c. Flemish art is represented by the famous double *portrait of Charles I of England and Henrietta of France*, works taken from prototypes by Van Dyck, as well as the *portrait of Isabella Clara Eugenia*, by Rubens (1625); near them is a *portrait of the grand duchess Vittoria Della Rovere* by Justus Suttermans (ca. 1640).

The Sala di Marte, or hall of Mars, contains two masterpieces by Rubens: *The Consequences of War** (1638), a powerful allegory that assigns responsibility for the destruction provoked by Mars, to Discord, or the Furies; the *Four Philosophers** (ca. 1611-12), a remarkably intense work abounding in literary and philosophical citations. Alongside these paintings is a group of major portraits: the *portrait of Cardinal Bentivoglio** by Van Dyck; a portrait of *Ippolito de' Medici*, by Titian (1532); a *portrait*, said

"Madonna del Granduca" by Raphael

to be of *Luigi Cornaro*, and now attributed to Tintoretto (1560-65); the stupendous **portrait of a man*** by Veronese (1550-60) – note the remarkably modern white and black brushstrokes.

In the next room, the Sala di Giove, or hall of Jove, you will find – alongside the *Velata**, or Veiled One, by Raphael (ca. 1516) – a picture of a woman idealized – and the *Three Ages of Man**, a masterpiece by Giorgione (ca. 1500) – a sizable selection of Tuscan paintings from the first half of the 16th c.

Among them note the famous *Lament over the Dead Christ* by Fra Bartolomeo (ca. 1511-12); compare this work with the pre-Mannerist *Annunciation* by Andrea del Sarto, painted in the same period (ca. 1512). Also by Andrea del Sarto is the renowned *St. John the Baptist* (1523), which provides an unusual depiction of the saint as an ephebe of classical beauty. Also note the *portrait of Guidubaldo Della Rovere* by Bronzino (1530-32) and the *Three Fates* (ca. 1537-38), a panel once thought to be by Michelangelo, now of uncertain authorship.

The Sala di Saturno, or hall of Saturn, contains a major body of works by Raphael; here you can trace the artist's entire career: the *Madonna del Granduca** (ca. 1506), which shows Raphael developing the teachings of Leonardo da Vinci; the **portraits of Agnolo*** and **Maddalena Doni*** (1506-7), which attain such great psychological and esthetic sweep that they remained prototypes of Renaissance portraiture; the **Madonna del Baldacchino*** (1507), unfinished, yet innovative, both in terms of composition and execution; the *portrait of Tommaso* (Fedra) *Inghirami** (ca. 1510); the **Madonna della Seggiola*** (ca. 1513-14), sublime in its monumentality; the *Vision of Ezekiel*, a late work (ca. 1518). Other works of considerable interest are the *Lament over the Dead Christ* by Perugino (1495), the *Salvator Mundi** by Fra Bartolomeo (1516) and two paintings by Andrea del Sarto: the *Debate over the Holy Trinity* (ca. 1517), with its rapid and vibrant brushwork, and the *Annunciation*.

In the Sala dell'Iliade, or hall of the Iliad, the Neoclassical installation underscores and enhances the presence of the portrait of a lady known as **La Gravida***, by Raphael (ca. 1506), with exquisite colors on a black background in the Flemish style. Two paintings by Andrea del Sarto – the Passerini *Our Lady of the Assumption* (1526) and the Panciatichi *Our Lady of the Assumption* (1522-23) – face each other on opposite walls, documenting two phases in the development of this artist toward a pre-Baroque style. Also note the *portrait of Valdemar the Christian*, prince of Denmark, a Flemish-inspired work by Suttermans, and the *Baptism of Christ* by Veronese (ca. 1575).

In the Sala dell'Educazione di Giove (or hall of the education of Jove) note the *Amore dormiente** by Caravaggio (1608), with a realism that completely overturns the classical subject of the Sleeping Cupid. On the left you enter the Sala della Stufa, or hall of the stove, which contained the ducts that served to heat the room of the grand duke, with frescoes of the *Four Ages of Man** by Pietro da Cortona (1637). On the right, through the Bagno di Napoleone, you can enter the Sala di Ulisse, or hall of Ulysses, where the **Madonna dell'Impannata*** hangs; by Raphael (ca. 1514): a recent restoration has returned this work to its former appearance, making it easier to understand the praise lavished upon it by Vasari. Hanging near it is a youthful masterpiece by Filippino Lippi (*Death of Lucretia*).

The installation of the Sala di Prometeo, or hall of Prometheus, sets a series of round paintings between two rows of rectangular paintings. Here you can see the oldest work in the entire Galleria Palatina: the Tondo Bartolini, with the **Virgin Mary and Christ Child*** by Filippo Lippi (ca. 1450) at the center, a masterpiece of the artist's mature period. In this room you will also find the few paintings by Botticelli and his workshop. An intense and powerfully modeled *Sacred Family* by Luca Signorelli should be compared with the tondo by Beccafumi that treats the same theme with a Michelangelesque grandeur, steeping it in a Mannerist atmosphere. Tuscan Mannerism is also represented by Pontormo (*Adoration of the Magi*, 1523; the *Eleven Thousand Martyrs*, ca. 1530).

After you walk through the Corridoio delle Colonne, or corridor of columns, with its small-format works of the Dutch and Flemish school of the 17th and 18th c., you will reach the Sala della Giustizia, or hall of justice, which largely features Venetian painters from the 16th c.; note the *portrait of Mosti*, a work done by a youthful Titian, with remarkable shades of grey and brown, and the *portrait of a gentleman* by Veronese (ca. 1570). In the next room, the Sala di Flora, you can admire works dating from the Florentine Cinquecento, including two *stories of Joseph* by Andrea del Sarto (1515). The Sala dei Putti contains Flemish and Dutch art, including: the *Three Graces* by Rubens (1622), monochrome on panel; two paintings, a *Still Life of Flowers* and a *Still Life of Fruit*, enlarged miniatures, by Rachel Ruysch (dated 1715 and 1716).

After you return to the Sala di Prometeo, you will walk through the Galleria del Poccetti, once an open loggia and now an exhibition space for works of the 17th c. Next comes the Sala della Musica, or hall of music, also known as the "Sala dei Tamburi," or hall of drums, because of the shape of the little pieces of Neoclassical furniture. Then you will reach the Sala di Castagnoli, with the round *table*, known as the *Tavolo delle Muse* (1851). On the right is the Quartiere del Volterrano, named after the artist whose real name was Baldassarre Franceschini, who frescoed the first hall, known as the Sala delle Allegorie, or hall of allegories. The four rooms that follow, overlooking the courtyard by Ammannati, are not part of the original arrangement of the Galleria Palatina, but were used after 1928, chiefly for works that came from the 19th-c. suppression of churches and convents. The last room, the Sala di Psiche, or hall of Psyche, is entirely devoted to Salvator Rosa (*Forest of Philosophers*, *Battle Between Turks and Christians*).

If you continue through the vestibule and the bathroom of Maria Luisa, you will reach the Sala della Fama, with works by Dutch and Flemish artists. Returning to the Sala delle Belle Arti, you can then enter the Sala dell'Arca, and from here, to the Cappella delle Reliquie.

Appartamenti Reali. These royal apartments are a suite of richly decorated and furnished rooms, on the second floor of the right wing of Palazzo Pitti; they served as the official residence of the Medici and the Lorraine families, as well as of Victor Emmanuel II in the years when Florence was the capital of a newly united Italy (1865-71). The current appearance of these rooms, which were recently restored, dates from the renovation done by Umberto and Margherita di Savoia. This royal couple of the House of Savoy crowded the rooms with furniture, paintings, tapestries, and other objects, largely taken from the palaces of Parma and Lucca. Recently reopened to the public, they can be seen only in guided tours; those tours follow a route that may be subject to variations.

The tour begins in the Sala Bianca, or white hall, an enormous room named for its bright light and stuccoed decorations, by the Albertolli brothers. Next you will see the Sala di Bona, the only room to survive intact from the early-17th c., with frescoes by Bernardino Poccetti and assistants. The series of rooms that follow this hall made up the apartment of King Umberto I di Savoia (or Savoy). The Sala dei Pappagalli, or hall of parrots, leads into the apartment of Queen Margherita; both apartments are decorated with rich old wall hangings and carpets and furniture, largely installed by

"Singing a Stornello" by S. Lega

the House of Lorraine.

After you return to the Sala dei Pappagalli, you pass into the chapel (until the turn of the 18th c. this was the bedroom in the apartment of Ferdinando de' Medici), one of the few examples of late-Baroque decoration in Palazzo Pitti. Next come the Sala Celeste (blue room), Sala del Trono (throne room), and Sala Verde (green room).

The tour ends in the Sala delle Nicchie, which is decorated in the Neoclassical style.

Galleria d'Arte Moderna. On the third floor of Palazzo Pitti, some 30 halls contain this remarkable collection, which offers a complete overview of Italian painting, from the Neoclassical period to the 20th c., as well as a few important sculptures, and several works by non-Italian artists. The current installation dates from 1972-79, and it organizes in chronological order and by subject matter the material, which ranges from the era of Pietro Leopoldo up to the First World War. Paintings from the 20th c. (up to 1945) will be installed on the top floor of the Galleria.

Among the most notable works are: *Samson* (1842; hall 2) and *The Two Foscari* (1851-52; hall 5) by Francesco Hayez; *Portrait of Diego Martelli*, by Federico Zandomeneghi (1879; hall 16); *Visit to the Wet-Nurse* by Silvestro Lega (1873; hall 17); *Leith* by Telemaco Signorini (1881; hall 23). There is a considerable presence of works by Giovanni Fattori (1825-1908).

Museo degli Argenti. Established in the second half of the 19th c., this museum possesses a rich and diversified collection of precious objects, semiprecious stones, crystals, and ivory that belonged to the grand dukes of Tuscany; it is installed in the summer quarters of the Medici court, with an entrance from the courtyard (by Buontalenti).

On the ground floor, the tour of the museum begins from Hall II (you can enter it through Hall IV); this hall contains works that predate the Tuscan principality, especially Roman, Sassanid, and Venetian vases, from the collection of Lorenzo the Magnificent. Among the most noteworthy items: a Byzantine *chalice*, a *double goblet* in amethyst, *Venus and Cupid*, a remarkable work in porphyry by Pier Maria Serbaldi da Pescia, known as the Tagliacarne. After Hall III, with a handsome wooden *relief* from the 17th or 18th c., you will retrace your steps to Hall IV, known as the Sala di Giovanni da S. Giovanni, after the painter who frescoed the room, with assistants (1634-42).

After the chapel (Hall V) you enter the apartment of the Grand Duke, with three rooms overlooking the square. These rooms were frescoed by the Bolognese artists Angelo Michele Colonna and Agostino Mitelli (1636-41). Of special note: in Hall VI, the *Stipo d'Alemagna* (or "German Cabinet," fashioned in Augsburg and a gift from the Archduke of the Tyrol) and a *kneeling-stool*, both made of ebony and semiprecious stones; in Hall VIII, a *cabinet* and a *Reliquary of the Saints of the Dominican Order*, both by Giovanni Battista Foggini. In Hall IX, there are stupendous German *vases*, in turned ivory; a *table* and a *cabinet*, masterpieces by a Dutch cabinetmaker; a *compass*, actually made by Czar Peter the Great, and given as a gift to Cosimo III. In the next room (Hall X) the earliest piece of turned ivory known is on display – a *sphere* with miniatures, contained in an ebony globe, by Giovanni Antonio Maggiore di Milano (1582). After the Sala delle Ambre (Hall XI, or hall of amber) you will reach Hall XII, with a collection of vases and goblets made of semprecious stones and rock crystal (16th/17th c.), with unusual and whimsical shapes. There are also many objects which belonged to Caterina de' Medici (or Catherine de' Medici).

On the mezzanine (entrance via the stairway linking halls X and XI) among the materials on display we should mention: a rich collection of cameos and intaglioes (Hall XIV); jewelry and precious trinkets (Hall XV); silver objects for liturgical use (Hall XVI) and silverware for dining (Hall XVII); curious exotic artifacts and products (Hall XIX); Chinese porcelain (Hall XX) and Japanese porcelain (Hall XXI).

Galleria del Costume. In a number of rooms in the Palazzina della Meridiana (entrance from the Bòboli gardens) you can admire this collection of historical clothing, which documents the development of men's and women's clothing from the turn of the 18th c. to the 1920s. The display of costumes (educational in intent) is changed every two years, with similar outfits from similar periods.

Donazione Contini Bonacossi. In 11 halls of the Palazzina della Meridiana this collection has been temporarily placed on display; it is part of a larger collection created at the turn of the 20th c. by a husband-and-wife team, the Contini Bonacossi, with the assistance of the art historian Roberto Longhi. The part on view was donated by them to the Italian state. The collection, which will in time be moved to the Uffizi, can now be seen by making a request to the Soprintendenza.

The collection includes furniture, majolica and terracotta by the Della Robbia family, important drawings, paintings, and statues, including: *Maestà with Saints Francis and Dominick* by Cimabue; *Madonna della Neve* by Sassetta (ca. 1432); *St. Jerome* by Giovanni Bellini (ca. 1479); *Martyrdom of St. Lawrence*, marble statue by Gian Lorenzo Bernini (ca. 1616); *Virgin Mary with Eight Saints* by Bramantino (1520-30); *Torero* by Goya (ca. 1800); *Madonna Pazzi* by Andrea del Castagno (ca. 1445).

Museo delle Porcellane. This porcelain museum exhibits, in rooms in the Casino del Cavaliere (located in the upper section of the Bòboli gardens), porcelain creations that belonged to the houses of Medici and Lorraine. Hall I features porcelain from the Real Fabbrica di Napoli (or Royal Factory of Naples; note the group of the *School for Bears* and the 18 *statuettes of Neapolitan common women*) and from the manufactory Ginori di Doccia (two *statuettes* depicting *Turkish women*), chiefly dating from the 18th c.; French porcelain from the manufactories of Tournai, Vincennes, Paris, and elsewhere. In Hall II there is a major collection of Viennese porcelain; hall III is chiefly dedicated to the porcelain manufactory of Meissen.

Museo delle Carrozze. This museum of carriages is being readied on the ground floor of the left roundabout of Palazzo Pitti; it features carriages from the courts of Lorraine and Savoy.

Giardino di Bòboli (plans 4 and 11). The Boboli gardens are one of the largest (45,000 sq. m.) Italian-style gardens in the world, as well as a remarkable open-air sculpture garden, with extraordinary pieces of architecture, as well. The main entrance is from the courtyard by Ammannati; a secondary entrance is in Via Romana (gate by Annalena); the entrance in Piazzale di Porta Romana is used only for leaving the gardens at closing time.

Fontana dell'Oceano: detail

The garden was created to plans by Niccolò Tribolo: the original, fairly simple plan evolved into a more complex and intricate layout with the passage of time, finally attaining its present size and layout in the 18th/19th c.

From the courtyard built by Ammannati, a stairway leads up to the esplanade, where the vast *amphitheater** opens out, formed of tiers with aedicules and statues (most of them are copies of ancient sculptures, now being restored); at the center, an Egyptian *obelisk* (1500 B.C.) and a granite basin taken from the Baths of Caracalla in Rome. Toward the rear of the palazzo, on the terrace, note the 17th-c. *Fontana del Carciofo*, literally, fountain of the artichoke, by Francesco Susini and Francesco del Tadda. Before you climb up the hill, you can follow a broad drive to the left, finally reaching a piazzale near the round about exit situated

to the right of the palazzo, where there is a little fountain, known as the *Fontanina del Bacchino* (the young Bacchus has been replaced with a copy) by Valerio Cioli (1560). If you continue along the little magnolia-lined drive, you will reach the *grotto*, known as the *Grotta del Buontalenti*, the product of a typically Mannerist flight of fancy (1583-88): before it extends a portico flanked by two niches, each with a statue by Bandinelli (*Ceres* and *Apollo*) and surmounted by a pediment with the Medici coat-of-arms. The entire complex is decorated with imitation stalactites and sponges. The three grottoes within (open by request) were inspired by the theme of the metamorphosis of matter, from chaos to the harmony of all creatures; at the four corners of the first grotto Michelangelo's *Prigioni*, or Prisoners, once stood (now replaced with copies; the originals are in the Galleria dell'Accademia); in the second grotto there is a group of marble statues depicting *Paris and Helen* by Vincenzo de' Rossi (1560); in the third grotto, note the exquisite *fountain* by Giambologna (ca. 1570). After you return to the upper esplanade, you can begin to climb the ramps at the end of the amphitheater. On the first terrace, note the *statues* from the Roman era; the next terrace is dominated by the *Vivaio di Nettuno** or *Fontana del Forcone*, a broad pond with a central "shoal" upon which stands a *statue of Neptune*, a bronze by Stoldo Lorenzi (1565-68).

On the highest tier, you will find the colossal *statue of Plenty*, begun by Giambologna (1608). If you turn to the right and follow the picturesque little drives, you will reach the base of the stairway that climbs up to the mansion known as the *Casino del Cavaliere*, built around 1700 for Gian Gastone de' Medici and rebuilt to its present-day appearance under the house of Lorraine; it now houses the porcelain museum, or Museo delle Porcellane.

A set of steps leads down to the *Prato dell'Uccellare*, a lawn surrounded by holm-oaks and cypress trees; this marks the beginning of the *Viottolone**, a long drive lined with old cypress trees, dotted with *statues* both ancient and from the 17th and 18th c. The drive cuts through an elaborate system of avenues and paths in the greenery, dotted with clearings and statues. At the end of the drive is the handsome **Piazzale dell'Isolotto***, a late-Mannerist complex begun in 1618 by Giulio and Alfonso Parigi. Much of this space – surrounded by tall hedges dotted with statues – is occupied by a circular basin, with a small island at its center, linked to the dry land by two walkways;

the beginnings of the walkways are marked by twin columns, flanked by fountains with figures of tritons; from the water emerge the statues of *Perseus* and *Andromeda*, from the school of Giambologna (1637). The islet, surrounded by a stone balustrade, has the *Fontana dell'Oceano*, a fountain depicting the Ocean, at its center; the original sculpture was carved by Giambologna in 1576 (copy; the original is in the Museo del Bargello).

If you continue, on a line with the Viottolone, you will cross the *Prato delle Colonne* – so-called for the two large columns in pink granite – surrounded by marble groups and colossal busts, and you will then reach the roundabout at the end of the drive (exit onto Piazzale di Porta Romana) and the large statue of *Perseus* by Vicenzo Danti.

You will then return toward Palazzo Pitti, skirting the enclosure wall and the large *limonaia*, or lemon grove (past the lemon grove, on the left, you will see the exit onto the Via Romana).

At the end of this uphill drive stands the large square overlooked by the *Palazzina della Meridiana*, a Neoclassical building begun by Gaspare Maria Paoletti (1778) and completed by Pasquale Poccianti (1822-40).

As you emerge once again into Piazza de' Pitti, if you turn to your left you can take a little detour into the Via Romana: notable features of this detour are the church of S. Felice in Piazza and the Museo Zoologico; your final destination will be the square of the Porta Romana.

Originally Romanesque (documented as early as 1066), the **church of S. Felice in Piazza** (4 E2) was rebuilt in the 14th c. and remodelled in the two centuries that followed. The simple Renaissance facade, believed to be the work of Michelozzo (1452-60), has a fine carved portal. Inside, the first half of the church is divided into a nave and two aisles, divided by Doric columns, with cross vaults (16th c.), while the second half has partly regained its original 14th-/15th-c. appearance following restoration done after the church was damaged by fire in 1926. On the side altars, note the artworks, largely dating from the 15th to 17th c. The main chapel, which was rebuilt by Michelozzo in 1458 (triumphal arch and large mullioned window), features a large painted wooden *Crucifix*, by Giotto and his workshop (prior to 1307-8).

Set in the venerable old Palazzo Torrigiani (at n. 17 in the Via Romana), the **Museo Zoologico "La Specola"** (4 E2) is a department of the Museo di Storia Naturale, or natural history museum, of the Università di Firenze, and was founded by the grand duke Pietro Leopoldo in 1775. The exhibition area is on the third floor; here visitors can see the most interesting specimens from the vast zoological collections, as well as a remarkable collection of anatomical preparations in wax, the creation of the museum workshop between the mid-18th c. and the end of the 19th c. On the second floor is the 19th-c. *Tribuna di Galileo*, comprising a vestibule and a hemicycle, with lavish decoration (marble, mosaics, and frescoes).

S. Felicita (4 D4). Set between Piazza de' Pitti and the Ponte Vecchio, this church, with S. Lorenzo, is one of the two oldest in Florence (4th c.). A first rebuilding took place – on the early-Christian foundations – during the Romanesque period, but the present-day building is a revision designed by Ferdinando Ruggieri and built between 1736 and 1739. Above the portico extending along the simple facade is a section of the Corridoio Vasariano.

At the beginning of the aisle, on the right, is all that survives of the Cappella Barbadori, designed by Brunelleschi (ca. 1420) and later renovated; inside are two Mannerist masterpieces by Pontormo (1525-28): the altar piece with the *Deposition*, with exquisitely diaphanous colors; and the stupendous fresco of the *Annunciation*.

From the right transept, you can reach the small sacristy, clearly inspired by the work of Brunelleschi, and built around 1470; it preserves a number of notable artworks, including a *polyptych* by Taddeo Gaddi (ca. 1355).

Via de' Bardi (4 D-E4-5-6). This thoroughfare, known in the Middle Ages as the "Borgo Pitiglioso" (this word meant "flea-bitten" or "miserable"), begins on a line with Ponte Vecchio, then runs beneath the Corridoio Vasariano; from that point on, in the first section, it is lined by mid-19th-c. buildings. Once you pass Piazza di S. Maria Soprarno (where the Costa di S. Giorgio begins, see below), you will see, on the left, at numbers 36-38, the notable *Palazzo Capponi*, with its tall rusticated ground floor, faced with ashlars (the other elevation, with its rebuilt facade, overlooks the Lungarno Torrigiani), built by Lorenzo di Bicci. A little further along you will find the *church of S. Lucia dei Magnoli* (4 E6), which dates from the 11th c. Inside, the single nave features a cusped panel by Pietro Lorenzetti depicting *St. Lucy* (1st altar on the left).

Costa di S. Giorgio (4 D-E-F5). It is possible to climb up to the hill, or Collina di Bòboli along this antique and picturesque street, which runs from Piazza di S. Maria Soprarno, steeply up between houses and garden walls. In the first section, on the uphill side, you will see the side of the *church of S. Giorgio and the Spirito Santo* (St.

George and the Holy Ghost; 4 D5), medieval in origin, but completely rebuilt at the turn of the 18th c. by G.B. Foggini. The exterior, bare and unfinished, contrasts sharply with the lavish interior, decorated with stuccoes and embellished with canvases and frescoes from the first decade of the 18th c. Now it holds a Rumanian Orthodox church. In the second part of the route, the road winds considerably; after the turn-off that leads to the entrance of the Forte di Belvedere, the road ends at the *Porta S. Giorgio* (4 F5), a gate that once formed part of the second walled perimeter; in the vault you can still admire a fresco by Bicci di Lorenzo (*Virgin Mary Enthroned with the Christ Child and Saints Leonard and George*, ca. 1430); the bas-relief on the exterior front is a cast of the original, from the late-14th c.

Forte di Belvedere (4 F4-5). This fortress, built at the end of the 16th c. at the wish of the grand duke Ferdinando I, was designed by Bernardo Buontalenti and Don Giovanni de' Medici; this fort fit into the overall defensive system of Florence as a bastion (providing four fortified fronts) both against attacks from without and to control possible uprisings within the city. The portal cut in the eastern side leads, up a ramp, to the upper level of the embankments, now partly covered with grass. From here you can see the inside part of the bastion dominating the city. If you walk along the ramparts of the perimeter, you can enjoy a magnificent close-up view* of Florence, the Arno valley and the surrounding hills.
At the center of the fort is the earlier *Palazzina di Belvedere*, built in 1560-70 to plans attributed to Bartolomeo Ammannati. Open only for special exhibitions, it can be reached along a stairway. The white plaster surfaces, set between angle stones in "pietra forte," are pierced by windows and doors designed for "bel vedere," or fine views – the essence, namesake, and meaning of the building.

With a short walk along the first section of Via di S. Leonardo – enclosed between plastered walls decorated with graffiti, atop which you can see the greenery of the garden behind it – you will reach the *church of S. Leonardo in Arcetri* (11 C5), a medieval parish church (11th or 12th c.) restored at the end of the 19th c. and the early part of the 20th c. Inside (accessible only during holiday and pre-holiday mass), note the marble and mosaic *pulpit* (13th c.), from the church of S. Pier Scheraggio; it is said that St. Antonino, Boccaccio, and Dante spoke from this pulpit.

Piazza de' Mozzi (4 E6). At the end of the Via de' Bardi, on a line with the Ponte alle Grazie, lies this geometric space, lined by handsome historic palazzi: at n. 2, behind the stern facades of the three *Palazzi de' Mozzi*, dating from the 13th c.; at n. 3, *Palazzo Lensi-Nencioni*, with a 15th-c. facade; at n. 4, *Palazzo Torrigiani-Nasi*, decorated with graffiti; at n. 5, *Palazzo Torrigiani*, built in the first half of the 16th c. by Domenico di Baccio d'Agnolo.

Museo Bardini (4 E6). Located at n. 1 in Piazza de' Mozzi, this museum is the result of the lifelong activity of the collector and antiquarian Stefano Bardini, who at the end of the 19th c. transformed a 13th-c. church into a palazzo, and installed in it a noteworthy collection of sculptures, paintings, furniture, ceramics, tapestries, and other material, dating from ancient times to the Baroque period. The museum was donated to the city of Florence in 1922.
Among the objects on display in the halls on the ground floor, we should point out: sculptures from Imperial Rome (Hall II); a capital depicting the *Nativity* and the *Adoration of the Magi* by a 12th-c. Campionese master, and *Charity**, a marble group by Tino di Camaino (Hall VII). In Hall X (you can enter it from the top of the first flight of the large staircase) is an old bracket support for an altar top, originally in the church of the Santissima Annunziata; in it is depicted the *Trinity with three faces*, from the workshop of Michelozzo. On the second floor you should note in particular: two polychrome terracottas (*Virgin Mary with the Christ Child and the Youthful Saint John the Baptist* by Benedetto da Maiano; *Virgin Mary with the Christ Child* attributed to Donatello) and a gilt and polychrome stucco by Donatello and his workshop, depicting the *Virgin Mary with the Christ Child and angels* (Hall XIV); a collection of 15th-c. chests, and the chest frontal with *Hercules at the crossroad between vice and virtue* by Domenico Beccafumi (Hall XV); *Saint John the Baptist* by Michele Giambono (Hall XVI); half figure of *Virgin Mary with the Christ Child*, a high relief in painted terracotta, from the workshop of Jacopo della Quercia (Hall XVII); *statue of Our Lady of the Annunciation*, a Siennese terracotta from the mid-15th c., and a canvas with *St. Michael Archangel* by Antonio Pollaiolo (Hall XVIII).

From Piazza de' Mozzi the route continues along the Via di S. Niccolò and, once you get past the first part, which is lined with historic palazzi, you will see, on the left, the *church of S. Niccolò Oltr'Arno* (5 E4), built in early times (12th c.), renovated in the Gothic style, and later rebuilt by Vasari. On the interior, with only a nave and with a truss roof, note the remains of 15th-c. frescoes, attributed to the Maestro di Signa (1st and 3rd altar on the right), and wooden *Crucifix* attributed to Michelozzo (2nd altar).

As an alternative, from Piazza de' Mozzi you may choose to follow the route along the banks of the river, on the 19th-c. *Lungarno Serristori* (5 E3-4). After a short distance, on the right, is Piazza Demidoff; at the center is the *monument to the count Nikolai Demidov (Nicola Demidoff)*, a Russian philanthropist who lived in Florence (1774-1828).

At the end of this thoroughfare, at n. 3, stands the *house-museum of Rodolfo Siviero* (1911-83; Siviero was very active in recovering artworks stolen by the Nazis), which contains his own private collection of artworks, from the Etruscan era to the 20th c., including drawings and paintings by Giorgio De Chirico.

6.2 From S. Spirito to Porta S. Frediano

This route runs from Piazza S. Spirito, dominated by the church of S. Spirito, one of Brunelleschi's masterpieces, along a fairly complex, zigzagging path.

First you head for the Arno, along Via Maggio, a thoroughfare built in the Middle Ages, and rebuilt along the same plan in the 16th c.; from here a detour off to the right allows you to walk through the remarkable medieval cityscape of Borgo S. Jacopo, while a turn-off to the left takes you down a panoramic promenade along the elegant Lungarno Guicciardini and then down Via de' Serragli and past S. Maria del Carmine, one of the "sanctuaries" of Renaissance painting (the frescoes of the Cappella Brancacci); after the unassuming Borgo S. Frediano, at the heart of a densely populated quarter, which perhaps more than any other has maintained its age-old atmosphere, the route turns back onto the Lungarni, or river-front promenades. They lead, in the western outskirts of Florence, to the Quartiere dell'Isolotto, a noteworthy piece of modern working-class housing.

Piazza S. Spirito (4 D2). Among the unassuming houses that surround this square, planted as a garden, stands the massive structure – at n. 10 – of **Palazzo Guadagni**, built at the turn of the 16th c., probably to plans by Cronaca. On the ground floor, note the center portal, surrounded by ashlars and square windows; on the two floors above it, centered windows and rusticated windows; on the fourth floor, a vast loggia with architraved columns.

S. Spirito* (4 C-D2). The unadorned 18th-c. facade of this Augustinian church conceals one of the purest pieces of Renaissance architecture. It was begun in 1444 by Brunelleschi and, following his death (1446), carried on by Antonio Manetti, Giovanni da Gaiole, and Salvi d'Andrea. The latter was also responsible for the construction of the cupola (1479-81), which had again been designed by Brunelleschi; the solid and elegant *campanile* was a creation of Baccio d'Agnolo (16th c.).

The **interior**, divided into nave and side-aisles with splendid monolithic columns topped by Corinthian capitals, imitates the basic design of S. Lorenzo, but in a livelier fashion, with the addition of the central dome and with the extension of the side-aisles into the smaller arms of the cross-vault. Around the perimeter of the church are forty semicircular apsidioles, occupied by aristocratic chapels. On the little altars once stood 15th-c. altar pieces. Many of them were replaced, over time.

The *main altar* was designed and built by Giovanni Caccini (1599-1607) with the assistance of Gherardo Silvani and Agostino Ubaldini. It is a Baroque complex of noteworthy complexity; note the elaborate architecture, the inlays, the sculptures, the marble screen, and the baldachin, covered by a fretwork cupola.

In two of the chapels in the right arm of the cross vault, note a panel by Filippino Lippi depicting the *Virgin Mary with Christ Child and the Young St. John, and St. Martin presenting the Patron Tanai de' Nerli and St. Catherine of Alexandria presenting his wife* (1493-94) and a marble *sarcophagus* attributed to Bernardo Rossellino (1458). In a chapel in the apse, *Virgin Mary with Christ Child and Four Saints*, a polyptych by Maso di Banco (ca. 1345).

The left arm of the cross-vault has preserved – on the whole and in the details – its original 15th-c. flavor. The Cappella Corbinelli (4th from the right) is a youthful work by Andrea Sansovino (1492), who also did the remarkable *altar of the Sacrament*, a decorative array in the classical style, inspired by Roman triumphal arches, with elegant carved pilaster strips, and niches containing statues and reliefs. The second-from-last chapel contains a *Virgin Mary with Christ Child, Enthroned, with Saints* by Raffaellino del Garbo (1501-5).

From the left aisle, through a rectangular

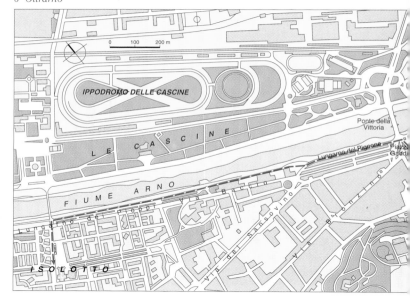

vestibule with an exceedingly lavish barrel vault with coffering, by Cronaca (1492-94) carried out to plans by Giuliano da Sangallo, you enter the octagonal *sacristy** (1489-92), with ribbing in "pietra serena," also designed by Giuliano da Sangallo; overhead is a ribbed dome and a lantern (1495-96; model by Antonio Pollaiolo and Salvi d'Andrea).

Cenacolo di S. Spirito (4 D2). To the left of the church (at n. 29) is the entrance to the 14th-c. refectory of the ancient convent, known as the Cenacolo di S. Spirito. An entire wall of this rectangular room, with a truss roof, is covered with a large *fresco** attributed to Orcagna (ca. 1365), depicting in the upper section a *Crucifixion with the Virgin Mary, the Pious Women, Longinus and other soldiers* (many sections are missing) and in the lower section a *Last Supper* (only a few fragments survive). The hall contains the **Fondazione Romano**, an interesting collection of sculpture, architectural elements, and polished and carved stones (from pre-Roman times to the late-15th c.), a gift made to the city of Florence in 1946 by the Neapolitan antiquary Salvatore Romano. Among the most notable works: *Virgin Mary with Christ Child*, a high relief by Jacopo della Quercia; two fragmentary stone bas-reliefs, depicting two *saints*, attributed to Donatello (ca. 1450); *caryatid* and *adoring angel*, marble sculptures by Tino di Camaino (1320-22).

Via Maggio (4 C-D-E3). The ancient "Via Maggiore," not far from Palazzo Pitti, was

one of the aristocratic roads of 16th-c. Florence, and was reconfigured in Medici times as the stately setting for official processions. As you follow it toward the Arno you may note the following buildings, among others: *Palazzo Zanchini-Corbinelli* (n. 13), designed by Santi di Tito; the *Palazzo di Bianca Cappello** (n. 26), built for the wife of Francesco I de' Medici, renovated by Bernardo Buontalenti (1570-74) and decorated with "graffito" grotesques by Bernardino Poccetti (1579-80); *Palazzo Michelozzi* (n. 11), also rebuilt in the second half of the 16th c.; *Palazzo Ricasoli-Firidolfi* (n. 7), dating from about 1520.

At the end of Via Maggio, from Piazza de' Frescobaldi runs the Borgo S. Jacopo (4 C3-4); at the mouth of this road is a handsome fountain with mascaron and basin with scrolls, a minor masterpiece by Buontalenti. At the beginning of this ancient thoroughfare, on the left, stands the church of S. Jacopo Sopr'Arno, which dates from the 10th c. but which has been rebuilt a number of times. Today it has been deconsecrated, and is used for cultural events. Before it extends a handsome Romanesque portico with three arches (12th/13th c.). The interior, with three aisles, still has an interesting set of 17th-/18th-c. paintings of the Florentine school. Further along, the street is dominated by a number of ancient *towers*. In the last stretch of this road, on the left, stands the 13th-c. *Torre dei Rossi-Cerchi*, and at its base, the *Fontana del Bacchino*, with a statue of a young Bacchus, attributed to Giambologna.

Lungarno Guicciardini (4 B-C2-3). Even in early times, this Lungarno was part of the

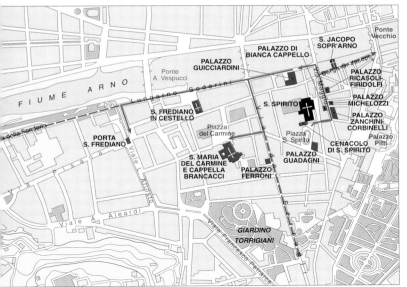

elegant promenade – very popular with the Florentines – along the two banks of the Arno, between the bridges of Ponte S. Trìnita and Ponte alla Carraia. Among the residences that overlook the Lungarno (with their earlier elevations on the interior Via di S. Spirito), particular note should be paid to: *Palazzo Capponi* (n. 1), which dates from the 15th c. but which was enlarged a number of times; *Palazzo Guicciardini* (n. 7), deprived of its garden in the 17th c. and then renovated in the 19th c.; the 16th-c. *Palazzo Lanfredini* (n. 9) with a facade by Baccio d'Agnolo, rebuilt in the 19th c.

Via de' Serragli (4 C-D-E-F1-2). This long straight thoroughfare links the bridge of Ponte alla Carraia to the gate of Porta Romana. Among the many buildings dating from the 15th and 16th c., at n. 8, note the

Palazzo Ferroni, begun around 1450, enlarged and rebuilt at the end of the 18th c. Further along, at n. 146, stands the entrance to the enormous *Giardino Torrigiani* (private; 9 E6), a garden designed by Luigi Cambrai-Digny and completed by Gaetano Baccani, who also built the Neo-Gothic tower (1821).

S. Maria del Carmine (4 C1). The construction of this church, known especially for the Cappella Brancacci, was begun in 1268 but completed only in 1476; after transformations in the 16th and 17th c., it was devastated by a fire (1771), and then rebuilt on the interior (1775), to plans by Giuseppe Ruggieri.
The interior is built to a Latin cross, and has a single nave, with five chapels on each side, and altars adorned with stuccoes. The

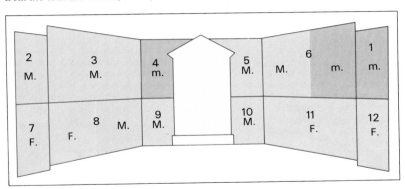

Layout of the frescoes in the Cappella Brancacci

right arm of the transept, with the Cappella Brancacci, can be reached from outside the church. At the head of the left transept is the *Cappella Corsini**, one of the earliest examples of Roman Baroque in Florence, built by Pier Francesco Silvani (1675). Among the decorations set upon the funerary monuments, note the *St. Andrea Corsini Leads the Florentines in the Battle of Anghiari*, a masterpiece by Giovanni Battista Foggini (1685-87).

Cappella Brancacci*. Although this chapel is part of the church of S. Maria del Carmine, the exterior entrance to the chapel – which continually draws crowds of tourists due to the presence of the frescoed masterpieces by Masaccio and Masolino – prevents the disruption of religious services.
The two artists began decorating the chapel in 1423-24, at the wish of Felice Brancacci, a leading Florentine citizen, and they continued until 1427-28, when Masaccio set out for Rome. The decoration was left unfinished, and was completed after 1480 by Filippino Lippi.
The **frescoes by Masaccio*** were, in the words of Vasari, "scuola del mondo," or "a school for the whole world," in that they were studied and emulated by all of the painters of the Renaissance. These frescoes offer – in a confidently created spatial context, clearly the work of a master of the techniques of perspective – human figures described with great realism and profound psychological insight; they are at once plastic and classical. The recent restoration (1983-90) has restored the authentic colors intended by Masaccio, revealing an artist with many points of contact with Fra Angelico; the restoration has also led to a new appreciation of the **frescoes by Masolino***, enhancing the delicate nuances of color and the exceedingly fine craftsmanship.
The plan shown on page 107 will assist you in locating and identifying the various scenes. 1, *Temptation of Adam and Eve*, by Masolino. 2, *Expulsion from the Garden of Eden**, Masaccio's masterpiece; critics and historians say that it was with this work that the painter broke definitively with the late-Gothic tradition, moving toward a new plastic form and a greater freedom of expression. 3, *Payment of the Tribute** by Masaccio; this is the best-known scene in the entire series of frescoes, as well as the earliest great Renaissance composition, and is broken up into three phases: Jesus shows Peter the lake where he will find a fish with a coin in its throat, the apostle bends down to take the coin out of the fish (left), and then

The Church of S. Frediano in Cestello

gives the coin to the tax collector (right). Masaccio paints the three separate phases of the Gospel story in a single space, punctuated by tree trunks and enclosed by mountains and a portico. 4, *Sermon of St. Peter*, di Masolino. 5, *Baptism of the Neophytes* by Masaccio; note the figure of the young man, naked and shivering with cold (praised by Vasari). 6, *The healing of the cripple and the resurrection of Tabitha*, by Masolino; the background depiction of a section of Florence has led some to suggest that Masaccio may have contributed to this scene. 7, *St. Peter in prison, visited by St. Paul* by Filippino Lippi. 8, *The resurrection of the son of Theophilus and St. Peter enthroned*; this is the last scene painted by Masaccio, and was completed by Filippino Lippi; in the scene with St. Peter enthroned, many of the figures are actually portraits of living contemporaries of Masaccio. 9, *St. Peter, followed by John, heals the sick with his shadow*, by Masaccio; in order to enlarge the scene, the architecture continues onto the splay of the window, with a remarkable optical effect. 10, *The distribution of alms and the death of Ananias*, by Masaccio. 11, *The debate of Simon Magus and the crucifixion of St. Peter*, by Filippino Lippi. 12, *The angel frees St. Peter from prison* by F. Lippi. From the Cappella Brancacci you can enter the sacristy, with its original Gothic structure (1394); among other works, it features 15th-c. frescoes and two lunettes, painted by the school of Agnolo Gaddi.

S. Frediano in Cestello (4 B1; 9 D6). Overlooking the Piazza di Cestello, open toward the Arno, the facade of this church, built between 1680 and 1689 and completed – with the elegant cupola, set on a high windowed tambour – by Antonio Maria Ferri.

The interior is built to a Latin-cross plan, and has three deep chapels on each side; these are decorated with stuccoes and paintings. Aside from various works from the 17th and 18th c., there is a wooden 15th-c. panel by Jacopo del Sellaio (left transept) and a wooden sculpture of the Florentine-Pisan school of the 14th c. (3rd chapel on the left).

Porta S. Frediano (9 C5-6). This gate formed part of the 14th-c. walled perimeter; now it stands alone at the end of Borgo S. Frediano. Built in 1332-34 and attributed to Andrea

Pisano, it has a remarkably broad opening (8 m.) and still has the original doors (more than 13 m. tall), covered with a number of studs.

Following the route of the Lungarni, after a long stretch heading out of the city (you will cross the Ponte della Vittoria and reach the Parco delle Cascine), you will reach the diagonal Viale delle Magnolie, the central thoroughfare of the *Quartiere dell'Isolotto* (9 A-B1-2), the first and largest developments that bear the name Ina{UNIF} Casa di Firenze, built in the Fifties. The developers used English models of garden-terraces, on a smaller scale, equipping the quarter with its own infrastructure and services; in particular note the *elementary school* (Via Giovanni da Montorsoli).

6.3 The Viale dei Colli

This is a spectacular and charming extension across the Arno of the 19th-c. ring roads designed by Giuseppe Poggi. The route begins at Piazza Francesco Ferrucci and climbs up Viale Michelangiolo – for the first stretch it is lined with small early-19th-c. villas – until it reaches Piazzale Michelangiolo; from here it continues toward the summit of the hill (known as the Monte alle Croci), crowned by the monumental complex of S. Miniato, a masterpiece of Romanesque architecture. The route continues along Viale Galileo Galilei, reaches Piazzale Galileo, and then turns off from the Viale dei Colli until it reaches – along the Viale E. Torricelli – the last stretch of Viale del Poggio Imperiale, which runs into the Villa del Poggio Imperiale, with a spectacular view.

Piazzale Michelangiolo (5 F5; 12 B2). This spot is exceedingly popular for its famed panoramic view* of Florence. Despite the fine view, this enormous plaza, built around 1875, is one of the less successful features of the Viale dei Colli, given its disproportionately monumental scale, and its location; together they have thrust out of kilter the delicate equilibrium of this setting. Even the *monument to Michelangelo* (1871), a blighted creation – set at the center of the plaza, and composed of bronze copies of the David and the statues from the Medici tombs in the church of S. Lorenzo – only serves to increase the artificial feeling of the place.

If you follow *Viale Giuseppe Poggi*, a series of ramps cut into the side of the hill allows you to descend toward the city, amidst grottoes and

Panoramic view from Viale Giuseppe Poggi

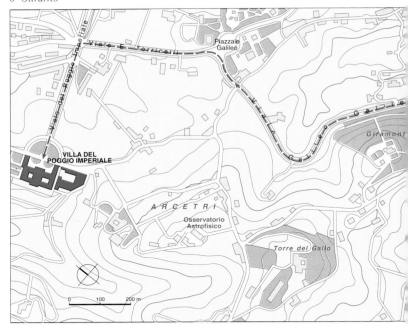

fountains, until you reach *Piazza Giuseppe Poggi* (5 E5), surrounded on all sides – as a result of the 19th-c. urban renovation – by uniform rows of buildings. The square is dominated by the 14th-c. *Porta S. Niccolò*, the only city gate that still has its original height; on the side facing the city, it has three stacked arches, with ramparts and stairways. In the entrance, note a 15th-c. fresco (*Virgin Mary with Christ Child and Saints*).

S. Salvatore al Monte (12 B2). From Piazzale Michelangiolo, a long stairway leads up to this church, built beween 1499 and 1504 by Cronaca, who enlarged a building erected in the preceding decade. The exceedingly simple facade has only a portal and pedimented windows.

The interior has only a single nave with side chapels. The walls are punctuated by a stacked double register of pilaster strips (used for the first time on the interior of a church), with an unusual use of "pietra forte"; almost all of the chapels have canvases dating back to the 17th and 18th c. From the right transept, you can enter the double chapel of Tanai de' Nerli (statesman of the 15th c.); note the panel, possibly of the Florentine school, turn of the 16th c. In the left transept, above the entrance to the large chapel (not open to the public), is a terracotta by Giovanni della Robbia (*Deposition*).

S. Miniato al Monte* (12 C2). This monument stands out on the horizon on the foothills to the south of the river Arno, and, with the Battistero di S. Giovanni, or baptistery, is a masterpiece of Florentine Romanesque architecture. The church of S. Miniato shares its perch atop the Monte alle Croci with its vast convent complex. Ruins of 16th-c. ramparts designed by Michelangelo stand uphill of the church, while a vast system of ramps, built in the 19th c., links the complex to the Viale dei Colli.

The church was built in a number of different phases, between 1018 and 1207 (the date is carved on the floor inside).

The **facade** is quite distinctive for the contrast between the white and green marble, a contrast which enhances the geometric proportions of the building. The lower register (11th c.) is simpler and is made up of five round blind arches, set on Corinthian semicolumns, with an alternation of solids and hollows. In the upper order, built later (12th c.), note the aedicule window at the center; it is classical in style and is surmounted by a mosaic depicting *Christ, enthroned between the Virgin Mary and St. Miniato, offering a benediction* (second half of the 13th c.). The facade has been restored a number of times, with replacement of the tiles, due to damage from atmospheric agents. The pediment is decorated with nine round false hanging arches and, above them, by inlaid allegorical figures (beginning of the 13th c.). On the cusp, note the eagle, symbol of the "Arte di Cali-

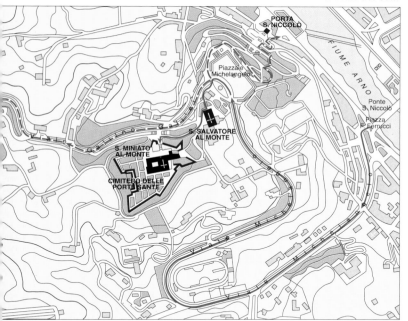

mala" (the Guild of Merchants) which had the patronage of the church.

To the left is the *campanile*, built in the first half of the 16th c. to plans by Baccio d'Agnolo, to replace the earlier bell tower, which collapsed in 1499.

The **interior**, spare and stern, covers three levels, with the presbytery sharply raised above the main level and the partly buried crypt; there is a nave and two aisles, punctuated by the rhythmic alternation of two columns for each pillar – in correspondence with the side arches – topped by round arches. The columns, except for those in the presbytery, were covered with "scagliola" during restoration in the 19th c. The white marble capitals, in Corinthian and composite orders, were taken from ancient buildings, while those made in terracotta painted white date from the Romanesque period. The entire building has a truss roof.

In the nave, the floor is decorated with exceedingly fine marble intarsia*, adorned with symbolic figures. At the end, the *Cappella del Crocifisso* stands alone, an aedicule designed by Michelozzo (1448) to enshrine the crucifix, or Crocifisso di S. Giovanni Gualberto (now in the church of S. Trìnita); it now contains panels by Agnolo Gaddi (*Saints Giovanni Gualberto and Miniato, Annunciation, and Stories of the Passion*), dating from 1394-96. The majolica decoration

of the barrel vault and the roof are by Luca della Robbia; the two eagles are by Maso di Bartolomeo.

In the right aisle the *frescoes* (13th/15th c.) represent – though with broad variations in quality – a unique array of types of faux architecture, with the various depictions linked by illusionistic friezes.

In the presbytery, on the right, is the entrance to the sacristy, a large square room with a cross vault (1387), entirely frescoed by Spinello Aretino and by his son Parri with a series of frescoes, the earliest in Tuscany, dedicated to the *stories of St. Benedict**. This series of frescoes stands out for the clear and orderly narrative, the essential lines of the decoration, and the plastic molding of the figures. After you return to the presbytery, on the right, note the altar with a cusped panel depicting eight *episodes from the life of St. Miniato*, masterpiece by Jacopo del Casentino (ca. 1320).

The presbytery area proper contains major Romanesque works (1207) with rich decoration in geometric patterns: aside from the *altar*, note the marble fretwork *screen* (about 3 m. tall) and the square *pulpit*. Above the main altar, *Crucifix* in glazed terracotta, attributed to Luca della Robbia.

The apse is punctuated by six semi-columns made of green marble, with five arches similar to those used in the facade; in the vault of the apse, note the large mosaic with *Christ Enthroned, Giving a Benediction, Be-*

tween the *Virgin Mary and St. Miniato and the Symbols of the Evangelists* (13th c.); it has been restored numerous times.

The *crypt* – the oldest part of the church (11th c.) – is made up of seven small aisles with cross-vaults, supported by 36 small columns made up of a broad array of materials, with different capitals, either Romanesque or re-used ancient ones. In the spandrels in the vaults of the presbytery, note the paintings, with gilt backgrounds, by Taddeo Gaddi, depicting, with remarkable color effects, *saints, martyrs, virgins, prophets, and evangelists* (1341).

If you climb back up to the left aisle, you will enter the *Cappella del Cardinale del Portogallo* (or chapel of the cardinal of Portugal; 1473), a homogeneous complex of architecture, painting, and sculpture, that is one of the most successful and best-preserved creations of the Florentine Renaissance. The architecture is by Antonio di Manetto

no. Note on the left wall the *Annunciation*, by A. Baldovinetti. Again, in the left aisle, a large painted *Crucifix* (end of the 13th c.), with handsome light effects on the drapery. To the right of the church stands the 14th-c. *Palazzo dei Vescovi*, the most important building in the convent complex (closed to the public), which belonged to the Olivetani. To the left is the entrance to the *Monumental Cemetery* (second half of the 19th c.).

If you continue along the hill roads, you will reach the Viale del Poggio Imperiale, which will take you to the spectacular entrance to the *Villa del Poggio Imperiale* (11 F4), rebuilt upon the site of older buildings by Giulio Parigi (1622-24), at the wishes of the grand duchess Maria Maddalena, sister of the emperor Ferdinand II of Hapsburg; following further major renovations in the 18th/19th c., it now has a largely Neoclassical appearance. Flanked by a chapel, also Neoclassical, the facade (1823) has a central loggia with two registers and side wings, and is deco-

The Church of S. Miniato al Monte

(a pupil of Brunelleschi), who clearly took his inspiration from the Sagrestia Vecchia of the church of S. Lorenzo. The vault, by Luca della Robbia, features four medallions made of glazed terracotta. On the right is the *Monument to the Cardinal*, a masterpiece by Antonio and Bernardo Rosselli-

rated with ancient *statues.* A tour of the villa – which now hosts a state-run boarding school – requires reservations (tel. 055/220151) and covers only a few rooms on the ground floor (*frescoes* * by Matteo Rosselli and other Florentine masters; 1623) and the "salone," or great hall, on the upper floor (*stuccoes* by Giocondo and Grato Albertolli; 1779-82).

The Places to Visit:
the Countryside Surrounding Florence

In the 4 chapters that follow, set outside of Florence, the 13 routes run through areas that are homogeneous in historical and environmental terms: the hill country (chapter 7), which is the charming landscape immediately surrounding Florence; the Mugello (chapter 8), which is the most interior and mountainous section of the territory around Florence, bordering the provinces of Bologna, Ravenna, Forlì, and the Casentino; the Valdarno (chapter 9), which covers the intermediate and more densely settled areas of the province, extending respectively toward Arezzo and Pisa; and Chianti (chapter 10), the wine-growing region par excellence, which fades into the Senese, or area around Siena. The territory of the province of Prato was established in 1992 and includes 7 townships broken off from the province of Florence. We describe here Carmignano and Poggio a Caiano.

The statistics concerning population of the towns are taken from Italy's official government publication, the Gazzetta Ufficiale of 24 June 1993, and refer to the legal population according to the Census of October 1991. The population of smaller towns and villages is not given.

Excursion key map   1 : 800 000 (1cm = 8000 m)

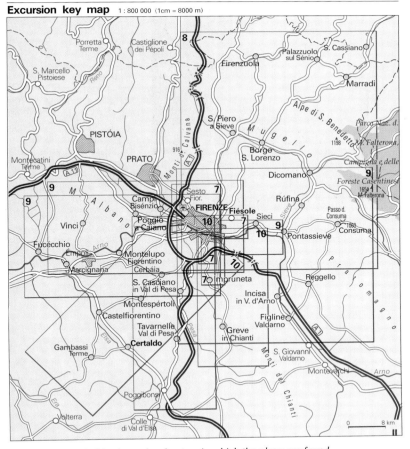

The numbers in bold refer to the chapters in which the plans are found.
The cities indicated in bold are illustrated by plans.

7 The Hills

Florence is much larger than just Florence. The "style" of the Florentines, their way of conceiving space and time, the way in which they organized their dealings with objects and animals, the measured and apparently simple idea they had of how to build houses and churches – all this radiated out from the city toward the hill country that surrounds Florence. The factor that most of all marks the countryside around Florence consists of a remarkable balance between man and nature, an equilibrium that has been established and maintained here over a great many centuries.

Panoramic view of Fièsole

Even as early as the 14th c. the great profusion of "rich palaces, towers, courtyards, and walled gardens" that could be found in the areas immediately surrounding Florence led more gullible travelers to think that – as the chronicler Giovanni Villani wrote – Florence was twice its actual size. Even more than this creeping urbanization, it was the management of land in accordance with the "sistema poderile," or system of allotments, that first cast the features of the landscape that we can admire today. Beginning in the 13th c., as the capital inhabited by the urban bourgeoisie spread out from the city center, extending into the countryside, the fields were studded with structures that were at once simple and classical. Their builders were inspired by the architectural models they had seen in town; they were immediately split into the two typologies of the "casa da lavoratore," or "laborer's house" and the "casa da padrone," or "proprietor's house," forerunners respectively of the "casa colonica," a true farmhouse, and the "villa-fattoria," or farming villa. This intertwining network of buildings and farmland became denser and closer-knit over time, and was never rent asunder. Indeed, time seems only to have strengthened the sort of "pact" between man and the land that created the Florentine landscape. It was not until the years following the Second World War that the spread of urban Florence and the breakdown and dismantling of traditional farming structures together contributed to alter the countryside.

This complex and ancient process did not follow the same lines everywhere, and the four routes suggested in this chapter will allow the traveler to discover, in the territory that closely surrounds Florence, the most notable differences.

In the area to the NE of Florence, particularly around the towns of Fièsole and Settignano, settlement concentrated along the course of the mountain rivers pouring into the Arno (the Mugnone, the Affrico, and the Mènsola). Over time, along the slopes of the valleys of these streams and rivers, a dense network of roads has sprung up, linking the marketplace in the city with the fertile countryside, studded with villas and farmhouses: the beauty of the landscape and towns, the wealth of vegetation, and the continuity of the traditions here – all these factors have contributed to making these hills some of the most sought-after resort areas for well-to-do Florentines, at least as far back as the time of the Medici.

A separate matter entirely is the village of Maiano, which specializes in quarrying and processing of "macigno," or hard sandstone, a special type of stone extracted hereabouts. In this area, entire generations of craftsmen and artists were born who in time made a major contribution to the physical appearance of the city of Florence.

To the south of Florence, the hills push quite close to the river Arno; naturally this affects human settlement and the environment here. There is exceedingly fine farmland here, and the produce of the earth drives thriving businesses, but the intertwining of rural and urban is closer than elsewhere; here you will see the parks and gardens of great Florentine families mixed, as if in a puzzle, with farmland and fields. The Colle di Bellosguardo is one of the most popular viewpoints from which to observe – one might almost say to contemplate – the city, and it owes to this fact the "wealth" in tourism that it has enjoyed for centuries. Further south, along the Via Romana (the modern-day Cassia, a highway that links Florence with Rome), stands the Certosa del Galluzzo, the bequest of the generous patronage of the great family of the Acciaioli, while, somewhat off the beaten path, the Santuario dell'Impruneta continues to represent the religious piety of the Tuscan people.

To the NW of Florence, at the boundary between hill country and plains, the presence of fertile farmland has long encouraged the construction of large country homes for the leading families of Florence, foremost among them the Medici. Here, unlike in many other areas, the environment – once quite rural and dotted with the large and lovely gardens of the villas, as well as with "pomari" (orchards) and intensely cultivated fields – has been badly damaged, due to extensive industrialization in the area.

7.1 Fièsole and Settignano

The two routes recommended here explore the NE section of Florence's outskirts; here a distinctive hilly landscape has managed to survive without excessive signs of modernization and urbanization.

The first route, which revolves around a visit to the little town of Fièsole, requires a short trip from Florence, which will allow you to visit the church of S. Domenico and the Badia Fiesolana, an abbey. Of the three recommended routes to the hill of Fièsole (all three roughly 5 km. long), the most popular one is the route followed by the city

bus n. 7; it is also the most scenic. The route begins from Piazza T.A. Edison (8 E5), and is at first called Via S. Domenico; it winds and curves easily, and is lined by numerous villas, until it finally reaches the village of S. Domenico. A second route runs along Via Giovanni Boccaccio (8 C-D3), first skirting the banks of the Mugnone through a quarter of relatively small houses; further along, on the right you may note the spectacular *Villa Palmieri* (8 B4), an ancient building reconstructed in its present form at the end of the 17th c., surrounded

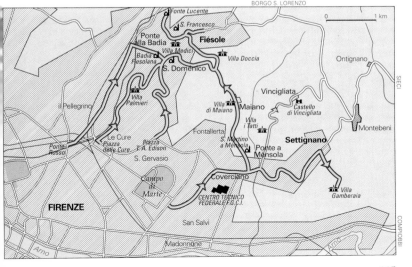

115

by a Romantic-style park laid out in the second half of the 19th c., in addition to the then-existing Italian-style garden. The third option is to follow the Via Faentina (8 A-B-C-D-E 1-2-3-4), in a network that becomes increasingly scattered, finally reaching the Ponte alla Badia, where you can turn right into the Via della Badia dei Roccettini. All three of the routes converge in the village of San Domenico, an offshoot of Fièsole; from here on, the route follows the Via Giuseppe Mantellini and the Via Fra Giovanni da Fiesole.

The route that leads to Settignano (3.5 km) sets out from the area around the Campo di Marte and then winds along the Via Gabriele D'Annunzio. The route cuts through Coverciano, where there is a soccer training camp, the *Centro Tecnico della Federazione Italiana del Gioco del Calcio*, equipped with eminently usable facilities built during the Fifties; you will then continue along through a pretty densely settled section, to the village of Ponte a Mènsola, and then you will begin to climb up the hill, or Colle di Settignano, amidst olive groves.

The two routes can be linked together by taking Via Benedetto da Maiano and Via di Poggio Gherardo.

Complex of the church and convent of S. Domenico

The church and the adjoining Dominican convent (where Fra Angelico lived, among others; plan on page 115: B1) stand, in the quarter of *San Domenico* (elev. 145 m.), midway up the slope of the Colle di Fièsole. Begun in 1406 and completed between 1418 and 1435, the church was enlarged and transformed in the 17th and 18th c. Before the facade extends an elegant portico built by Matteo Nigetti (1635).

The interior has only the nave with three chapels on either side, and dates from the 15th/16th c. The presbytery and the choir date from the 17th c. On the right side of the nave, note the wooden *Crucifix* from the 14th c. (1st chapel), *Baptism of Jesus* by Lorenzo di Credi (2nd chapel). In the raised presbytery, at the main altar, note the large 17th-c. tabernacle made of gilt wood, with *statues of saints of the Dominican order.* In the 1st chapel on the left, *Virgin Mary with Christ Child, angels, and saints Thomas Aquinas, Barnabas, Dominick, and St. Peter martyr*, a triptych by Fra Angelico (a painting of his youth, in 1425) which reveals the influence of Masaccio and Gentile da Fabriano; it was transformed into a rectangular panel by Lorenzo di Credi (1501), who added the architectural background and

the landscape.

If you speak to the sacristan, you can visit a part of the convent; here, in the Sala Capitolare, or chapter hall, is a *Crucifix* frescoed by Fra Angelico (ca. 1430) and a *Virgin Mary with Christ Child*, a detached fresco from the workshop of Fra Angelico, with a preparatory drawing, from the hand of the master.

Badia Fiesolana

A little beyond the church of S. Domenico, on the left, Via della Badia dei Roccettini leads directly to the Badia Fiesolana (elev. 122 m.; plan on page 115: B1). This handsome construction, which served as the cathedral of Fièsole until 1028, was given the appearance that it has today when Cosimo the Elder ordered it rebuilt (1456); clearly the inspiration was the work of Brunelleschi, and especially his church of S. Lorenzo. The facade, which is still rough and unfinished, incorporates the Romanesque facade from the 12th c., made of green and white marble. This facade borrows decorative motifs from the the baptistery, or Battistero di S. Giovanni and the facade of S. Miniato; the lower register of the facade has three blind arches; the upper register has three small pedimented windows.

The interior (1461-64) has only a nave, with side chapels with 16th-c. altars and a raised transept; the architect clearly took his inspiration from the work of Brunelleschi (white walls punctuated with pilaster strips made of "pietra serena"). At the end of the right transept, note the *Crucifixion* attributed to Bernardino Campi, a rare example of 16th-c. Lombard art in Florence. Through two elegant 15th-c. stone portals, you can enter either a small chapel with a fresco from the workshop of Raffaellino del Garbo (*Annunciation*) or a vestibule with a marble *lavabo* by Gregorio di Lorenzo (1461). In the 1st chapel on the left, a relief depicts the *Virgin Mary with Christ Child*, a work from the school of Jacopo della Quercia.

On the right of the church is the entrance of the former *convent*, now the site of a school, the Istituto Universitario Europeo. On the left a staircase leads into the huge Renaissance cloister, with handsome arches on columns, and a loggia on the upper floor. In the refectory, note the ornate semicircular stone pulpit and the large fresco by Giovanni da S. Giovanni (*Christ being fed by angels*, 1629).

After you return to Piazza S. Domenico, you continue toward Fièsole along the broad Via

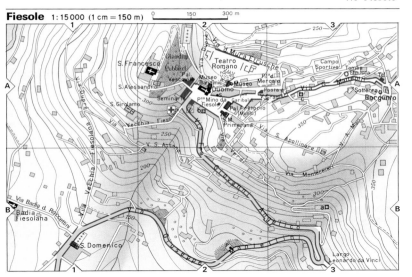

Giuseppe Mantellini. At the curve in the road marked by the bus-stop "Mantellini 3," a narrow lane runs down to the *Villa Bellagio*, the last residence (1894-1901) of the Swiss painter Arnold Böcklin. At the next sharp turn begins Via Fra' Giovanni da Fiesole. There, immediately to the right, a turn-off leads up to the *Villa S. Michele* (now a hotel; plan above: B3); it once belonged to the Davanzati family and was later made into a convent.

Fièsole*

This little town (elev. 295 m., pop. 15,096) – perched in a panoramic setting atop the hill that dominates the river valleys of Arno and Mugnone – is the most interesting of the various towns surrounding Florence, both for the beauty of the landscape and for the wealth of artistic and historical relics, dating back without interruption to the earliest times.

Originally an ancient Etruscan city, in Roman times "Faesulae" was the center of the region; its prosperity began to decline with the barbarian invasions, and it was finally conquered by its more powerful neighbor, Florence (1125). Fortified in 1325 to deal with the onslaught of foreign enemies, Fièsole was one of the Medici's favorite spots in the 15th c. In the 18th and 19th c., new villas and gardens were built in Fièsole, making it one of the most popular resorts around Florence for foreign visitors.

There are numerous major cultural institutions here, including the Istituto Universitario Europeo (Badia Fiesolana) and Harvard University (Villa i Tatti). Note the summer theatrical performances of the Estate Fiesolana, in the Roman theater and in other locations.

Starting from the centrally located Piazza Mino da Fiesole, a square that is lined by some of the most interesting structures in this little town (Duomo, Palazzo Pretorio, church of S. Maria Primerana), the walking route runs north of the square, in Via Giovanni Duprè, with a tour of the various museums (Museo Bandini, Antiquarium) and the excavations of the Etruscan-Roman city. After returning to Piazza Mino da Fiesole, you will climb up the steep Via S. Francesco and to the Colle di S. Francesco, a hill, corresponding to the site of the Acropolis of Fiesole; of particular interest, besides the views of Florence, is the Basilica di S. Alessandro and the convent complex of S. Francesco.

Piazza Mino da Fiesole (A2). The far end of this square is closed off by the handsome *Palazzo Pretorio* (town hall) built in the 14th c. and renovated in later centuries, adorned with the heraldic crests of various "podestà," or local rulers. Nearby stands the old *church of S. Maria Primerana*, with its facade rebuilt at the end of the 16th c., in Mannerist style. Inside, note faded surviving frescoes with *stories of the Virgin Mary* by Niccolò di Pietro Gerini, and a large *Crucifix* on wooden panel, attributed to Bonaccorso di Cino (14th c.).

Duomo (A2). Dedicated to St. Romulus, this Romanesque cathedral was built from the 11th c. onward, and enlarged in the 13th and 14th c. The facade received its present appearance in 1878-83; the handsome *cam-

panile (1213) was rebuilt during the 18th
and 19th c.

The interior has a basilican plan, a nave and
two aisles, and arcades set on columns
with handsome capitals; also note the truss
roof and a presbytery, raised over the crypt.
In the presbytery, to the right, is the Cappella Salutati, a chapel with frescoes by
Cosimo Rosselli and the *tomb of the bishop
Leonardo Salutati*, by Mino da Fiesole, who
also executed the altar frontal. On the main
altar, note a polyptych with the *Virgin Mary
Enthroned, the Christ Child, and Saints* by Bicci di Lorenzo (1450).

To the left is the Cappella dei Canonici, a
chapel, with a marble altar-frontal by Andrea Ferrucci (1493), containing *statues of
Saint Romulus and Saint Matthew*.

In the 13th-c. crypt, divided into a nave
and two aisles by slender columns, a handsome iron grate (1349) surrounds the 15th-
c. altar dedicated to St. Romulus (S. Romolo). Recently (1990), remarkable new archeological finds have documented the existence here of the ancient Roman "Capitoli-
um," which had long been thought to have
stood in a number of points throughout
the city.

Museo Bandini (A2). With an entrance at n.
1 in Via Giovanni Duprè, this museum contains the collection of the canon Angelo
Maria Bandini (an 18th-c. man of letters,
the librarian of the Biblioteca Marucelliana
and the Biblioteca Laurenziana). His collection consisted largely of panels of the
Tuscan school from the 13th and 14th c. as
well as canvases from the 15th c., objects of
the applied arts, and sculptures – including
many items of the school of the Della Robbia – from the 14th/16th c. Among the paintings, let us point out a small *Crucifixion* by
Lorenzo Monaco and four panels of a chest,
with *Triumphs* (*Triumph of Love, Triumph of
Chastity, Triumph of Time*, and *Triumph of Divinity*) attributed to Jacopo del Sellaio.

Area Archeologica* (A2). In this archeological area, identifiable with the part of
the Roman city that lay to the north of the
Forum (present-day Piazza Mino da Fiesole),
are concentrated the chief urban remains of
the Etruscan city and of Roman "Faesulae."
The tour of the excavations, of considerable
interest for the archeological material, is also notable in terms of the landscape and environment in which the ruins are set.

The entrance (in Via Giovanni Duprè, across
from the Museo Bandini; plan shown below) leads onto a small clearing. From here,
a short stairway takes you to the *Teatro
Romano** or Roman Theater, begun under
Augustus and completed under Claudius. It
has a cavea capable of seating 3,000 (34 m.
in diameter), carved into the side of the
hill, and split up into four sectors by three
little flights of steps.

To the right of the theater, a trail leads to the
ruins of the *Terme*, or baths, which may
have been founded under the reign of Au-

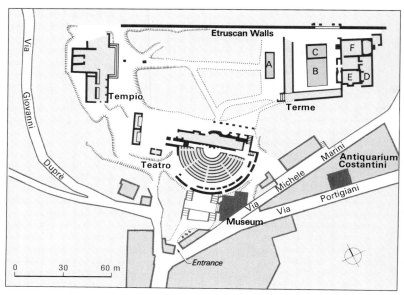

The archeological area of Fièsole: plan

gustus, but were rebuilt and enlarged in ensuing centuries. At their greatest expanse, they covered a surface area of about 4,500 sq. m. You can observe (on the left) an enormous courtyard with a large rectangular swimming pool (plan, A) and, on a terrace set higher up, two more rectangular pools, either for filtering water or for swimming (B and C); to the right, if you descend a few steps, you will find a number of rooms, including the "hypocausis" (D), with the burners and the pipes that served respectively to heat and to distribute the hot water and hot air into the adjoining room (the "calidarium"; E). Three tall arches, largely the product of restoration, define the "frigidarium" (F).

If you follow the "vialetto" westward, you will walk past the *Etruscan walls** (248 m. long and 4.8 m. tall), composed of closely hewn colossal parallelepiped blocks. You then reach the sacred area of Fièsole, with the ruins of the *Tempio Romano*, a Roman temple that was rebuilt in the 1st c. B.C. after a fire. After the fire, it was enlarged but the pediment had the same decoration used in the prior Etruscan temple, with figures in terracotta (now in the Museum: see below). The cella was tripartite, with a tetrastyle pronaos. The steps, facing east, are 23 m. wide at the base; the right stylobate is 11 m. long, while the left one extends into a terrace that once had a portico (now vanished; the bases of five columns remain).

Climb up to your left, beyond the theater and, on the upper esplanade, you enter the *Museum*, a building dating from the turn of the 20th c., shaped like a little Ionic temple. In the first four halls on the ground floor are exhibits of Etruscan and Roman archeological finds, from Fièsole and surrounding territory; on the upper floor, the fifth hall contains chalices, tankards, and weapons from the high Middle Ages. The last three rooms contain the Antiquarium, with artifacts and archeological finds that do not come from Fièsole.

After you leave the area of excavations, climb up to the left along Via Portigiani and note, at n. 9, the *Palazzina dell'Antiquarium Costantini*, where there is a remarkable collection of ancient ceramic objects (about 170 items), donated to the town of Fièsole in 1985 by Alfiero Costantini.

Basilica di S. Alessandro (A2). This basilica is traditionally said to have been founded upon the site of a pagan temple, transformed in the 6th c. into a Christian church,

renovated in the 11th c., and repeatedly modified. The Neoclassical facade dates from the second decade of the 19th c. The interior is basilican in style, with a nave and two side aisles, and a truss roof; the interior is divided up by sixteen ancient columns in cipollino, with Ionic bases and capitals.

S. Francesco (A2). On the peak of the hill (elev. 346 m.), where the acropolis once rose, stands the church of S. Francesco, built in the 14th c. as the oratory of a convent, later enlarged and modified over the centuries that followed, and completely restored at the turn of the 20th c. The facade dates from the turn of the 15th c. The interior has only a nave, with three large pointed arches; note the *Annunciation* by Raffaellino del Garbo (2nd altar on the left). Adjacent to the sacristy is a small 15th-c. cloister; from it you can enter the *Museo Etnografico Missionario* (an ethnographic museum set up by missionaries; there are Etruscan, Chinese, and Egyptian objects). To the right of the entrance is the entrance to the two oldest cloisters in the convent (14th and 15th c.); overlooking the first cloister is the "dormitorium," where St. Bernardino of Siena lived.

The trip to Fonte Lucente is particularly pleasant because of the lovely landscape through which you pass. From Piazza Mino da Fiesole, if you proceed along the Via Vecchia Fiesolana, you will soon find the *Villa Medici* (A2), built by Michelozzo (1458-61) for Cosimo the Elder; here Lorenzo the Magnificent offered hospitality to the literati in his entourage. The building was completely rebuilt in 1780, and only scattered fragments of the original structure survive. If you continue along the road, amidst tall cypress trees, you will reach the fork in the road with Via di Fonte Lucente; this road leads (after just 600 m.) to Fonte Lucente, with its 18th-c. oratory, the *Oratorio del SS. Crocifisso* (A1, off map), with the spring that gives its name to the town, and a 16th-c. stone *Crucifix*, said to be miraculous.

Settignano
This small village stands at an elevation of 178 m., and is set in a stupendous landscape, surrounded by gentle rolling hills studded with villas. Settignano is known especially as the birthplace of numerous artists, including Desiderio da Settignano, the Rossellino brothers, and Bartolomeo Ammannati. In the central Piazza Tommaseo is the *church of S. Maria*, documented as early as the 12th c., but rebuilt and enlarged in the 16th c. and completely restored in the late-17th c. Inside, there is a

Settignano: Villa Gamberaia

nave and two aisles, an arrangement which dates from the end of the 16th c.

Villa Gamberaia. Built as a modest country home (at n. 72 in Via del Rossellino) for the Rossellino family, it was entirely rebuilt in the 17th c.; in particular the splendid Italian-style *garden** was embellished with numerous statues, fountains, and sprays (you can visit the garden if you call ahead and ask the owners; tel. 055-697205).

S. Martino a Mènsola. Located not far from the main road that runs from Via Gabriele D'Annunzio to Maiano, this church (documented as early as the 11th c.) has a 15th-

c. appearance. Before it extends an 18th-c. portico. The interior, with a nave and two aisles and a truss roof, has a number of outstanding works of art, including a triptych by Taddeo Gaddi, with the *Virgin Mary enthroned, between two saints*, set in the midst of four *Prophets* during the 15th c. (altar at the head of the right aisle).

As you drive along the hillsides, heading for Vincigliata, at a distance of 2.8 km. from S. Martino a Mènsola, stands the *Villa i Tatti*, which belonged (1905-59) to the art historian Bernard Berenson, who assembled a noteworthy **collection of Italian paintings**, dating especially from the 14th, 15th, and 16th c. (open only to scholars doing research). The entire complex (villa, art collection, library, and park) was left in a bequest to Harvard University.

The road continues uphill, among dense stands of pines and cypresses, to the *Castello di Vincigliata*, a castle that has been entirely rebuilt – upon the ruins of the 14th-c. castle – in the Gothic style by Giuseppe Fancelli (1855-65) for the owner, John Temple Leader.

A kilometer-and-a-half past S. Martino a Mènsola, if you head toward Fièsole, along Via di Poggio Gherardo and Via Benedetto da Maiano, at n. 26 in the latter road, you will pass the *Villa di Maiano*, long ago an estate owned by the Pazzi family, and completely restored in the 19th c. – in accordance with the architecture of Michelozzo, at the wishes of the owner, John Temple Leader. A little further along is the small settlement of **Maiano** (elev. 173 m.), a village with a long tradition of stonecarvers and sculptors (including Benedetto and Giuliano da Maiano).

7.2 Impruneta

The route suggested for reaching the village of Impruneta runs through the area to the south of Florence, distinguished by hills, largely covered with olive trees, over which centuries of human settlement have extended a dense network of roads and country lanes, often dating from the Middle Ages; one curiosity is represented by the many tabernacles, often decorated with locally made terracotta, set at the crossroads.
The route (9.7 km. long) – scenic, but full of sharp turns and in some stretches quite narrow— begins in Poggio Imperiale (11 F4) and then runs down, amidst enclosure walls and aristocratic buildings, to the village of San Felice a Ema. After you cross the river Ema, the road runs back up the villa-dotted hill. At the top of the hill is the little town of Pozzolàtico; after you pass the Autostrada del Sole (highway); finally, the road reaches Mezzomonte and, after a last flat stretch, you roll into Impruneta.

S. Felice a Ema
The church of S. Felice a Ema, with documentation as early as the 11th c., gave its name to the village of S. Felice a Ema (elev. 75 m.). In the facade there is still a Romanesque lunette. The interior, with nave and two aisles, was rebuilt in Neoclassical style at the end of the 18th c.; the altars are decorated with altarpieces dating from the 17th and 18th c.; in the sacristy, note the *Virgin Mary with Christ Child* by Giovanni del Biondo (1387). In the nearby cemetery, the Nobel laureate and poet Eugenio Montale is buried.

Impruneta
Before you reach the large village on the ridge between the Greve and the Ema, the road runs through Pozzolàtico (elev. 143 m.) and Mezzomonte (elev. 237 m.), where the enormous **Villa Corsini** (privately owned and difficult to visit) stands isolated on the

left; it dates from the 16th c., and is lavishly decorated inside with 17th-c. frescoes.
The small town of Impruneta (elev. 275 m., pop. 15,028), with its distinctive spoke-shaped structure, is a traditional Tuscan farming town; it also produces terracotta for the building trades. In more recent years it has become something of a resort town. The development of the village – which may have been founded as early as the 8th or 9th c., around the parish church of S. Maria – in the Middle Ages and in modern times was a result of its role as a religious center, a role bound up with the image of the Madonna dell'Impruneta, believed to be miraculous, and now found in the basilica/sanctuary that overlooks the Piazza Buondelmonti. Dating back to the earliest times is the "Fiera di S. Luca" (a fair, held in mid-October); more recent is the "Festa dell'Uva" (a wine festival, held on the last Sunday in September), with processions of allegorical carts.

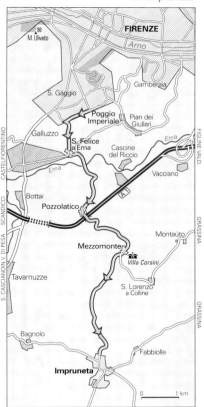

GREVE IN CHIANTI   GREVE IN CHIANTI

Basilica Santuario di S. Maria all'Impruneta.
This basilica/sanctuary stands on the site of an Etruscan-Roman sanctuary. In the high Middle Ages a church was built on the same site. The early Romanesque parish church was consecrated in 1060; it was then enlarged in the 14th c., completely rebuilt in the middle of the 15th c., and further renovated in the centuries that followed. The facade is sheltered by a *portico* surmounted by a large hall ("salone"), the work of Gherardo Silvani (1634), and is flanked by the crenelated *bell tower* (13th c.), one of the few surviving features of the Romanesque buildings, as well as by an 18th-c. *turret*, with a clock.
The interior, which has only the single nave, was seriously damaged by bombing in 1944; following extensive restoration, it has acquired its original Renaissance appearance. On the four side-altars, note the remarkable 17th-c. altar-pieces, including: *Nativity of the Virgin Mary* by Passignano (2nd on the right); *Vocation of St. Peter* by Empoli (1st on the left). On either side of the presbytery, two *aedicules** attributed to Michelozzo and decorated with glazed terracottas* by Luca della Robbia: the one on the right, called the Cappella della Croce, or chapel of the cross, contains a relic of the True Cross and, on the altar, Delle Robbia terracottas depicting the *Crucifixion* between two *statues of saints*; the aedicule on the left, known as the Cappella della Madonna, preserves – set in a 15th-c. marble tabernacle – a gilt panel with the image (sometimes covered) of the *Madonna dell'Impruneta*, repainted by

Ignazio Hugford (1758). It is surrounded by Delle Robbia terracottas depicting *St. Peter and St. Paul*. On the main altar, note the 14th-c. polyptych painted by Pietro Nelli with the assistance of Niccolò di Pietro Gerini – depicting the *Virgin Mary with Christ Child and Apostles* – shattered into fragments by bombing, and later reassembled. A 15th-c. portal on the right of the portico on the facade leads into the cloisters. From the second cloister, you can pass into the crypt, a small room with an apse.

Museo del Tesoro di S. Maria all'Impruneta.
This museum of the treasure of the basilica has a collection comprised chiefly of creations in gold and silver, as well as illuminated codices and other objects that form part of the history of this sanctuary. Of particular note is a marble bas-relief depicting the *Discovery of the Image of the Madonna* (ca. 1430), attribution disputed (Michelozzo, Filarete, or Luca della Robbia). Among the various pieces of goldwork and silverwork, let us point out a *Reliquiario della S. Croce*, or reliquary of the Holy Cross (17th c.).

7.3 Bellosguardo and the Certosa del Galluzzo

Running over the hill country just south of Florence, this route breaks down into two branches leading to the areas mentioned in the title.

The point of departure for the first section of this route – actually a short stroll: just 1.3 km. in length – is Piazza Torquato Tasso (9 D6). From here, if you take Via Villani, you will reach Piazza S. Francesco, which marks the beginning of Via di Bellosguardo, which in turn runs up Monte Rimorchi and leads to the Colle di Bellosguardo. In the 19th c., this town, which overlooks the SW section of Florence, became the most popular resort, after Fièsole, for the intellectual elite of Italy and elsewhere.

The second thoroughfare (4.3 km.) will take you to the Certosa del Galluzzo, a charter house and one of the most interesting monuments in the area around Florence; to get there, you will travel through a landscape swathed in olive groves and dotted with aristocratic villas. The route begins in Piazzale di Porta Romana (to get there from Piazza T. Tasso, just take Viale F. Petrarca; 9 F6) and then turns onto the Via Senese – an urban extension of the state road, Statale 2, Via Cassia – which will take you to Due Strade, a village. Here the thoroughfare for the Certosa del Galluzzo forks in two directions: on the right, you can take the "new" Via Senese, which runs past an Evan-

gelical cemetery at one point; on the left – the more interesting one – is the old "Via Romana," now called Via del Podestà, a road lined with old buildings, villas, and a convent. These two alternative routes hook up again in the town of Galluzzo, and from there it is just a short hop to the Certosa del Galluzzo itself.

To Bellosguardo

Climbing up to the hill of Bellosguardo, the Via di Bellosguardo runs through the "Prato dello Strozzino," a field overlooked by the *Villa le Lune* (or *Villa dello Strozzino*; 9 E4), a Renaissance construction with a corner loggia, once the property of the Strozzi family.

A detour from Prato dello Strozzino runs down along the Via di Monte Uliveto (you really should walk this part) to the *convent of S. Bartolomeo in Monte Uliveto* (9 C4). The church (open only Sunday morning) was built at the end of the 14th c., and was then rebuilt to plans by Michelozzo (1472) and further renovated in the 17th and 18th c. The facade still boasts a carved stone portal, surmounted by a large twin-light mullioned window. The interior has a single nave with cross vaults. There are paintings dating from the 16th and 17th c.

As you continue to climb from the Prato dello Strozzino, you reach the handsome Piazza del Colle di Bellosguardo. Directly before that, a short detour along Via Roti Michelozzi will take you to the *Torre di Bellosguardo* (9 E4), a 14th-c. castle transformed into a villa after 1583, then renovated between the 19th and 20th c., and finally converted into a hotel. Adjoining it, but with an entrance at n. 12 of the Piazza del Colle di Bellosguardo, is the *Villa dell'Ombrellino* (another hotel; 9 E4), where Galileo Galilei lived from 1617 until 1631.

The Galluzzo

From the Due Strade, if you follow the *Via del Podestà*, which runs between two rows of buildings and walls, you will pass, at n. 79, the *Villa dei Corboli* (16th/17th c.); a little further along, at n. 86, note the 14th-c. *Convento del Portico*; still further along, on the hill on the right, note the 18th-c. *Villa la Favorita*. As you enter the village of Galluzzo, on the left note the *Palazzo Podestarile*, with a facade marked by a number of crests in stone and in glazed terracotta.

Certosa del Galluzzo*

Soon after you leave the town of Galluzzo, you will see on the Monte Acuto (elev. 110

The Charter House, or Certosa del Galluzzo

m.) the stern silhouette of this complex, walled as if it were a fortress. This charter house is also known as the *Certosa di Firenze* or the *Certosa di Val d'Ema*, and was founded in 1342 by Niccolò Acciaioli, a member of one of the most prominent families in Florence; in later times, it was enlarged and embellished with artwork through the bequests of many citizens of Florence.

At the entrance is the compact block of *Palazzo Acciaioli*, the original core of the complex, begun to plans by Fra Jacopo Passavanti and Fra Jacopo Talenti; work was interrupted upon the death of Acciaioli and was only completed in the mid-16th c. It is now used as a *Pinacoteca* or art gallery; among some of the lesser known works are five large frescoed lunettes, with *scenes of the Passion**, by Jacopo Pontormo (1523-25), detached from the large cloister.

Note the vast proportions of the "piazzale," or plaza, overlooked by the 16th-c. facade of the *church of S. Lorenzo*, founded in the 14th c., but rebuilt in the 16th c.; after you cross through the Coro dei Conversi, a vestibule that was added in 1556-58 and decorated with paintings in the 17th c., you enter the church of the Monaci, which still maintains its original 14th-c. plan; on three walls, note the carved and inlaid walnut-wood *stalls* (ca. 1570-90).

The next series of rooms in the church are not always open to the public. At the end of the nave, on the right, note the 14th-c. Cappella delle Reliquie, or chapel of relics, rebuilt in the 17th c. and frescoed by Poccetti and by Lucio Massari; to the left, set symmetrically, is the refined and elegant sacristy, with 18th-c. decoration. Among the chapels along the right side of the church, note the 14th-c. Cappella di S. Maria, or St. Mary's chapel, with a Greek-cross plan; renovated at the turn of the 17th c. The Neo-

Gothic appearance is the result of a 19th-c. restoration. From the Cappella di S. Maria you can descend to the Cappella di Tobia, the burial crypt of the Acciaioli family: on the left wall, *funerary monument to Niccolò Acciaioli* (second half of the 14th c.), attributed to the workshop of Andrea Orcagna; on the floor, note the three *tombstones*. The adjoining crypt of the Cappella di S. Maria preserves the *tombstone of Angelo Cardinal Acciaioli*, by Francesco da Sangallo (ca. 1550).

From the church of the Monaci you enter the convent, starting in the Colloquio, with 16th-c. "grisaille" stained-glass windows, and a *Christ Carrying the Cross*, glazed terracotta by Gerolamo della Robbia (ca. 1514). Next comes a small cloister, the Chiostrino dei Monaci (rebuilt in 1558-59), which preserves a lunette with *St. Lawrence Between Two Angels* by Benedetto da Maiano (1496). Above the door that leads into the Sala Capitolare, two lunettes by Bronzino (*Pietà, with Two Angels* and *St. Lawrence*). The Capitolo contains a *Crucifixion* frescoed by Mariotto Albertinelli (1506); on the floor, note the *tomb of the prior Leonardo Buonafede*, by Francesco da Sangallo (1545).

You emerge through the Renaissance *great cloister** (16th c.), surrounded by a harmonious loggia set on slender columns with composite capitals; in the spandrels, note 66 busts made of glazed terracotta from the workshop of Giovanni della Robbia.

On three sides of the cloister are the rows of monks' cells, each comprising a small antechamber, a room that served for eating, a bedroom, a room on the upper floor, a covered loggia, a little garden, and a storeroom. Outside of every cell, a letter of the alphabet and a frescoed lunette mark the various residences of the monks (the lunette with the *Good Shepherd* by Tommaso Redi and the letter A indicate the apartment of the prior).

7.4 Careggi, Castello, Sesto Fiorentino

The route sets out from Piazza Dalmazia (7 B3) and explores the area to the north and NW of Florence, initially following the line of Viale G.B. Morgagni and Viale Gaetano Pieraccini to the Colle di Careggi, then Via Reginaldo Giuliani and Via delle Panche to Castello, and lastly Via Antonio Gramsci to Sesto Fiorentino, situated six Roman miles from the center of Florence, equivalent to 9 km. The areas of Careggi and Castello are located on the lowest rolling hills, dotted with venerable old aristocratic villas, including a number of major Medici estates (Villa di Careggi, Villa della Petraia, Villa di Castello), part of a major network of landholdings in the area.

The territory of Sesto Fiorentino occupies the foothills along the plains. This area abounds in archeological finds, fine art, and relics of history. The area has also been intensely settled and built up; there is much manufacturing. From Sesto Fiorentino you may choose to extend your explorations to Calenzano, or take the scenic and panoramic Strada dei Colli Alti (literally, road of the

high hills), which allows you to enjoy the remarkable views and landscape of the wooded amphitheater of Monte Morello.

Careggi

As you follow the Viale Gaetano Pieraccini, skirting the area of the hospital, or *Ospedale di Careggi* – a complex of wards and clinics clustered along the side of the hill, or Collina di Careggi – you will encounter the **Villa Medicea di Careggi** (entrance at n. 21), now containing the offices of the public health administration, or USL 10 D. The original 14th-c. fortified "casa da signore," or aristocratic residence, was purchased by the Medici at the turn of the 15th c. and rebuilt in accordance with a plan attributed to Michelozzo; it became one of the Medici family's favorite residences. The facade is slightly irregular in its perimeter, a reflection of the old road that ran past this side in the 15th c. The building still conserves a number of features typical of medieval military architecture. Inside (open to visitors who ask permission from the administrative

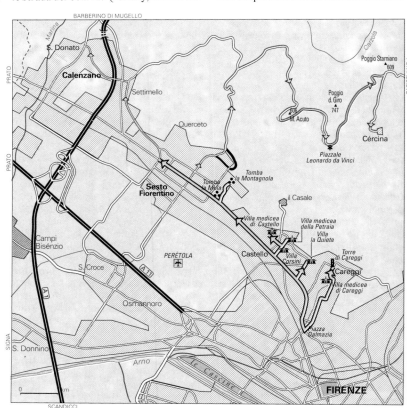

offices of USL 10 D), the courtyard is trapezoidal in shape. The rear facade, slightly more complex in structure, extends toward the garden with two loggias, each with three arches. Above the right arcade is a loggia with little architraved Ionic columns, believed to be by either Michelozzo or Giuliano da Sangallo.

Climb still further, and you will reach the Piazza di Careggi, with the old tower, or *Torre di Careggi*, a medieval construction surrounding the crenelated tower, dating from the 14th c. but rebuilt at the end of the 16th c. It belonged to the Medici, who used it as guest quarters and farmhouse for their nearby villa; beginning in 1936 it was incorporated into the convent of the Oblate nuns. Inside (open to the public, with written permission from the Amministrazione della USL 10 D, Italian department of health) there are notable artworks, such as two *Crucifixes* on panels (one dating from the 13th c., the other from the 14th c.); a *Virgin Mary with Christ Child* by Niccolò Gerini; a two-part panel with *Virgin Mary Enthroned, Christ Child, Four Saints, and Crucifixion*, attributed to Giottino.

Villa la Quiete

This old noble residence was, at various times, also owned by the Medici and the Lorraine (Lorena), and was converted in the mid-17th c. into a conservatory for young aristocratic women; it stands at the end of the Via delle Montalve, a cross-street of Via delle Panche. Since 1937 it has housed a convent of the Montalve nuns (open by request) and an educational institution.

The oldest core of the complex is the structure surrounding the first courtyard, where the 17th-c. church was added. The "salone," or great hall, the wings on the east side, and the second roof terrace, or "altana" all date from the end of the 19th c. The church comprises two levels, and the upper level is protected by grates; on the right altar, note the 13th-c. *Crucifix* on panel. Behind the church, a vestibule leads into the two frescoed parlors, and then into the "salone," or great hall, which contains most of the artworks in the convent. Note the *Coronation of the Virgin Mary and Saints* by Sandro Botticelli and workshop, and the *Wedding of St. Catherine* by Ridolfo del Ghirlandaio.

To the south of the villa extends an 18th-c. Italian-style garden, virtually intact, with tall enclosure walls.

Castello

Once an outlying section of Florence, and since absorbed by the expansion of the Florentine outskirts, Castello takes its name from the fact that in ancient times there was a cistern here (in Latin, "castellum"). The buildings that make up the "borgo," or hill town, are lined densely along the last stretch of Via Reginaldo Giuliani, while the three splendid villas that constitute its chief and monumental attraction, line the slopes of the small hill.

Villa Corsini. This spectacular reconstruction of existing buildings (15th/16th c.) dates from the late-17th c., and serves as a backdrop to the end of the Via di Castello with its imposing late-Baroque facade. The facade, comprising two levels, is punctuated by pilaster strips covering the entire height of the register, and is enriched by stuccoes and a crowning scroll-work, incorporating a clock. Above the balcony that projects over the portal is the heraldic crest of the Corsini family. Note the handsome, Italian-style garden and park, with a sculpture by Tribolo.

Villa Medicea della Petraia*. To the left of Villa Corsini, Via della Petraia runs up to this superb Medici residence. With its distinctive square shape and plan, with a central courtyard, and its massive central tower with a jutting battlement looming over all, the villa stands out in the hilly landscape. The *garden** is extremely handsome. The three levels date from the 16th-c. renovation, though changes have certainly been made since then. The lower level of the garden is in the Italian style, with a circular fountain; the intermediate level features a large fish-pond, spanned by a stairway leading up to the upper terrace where – on the right of the villa – there is a hanging garden, called the "Piano della Figurina." The Figurina is a clear reference to the feminine figure depicted in the *Fountain of Venus-Fiorenza* – Fiorenza being the personification of the city of Florence. The fountain was built by Tribolo with the assistance of Pierino da Vinci in the mid-16th c. It was placed here in 1788. Today all that remains is the lower basin; the bronze statue that once crowned the basin, by Giambologna, is now on display on the second floor of the villa.

The courtyard, with loggias on two sides, was covered in the 19th c. by an iron-and-glass structure. On the two sides without loggias, note frescoes by Cosimo Daddi (1591-94), depicting *deeds of Godfrey of Bouillon*; beneath the two loggias, the series of the *glories of the house of Medici**, frescoed by the Volterrano (1636-48).

The interior was renovated – when this

The Medici Villa della Petraia

building became a hunting lodge of the new Italian king, Vittorio Emanuele II (Victor Emmanuel II) in 1865 – with reconstruction of floors and ceilings, and enriched with wallpaper, upholstery, and new furniture. On the second floor, in the "studiolo," or study, note the bronze statue of *Venus-Fiorenza, Wringing from Her Hair the Waters of the Arno and the Mugnone*, by Giambologna (ca. 1572); the statue originally stood atop the fountain in the garden.

Villa Medicea di Castello*. This was one of the Medici family's favorite residences; it is set on a hill where an exceedingly old cistern ("castellum") once stood; it gave the entire area its name. The original fortified home (12th/13th c.), which had already been rebuilt before the Medici acquired it in 1477, was thoroughly renovated, especially under the rule of Cosimo, following his selection as duke (1537). Cosimo commissioned Tribolo to do the renovation; Tribolo revised the elevations, standardizing them with a series of windows on two floors with a mezzanine. The central portal with its stout rusticated cornicework, surmounted by a balcony, dates from the later renovation and enlargements carried out under the supervision of Bernardo Buontalenti (late-16th c.). The villa (closed to the public) has held the offices of the *Accademia della Crusca* since 1974; this institution was founded in 1583 in order to publish the "Vocabolario," Italy's counterpart of the Oxford English Dictionary, the touchstone of proper Italian style and usage.

Behind the villa, note the magnificent *garden**, built at the wishes of Cosimo as a symbolic depiction of the territory of the duchy, and as a celebration of the Medici dynasty. All that survives of the ideal and metaphorical route designed by Benedetto Varchi and the Tribolo are a few scattered traces; the path originally set out from the highest point in the garden (it can be reached by following the drive that starts at the large entrance gate on the right side of the villa), a stand of cypress trees and holm-oaks surrounding a basin of water, at the center of which stands a statue by Bartolomeo Ammannati (ca. 1563), depicting either the *Apennines* or else the month of *January* (Cosimo was chosen as duke in the month of January). You can then climb down into the Italian-style garden; note the whimsical *Grotta degli Animali*, or grotto of animals, a manmade cave built by Tribolo (ca. 1545) and adorned with stalactites, sponges, and seashells; the water in the basin above poured down into this grotto, causing sprays to jet across and into the two side basins, adorned with marine animals; the decoration was completed, under the supervision of Vasari, by Ammannati, the Lorenzi brothers, and others; note the remarkable array of petrified animals. On the central axis of the garden, at the center of a small square, surrounded by ancient Roman statues, is the *Fontana di Ercole e Anteo**, or fountain of Hercules and Antaeus, by Tribolo (ca. 1545), with an octagonal basin and two circular tazzas, adorned with putti: originally, the fountain was surmounted by a marble group depicting *Her-*

cules Crushing Antaeus by Ammannati (1558-59); this group is now in storage.

Sesto Fiorentino

This major industrial town (elev. 55 m., pop. 47,406) was originally a Roman settlement, and is known especially for the porcelain manufactory, the Manifattura di Porcellane Ginori di Doccia. The ancient town, developed heavily over recent decades, has progressively swallowed up many surrounding smaller towns.

Not far from the village of *Quinto*, at n. 95 in the Via Fratelli Rosselli, in the park of the Villa Manfredi, stands the **Etruscan tomb of Montagnola** (for access, contact the gardener), one of the most noteworthy and well-preserved Etruscan monuments in the area. It dates from the 7th c. B.C., and comprises a corridor, or "dròmos," without a roof, a covered corridor with a false vault, flanked by two cellae also with false-vault roofs, and a "thòlos" with a false cupola with a central pillar. The material found in it is now in the Museo Archeologico in Florence. In the same area, in Via della Mula n. 2, inside the estate of the Villa La Mula is an **Etruscan tomb** that dates from the 7th c. B.C.; all that still stands is the large "thòlos" with a false cupola, without a central pillar. At the NW extremity of Sesto, in Via Pratese n. 31, you will find the **Museo delle Porcellane di Doccia**; inaugurated in 1965, this museum contains complete documentation of the "historic" production of the Manifattura Ginori, a porcelain manufactory founded in 1737. The exhibits include numerous objects of remarkable quality and workmanship. It is evident that the craftsmen were trying to merge the classical and the Florentine traditions of art with the newest developments of the European decorative arts of the time.

To the NE, beyond the Borgata Colonnata, begins the **Strada dei Colli Alti**, or road of the high hills, a lovely scenic route that runs along the slopes of Monte Morello. The road runs through the villages of Collina and Gualdo, and then around Monte Acuto (elev. 606 m.), skirting the Poggio Balletto (elev. 670 m.), on the slopes of which extends the *Piazzale Leonardo da Vinci* (elev. 595 m.); from here you can enjoy a splendid view of Florence and the Arno valley. After Ceppeto, a turn-off on the right descends (at a distance of 14 km. from Sesto Fiorentino) to *Cercìna* (elev. 353 m.), and the Romanesque *parish church of S. Andrea**. The interior has a nave and two aisles, with truss roofs; in the right apse, note the fresco by Domenico and Davide Ghirlandaio (*St. Jerome, St. Barbara, and St. Anthony Abbot*); in the chapel at the end of the left aisle, note the *Madonna*, a polychrome wooden statue (12th/13th c.) that is greatly venerated; near the entrance is the *funerary monument to the Catellini da Castiglione* (turn of the 14th c.).

A 4.5-km. drive takes you from Sesto Fiorentino to **Calenzano** (elev. 108 m., pop. 14,959), a town with ancient origins, now a manufacturing center. The modern town extends along the plain, between two hills – S. Donato and Castello – upon which the ancient settlements were clustered. On the western hill stands the *Castello**, a picturesque fortified village, which still has major sections of medieval walls, with two turreted towers (14th and 15th c.). Among the older buildings, note the *Pieve di S. Niccolò*, a country parish church, and the *Oratorio della Compagnia del Santissimo Sacramento*, an oratory.

8 The Mugello and the Vallombrosa

The Mugello is an enormous hollow spreading out between two mountain chains to the NE of Florence; on the far side of the Apennine passes, this area takes the name of the Alto Mugello, or upper Mugello. The part of the valley to the east of the town of Vicchio is known, instead, as the Val di Sieve; through this river valley runs the river Sieve, the largest tributary to the upper course of the river Arno. The entire area is noteworthy for the broad expanses in which the natural environment has been left virtually intact, with woods of Turkey oaks and chestnut trees, pine forests and mountain meadows.

When the Florentine Republic, in the course of its great expansion, began to cast covetous eyes upon the Mugello in the 14th c., it encountered fierce and combattive feudal lords; Florence eventually wrested control of the territory and, with it, strategic control of communications with Romagna through the construction of the so-called "new towns" ("terre nuove"; or "walled towns" – "terre murate"): Scarperìa, Firenzuola, and Vicchio. These were settlements with a regular, well-aligned urban structure, surrounded by a solid, well-planned system of walls. They were founded with the intention of ensuring the security of trade with the Po Valley. Alongside these towns, there were others, of course, which had sprung up at the crossroads of the most important arteries of communication in the region (San Piero a Sieve, Borgo San Lorenzo). In the town layout, you can still see how the original settlement revolved entirely around the marketplace and trade.

The prosperity of the Mugello began to decline in the 18th c., when new, more-direct roads were built across the Apennines; a shift in the political and economic landscape of the Grand Duchy of Tuscany also helped to push this territory out of the picture. The process of decline sharpened in the 19th and 20th c., when the great hollow of Mugello became little more than a reservoir of laborers for the city of Florence. It was not until the 1980s that the situation improved here, with a new appreciation for the area's environmental resources.

To the SE of the Val di Sieve is the broad mountainous territory of the Pratomagno, an area of considerable natural attractions; here, surrounded by age-old forests, stands the famous abbey of Vallombrosa.

8.1 From Florence to Scarperìa

The route recommended here (30.4 km. long) exits Florence along the Via Bolognese ("Statale 65 della Futa," a state road) which runs across the bridge known as the Ponte Rosso (8 E1). The route runs through an urban area mostly occupied by gardens and large villas: *Villa La Pietra* (n. 120), set amidst a spectacular garden; *Villa Finaly* (n. 134), which now houses a branch of the University of Paris; *Villa La Loggia* (N. 165), with a loggia in the Renaissance style; *Villa Salviati*, in the style of Michelozzo, set in a vast park. You then continue through an area where stunning landscapes alternate with notable historical landmarks (Medici villas, convent of Monte Senario).

At San Piero a Sieve you turn on to the Statale 503 toward Scarperìa, a "borgo," or old village, of particular interest. Also, note the surrounding areas (convent of the Bosco ai Frati, Pieve di S. Agata). The road to Firenzuola runs up into the Apennines. The route looks increasingly like a mountain road, twisting and steep, but you can often enjoy glimpses of astounding and beautiful landscapes.

Medici Villas
As you follow the Statale 65, you will drive past a number of sites of major Medici residences. Not far from the town of *Pratolino*, is the **park of the Villa Medici-Demidoff***. The park now belongs to the government of the province of Florence. The park was originally part of the estate of an enormous Medici villa, designed and built by Bernardo Buontalenti at the wishes of Francesco I de' Medici. When the House of Lorraine became the ruling dynasty of Tuscany, the building began to be neglected, and it was demolished in 1824; in the same period the park was transformed into one of the most noteworthy Romantic gardens in all of Tuscany. Finally, the estate became property of Paolo Demidoff, who established his residence in the old pages' quarters, of the villa. The focal point of the original project, as designed by Buontalenti, was the giant *Fontana dell'Appennino**, or Fountain of the Apennines; this fountain was built by Giambologna (1579-89). It was a three-story edifice, with rooms made to look like grottoes, and containing water games.

At Pratolino, if you take the road toward Bivigliano, a short detour on your left leads to the *little church of S. Cresci a Macioli*, a building founded in the high Middle Ages and completely rebuilt around 1450. The interior has a nave and two aisles, divided by columns with Ionic capitals; it resembles the style of Giuliano da Maiano.

The other Medici villas of the Mugello can be reached by continuing along the Statale 65 past the crossroads of Nòvoli. A detour on the left (2 km.) leads directly to the **Castello di Trebbio***, a castle set atop a hill, amidst a cypress grove. Built by Michelozzo (1427-36) for Cosimo the Elder, it comprises a crenelated tower and a massive square central structure, surmounted by corbels and set around a rectangular courtyard. Further along, but still on the state road, or "statale," you will see the **Villa di Cafaggiolo***, also by Michelozzo (1454), one of the favorite residences of Lorenzo the Magnificent. Set atop the broad elevation, crowned with corbels and merlons, is a large crenelated tower, with a monumental portal.

Convent of Monte Senario
A road that splits off from the Statale 65, on a line with Vaglia, leads up (7.2 km.) to the convent, climbing and winding to an altitude of 815 m. Built in 1234 by the seven Florentine noblemen who founded the order of the Servi di Maria, or Servites, this convent was enlarged and renovated repeatedly between the 15th and 19th c. Overlooking the little square of the complex is the *church of the Addolorata*, built in 1412 but entirely rebuilt at the turn of the 18th c. The facade is preceded by a portico; beside it stands a 17th-c. campanile, which was renovated at the end of the 18th c. The interior – with a single nave and side chapels – is lavishly decorated in the Baroque style, with stuc-

coes on the barrel vault. To the right of the choir is the Cappella dell'Apparizione, or chapel of the Apparition, the oldest section of the convent. On this site in 1240 it is said that the Virgin Mary appeared to the founders of the order of the Servites. In the sacristy, note the 17th- and 19th-c. paintings. To the left of the church is the entrance to the *convent*, with a small 15th-c. cloister. Running all around the complex is a terrace with a fine view of the Mugello valley and the Apennines.

San Piero a Sieve
This small town (elev. 212 m., pop. 3,770) marks a turnoff for traffic from Florence and the Val di Sieve. The modern town extends on flatland around the ancient *Pieve di S. Pietro*, a church that dates from the 11th c. and was repeatedly modified, and then completely transformed in 1776. In the interior, with nave and two aisles, note the *baptismal font* in glazed terracotta, by the school of Giovanni della Robbia. Dominating the old center of town is the 16th-c. *Fortezza di S. Martino* (elev. 337 m.), with massive bastions and ramparts that enclose the keep; this fortress was built at the wishes of Cosimo I to protect the pass over the Apennines.

If you continue along the "Statale 503 del Passo del Giogo," a state road, toward Scarperìa, almost immediately on your left you can make a turn onto the road that runs up to the **Convento del Bosco ai Frati** (elev. 274 m.). This ancient hermitage of the Basiliani (11th c.) was almost entirely rebuilt – at the wishes of Cosimo the Elder – by Michelozzo; this architect's hand can be detected in the portico, with stout columns, set before the facade of the church, and inside, in the

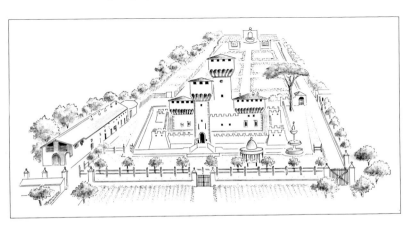

The Medici Villa of Cafaggiolo. This illustration is taken from one of the lunettes painted by Justus Utens in 1599 (Museo di Firenze Com'Era).

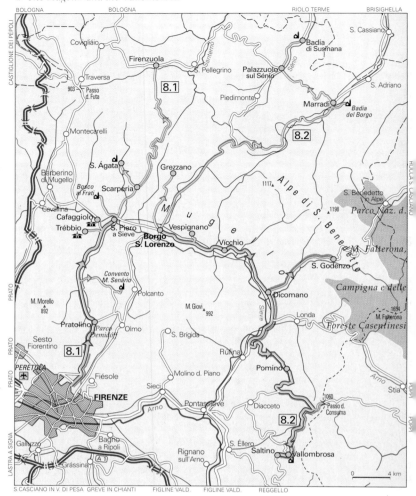

cross-vault covering, with ribbing made of "pietra serena," and in the choir, with its vast polygonal shape. In the adjoining cloister you will find the chapter hall, which has been turned into a museum of religious art; note the wooden *Crucifix*, discovered in 1950 and attributed to Donatello.

Scarperìa

The "borgo" (elev. 292 m., pop. 5,852) is one of the most important small towns in the hollow of the Mugello; here a thriving crafts tradition of knife-smithery is carried on. The town still has the regular medieval walled layout; the walls are still partly visible. It was founded in 1306 by the Florentine Republic, in order to contrast the Ubaldini, feudal lords of the Mugello, and in order to control the roads leading to Bologna. For centuries this was a major way station; it suffered economic decline when the road running over the Passo della Futa was

opened around 1750.

The spacious central square takes its name from the 14th-c. **Palazzo dei Vicari**, with a tall crenelated tower and a facade decorated with numerous heraldic crests of the "Vicari," who once ruled the town; its present-day appearance, however, is the result of careless 19th-c. restorations. The interior is decorated with frescoes dating from the 14th to 16th c. Facing the palazzo is a fresco of the *provostry of St. James and St. Philip*; this work dates from the 14th c., but was completely transformed by restorations and enlargements, during the 19th and 20th c. Inside, with only a single nave, with side altars and a choir with apse, you may admire – among other things – a delicate *Virgin Mary with the Christ Child*, a marble tondo by Benedetto da Maiano. Also overlooking the Piazza dei Vicari is the *Cappella della Madon-*

na di Piazza, a chapel. Inside, beneath the roof vaults, is a panel by Jacopo del Casentino, clearly inspired by Giotto.

With a short detour (3.5 km.) along the cultivated highlands, you will reach *Sant'Agata* (elev. 341 m.), an exceedingly old village; nearby is the **Pieve di S. Agata**, a parish church, the most important and one of the oldest religious buildings (A.D. 984) in the Mugello, made of ashlars with the typical coloring of Tuscan Romanesque. The interior – with nave and two aisles and a truss roof – ends in a choir flanked by two chapels; in the right chapel is a panel by Bicci di Lorenzo (*Marriage of St. Catherine of Alexandria*). At the end of the main road of the little town, in the Centro Polivalente is a *permanent exhibiton* of small "automatons," which reproduce

scenes of daily life in the old days in the village of Sant'Agata.

Just outside of Scarperìa, the state road winds and climbs up to the Passo del Giogo (a pass; elev. 882 m.), and then runs down into the valley of the river Santerno and on the broad mountain hollow of *Firenzuola* (elev. 422 m., pop. 4,844), another "borgo" founded in 1332 by the city of Florence; this settlement too was intended as a blow against the Ubaldini family and an outpost to help control the route across the Apennines. The village was virtually destroyed during WWII, and was entirely rebuilt, to its original regular layout. To the south and the east, part of the ring of walls, with corner bastions and ramparts, has been preserved; these fortifications were designed and built by Antonio da Sangallo the Elder (late-15th c.) for Lorenzo de' Medici.

8.2 From Borgo San Lorenzo to Vallombrosa

This route starts out from Borgo San Lorenzo, a little town connected with Florence by the Via Faentina (Statale 302; 27.8 km.). From here, it turns through the eastern part of the hollow of the Mugello and a stretch of the Val di Sieve, following the state roads Statale 551 and Statale 67; the route then reaches the abbey of Vallombrosa, making use of stretches of pretty bad road (including the so-called Strada di Pomino).

The main route (55.3 km) and the detours suggested alternate stretches of lovely hill country with stern mountain lanscapes, with splendid woods (including the forest of Vallombrosa). Less easy to enjoy – outside the major towns – is the artistic and monumental dimension: the castles and churches that date from the Middle Ages are often inaccessible or badly restored following damage from the earthquake of 1919 and damage during WWII.

Borgo San Lorenzo

This is the most important town in the Mugello (elev. 193 m., pop. 15,285) and it extends over the broad hollow formed by the river Sieve, at the intersection of two main routes of communications; it boasts a solid manufacturing sector. Founded by the Romans, this town was once property of the Ubaldini family and the bishops of Florence before becoming a holding of the city of Florence (late-13th c.). Florence fortified the town in 1351 (portions of the town walls and two of the four gates survive).

Not far from the central Piazza Garibaldi, with the facade – studded with heraldic crests – of the rebuilt *Palazzo Pretorio*, is the Romanesque **Pieve di S. Lorenzo**, a parish

church (1263), with a 13th-c. hexagonal campanile. Inside, amidst the nave and two aisles with pillars and columns, note the major artworks, including a panel with a *head of the Virgin Mary*, believed to be a youthful work by Giotto (ca. 1300). From Piazza Garibaldi, follow Corso Matteotti and you will reach the 18th-c. sanctuary, the *Santuario del Santissimo Crocifisso dei Miracoli*, rebuilt following the earthquake of 1919; inside, 18th- and 19th-c. canvases. In the adjoining chapel, note the remarkable polychrome wooden *Crucifix* (14th c.), long believed to be miraculous.

At a distance of 7.5 km, near the town of *Grezzano* (elev. 358 m.), an old farm house has been used to house the *Museo della Civiltà Contadina*, or museum of peasant culture; the museum displays farm tools, everyday objects, and machinery, all still functional.

If you follow the state road Statale 302 northward, you will come to the exceedingly old *Pieve di S. Giovanni Maggiore* – a parish church rebuilt (16th c.) and transformed (19th/20th c.) – with an original octagonal bell tower (11th c.). Further along, in Ronta, is the *church of S. Michele* (18th c.), with interesting altar pieces dating from the 17th/18th c. After you cross the Colla di Casaglia (elev. 913 m.), you descend (after 36 km.) to the picturesque village of **Marradi** (elev. 328 m., pop. 3,895), set on a number of different levels, and studded with aristocratic palazzi and old homes. A short detour will take you to the *Badia del Borgo*, an ancient religious complex that was rebuilt in the mid-18th c., except for the Romanesque campanile (note the collection of paintings by the Maestro di Marradi).

From Marradi, split off from the Statale 302, and continue on toward **Palazzuolo sul Senio** (elev. 437 m., pop. 1,323; 11.5 km. from Marradi), a popular holiday resort. In the 14th-c. *Palazzo dei Capitani*, with a distinctive corner portico and raised entrance way, is the *Museo della Civiltà Contadina e Artigiana*, a museum of peasant ways and crafts.

The Val di Sieve

If, from Borgo San Lorenzo, you follow the state road Statale 551, you will reach *Vicchio* (elev. 203 m., pop. 6,271), a town with an old center surrounded by five-sided walls (still visible); this was the home of Fra Angelico. In fact the town *museum* is named after "Beato Angelico"; this museum however has none of Angelico's work, but rather religious art from the Mugello area. Three km. before Vicchio is the turnoff for *Vespignano* (elev. 264 m.), where you can see the *birthplace of Giotto*; there is a collection of documents and memorabilia of Giotto's life.

At the edge of the town of *Dicomano* (elev. 162 m., pop. 4,570) – an ancient medieval "borgo," or village, rebuilt after WWII – is the Romanesque *Pieve di S. Maria* (11th c. parish church), with a massive campanile. Inside, in the nave and two aisles, are many canvases and panels from the 15th to 18th c. On the far side of town is the *Oratorio di S. Onofrio* (late-18th c.), a Neoclassical building, with an Ionic pronaos, and a lovely interior (being restored).

From Dicomano, a detour along the Statale 67 will take you to *San Godenzo* (elev. 404 m., pop. 1105), a picturesque little town perched on a tall crag, and dominated by the Benedictine **Badia**, or abbey, of **S. Godenzo**. The abbey was founded in the 11th c., enlarged in the 12th c., and repeatedly renovated (17th and 18th c.). Inside, note the nave and two aisles set on square pillars and the three-apse presbytery, raised over the crypt, as well as a wooden statue of *St. Sebastian*, by Baccio da Montelupo (1506).

As you descend the valley of the Sieve, after Scopeti you continue to the left along the road that runs up to *Pomino* (elev. 585 m.) (Romanesque *Pieve di S. Bartolomeo*, from the 12th c., with facade and campanile from the earliest 13th c.). Further along, you will pass the *Fattoria del Palagio*, a late-16th-c. villa; you will then turn onto the state road ("statale") toward and over the Passo della Consuma.

Forest of Vallombrosa*

Numerous – and all charming – are the roads that run through the stupendous forest of Vallombrosa, one of the most notable areas in the Florentine mountains; since 1973 it has been an Italian "Riserva Biogenetica Naturale," literally, natural biogenetic preserve, extending across the western slope of the massif of the Pratomagno for roughly 2,400 hectares; it consists largely of the pine trees planted by the monks of the abbey, to replace the original beech and chestnut trees.

Abbey of Vallombrosa

Immersed in the age-old forest, this abbey is the original home of the Vallombrosan congregation, an offshoot of the Benedictine order, founded by St. Giovanni Gualberto in the 11th c., taking inspiration from two different religious ideals: Benedictine cenobitism and hermitry. Giovanni Gualberto, a Benedictine monk, retired with a few followers to Vallombrosa, creating the first core of the cenobium and tested a radically new approach: isolated in the Apennine forest, the monks readied themselves in prayer for their upcoming venture into life in Florence, and in particular, for their battle against simony, the practice of buying or selling church offices and preferences. The abbey expanded greatly over time thanks to the support of the Florentine Republic, and it also acquired considerable political power. Following the events of the 19th c. (Napoleonic suppression of the monastery, municipal seizure of the estate), between 1949 and 1963, the Vallombrosan congregation progressively regained ownership of the monastic complex.

A rusticated portal in the elegant 17th-c. facade, by Gherardo Silvani, leads into an open atrium, with the front elevation of the *church*, also by Silvani, dominated by the 13th-c. bell tower. The interior, chiefly Baroque in appearance, built to a Latin-cross plan, preserves the outer walls of the Romanesque construction; on the walls, 18th-c. canvases; behind the main altar, wooden 15th-c. *choir*. In the Renaissance sacristy, note panel by Raffaellino del Garbo (*St. Giovanni Gualberto and other saints*, 1508); from here you can enter the *monastery* (open only by appointment).

A short walk takes you past several chapels (badly neglected), dedicated to events or personages from the history and mythology of the congregation, reaching the *Eremo delle Celle*, a hermitage that was known as the *Paradisino*. From here you can enjoy a panoramic view of the abbey.

A detour (1.6 km) to the right of the monastery runs to the *Saltino*, or "little leap" (elev. 995 m.), the earliest resort built in the Pratomagno.

9 The Valdarno and the Monte Albano

The valley of the Arno in its middle course can be split up into four areas: upstream of Florence, the Valdarno Superiore (on the right bank of the river) and the Pian di Rìpoli (a strip of territory between the river and the hills of Chianti); downstream of Florence, the Florentine plains, which the Gola della Golfolina divides from the Valdarno Inferiore.

In this long and narrow strip of territory, between the 13th and 14th c., a series of "terre murate," or walled towns, were founded (Figline, Signa, Lastra a Signa, Montelupo, Empoli, Fucecchio), fortified villages strategically located over the main routes of the period.

Beginning in the 19th c., the Valdarno Superiore – previously a farming preserve belonging to the city of Florence – became an industrial area, resulting in a vast difference in the valley floor. The ancient equilibrium between man and nature can now only be found on the surrounding hills.

Even the Monte Albano – a range of hills (maximum elevation 633 m.) running NW to SE, which divides the plain between Florence and Pistoia from the lower Valdarno Empolese – in its agrarian economy, largely devoted to wine-making, has a lovely landscape, with historical landmarks dating back to the Etruscans.

9.1 From Florence to Figline Valdarno

This route starts out from the bridge, or Ponte S. Niccolò (10 E1) and runs through the upper Arno valley, or Valdarno Superiore, following the main thoroughfare of the "Via Aretina" (Statale 67 Tosco Romagnola and Statale 69 di Val d'Arno). The drive (41.7 km.), after you emerge from the outskirts of the regional capital, runs up the right bank of the river Arno as far as Incisa, then crosses the river and ends at Figline Valdarno. Of particular historic and monumental importance is the medieval "Via Setteponti" (a variant on the Statale 69 in the stretch from Sant'Ellero to Figline). The riv-

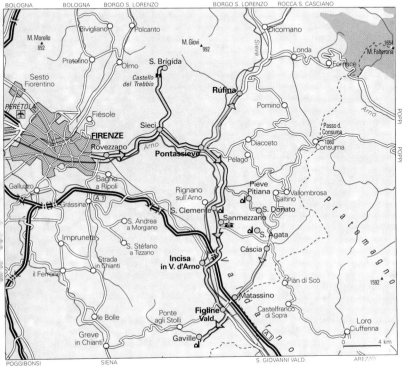

Mills at Rovezzano

er plain is now heavily industrialized, while the surrounding hilly and mountainous areas have a great deal of charm, and are largely unspoilt.

Rovezzano

This outlying village, elev. 58 m., features the ancient *church of S. Michele a Rovezzano*, renovated in 1840, with a stone *portal* attributed to Baccio d'Agnolo. Inside, note the *Virgin Mary Enthroned*, a panel by the Maestro della Maddalena (late-13th c.).

As you continue along the Via Aretina you drive past the park and the stables of the *Villa Favard*, built by Baccio d'Agnolo.

S. Giovanni Battista a Rèmole

Along the Statale, or state road, at the center of the town of *Sieci* (elev. 80 m.), stands the Romanesque parish church (11th/12th c.), with a tall campanile. Inside, nave and side-aisles with square pillars; also, *Virgin Mary Enthroned with Christ Child, Angels and Saints*, a panel of the 13th-c. Florentine school.

As you enter Sieci, a detour on the left leads to Molino del Piano and, on the road for Santa Brigida, to the **Castello del Trebbio** (not open to the public), a 13th-c. construction, rebuilt in the 15th c.

From *Pontassieve* (elev. 108 m., pop. 20,439), a detour along the Statale 67 leads (in 7.5 km.) to *Rùfina* (elev. 115 m., pop. 5,922), a town known for its wines; in the late-16th-c. *Villa di Poggio Reale* is the *Museo della Vite e del Vino*, a museum of wine making.

The "Via Setteponti"

This is the old and winding "Cassia Vetus," a parallel and alternative route to the Statale 69 (crossroads on a line with Sant'Ellero); it runs from Donnini to Figline Valdarno, skirting the slopes of the Pratomagno, in a farming landscape, with terraces cultivated in olive trees and grape vines. There is an interesting succession of medieval churches:

the *Pieve Pitiana*, with Romanesque campanile and 16th-c. portico (inside, an *Annunciation* on panel, attributed to Ridolfo del Ghirlandaio); in the village of San Donato, note the *church of S. Donato in Fronzano*, renovated in the 17th/18th c.; at Pietrapiana, on a secondary road, note the Romanesque *Pieve di S. Agata in Arfoli* (12th/13th c.), flanked by a 13th-c. cloister; it features 15th-c. paintings and a sandstone *pluteus* (8th/9th c.); lastly, in the village of Cascia, the Romanesque *Pieve di S. Pietro* (end of the 12th c./beginning of the 13th c.); inside, nave and two side-aisles, set on monolithic columns with noteworthy capitals, a triptych with the *Virgin Mary Enthroned, the Christ Child, and Adoring Angels, between St. Bartholomew, St. Blaise, St. Juvenal, and St. Anthony**, the first known painting by Masaccio (1422).

If you keep to the state road ("statale,") you will see, on your left, the *church of S. Clemente a Sociana*, which features a marble relief (*Virgin Mary with Christ Child*) attributed to Antonio Rossellino. Further along, also on the left, you can look up to the *Villa di Sammezzano* (now a hotel), a 19th-c. transformation, in the Romantic eclectic style, of a castle dating from the high Middle Ages; note the English-style park. You will then reach *Incisa in Val d'Arno* (elev. 122 m., pop. 5,312), a village set in a canyon dug out by the river, with a few houses dating back, in part, to the Middle Ages.

Figline Valdarno

The town (elev. 126 m., pop. 15,699), with one of the most interesting townscapes in the entire Florentine territory, has an old center that is still entirely surrounded by 14th-c. walls. Once known as the "bread-basket of Florence," it is now a major industrial center.

In the centrally located *Piazza Marsilio Ficino*, with porticoes, note the 17th-c. *loggia* of the old Ospedale Serristori, a hospital; on the opposite side is the *Collegiata di S. Maria* (a collegiate church founded in 1252-57), which contains a cusped 14th-c. panel (*Virgin Mary Enthroned with Christ Child, among angels, St. Elizabeth of Hungary and St. Louis of Toulouse*) by the Maestro di Figline. In the adjacent Piazza S. Francesco d'Assisi are the 14th-c. *Palazzo Pretorio*, rebuilt with eclectic taste in the 1930s, and, with portico extending before it, the **church of S. Francesco**, documented as far back as 1229 but rebuilt during the 14th c. Inside, there is just the nave, covered with a truss roof, with 15th-c. frescoes. You will then return to Piazza Marsilio Ficino, and then you will follow Corso Mazzini, at the end of which stands the old *Villa di S. Cerbone*, rebuilt in the 16th and 17th c. Since 1890 it has housed the *Ospedale Serristori*, a hospital; note the interesting pharmacy – from the old hospital on the square – with majolica vases, glass, and paintings.

From the Ospedale Serristori a road runs past Gaville and reaches (in 6.5 km.) the **Pieve di S. Romolo**, which dates back to the 12th or 13th c., with an older campanile (11th/12th c.); inside, note the capitals. In the rectory is the *Museo della Civiltà Contadina*, or museum of peasant culture, which contains traditional furniture and tools used in the Tuscan countryside.

9.2 From Florence to Rosano

This short route (15.4 km.) also runs from the bridge, or Ponte S. Niccolò (12 B3), up the left bank of the Arno as far as Rosano (Via di Rìpoli, Strada Provinciale 1 Aretina and, from Bagno a Rìpoli, Via di Rosano). The section that is closest to Florence has been changed by the creation of new settlements and by the opening of modern thoroughfares. After you reach the terminus of the route, you can take a bridge to reach Pontassieve, and then rejoin the preceding route.

Badia di Rìpoli
Arrayed along the Via di Rìpoli is the oldest monastery in the territory around Florence (7th/8th c.). The church, with a 16th-c. portico, has a cusped campanile; inside, paintings dating from the 16th/18th c.
A little further along, on the right, is the *Quartiere di Sórgane*, built in the 1960s, with a number of notable buildings, like large urban sculptures.

Pieve di S. Pietro a Rìpoli
The Romanesque church, documented as far back as the 13th c., has a nave and two side aisles, a colorful truss roof, and 14th-c. frescoes.

If you continue straight, you will reach the town of *Bagno a Rìpoli* (elev. 75 m., pop. 27,382), where there is a small archeological area, with ruins of Roman buildings (one of which may have been a bath house) and of a large cistern, dating from the Empire (to see it, contact the Gruppo Archeologico, Via della Nave 1).

From here, as you shift toward the Via di Rosano, you will encounter a short detour through Vicchio di Rimaggio, where you should stop to visit the little **church of S. Lorenzo** (12th c.), with 14th-c. frescoes and a panel (*Virgin Mary with Christ Child*) dating from around 1300.

S. Donnino
In the village of *Villamagna* (elev. 326 m.), accessible along a detour of 4.3 km. from Candeli, you will find the simple and stern 10th-c. Romanesque parish church, or *Pieve di S. Donnino*. Inside are major works of art: triptych by Mariotto di Nardo (*Virgin Mary with Christ Child and Saints*, 1395) and *Virgin Mary with Christ Child, between St. Gerard and St. Donnino* by Francesco Granacci (ca. 1520-30).

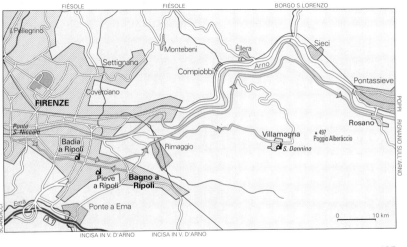

Monastery of S. Maria a Rosano

Before reaching *Rosano* (elevation 84 m.), the Via di Rosano runs along the banks of the river Arno, skirting, on the left, the *Gualchiere di Rèmole*, a significant piece of industrial archeology (14th/15th c.), the only building surviving of the complex devoted to the "gualcatura" (strengthening of fabrics) which once stood along the river banks.

This Benedictine monastery, surrounded by the houses of the little village, is said to have been founded in A.D. 780; the structures that you can see date back to the 12th/13th c., 16th, and 18th c. (inhabited by cloistered nuns; strict limitations on the tour). The church, renovated repeatedly over the centuries, has been restored to its medieval structure; on the facade, 16th-c. portal; alongside it, bell tower from the 12th c. Inside – nave and two side aisles, truss roof – note the *triptych* by Giovanni del Ponte (1434) and the *Crucifix with Stories of the Passion* by the Maestro di Rosano (12th/13th c.).

9.3 From Florence to Vinci

The territory through which this route runs (44.8 km.), to the NW of Florence and on the right bank of the Arno, presents a diverse array of environmental features: as far as Poggio a Caiano it is reasonably flat and heavily developed; thereafter, one runs along the southern slopes of the Monte Albano, a range of hills of considerable charm and natural beauty.

The main thoroughfare of this route – which begins not far from Perétola – is the Statale 66 Pistoiese (6 B-C1-2), as far as Poggio a Caiano; in the second section of the route, you will take provincial roads, which are in some places steep and twisting, but which offer spectacular views.

Worthy of note, although not officially part of the route, is the *church of the Autostrada del Sole* (*S. Giovanni Battista*, or St. John the Baptist), one of the best known and most successful creations of Giovanni Michelucci (1961-68), located in the service area of the Firenze Nord highway station.

The Piana del Bisenzio

At the mouth of the Statale 66 stands the suburban town of *Perétola* (elev. 40 m.), the site of the airport, or *Aeroporto "Ameri-go Vespucci"*. In Piazza Garibaldi (6 B1) is the *church of S. Maria* (12th c.), restored in 1888, with a marble and glazed terracotta *ciborium* by Luca della Robbia (1441-43). Other towns in this same plain are *Brozzi* (elev. 36; with the *Pieve di S. Martino*, dating back before the year 1000, but rebuilt in the 15th and 17th c.), and *San Donnino* (elev. 36 m.). Here, standing in the main square, is the *church of S. Andrea a Brozzi*, of early origin; inside, note the *triptych* by the Maestro dell'Annunciazione di Brozzi, *Crucifix* by Giovanni di Francesco, an aedicule with frescoes by Davide and Domenico Ghirlandaio.

A detour of 2.5 km. from the Statale, or state road, leads to *Campi Bisenzio* (elev. 38 m., pop. 34,444), an apparently modern town with traces of the older settlement (*Palazzo Pretorio* and *Pieve di S. Stefano*, both in the Piazza Matteotti). After the bridge over the Bisenzio, note the *Rocca degli Strozzi*, a 15th-c. residence that was transformed into a large farmhouse in the 17th c.

The Medici Villa of Poggio a Caiano*

On the Via Pistoiese, which runs through

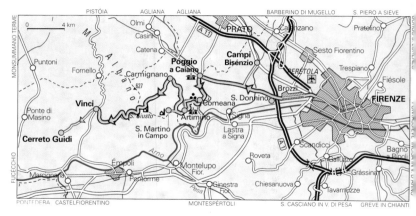

he town of *Poggio a Caiano* (elev. 45 m., oop. 7,941), is the entrance to the splendid villa, once a medieval fortress, purchased (around 1480) by Lorenzo the Magnificent, and rebuilt by Giuliano da Sangallo. The ouilding – prototype of the vacation villas of Humanistic inspiration – was later renovated: the original entrance stairway, with straight ramps of stairs, was replaced with a 19th-c. stairway with curving ramps.
On the second floor, the central *Salone*, or great hall, is covered with a stupendous oarrel vault with gilt coffering, decorated by Andrea Feltrini and by Franciabigio (1518); on the walls is a *series of frescoes* * (Andrea del Sarto, Franciabigio, and Pontormo, 1519-21; Alessandro Allori, 1579-82), celebrating the glories of the Medici. From the terrace adjoining the loggia you can see a modern copy of the *frieze* * on the pediment (the original will be placed on the interior), in enameled terracotta in a bas-relief, attributed to Andrea Sansovino.

The Etruscan Tombs of Comeana

In the territory of this town (elev. 51 m.) there are major Etruscan relics, mostly tombs: the *Tomba dei Boschetti* (along the climb up toward the town, near the cemetery) is a double-chamber structure that dates back to the 7th c. B.C.; the mound, or *Tumulo di Montefortini* (on the road to Signa) features two tombs, one of which – with a double chamber covered by a false vault – can be toured.

Medici Villa of Artimino*

On a hill across from Artimino is the lovely *villa* known as *La Ferdinanda*, the "villa dei cento camini," or the villa of the 100 chimneys. Built by Bernardo Buontalenti for Ferdinando I de' Medici (1594-98), and frequented by the grand ducal court for hunting expeditions, the villa has a broad facade extending between two scarped corner towers.
In the cellars of the villa is a temporary installation of the *Museo Archeologico Comunale*, which chiefly features Etruscan artifacts (including a *krater* and a *thurible*) from the surrounding area and from other necropolises in the zone.
After the village of *Artimino* (elev. 260 m.), you will see the Romanesque parish church, or **Pieve di S. Leonardo**, founded – according to tradition – by the Countess Mathilda (1107); before it extends a portico, and it is marked by a tall bell tower and three apses with small arches.
Another interesting church is (at a distance of 1.5 km.) *S. Martino in Campo* (originally

The Medici Villa of Artimino

dating from the 10th/11th c., and rebuilt in the 12th c.), with a handsome apse.

Carmignano

The town (elev. 189, pop. 9,584) is dominated by the ruins of the old castle, destroyed by the Florentines in 1228. The *church of S. Michele* (13th c.), with its Renaissance portico, features a notable *Visitation* *, a masterpiece by Pontormo (ca. 1528-30).
Along the road to Vinci, if you pass Santa Cristina a Mezzana, you will see the Romanesque *Badia di S. Giusto* (12th c.), with marble inlays on the facade.

Vinci

This town (elev. 97 m., pop. 13,747) is well known as the birthplace of Leonardo. The **Castello dei Guidi** (12th c.), with its unusual almond shape, contains the notable *Museo Leonardiano*, with a series of models of machines, clocks, and instruments, built to plans by Leonardo himself. The visit is completed by a tour of the *birthplace of Leonardo*, at Anchiano (2.5 km. to the north).

At a distance of 5.4 km. is *Cerreto Guidi* (elev. 123 m., pop. 8,953), with its distinctive circular layout, culminating in the **Villa Medicea**, or Medici villa, to which immense ramps lead – the so-called *Ponti Medicei* – built by Alfonso Parigi the Elder to plans by Buontalenti. Both sumptuous and austere, it was built in 1565-67 for Cosimo I de' Medici.

9.4 From Florence to Fucecchio

This route (41 km.) runs from Piazza Taddeo Gaddi (9 C4) and through the Valdarno Inferiore along the main thoroughfare of the Statale 67 Tosco Romagnola. The first section of the route, of minor interest, is within the greater Florence area, and is largely outskirts, with the large town of *Scandicci* (elev. 47 m., pop. 53,523); the intense buildup continues as far as Le Signe, and it is not until the next stretch of road, along the winding course of the river Arno, that the route once again becomes lovely and scenic.

The second part of this route runs through a series of major medieval "terre murate" or walled towns: Montelupo and Empoli on the left bank of the Arno, Fucecchio on the right bank.

Badia di S. Salvatore a Settimo

This vast complex – accessible from the Statale 67 with a 2-km. detour that first runs past the parish church, or *Pieve di S. Giuliano a Settimo* (12th c.), with a 17th-c. portico – is documented as early as A.D. 988; Cistercian monks renovated the church, with a nave and two side aisles and with a truss roof, and added a rose window to the facade, as is their custom. Inside, among other things, note the *tabernacle* by Giuliano da Maiano and 17th-c. frescoes by Giovanni da S. Giovanni, as well as a rare *sarcophagus* from the high Middle Ages.

Lastra a Signa

This large town (elev. 36 m., pop. 17,416) still features the urban layout and walls built in 1377 by the Florentine Republic, to create a stronghold against the Pisans, with more reinforcement carried out later by Brunelleschi. In Corso Manzoni note the *church of S. Maria alla Lastra* (1404), transformed in the 17th and 18th c. On the central Piazza Garibaldi is the elegant *Ospedale di S. Antonio* (1411), believed to be a youthful work of Brunelleschi, with a seven-arcade loggia.

Pieve di S. Martino a Gangalandi

This church – a short distance from Lastra in the direction of Empoli – is a Romanesque construction (12th c.), remodeled in several phases. Inside, in the Cappella del Battistero, frescoed by Bicci di Lorenzo and school (1433), note the marble *baptismal font* (1423); the apse is attributed to Leon Battista Alberti.

In the small adjoining *Museo Vicariale*, there is, among other artwork, a painting by Lorenzo Monaco (*Madonna dell'Umiltà*).

Just beyond Lastra a Signa, on a line with Ponte a Signa, on the far side of the river Arno, stands the large industrial town of *Signa* (elev. 46 m., pop. 14,375). We should point out here, in the upper section of the town, the *church of S. Maria in Castello*, documented as early as A.D. 746; in the lower section, in the Piazza Cavour, the *Pieve di S. Giovanni Battista*, with a facade in the distinctive 15th-c. style, and the *Oratorio di S. Lorenzo*, an oratory rebuilt in the 12th c., which features a handsome *pulpit* (12th c.).

After Ponte a Signa, the Statale runs along the winding course of the river Arno and enters the *Gola della Golfolina*, a canyon carved out by the river over the course of the millennia; at the narrowest point, an enormous sandstone boulder forms a small grotto, with dates carved in the stone from the 16th and 17th c.

Montelupo Fiorentino

This large village (elev. 35, pop. 10,064), renowned ever since the Middle Ages for its production of ceramics, was fortified (castle) in 1203 by the Florentines as a stronghold against the Pistoian Capraia, across the river Arno.

In Via Baccio Sinibaldi you will see the *Pieve di S. Giovanni Evangelista*, rebuilt in 1756, with a handsome panel painting from the workshop of Botticelli; immediately after is the 14th-c. *Palazzo del Podestà*, with a portico and loggia adorned with heraldic crests; this is the site of the *Museo Archeologico e della Ceramica*, with prehistoric exhibits and Italian ceramic products, from antiquity to the 18th c. At the summit of the hill is the priory, or *Prioria di S. Lorenzo*, with 13th-c. frescoes.

Across the river Pesa is a **Medici villa** known as the **Ambrogiana**, with a square plan and corner towers, built at the orders of Ferdinando I and designed by Buontalenti (closed to the public).

Empoli

The city (elev. 28, pop. 43,522), extending over the plain on the left bank of the Arno, lies at the intersection of several main thoroughfares, and is a major commercial and industrial center (clothing, glass). The ancient center features the remains of 15th-c. walls.

After a tour of the historical center, a long detour leads to the western outskirts of town, where, at the end of the Via della Repubblica, you will see the church of S. Maria a Ripa.

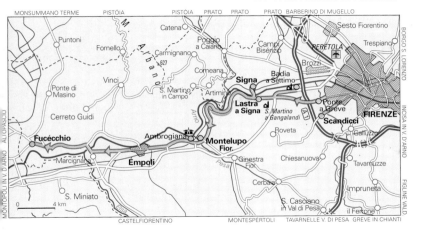

Collegiata di S. Andrea. All that survives of the Romanesque structure is the lower section of the facade, with five arches; the upper section was completed in the 18th c. The campanile is a faithful reconstruction of the Romanesque-Gothic original – destroyed in WWII – with a 17th-c. cusp. The interior, which was also badly damaged, is a restoration of the 18th-c. version; at the main altar, note a triptych by Lorenzo di Bicci and Bicci di Lorenzo.

Museo della Collegiata. This museum contains artworks by Florentine and Tuscan artists, especially from the 14th and 15th c., including: *Christ, in "pietà"*, a fresco, detached, by Masolino da Panicale (hall I); two sculptures of the *Virgin Mary with the Christ Child*, by Tino di Camaino and Mino da Fiesole (hall II); three *Virgins Mary*, by Bicci di Lorenzo, Lorenzo Monaco, and Filippo Lippi (hall IV); two monumental wooden *tabernacles*, respectively by Antonio Rossellino and Francesco Botticini (hall V) and by Francesco Botticini with his son Raffaello (hall VI).

S. Stefano. This church was built in the 14th c., and was frescoed after 1424 by Masolino da Panicale and his workshop (fragments survive in the 1st and 4th chapels on the right and in the right transept). Among the other artworks, note the *Annunciation*, a masterpiece of sculpture by Bernardo Rossellino (ca. 1447), an *Adoration of the Shepherds* by Passignano, and *St. Nicholas of Tolentino Protects Empoli from the Plague* by Bicci di Lorenzo.

S. Maria a Ripa. Documented as early as the 12th c., this church is marked by a Renaissance portico with fragments of 17th-c. frescoes. Inside are artworks by Empoli, Benedetto and Santi Buglioni, and Giovanni Antonio Sogliani.

Fucecchio

A market and manufacturing town (elev. 25, pop. 20,540), Fucecchio dates from the 10th c. and was a free Commune, before yielding (1330) to Florence. The tour focuses on the Piazza Vittorio Veneto, overlooked by a number of historical buildings: the former *Villa Corsini*, which will soon house the Museo Cittadino, or town museum; the *Palazzo del Podestà*, with a portico and with heraldic crests; the exceedingly old *Collegiata di S. Giovanni Battista*, with a stairway, heavily renovated in the 18th c. In the adjoining scenic square stands the *Abbazia di S. Salvatore*, an abbey founded in the 10th c.

10 The Florentine Chianti Region and the Valdelsa

Chianti is a hilly, wine-growing region set between Florence and Siena and, in the modern-day significance of the name, it extends approximately from the mountains – the Monti del Chianti – on the left slope of the Valdarno Superiore to the valley of the river Elsa.

This region is a vast expanse of hills crisscrossed with valleys, which originate from the Chianti mountain chain. The landscape is for the most part wooded, in some areas with sharp slopes that are not particularly well suited for farming; all the same, the work of generations of peasants has shaped and transformed the land, succeeding finally in making it productive. The transformation of agriculture in the Chianti area, which began in the middle of the 1960s, led to the reconstitution of the heritage of vines yielding wine grapes in this region, with modernization and mechanization; as a result, there has been a modification in the structure of the agrarian landscape: the dense mosaic of "poderi mezzadrili," or small lots farmed by family units, has been infiltrated by major specialized vineyards run by large corporations.

The area that produces the Chianti Classico "Gallo Nero" – a wine blended from four fundamental grapes (Sangiovese, Malvasia, Trebbiano, and Canaiolo) – was established officially in 1932 and includes the townships of Greve, Castellina, Radda, and Gaiole, and part of the territories of San Casciano in Val di Pesa, Tavarnelle, Barberino Val d'Elsa, Poggibonsi, and Castelnuovo Berardenga.

The Palazzo Pretorio in Certaldo

Prior to the 13th c., the regional term "Chianti" indicated nothing more than a valley, in Siennese territory. At the turn of the 13th c., the surrounding area – corresponding roughly to the modern-day towns of Radda, Gaiole, and Castellina – was bitterly fought over by Siena and Florence, and was finally conquered by the latter city, which organized it into an administrative district, assigning it as an emblem a black rooster, which nowadays adorns the bottles of the Consorzio Chianti. Beginning in the 18th c., the term began to be used to indicate a geographic area that was increasingly vast; for the past few decades it has been used generically to refer to the territory between Florence and Siena.

The Valdelsa, running diagonally (from SE to NW) along the western boundaries of the Chianti area, became historically important when traffic from Rome northward through to the Po valley and beyond the Alps in the Middle Ages began to run along the flat flood plain of the river Elsa. The Via Francigena, which was the only international road running the length of the peninsula, was the only route available to pilgrims heading to and returning from Rome, and the same was true of merchants and heavy transport. Because of its strategic importance, the Valdelsa became the theater of continual conflict between Florence and Siena, until Florence finally triumphed definitively.

10.1 From Florence to Panzano

The route recommended here begins from the Badia di Rìpoli (page 135) and makes use of the old Via Chiantigiana, Statale 222, as a thoroughfare running into the classic wine region lying between the Monti del Chianti (to the east) and the Val di Greve (to the west).

After Gràssina, the route runs uphill, winding through switchback curves, until it reaches the panoramic highlands of Strada, running past a succession of buildings, many of them founded long ago; it runs on through a landscape covered with extensive vineyards and studded with isolated farm houses; once you pass the hill, or Poggio di Collegalle, you will descend quickly toward the valley bottom of the river Greve, which then climbs back up and spreads out into the "conca" that contains the village of Greve. The route comes to an end, after 31 km., at the border with the province of Siena, near the village of Panzano.

Of special interest are the landscapes and countryside; most of the detours run through the territory to the east of the main route, which abounds in medieval landmarks and monuments.

Oratorio di S. Caterina dell'Antella
The 14th-c. church stands in the fields near Ponte a Ema. The interior has only a nave, with pointed arch vaults and a square "scarsella," and is decorated with major 14th-c. **frescoes***, including *stories of St. Catherine of Alexandria* and *Evangelists* by Spinello Aretino, and other frescoes by the Maestro di Barberino.

Just outside of the town of Ponte a Ema, a detour running some 2.4 km. leads to *Antella* (elev. 114 m.), in the central square of which stands a parish church, or *Pieve di S. Maria*, a Romanesque structure mentioned as early as the 11th c. and rebuilt in the 13th c., with a campanile with three-light mullioned windows. Inside, a single nave with wooden trusses, 17th-c. altars, and a *Virgin Mary with the Seven Founding Saints* by Lorenzo Lippi (1660).

As you continue along you will reach the local road, or "provinciale" toward Incisa in Val d'Arno, on a line with the village of Osteria Nuova; nearby is the *church of S. Giorgio a Ruballa*, documented as early as 1273 but entirely rebuilt in 1707 (interior) and 1863 (exterior); it possesses two noteworthy 14th-c. works: *Virgin Mary with Christ Child*, *Angels and Saints*, by a painter close to Maso di Banco and a *Crucifix* by Taddeo Gaddi.

The Via di Tizzano
From *Gràssina*, at an elevation of 87 m., a detour branches off (about 9 km.) that runs through a territory which still largely has the traditional features of this area. The road runs past the *Villa di Lappeggi* (now a farm), rebuilt on the site of a Medici family residence, with 16th-c. frescoes. Further along, a branch leading off to the left will take you to the *church of S. Andrea a Morgiano* (11th c.), heavily restored in 1960. From the main road, two further minor detours branch off: to the left, you can reach the *church of S. Bartolomeo a Quarate* (1433-35), totally rebuilt in the 18th c., and the remains of the *Castello di Quarate*, with the noteworthy detail of an olive tree atop the tower; on the right, a dirt road leads to the *church of S. Stefano a Tizzano*, with two small panels attributed to the Cigoli. Lastly, to the north of San Polo in Chianti is the parish church, or *Pieve di S. Miniato di Rubbiana* (11th c.), heavily restored.

Villa l'Ugolino
The Via Chiantigiana passes the front elevation, with its 18th-c. portico; the elegant building as a whole dates from the 17th c. and was built by Gherardo Silvani.

A little further along is the entrance to a golf course known as the *Golf dell'Ugolino*, with 18 holes on rolling terrain, amidst cypresses, pine trees, and olive groves.

After you drive through the town of *Strada in Chianti*, elev. 245 m., you can follow the local road, or "provinciale" toward La Panca, a route of some 7.8 km., remarkably lovely due to the unspoilt nature, with a delicate equilibrium between nature and medieval settlements. Almost immediately, you will see the *Castello di Mugnana* (13th c.), which has been a villa-farm for centuries, with a masonry facing made of small blocks of "alberese" stone. On the opposite side of the valley, you can see the *Castello di Sezzate*, elev. 284 m., a small village of medieval appearance. If you continue, you can see the *Castello di Cintoia*, a rural village – possibly of Longobard origins – which still has its 13th-/14th-c. appearance. Before you reach the town of La Panca, a steep and badly maintained road leads up to the Vallambrosan *Abbey of Montescalari* (now a farm), a large square building containing numerous 17th-c. structures as well as a late-Romanesque church.

Villa-farms in Val di Greve
The presence of villa-farms along the Via Chiantigiana becomes more abundant between Strada and Greve. These are often historical complexes, built upon the remains of medieval castles or 13th-/14th-c. "case da padrone."
In the small town of Le Bolle, a road leads up

(elev. 236 m., pop. 11,139), a modest settlement in the Middle Ages, developed as a market town, because it lay at the intersection between the old Via Chiantigiana and another road linking up with the Valdarno Superiore. The layout of the town still reflects these origins; the town is arranged around the distinctive *Piazza Giovanni da Verrazzano*, a vast elongated triangle, with porticoes that were used to display merchandise. At the end of the square is the parish church, or *Parrocchiale di S. Croce*, rebuilt in the Neoclassical style in the mid-19th c.; inside, note the triptych (*Virgin Mary and Saints*) by Bicci di Lorenzo.

Fortified Villages, or Borghi
Not far from Greve, on the left slope of the valley stands **Montefioralle** (elev. 352 m.), a handsome castle set within medieval walls, lined with narrow cobblestone roads twisting and winding, passageways, and stone buildings. In the center of the town is the *church of S. Stefano*, with noteworthy artworks, including a 13th-c. panel of the *Virgin Mary with Christ Child*.
After leaving Greve, the Via Chiantigiana, after running along the course of the river, runs up the hill upon which **Panzano** extends (elev. 498 m.), a resort standing at the edge of the old center, with the ruins of the castle, a roughly rectangular construction of which two sides survive, along with the entranceway and the tower of the keep.

Pieve di S. Leolino
This parish church, known also as the Pieve di Panzano and documented as early as the 10th c., was rebuilt in handsome Romanesque style; before it extends a 16th-c. portico on slender Tuscan-style columns made of sandstone. Inside, the nave and two aisles feature square pillars and numerous artworks of the Florentine school; in particular, one should note two frescoes (*Baptism* and *Virgin Mary between Two Angels*) by Raffaellino del Garbo, and an exquisite panel with the *Virgin Mary Enthroned, with St. Peter and St. Paul*, attributed to Meliore (second half of the mid-13th c.).

to the hill upon which stands the *Castello di Vicchiomaggio* (13th c.), transformed into a villa in the 16th c.; what survives of the original structure is a 13th-c. tower with a gallery. At the beginning of the town of Greti, a detour leads to the *Castello di Verrazzano*, a villa-farm that stands on the site of a "casa da padrone" (13th c.), which belonged to the family of the great navigator Giovanni da Verrazzano; a crenelated tower survives. From the beginning of the town of Greve you will reach the *Castello di Uzzano*, which preserves much of the enclosure walls, with a rectangular plan; inside, a villa-farm with a monumental appearance.

Greve in Chianti
Situated in a broad valley, this large village

10.2 From Florence to the Pieve di S. Appiano

This route runs from the Porta Romana (11 C3), along the Statale 2, Via Cassia (in the urban section, the Via Senese), the main thoroughfare constituting the route, as far as Barberino Val d'Elsa. This is the first stretch of the "strada regia romana," which was the main artery of communication between

Florence and Rome. After Barberino, this route runs along secondary roads and, at the end of the 37.6 km. distance, reaches the parish church, or Pieve di S. Appiano.
The landscape here is in many ways similar to that of the preceding route, differing only in the fact that overall it is less rural,

and runs past larger towns and as a consequence, the traffic also tends to be slightly more chastic and stressful.

After Tavarnuzze, you climb back up along the course of the river Greve in an increasingly narrow valley, set about by steep hills covered with a woody blanket of cypresses, poplars, oaks, and pine trees, along the edge of the large *Cimitero di Guerra Americano* (American War Cemetery; 1959), a major instance of landscaping. Once you have passed the bridge, or Ponte dei Falciani, the route begins to climb and dip rather more sharply, crossing in succession the hills that separate the valleys of the rivers Greve, Pesa, and Elsa.

The detour along the old Via Certaldese is of interest for its hilly landscape and for the abundance of medieval settlements (from San Casciano to Certaldo). Also significant is the detour along another medieval route, the old route toward Siena called the "strada senese del Sambuco," which allows one to reach the Badia di Passignano and San Donato in Poggio.

San Casciano in Val di Pesa

This little town (elev. 310 m., pop. 16,012), one of the most important places in the Chianti area as far as the production of wine is concerned, still reflects its origins in

The Chianti consortium trademark: a black cock

its urban layout – arrayed around two main thoroughfares that intersect in the center of the town – set at a strategic location at the intersection of the "strada regia romana," or Roman main road, and a cross-route linking up with the Val di Greve. Once the fief of the bishops of Florence, in 1272 it came under the dominion of the Florentine Republic, and a few years later gaining the title of

"capoluogo di podesteria"; in the mid-14th c., it was enclosed by a walled perimeter with a polygonal plan, of which notable traces remain.

From the centrally located Piazza Orazio Pierozzi you will climb up to the *Collegiata di S. Cassiano* (1793-96), with – on the interior, with nave and two aisles – a *Crucifix* from the workshop of Baccio da Montelupo (main altar).

From the same square, take the Via Morrocchesi and you will reach the *church of S. Maria del Prato*, built in the 14th c., transformed in the 17th c., and restored following heavy damage sustained in WWII. Of some interest, inside, is the considerable number of artworks belonging to the Compagnia della Misericordia, now installed in the **Museo della Misericordia**. Note in particular: *pulpit** by Giovanni di Balduccio (1336-39); *Crucifix** by Simone Martini (ca. 1321-25); three panels (*Virgin Mary with Christ Child, St. Peter, St. Francis*) by Ugolino di Nerio.

Starting once again from Piazza Pierozzi, the Via Roma will take you to the former *church of S. Maria del Gesù*, site of the **Museo Vicariale di Arte Sacra**, a museum of sacred art, which features artworks and liturgical objects taken from churches (isolated, abandoned, or demolished) in the surrounding countryside. On the altars, you can see original works, including an exquisite *Virgin Mary with Christ Child* by Lippo di Benivieni (ca. 1310). In the museum area, note two masterpieces of early Tuscan painting: *St. Michael Archangel**, attributed to Coppo di Marcovaldo, and the *Virgin Mary with Christ Child** by Ambrogio Lorenzetti (1319). Of considerable note is a collection of 14th-c. paintings of the *Virgin Mary with Christ Child* and a *Coronation of the Virgin Mary*; note the *carved shaft*, by the Maestro di Cabestany (12th c.).

The Via Certaldese

The old hill road, winding but of particular interest because it is lined by parish churches and "castelli," links San Casciano with Certaldo (it runs over the first 15 km.). In the village of San Pancrazio is an important parish church, or **Pieve di S. Pancrazio a Lucardo** (11th c.), a building in the most archaic Romanesque style, despite the restoration and integration done at the turn of the century; the two surviving apses feature small inset hanging arches, clearly of Lombard derivation. Inside, three aisles set on corner pillars, with the *Madonna del Latte* attributed to Cenni di Francesco (1400) and a *Crucifixion* by Santi di Tito (1590).

in the Lombard Romanesque style, belong to the original construction.

Badia di Passignano

In an isolated and lovely site, accessible from the Via Cassia along a stretch of the "Strada Senese del Sambuco" and a later detour (overall 5.4 km., from the intersection with the state road, or "statale"), stands this major abbey, founded in 1049 in the context of the Vallombrosan reformation. It is a magnificent monastic complex, fortified in the 15th c., with a square plan and corner towers. Overlooking the wide courtyard are the principal buildings, including the *church of S. Michele Arcangelo* (13th c.), built upon an existing Romanesque building, of which the crypt survives. The elevation is faced with long stringcourses of "alberese" stone; note the massive bell tower (largely rebuilt).

The interior, with a single nave on a Latin-cross plan, was rebuilt more than once (16th, 18th, and 19th c.). The lavish frescoes date from the 16th/18th c.: of special note is the decoration of the main chapel (frescoes and paintings), by Passignano (1601), and the frescoes in the left transept (Alessandro Allori, 1581). The church is split up by a handsome wooden screen (1549), adorned with two panels (*Archangels Michael, Raphael, and Gabriel* and a *Nativity*) attributed to Michele di Ridolfo del Ghirlandaio. The wooden *choir* (dating from the same period as the screen) features inscriptions in Greek and Hebrew (Passignano was also a major center for the study of eastern languages).

Before the church is the entrance – through a stone 15th-c. portal, with wooden doors from the same period, carved and inlaid – to the *monastery*, still inhabited by a Vallombrosan community. The monumental rooms that can be seen are: the refectory, with a *Last Supper* by Domenico and Davide Ghirlandaio (1476-77), surmounted by two large 15th-c. lunettes, frescoed by Bernardo di Stefano Rosselli; the old kitchen; the chapter hall.

After descending back down to the "Strada Senese del Sambuco," you can continue on to *San Donato in Poggio*, elev. 418 (at a distance of 5.9 km. from the intersection for the Badia di Passignano), a village that still reveals the structure of the medieval "terre murate," with the enclosure wall and an urban layout crossed by the main thoroughfare, which links the two entrance gates. Just outside of the town is the parish church, or *Pieve di S. Donato in Poggio*, a model for the Romanesque religious architecture of the 12th c. in the territory of Florence. The simple geometric

As you continue you will drive through *Lucardo* (elev. 422 m.), an exceedingly old medieval village (8th c.), with the remains of a *castle* from which you can enjoy a splendid view of the Val di Pesa and the Valdelsa. Adjacent is the *church of S. Martino a Lucardo*, originally Romanesque, with the interior rebuilt and decorated in the 18th c.

After you pass, on your right, the Romanesque *church of S. Donato a Lucardo* and you reach the town of Fiano, a detour to the left along the road toward Tavarnelle leads to the imposing and turreted **Fattoria di S. Maria Novella**, a farm that stands upon the square walled perimeter of a medieval castle (11th c.), later transformed into a fortress.

Once again on the Via Certaldese, you will run past the crossroads, or Bivio del Pozzo, where a brief detour to the left ends at the parish church, or *Pieve di S. Lazzaro a Lucardo* (8th c.), rebuilt after the year 1000 and modified more than once; the three apses, shapes are unadorned by elements of decoration: there is only a facing in stringcourses of "alberese" stone. The interior, with a nave and two side aisles, has three apses and simple pillars; there is a *baptismal font* in glazed terracotta with *stories from the life of St. John the Baptist*, by Giovanni della Robbia (1513), and a number of 14th-c. panels.

Tavarnelle Val di Pesa

This town (elev. 378, pop. 6,911) has the distinctive structure of a "borgo di strada," the product of the convergence of a number of villages scattered along the "via regia romana." Just before the town, a short detour on the left leads to the **Pieve di S. Pietro in Bòssolo**, an old building dating from the earliest Romanesque period. One of the main features of interest of the site is the *Museo d'Arte sacra*, a museum of religious art with collections of local art, located in the Canonica; among the most noteworthy works: three panels (*Virgin Mary with Christ Child and Saints*, *Lamentation over the Dead Christ* and fragments of a third panel) by Neri di Bicci (1473); *Virgin Mary with Christ Child* by Lorenzo di Bicci; *Virgin Mary with Christ Child and Young St. John* by Empoli.

At the far end of the town of Tavarnelle stands a former Franciscan convent, with the *church of S. Lucia al Borghetto* (second half of the 13th c.), one of the finest pieces of Gothic architecture in the area, consisting of a distinctive Franciscan layout with a nave and no side aisles, pointed-arch windows, truss roof, and a square "scarsella." The Neogothic facade dates from the turn of the 20th c. The interior still features fragments of a series of frescoes from the second half of the 14th c.

Pieve di S. Appiano

You reach it by driving through *Barberino Val d'Elsa* (elev. 373 m., pop. 3,542), where the old town center is of considerable interest, perched as it is high in a strategic location upon a hill of the ridge that runs between the Val di Pesa and the Valdelsa and

along the old "via regia romana." It preserves many of the distinctive features of a medieval fortified hilltop settlement, with a nearly elliptical plan, cut diagonally by the main thoroughfare that links the two entrance gates.

Just outside of the town, you leave the Via Cassia and, heading off toward the right through an intensely cultivated countryside punctuated with farmhouses, you will reach the parish church, or Pieve di S. Appiano, one of the oldest Romanesque churches of the Florentine territory. The oldest structures of this church (left aisle and apse), which date from the 11th c., are made of stone, while the rest of the building (12th c.) is made of brickwork, with arches

Barberino Val d'Elsa

set on stout terracotta columns with capitals in the classical style. Inside are fragments of 15th-c. frescoes. Before the church once stood the old baptistery (demolished in 1805, following damage from an earthquake), of which survive only four cross-shaped pillars with capitals carved into symbolic motifs. A variety of archeological material is housed in the small "antiquarium" that stands to one side of the church.

10.3 From Florence to Certaldo

This route, which starts from the village of Galluzzo (page 120) and leads (after 43.6 km.) to the town of Certaldo, is divided sharply into two sections.

The first section, running from the Galluzzo to Castelfiorentino, follows the Strada Provinciale 4, the exceedingly old Via Volterrana, which has linked Volterra with Fièsole ever since the earliest times; this road was of

great importance in the Middle Ages as well, as is indicated by the presence of parish churches and castles. The twisting hillside route – surrounded on the whole by a pristine landscape and with some particularly lovely scenic areas – is lined, especially at the beginning, by numerous monuments and landmarks: the 15th-c. villas, *Villa La Sfacciata* and *Villa Il Melarancio*; the Romanesque

Pieve di S. Alessandro a Giògoli (11th c.); the two handsome 16th-c. villas, *I Collazzi*, built to plans by Santi di Tito, and *I Tàttoli*, surrounded by an Italian-style garden.

The second stretch of this route, from Castelfiorentino to Certaldo, runs along the Statale 429 – the medieval Via Francigena – which runs up the valley floor of the Valdelsa, now dotted with small and medium-sized factories; the traffic is very heavy.

Lastly, of considerable interest, in terms of views and artistic heritage, is the stretch that runs from Certaldo along secondary roads, penetrating into the hilly area on the left bank of the river Elsa, and running through the small towns of Gambassi and Montaione and past the convent of S. Vivaldo.

Pieve di S. Giovanni in Sugana

From *Cerbaia* (elev. 86 m.), a large modern village, you take a short stretch of the road to San Casciano, and then you reach the parish church, or Pieve di S. Giovanni in Sugana, a late-Romanesque construction with only a nave. The interior, renovated in the 16th c., features a *Pietà* in glazed terracotta from the school of Giovanni della Robbia. In the 16th-c. cloister, note the handsome portals made of "pietra serena."

Pieve di S. Pietro in Mercato

Not far from *Montespèrtoli* (elev. 257 m., pop. 9,432), a major market town and wine-making center on the summit of a hill, you will find the Pieve di S. Pietro in Mercato, a house of worship dating from the 11th c., flanked by a bell tower that preserves a Romanesque style: basilican plan, with a nave and two aisles covered with wooden trusses and with three apses. Inside, note 15th- and 16th-c. paintings of the Tuscan school, including a *Virgin Mary with Christ Child and St. Anthony and St. Julian* by Neri di Bicci, and an hexagonally shaped *baptismal font*, decorated with marble intarsia (late 11th c./early 12th c.).

Castelfiorentino

This little town (elev. 50 m., pop. 17,155), capital of the Valdelsa and noteworthy industrial center on the right bank of the river Elsa, consists of a modern section (lower down) and an older settlement (on the high ground), whose importance in the past was linked to its strategic location along the Via Francigena. The early feudal settlement passed over to the Florentines (1149), who fortified it as an outpost against Siena; in 1260, following the great battle of Montaperti, a peace treaty between Florence and Siena was signed here. Much fighting went on here until the first few decades of the 16th c., when its strategic importance began to diminish.

In the lower section of town, at the end of a green and tree-lined square, stands the **church of S. Verdiana**, one of the most significant examples in this region of integration of Baroque architecture and art. Built at the turn of the 18th c., it was later completed with facade (1771), portico (1778), and statues (1810). The interior, designed by Giovanni Battista Foggini, has a nave and two aisles; decorated with 18th-c. frescoes, stuccoes (chapels at the foot of the aisles and nave) and 17th-c. canvases (side altars). Adjoining the church is a small *Pinacoteca*, or gallery, with interesting paintings, among which: two paintings of the *Virgin Mary with Christ Child*, one by an artist midway between Cimabue and Duccio, the other one attributed to Taddeo Gaddi; three small panels depicting *St. John the Evangelist*, *St. Andrew*, and *St. Catherine*, attributed to Jacopo del Casentino.

From the Piazza del Popolo, center of the high section of town, Via Tilli splits off; at n. 41 is the Centro Culturale Comunale, a cultural center, which contains the *Raccolta Comunale d'Arte*, or town art collection, of special interest for the two series of *frescoes** by Benozzo Gozzoli (1484 and 1490), with preparatory drawings; one comes from the Tabernacolo della Visitazione (in Castelfiorentino), the other from the Cappella della Madonna della Tosse (near Castelnuovo d'Elsa).

Overlooking the Piazza del Popolo is the *church of the Ss. Lorenzo e Leonardo*, the old oratory of the Commune, or medieval township, rebuilt more than once (16th/18th c.); note the refined decorative detail in terracotta with the cross (on the right side, up high). After you enter the Via S. Ippolito and climb the facing stairway, you will reach the summit of the hill, dominated by the *Pieve dei Ss. Ippolito e Biagio* (1195), a parish church whose facade is distinguished by a terracotta facing with elements in ceramics; in the campanile are two very old bells. A stretch of the enclosure wall and two towers are all that survive of the medieval fortifications of Castelfiorentino.

Certaldo*

This handsome little town (elev. 67 m., pop. 15,942) of Etrusco-Roman origins comprises a higher and older section (Certaldo Al-

to or Castello), and a lower, more modern area (Certaldo Basso or Borgo), also dating from the Middle Ages (13th/14th c.), which sprang up along the Via Francigena (now Via Roma). The town, once a fief of the counts Alberti, began to lose its independence in 1184, and finally became a subject of Florence in 1293; from 1415 on, it was the site of a vicariate that finally wound up controlling the Val di Pesa and part of the Valdelsa and the Valdarno Inferiore. Certaldo Alto has preserved intact – with its walled perimeter – the medieval city layout, distinguished by the warm red color of its brick architecture. This is the place of origin of the family of Giovanni Boccaccio, who died and was buried here (1375).

The tour of Certaldo Alto – accessible from the Via Roma along the Via del Castello – sets out from the Piazza SS. Annunziata and extends the length of the Via Boccaccio (Casa del Boccaccio, church of Ss. Jacopo e Filippo), and ends at the summit of the hill, in the Piazzetta del Vicariato, near the Palazzo Pretorio.

Casa del Boccaccio (plan below: A2). The house, of which only segments of the original medieval sturcture survive, was rebuilt in period style after the damage sustained in WWII; it houses a library, with precious volumes of all the various editions and

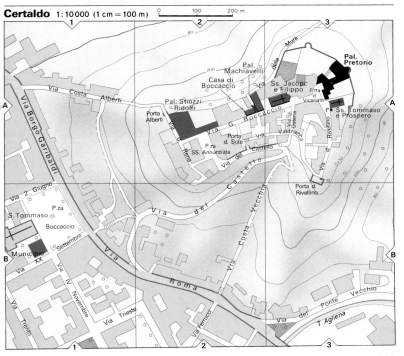

Certaldo 1:10 000 (1 cm = 100 m)

translations of the "Decameron," as well as related studies.

Ss. Jacopo e Filippo (A3). This simple brick church was built at the turn of the 13th c. Inside, in the single nave with semicircular apse, is the Cenotaph of Giovanni Boccaccio; a terracotta Della Robbia altar piece of the *Madonna della Neve*; two remarkable Della Robbia tabernacles (1499 and 1502). Alongside is a 14th-c. cloister, with two registers of columns.

Palazzo Pretorio* (A3). The building that now stands here is a 15th-c. reconstruction of the original 12th-c. building, of which

One of the heraldic shields of the facade

only the donjon survives. The facade, densely adorned with heraldic shields, has two registers of basket-arch windows, and is crowned with a crenelation. Inside, note the frescoes from the 15th and 16th c. The courtyard in the Renaissance style is quite charming, decorated as it is with stone and ceramic heraldic crests; one side is framed by a portico with uneven arches, surmounted by a loggia; under the portico, note the detached 15th-c. frescoes, including a handsome *Annunciation*.

Ss. Tommaso e Prospero (A3). Set next to the Palazzo Pretorio and no longer consecrated, this church dates from the 13th c. Inside, the *Tabernacolo dei Giustiziati* has been reassembled, and is decorated with a major series of **frescoes*** by Benozzo Gozzoli (1466-67) and assistants, depicting the theme of the *Passion of Jesus Christ*.

From the ring road around Certaldo Basso you can take a road that runs over scenic hills swathed in vineyards, leading in 8 km. to *Gambassi Terme* (elev. 332, pop. 4,215), a town long devoted to farming and handicrafts (glassmaking), which has recently become something of a resort (hot springs: Acqua di Pillo). A short detour, in the general direction of Castelfiorentino, will take you to the **Pieve di S. Maria a Chianni** (13th c.), a structure with handsome Pisan-Romanesque and Luccan design, containing a facade with three registers of arches and little blind loggias. In the charming interior, with a nave and two aisles, a raised presbytery and a semicircular apse, note the remarkable capitals with symbolic depictions.

Continuing along, after another 6.5 km., you will reach *Montaione* (elev. 342 m., pop. 3,390), an old "terra murata" which in part preserves the structure of the medieval village (urban layout focusing on three parallel streets, pieces of surviving wall, ruins of towers). In the center of the town is the *church of S. Regolo*, dating from the 12th c. but rebuilt in the 17th c., with a *Virgin Mary and Christ Child*, of the school of Cimabue; next to it stands the *Palazzo Pretorio* (15th c.), with heraldic shields upon the facade.

Just before Montaione, leading from the "strada provinciale" is a winding road that leads to the **Convento di S. Vivaldo**, a handsome Franciscan complex built (15th/16th c.) on the site of a small 14th-c. church, surrounded by a dense wood. The church features a panel depicting the *Virgin Mary and St. John the Baptist, St. Jerome, St. Francis, and St. Vivaldo*, by Raffaellino del Garbo. Adjoining the convent, like in the "sacri monti," or holy hills, of northern Italy, is a series of 16th-c. chapels (now 17, originally, 33), which feature terracotta tableaux, depicting *episodes from the life of Jesus*, largely the creation of local craftsmen.

Information for Travellers:
Hotels, Restaurants, Curiosities

n the listings that follow, the information concerning Florence is split into two sections: *The city within the walls* and, beginning on page 157, *The outlying quarters and the low-lying hills*. Beginning on page 159 is the section dealing, township by township, with the territory around Florence.

The hotels, camping areas, and resort villages recommended here are indicated with official classification, expressed by number of stars as required by the Italian law (from ★★★ to ★). The restaurants listed are accompanied by the customary "fork" ratings, TCI's traditional way of ranking restaurants (from ¶¶¶ to ¶). This classification is based on price, comfort, service, and appeal of the setting. Hotels and restaurants are followed by a capital letter and number (E5) followed by one (or two) bold letters (**ab**) which should refer you to its location on the maps, identified by a number.

Florence
✉ 50100 ☎ 055

i *Tourist information offices, page 26*

The city within the walls

Hotels

★★★★★ **Excelsior.** Piazza Ognissanti 3, tel. 264201, fax 210278. Number of rooms: 192. Air conditioning, elevator; parking area (4, A2, **ac**).

★★★★★ **G.H. Ciga.** Piazza Ognissanti 1, tel. 288781, fax 217400. Number of rooms: 107. Handicap-friendly. Air conditioning, elevator; parking area, special parking garage for guests (4, A1, **ag**).

★★★★★ **Helvetia e Bristol.** Via dei Pescioni 2, tel. 287814, fax 288353. Number of rooms: 52. Air conditioning, elevator; parking area, special parking garage for guests (1, D2, **ao**).

★★★★★ **Regency.** Piazza D'Azeglio 3, tel. 245247, fax 245247. Number of rooms: 35. Air conditioning, elevator; parking garage, garden (3, D6, **bl**).

★★★★★ **Villa Medici.** Via il Prato 42, tel. 2381331, fax 2381336. Number of rooms: 103. Air conditioning, elevator; special parking garage for guests, garden, pool (9, B6, **bu**).

★★★★ **Anglo-American.** Via Garibaldi 9, tel. 282114, fax 268513. Number of rooms: 107. Air conditioning, elevator; special parking garage for guests, garden (9, B6, **e**).

★★★★ **Astoria Palazzo Gaddi.** Via del Giglio 9, tel. 2398095, fax 214632. Number of rooms: 90. Air conditioning, elevator; special parking garage for guests (1, B2, **bi**).

★★★★ **Augustus & dei Congressi.** Vicolo dell'Oro 5, tel. 283054, fax 268557. Number of rooms: 62. Lodging only; no board. Handicap-friendly. Air conditioning, elevator; special parking garage for guests (1, E2-3, **l**).

★★★★ **Berchielli.** Lungarno Acciaiuoli 14, tel. 264061, fax 218636. Number of rooms: 76. Lodging only; no board. Handicap-friendly.

Air conditioning, elevator; special parking garage for guests (1, E2, **o**).

★★★★ **Bernini Palace.** Piazza S. Firenze 29, tel. 288621, fax 268272. Number of rooms: 86. Lodging only; no board. Handicap-friendly. Air conditioning, elevator; parking garage (1, D-E4, **p**).

★★★★ **Brunelleschi.** Piazza S. Elisabetta 3, tel. 562068, fax 219653. Number of rooms: 96. Air conditioning, elevator (1, D3, **q**).

★★★★ **Continental.** Lungarno Acciaiuoli 2, tel. 282392, fax 283139. Number of rooms: 48. Lodging only; no board. Handicap-friendly. Air conditioning, elevator; special parking garage for guests (1, E3, **x**).

★★★★ **Croce di Malta.** Via della Scala 7, tel. 218351, fax 287121. Number of rooms: 98. Handicap-friendly. Air conditioning, elevator; special parking garage for guests, garden, pool (2, F3, **y**).

★★★★ **De la Ville.** Piazza Antinori 1, tel. 2381805, fax 2381809. Number of rooms: 75. Lodging only; no board. Handicap-friendly. Air conditioning, elevator; special parking garage for guests (1, C2, **bw**).

★★★★ **Executive.** Via Curtatone 5, tel. 217451, fax 268346. Number of rooms: 38. Lodging only; no board. Air conditioning, elevator; parking area, special parking garage for guests (9, B-C6, **ad**).

★★★★ **G.H. Baglioni.** Piazza Unità Italiana 6, tel. 23580, fax 2358895. Number of rooms: 196. Handicap-friendly. Air conditioning, elevator; special parking garage for guests (1, B2, **af**).

★★★★ **G.H. Majestic.** Via del Melarancio 1, tel. 264021, fax 268428. Number of rooms: 103. Handicap-friendly. Air conditioning, elevator; parking garage (2, E4, **ah**).

‡ **G.H. Minerva.** Piazza S. Maria Novella 16, tel. 284555, fax 268281. Number of rooms: 99. Air conditioning, elevator; special parking garage for guests, garden, pool (2, E3, **ai**).

‡ **J and J.** Via di Mezzo 20, tel. 2345005, fax 240282. Number of rooms: 19. Lodging only; no board. Handicap-friendly. Air conditioning; parking area, garden (5, A5, **ar**).

‡ **Jolly Carlton.** Piazza Vittorio Veneto 4/A, tel. 2770, fax 294794. Number of rooms: 167. Air conditioning, elevator; pool (9, B5, **at**).

‡ **Kraft.** Via Solferino 2, tel. 284273, fax 2398267. Number of rooms: 78. Air conditioning, elevator; special parking garage for guests, pool (9, B6, **au**).

‡ **Laurus.** Via Cerretani 8, tel. 2381752, fax 268308. Number of rooms: 55. Lodging only; no board. Handicap-friendly. Air conditioning, elevator; special parking garage for guests (1, C2, **av**).

‡ **Lungarno.** Borgo S. Jacopo 14, tel. 264211, fax 268437. Number of rooms: 66. Lodging only; no board. Air conditioning, elevator; special parking garage for guests (1, F2, **ay**).

‡ **Montebello Splendid.** Via Montebello 60, tel. 2398051, fax 211867. Number of rooms: 54. Air conditioning, elevator; special parking garage for guests, garden (9, B6, **bb**).

‡ **Pierre.** Via de' Lamberti 5, tel. 217512, fax 2396573. Number of rooms: 39. Lodging only; no board. Elevator; special parking garage for guests (1, D3, **be**).

‡ **Plaza Hotel Lucchesi.** Lungarno della Zecca Vecchia 38, tel. 26236, fax 2480921. Number of rooms: 97. Air conditioning, elevator; parking area (5, D4-5, **bf**).

‡ **Principe.** Lungarno Vespucci 34, tel. 284848, fax 283458. Number of rooms: 20. Lodging only; no board. Air conditioning, elevator; special parking garage for guests, garden (9, C6, **bg**).

‡ **Ritz.** Lungarno della Zecca Vecchia 24, tel. 2340650, fax 240863. Number of rooms: 32. Lodging only; no board. Air conditioning, elevator; special parking garage for guests (5, D5, **cd**).

‡ **Rivoli.** Via della Scala 33, tel. 282853, fax 294041. Number of rooms: 65. Lodging only; no board. Handicap-friendly. Air conditioning, elevator; special parking garage for guests, garden (2, E2, **bm**).

‡ **Savoy.** Piazza della Repubblica 7, tel. 283313, fax 284840. Number of rooms: 101. Handicap-friendly. Air conditioning, elevator; special parking garage for guests (1, C-D3, **bp**).

‡ **Starhotel Michelangelo.** Viale F.lli Rosselli 2, tel. 2784, fax 2382232. Number of rooms: 138. Handicap-friendly. Air conditioning, elevator; parking area (9, B5, **ba**).

★★★ **Alba.** Via della Scala 22, tel. 211469, fax 288358. Number of rooms: 24. Lodging only; no board. Air conditioning, elevator; special parking garage for guests (2, E2, **a**).

★★★ **Albion.** Via il Prato 22/r, tel. 214171, fax 283391. Number of rooms: 21. Air conditioning, special parking garage for guests (9, B6, **b**).

★★★ **Ambasciatori.** Via Alamanni 3, tel. 287421, fax 212360. Number of rooms: 93. Lodging only; no board. Air conditioning, elevator; special parking garage for guests (2, D2, **c**).

★★★ **Andrea.** Piazza dell'Indipendenza 19, tel. 483890, fax 461489. Number of rooms: 15. Lodging only; no board. Air conditioning, elevator; special parking garage for guests (2, B5, **d**).

★★★ **Aprile.** Via della Scala 6, tel. 216237, fax 280947. Number of rooms: 29, of which 21 have a bath or shower. Lodging only; no board. Elevator; garden (2, E-F3, **g**).

★★★ **Argentina.** Via Curtatone 12, tel. 215408, fax 216731. Number of rooms: 30, of which 27 have a bath or shower. Lodging only; no board. Air conditioning, elevator; special parking garage for guests (9, B-C6, **h**).

★★★ **Arizona.** Via Farini 2, tel. 245321, fax 2346130. Number of rooms: 21. Lodging only; no board. Elevator (3, F5, **i**).

★★★ **Balestri.** Piazza Mentana 7, tel. 214743, fax 2398042. Number of rooms: 50. Lodging only; no board. Air conditioning, elevator; special parking garage for guests (5, D2-3, **n**).

★★★ **Byron.** Via della Scala 49, tel. 280852, fax 213273. Number of rooms: 45. Lodging only; no board. Elevator; parking area (2, E2 **r**).

★★★ **Calzaiuoli.** Via Calzaiuoli 6, tel. 212456, fax 268310. Number of rooms: 46. Lodging only; no board. Handicap-friendly. Air conditioning, elevator (1, D3, **s**).

★★★ **City.** Via S. Antonino 18, tel. 211543, fax 295451. Number of rooms: 18, of which 16 have a bath or shower. Lodging only; no board. Air conditioning, elevator; special parking garage for guests (1, A-B2, **w**).

★★★ **Della Signoria.** Via delle Terme 1, tel. 214530, fax 216101. Number of rooms: 27. Lodging only; no board. Air conditioning, elevator (1, E3, **aa**).

★★★ **Goldoni.** Via Borgo Ognissanti 8, tel. 2396983, fax 282576. Number of rooms: 20. Lodging only; no board. Elevator (4, A2, **al**).

★★★ **Golf.** Viale F.lli Rosselli 56, tel. 281818, fax 268432. Number of rooms: 45. Lodging only; no board. Handicap-friendly. Air conditioning, elevator; parking area (9, A6, **am**).

★★★ **Hermitage.** Vicolo Marzio 1 ang. piazza del Pesce, tel. 287216, fax 212208. Number of rooms: 22. Lodging only; no board. Air conditioning, elevator; special parking garage for guests, garden (1, E3, **ap**).

★★★ **Il Guelfo Bianco.** Via Cavour 29, tel. 288330, fax 295203. Number of rooms: 21. Lodging only; no board. Handicap-friendly. Air conditioning, elevator; special parking garage for guests (3, D2, **aq**).

★★★ **Loggiato dei Serviti.** Piazza SS. Annunziata 3, tel. 289592, fax 289595. Number of rooms: 29. Lodging only; no board. Air conditioning, elevator; special parking garage for guests (3, D3, **ax**).

★★★ **Mario's.** Via Faenza 89, tel. 216801, fax 212039. Number of rooms: 16, of which 15 have a bath or shower. Lodging only; no board. Air conditioning (2, C3, **az**).

★★★ **Palazzo Benci.** Via Faenza 6/r, tel. 213848, fax 288308. Number of rooms: 34. Lodging only; no board. Air conditioning, elevator; garden (1, B2, **bd**).

★★★ **Privilege.** Lungarno della Zecca Vecchia 26, tel. 2341221, fax 243287. Number of rooms: 18. Lodging only; no board. Air conditioning; parking area, special parking garage for guests, garden (5, D5, **bh**).

★★★ **Royal.** Via delle Ruote 52, tel. 483287, fax 490976. Number of rooms: 39. Lodging only; no board. Air conditioning, elevator; parking area, garden (7, F6, **bn**).

★★★ **San Remo.** Lungarno Serristori 13, tel. 2342823, fax 2342269. Number of rooms: 20. Lodging only; no board. Air conditioning, elevator (5, E5, **bo**).

★★★ **Splendor.** Via S. Gallo 30, tel. 483427, fax 461276. Number of rooms: 31, of which 25 have a bath or shower. Lodging only; no board. Elevator (3, B2-3, **br**).

★★★ **Villa Azalee.** Viale F.lli Rosselli 44, tel. 214242, fax 268264. Number of rooms: 24. Lodging only; no board. Handicap-friendly. Air conditioning; special parking garage for guests, garden (9, A6, **bs**).

★★ **Apollo.** Via Faenza 77, tel. 284119, fax 210101. Number of rooms: 15. Lodging only; no board. Air conditioning (2, C3-4, **f**).

★★ **Casci.** Via Cavour 13, tel. 211686, fax 2396461. Number of rooms: 25. Lodging only; no board. Elevator; special parking garage for guests (1, A4, **u**).

★★ **Centro.** Via de' Ginori 17, tel. 2302901, fax 2302902. Number of rooms: 16, of which 13 have a bath or shower. Lodging only; no board. Elevator; special parking garage for guests (2, C-D5, **v**).

★★ **Delle Camelie.** Via di Barbano 10, tel. 490467, fax 461229. Number of rooms: 12, of which 11 have a bath or shower. Lodging only; no board. (2, A-B4, **ab**).

★★ **Desirée.** Via Fiume 20, tel. 2382382, fax 2382382. Number of rooms: 20. Lodging only; no board. Elevator; special parking garage for guests (2, C3, **by**).

★★ **Liana.** Via Alfieri 18, tel. 245303, fax 2344596. Number of rooms: 18. Lodging only; no board. Handicap-friendly. Parking area, garden (10, B1, **aw**).

★★ **Lombardi.** Via Fiume 8, tel. 283151, fax 284808. Number of rooms: 15. Lodging only; no board. Elevator; special parking garage for guests (2, D3, **bz**).

★★ **Mearini.** Via Guelfa 110, tel. 471177. Number of rooms: 9, of which 7 have a bath or shower. Lodging only; no board. (2, B3-4, **ca**).

Restaurants

🍴🍴🍴 **Relais Le Jardin.** Piazza D'Azeglio 3, tel. 2342936, fax 2342936. Closed Sunday. Air conditioning, garden. Fine Tuscan cuisine (3, D6, **bl**).

🍴🍴🍴 **Alle Murate.** Via Ghibellina 52/r, tel. 240618. Closed Monday, August. Air conditioning. Fine cuisine (5, B5, **rw**).

🍴🍴🍴 **Cantinetta Antinori.** Piazza Antinori 3, tel. 292234, fax 2359877. Closed Saturday and Sunday, Christmas-Epiphany (6 Jan.) and August. Air conditioning. Tuscan cuisine (1, C2, **rg**).

🍴🍴🍴 **Don Chisciotte.** Via Ridolfi 4/r, tel. 475430, fax 485305. Closed Sunday and midday on Monday, August. Air conditioning. Fine Tuscan cuisine (2, A-B4, **rn**).

🍴🍴🍴 **Harry's Bar.** Lungarno Vespucci 22/r, tel. 2396700. Closed Sunday, mid-December/Epiphany (6 Jan.). Air conditioning. Tuscan and classical cuisine (4, A-B2, **rq**).

🍴🍴🍴 **Oliviero.** Via delle Terme 51/r, tel. 287643, fax 2302407. Closed Sunday, August. Air conditioning. Fine Tuscan cuisine (1, D-E2, **rx**).

🍴🍴🍴 **Paoli.** Via dei Tavolini 12/r, tel. 216215. Closed Tuesday, for a certain period in August. Tuscan cuisine (1, D3, **sa**).

🍴🍴 **Acquerello.** Via Ghibellina 156/r, tel. 2340554. Closed Thursday. Air conditioning. Florentine cuisine (1, D5, **ra**).

🍴🍴 **Buca Lapi.** Via del Trebbio 1/r, tel. 213768. Closed Sunday, for a certain period between December and January. Tuscan cuisine (1, C2, **rc**).

🍴🍴 **Buca Mario.** Piazza Ottaviani 16/r, tel. 214179. Closed Wednesday, August. Air conditioning. Tuscan cuisine (1, C1, **rd**).

🍴🍴 **Cammillo.** Borgo S. Jacopo 57/r, tel. 212427. Closed Wednesday and Thursday, mid-December/Epiphany (6 Jan.) and for a certain period in August. Air conditioning. Tuscan cuisine (4, C3, **rf**).

🍴🍴 **Cibreo.** Via dei Macci 118, tel. 2341100. Closed Sunday and Monday, New Year's Day-Epiphany (6 Jan.) and August. Garden. Tuscan and classical cuisine (5, A6, **rl**).

🍴🍴 **Dino.** Via Ghibellina 51/r, tel. 241452. Closed Sunday evening and Monday, for a certain period in August. Air conditioning. Tuscan cuisine (5, B5, **rm**).

🍴🍴 **I' Toscano.** Via Guelfa 70/r, tel. 215475. Closed Tuesday, for a certain period in August. Air conditioning. Tuscan cuisine (2, C5, **rs**).

🍴🍴 **Latini.** Via dei Palchetti 6/r, tel. 210916.

151

¶¶ Closed Monday, Christmas-Epiphany (6 Jan.). Air conditioning. Tuscan cuisine (1, D1, **rt**).

¶¶ **Mamma Gina.** Borgo S. Jacopo 37/r, tel. 2396009. Closed Sunday, for a certain period in August. Air conditioning. Tuscan cuisine (1, F2, **rv**).

¶¶ **Posta.** Via de' Lamberti 20/r, tel. 212701. Closed Tuesday. Air conditioning, garden. Classical cuisine (1, D3, **sc**).

¶¶ **Quattro Amici.** Via degli Orti Oricellari 29, tel. 215413. Closed Wednesday, for a certain period in August. Air conditioning. Classical cuisine – fish (2, D2, **rz**).

¶¶ **Sagrestia.** Via Guicciardini 27/r, tel. 210003. Closed Monday. Air conditioning. Classical cuisine (4, D4, **sg**).

¶¶ **Sasso di Dante.** Piazza delle Pallottole 6/r, tel. 282113. Closed Thursday and Friday, mid-December/February. Garden. Classical cuisine (1, C4, **sf**).

¶¶ **Taverna del Bronzino.** Via delle Ruote 25-27/r, tel. 495220. Closed Sunday, August. Air conditioning. Classical cuisine (2, A6, **sh**).

¶¶ **Trattoria Vittoria.** Via della Fonderia 52/r, tel. 225657. Closed Wednesday, for a certain period in August. Air conditioning. Classical cuisine – fish (9, C4-5, **si**).

¶ **Carabaccia.** Via Palazzuolo 190/r, tel. 214782. Closed Sunday and midday on Monday, for a certain period in August. Tuscan cuisine (9, B6, **ri**).

¶ **Carmine.** Piazza del Carmine 18/r, tel. 218601. Closed Sunday, August. Florentine cuisine (9, D6, **rj**).

¶ **Cavallino.** Via delle Farine 6/r, tel. 215818. Closed Wednesday. Air conditioning. Tuscan and classical cuisine (1, D-E4, **rk**).

¶ **Fagioli.** Corso dei Tintori 47/r, tel. 244285. Closed Saturday in summer and Sunday, August. Tuscan cuisine (5, C-D3, **ro**).

¶ **Pierot.** Piazza Gaddi 25/r, tel. 702100. Closed Sunday, for a certain period in July. Air conditioning. Tuscan and classical cuisine – fish (9, B-C4, **sb**).

¶ **Quattro Stagioni.** Via Maggio 61/r, tel. 218906. Closed Sunday, August. Air conditioning. Tuscan and classical cuisine (4, E2-3, **se**).

¶ **Vecchia Bettola.** Viale L. Ariosto 32/r, tel. 224158. Closed Sunday and Monday, Christmas-New Year's Day and for a certain period in August. Garden. Tuscan cuisine (9, D5, **sj**).

Cafes, pastry shops, ice cream shops, and the many flavors of Florence

Antica Mescita S. Niccolò. Via S. Niccolò 60-62/r, tel. 2342836. Closed Sunday. **Antico Vinaio "I Fratellinil."** Via dei Cimatori 38/r, tel. 2396096. Closed Sunday. **La Fiaschetteria.** Via dei Neri 2/r, tel. 216887. Closed Sunday. These are a few of the most distinctive little "fiaschetterie," or wine

taverns, in the historical center; good wine is served, with flavorful "panini," or sandwiches.

Badiani. Viale dei Mille 20/r, tel. 578682. Closed Tuesday. This is a historic ice cream shop of Florence; it is justly renowned for the "Buontalenti" ice cream, named after the 16th-c. artist who is said to have invented the recipe.

Cantinetta dei Verrazzano. Via dei Tavolini 18-20/r, tel. 268590. Closed Sunday. This is an elegant wine tavern in full 19th-c. style, in the heart of Florence. Wines from Chianti are served with delicious and aromatic turnovers: an alchemistic combination of flavors.

Friggitorie. Via S. Antonino 50/r, tel. 211630. Closed Sunday. One of the oldest Florentine "friggitorie," literally "fry shops" – try the frittelle, polenta fritta, bomboloni, ciambelline – an array of doughnuts and other delights.

Gilli. Piazza della Repubblica 39/r, tel. 213896. Closed Tuesday. This cafe has all the charm of a trip to another era; particularly good aperitifs.

Giubbe Rosse. Piazza della Repubblica 13-14/r, tel. 212280. Closed Wednesday. This historic literary cafe dates from the early-20th c. Nowadays, monthly exhibits and conferences are held here, and it is possible to eat light snacks.

Palazzo dei Vini. Piazza Pitti 15, tel. 288323. Closed Sunday and Monday. In the historic Palazzo Temple Leader, Tuscan wine is promoted in a cultural context, in an original and innovative wine cellar. Wine tasting and sale; museum and data bank.

Rivoire. Piazza della Signoria 5/r, tel. 214412. Closed Monday. This little cafe offers an excellent view of the Palazzo Vecchio. The delicacy here is an excellent hot chocolate, made in the traditional fashion.

"Trippai," or tripe shops. Piazza dei Cimatori, Piazza S. Ambrogio, Via dell'Ariento, Loggia del Mercato Nuovo. In fall and winter especially, strolling tripe vendors sell tripe and "lampredotto," cut into small bits, which you eat hot, wrapped in heavy paper.

Vivoli. Via Isole delle Stinche 7/r, tel. 292334. Closed Monday. This is the unrivalled historic king of ice cream in Florence, and has been for three generations. It is faithful to the classic flavors.

Museums and cultural institutions

Accademia di Belle Arti. Via Ricasoli 66, tel. 2398350.

Accademia di Scienze e Lettere "La Colombaria." Via S. Egidio 21, tel. 2396628.

Appartamenti Reali. Palazzo Pitti, Piazza de' Pitti tel. 2388611. Closed Monday. *Tours by request.*

Arciconfraternita della Misericordia. Piazza del Duomo 19, tel. 287788. *Tours by request.*

Biblioteca Comunale Centrale. Via S. Egidio 21, tel. 219194.

Biblioteca Marucelliana. Via Cavour 43, tel. 210602.

Biblioteca Medicea Laurenziana. Piazza S. Lorenzo 9, tel. 214443.

Biblioteca Nazionale Centrale. Piazza dei Cavalleggeri 1, tel. 244442.

Biblioteca Riccardiana. Palazzo Medici-Riccardi, Via de' Ginori 10, tel. 212586.

Campanile di Giotto. Piazza del Duomo, tel. 2302885. *Weekdays, weekends, and holidays: summer 9-6:50, winter 9-4:20.*

Cappella Brancacci. Piazza del Carmine, tel. 2382195. Closed Tuesday. *Weekdays 10-5, weekends and holidays 1-5.*

Cappelle Medicee, or Medici Chapels. Piazza Madonna degli Aldobrandini 6, tel. 23885. Closed Monday. *Weekdays, weekends, and holidays 9-2.*

Casa Buonarroti. Via Ghibellina 70, tel. 241752. Closed Tuesday. *Weekdays, weekends, and holidays 9:30-1:30.*

Casa di Dante. Via S. Margherita 1, tel. 219416. Closed Tuesday. *Summer 10-5, winter 10-4.*

Casa-Museo di Rodolfo Siviero. Lungarno Serristori 3. *Monday, Wednesday, and Friday, 10-12.*

Cenacolo della Calza. Piazza della Calza 6, tel. 222287. *Weekdays, weekends, and holidays 9-1:30.*

Cenacolo del Ghirlandaio. Borgo Ognissanti 42, tel. 2396802. *Monday, Tuesday, and Saturday 9-12.*

Cenacolo delle Monache di Foligno. Via Faenza 42, tel. 286982. *Tours by request.*

Cenacolo di S. Apollonia. Via XXVII Aprile 1, tel. 2388607. Closed Monday. *Weekdays, weekends, and holidays 9-2.*

Cenacolo di S. Spirito and **Fondazione Romano.** Piazza S. Spirito 29, tel. 287043. Closed Monday. *Weekdays 9-2, weekends and holidays 8-1.*

Chiostro dello Scalzo. Via Cavour 69, tel. 2388604. *Monday and Thursday 9-1.*

Conservatorio di Musica "Luigi Cherubini," a conservatory. Piazza delle Belle Arti 2, tel. 292180.

Museo degli Strumenti Musicali, a museum of musical instruments. Closed for restoration.

Forte di Belvedere (or Forte di S. Giorgio). Via di S. Leonardo, tel. 2342822. *Winter 9-4:30, summer 9-8.*

Fortezza di S. Giovanni (or Fortezza da Basso). Viale Filippo Strozzi. Temporary exhibitions and cultural events are held here.

Gabinetto dei Disegni e delle Stampe degli Uffizi, a noteworthy collection of drawings and prints. Via della Ninna 5, tel. 23885. Temporary exhibitions are held here.

Gabinetto G. P. Vieusseux. Palazzo Strozzi, Piazza degli Strozzi, tel. 215990.

Galleria dell'Accademia. Via Ricasoli 60, tel. 2388612. Closed Monday. *Weekdays 8:30-7, holidays 8:30-2.*

Galleria d'Arte Moderna. Palazzo Pitti, Piazza de' Pitti, tel. 287096. Closed Monday. *Weekdays, weekends, and holidays 9-2.*

Galleria Corsini. Palazzo Corsini, Via del Parione 11, tel. 218994. *Tours by appointment.*

Galleria del Costume. Palazzo Pitti, Piazza de' Pitti, tel. 212557. Closed Monday. *Weekdays, weekends, and holidays 9-2.*

Galleria Palatina. Palazzo Pitti, Piazza de' Pitti, tel. 238611. Closed Monday. *Weekdays 8:30-7, holidays 8:30-2.*

Galleria degli Uffizi. Piazzale degli Uffizi 6, tel. 23885. Closed Monday. *Weekdays 9-7, weekends and holidays 9-2.*

Giardino di Bòboli. Piazza de' Pitti, tel. 213440. Closed the first and the last Monday of the month. *Opens at 9; closing time may vary by season.*

Giardino dei Semplici (Orto Botanico, or botanical garden). Via P.A. Micheli 3, tel. 2757402. *Monday, Wednesday, Friday 9-12.* Reservations obligatory for groups.

Istituto Britannico (British Institute). Palazzo Ferroni, Via de' Tornabuoni 2, tel. 284033 (secretariat). Lungarno Guicciardini 9, tel. 284031 (library).

Istituto Francese. Piazza d'Ognissanti 2, tel. 287521.

Istituto Nazionale di Studi sul Rinascimento, an institute for Renaissance studies. Palazzo Strozzi, Piazza degli Strozzi, tel. 287728.

Kunsthistorisches Institut in Florenz (German Institute for the History of Art). Via Giusti 44, tel. 2479161.

Museo Nazionale di Antropologia ed Etnologia. Via del Procònsolo 12, tel. 2396449. *Thursday, Friday, Saturday, and the third Sunday of the month 9-1.*

Museo Archeologico. Via della Colonna 38, tel. 23575. Closed Monday. *Weekdays 9-2, weekends and holidays 9-1.*

Museo degli Argenti. Palazzo Pitti, Piazza de' Pitti, tel. 212557. Closed Monday. *Weekdays, weekends, and holidays 9-2.*

Museo Bardini. Piazza de' Mozzi 1, tel. 2342427. Closed Wednesday. *Weekdays 9-2, weekends and holidays 8-1.*

Museo Nazionale del Bargello. Via del Procònsolo, tel. 23885. Closed Monday. *Weekdays, weekends, and holidays 9-2.*

Museo Botanico ed Erbario Tropicale. Via La Pira 4, tel. 27571. Closed weekends and holidays, days before holidays, and in August. *Monday-Friday 9-12.* Tours by reservation.

Museo delle Carrozze. Palazzo Pitti, Piazza de' Pitti, tel. 213440-216673.

Museo della Casa Fiorentina Antica. Palazzo Davanzati, Via Porta Rossa 13, tel. 2388610. Closed Monday. *Weekdays, weekends, and holidays 9-2.*

Museo di Firenze Com'Era. Via dell'Oriuolo 24, tel. 2398483. Closed Thursday. *Weekdays 9-2, weekends and holidays 8-1.*

Museo di Geologia e Paleontologia. Via La Pira 4, tel. 27571. Closed weekends and holidays and August. *Monday 2-6; Tuesday, Wednesday, Thursday, and Saturday 9-1.* Tours by reservation.

Museo Horne. Via de' Benci 6, tel. 244661. Closed Sunday and holidays. *Weekdays 9-1.*

Museo Marino Marini. Piazza di S. Pancrazio, tel. 219432. Closed Tuesday. *June, July, and August, Weekdays, weekends, and holidays 10-1, 4-7; during other months, weekdays, weekends, and holidays 10-1, 3-6.*

Museo di Mineralogia e Litologia. Via La Pira 4, tel. 27571. Closed weekends and holidays and August. *Weekdays 9-1; Wednesday 9-1, 3-6.* Tours by reservation.

Museo dell'Opera di S. Croce, cloisters and the **Cappella Pazzi.** Piazza di S. Croce 16, tel. 244619. Closed Wednesday. *Weekdays, weekends, and holidays, summer 10-12:30, 2:30-6:30; winter 10-12:30, 3-5.*

Museo dell'Opera di S. Maria del Fiore. Piazza del Duomo 9, tel. 2398796. Closed weekends and holidays. *Weekdays: summer 9-6:50, winter 9-5:20.*

Museo dell'Opificio delle Pietre Dure. Via degli Alfani 78, tel. 210102. Closed holidays. *Weekdays 9-2, Saturday 9-7.*

Museo delle Porcellane. Giardino di Bòboli, Piazza de' Pitti, tel. 212557. *It can be toured by appointment.*

Museo e Istituto Fiorentino di Preistoria. Via S. Egidio 21, tel. 295159. Closed holidays. *Weekdays 9:30-12:30.*

Museo di S. Marco. Piazza S. Marco 1, tel. 23885. Closed Monday. *Weekdays, weekends, and holidays 9-2.*

Museo di S. Maria Novella. Piazza S. Maria Novella, tel. 282187. Closed Friday. *Weekdays 9-2, weekends and holidays 8-1.*

Museo di Storia della Fotografia Fratelli Alinari. Palazzo Rucellai, Via della Vigna Nuova 16, tel. 213370. Closed Wednesday. *Weekdays, weekends, and holidays 10-7:30.*

Museo di Storia della Scienza. Piazza dei Giudici 1, tel. 293493. Closed weekends and holidays. *Monday, Wednesday, and Friday 9:30-1, 2-5; Tuesday, Thursday, and Saturday 9:30-1.*

Museo Zoologico "La Specola." Via Romana 17, tel. 222451. Closed Wednesday. *Weekday 9-12, holidays 9-1.*

Palazzo Medici-Riccardi. Via Cavour 1, tel. 2760340. **Cappella dei Magi.** Closed Wednesday. *Weekdays 9-1, 3-6, weekends and holidays 9-1.* Reservations recommended.

Palazzo Vecchio. Piazza della Signoria. tel. 27681. City government offices and the **Quartieri Monumentali.** Closed Thursday. *Weekdays 9-7, weekends and holidays 8-1.*

Pinacoteca dell'Ospedale degli Innocenti. Piazza SS. Annunziata 12, tel. 2478997. Closed Wednesday. *Weekdays 8:30-2, weekends and holidays 8-1.*

Raccolta d'Arte Contemporanea "Alberto della Ragione." Piazza della Signoria 5, tel. 283078. Closed Tuesday. *Weekdays 9-2, weekends and holidays 8-1.*

Università degli Studi di Firenze (information offices for university activities in Florence). Piazza S. Marco 4, tel. 27571.

Monumental churches

Badia Fiorentina. Via del Procònsolo, tel. 287389. *Weekdays 9-12, 4-6; weekends and holidays 4:30-6.*

Basilica di S. Croce. Piazza di S. Croce, tel. 244619. *Weekdays: summer 8-6:30, winter 8-12:30, 3-6:30; weekends and holidays: summer 8-12:30, 3-6:30, winter 3-6.*

Basilica di S. Lorenzo. Piazza S. Lorenzo, tel. 216634. *Weekdays, weekends and holidays 7-12:30, 3:30-6:30.*

Basilica di S. Maria del Fiore. Piazza del Duomo, tel. 294514. *Weekdays 10-5; weekends and holidays 7-12, 2:30-6.* **Cripta di S. Reparata,** tel. 294514. Closed weekends and holidays. *Weekdays 10-5.* **Cupola del Brunelleschi,** tel. 294514. Closed weekends and holidays. *Weekdays 10-5.*

Basilica della SS. Annunziata. Piazza della SS. Annunziata, tel. 2398034. *Weekdays, weekends and holidays 7:30-12:30, 4-6:30.*

Battistero di S. Giovanni. Piazza di S. Giovanni, tel. 2302885. *Weekdays 1:30-6; weekends and holidays 9-1:30.*

Orsanmichele. Via dell'Arte della Lana, tel. 284715. *Hours: 9-12, 4-6.*

S. Felicita. Piazza di S. Felicita, tel. 213018. *Hours: 7:30-12, 3:30-6.*

S. Maria del Carmine. Piazza del Carmine, tel. 212331. *Hours: 9:30-5:30.*

S. Maria Maddalena de' Pazzi and **chapter hall** with Crucifixion by Perugino. Borgo Pinti 58, tel. 2478420. *Weekdays, weekends, and holidays 9-12, 5-7.*

S. Maria Novella. Piazza S. Maria Novella, tel. 210113. *Hours: 7-11:30, 3:30-6.*

S. Spirito. Piazza S. Spirito, tel. 210030. *Hours: 8-12, 4-6.*

S. Trìnita. Piazza S. Trìnita, tel. 216912. *Weekdays 8:30-11, 4-6; weekends and holidays 4-6.*

Ss. Apostoli. Piazza del Limbo, tel. 290642. *Hours: 3:30-5:30.*

Tempio Israelitico (synagogue). Via L.C. Farini 4, tel. 245252. Closed Saturday. *October-March Monday-Thursday 11-1, 2-5; Friday 11-1; Sunday 10-1. April-September one hour earlier than the winter schedule, and Sunday open in the afternoon.* **Museo Ebraico di Firenze (Jewish Museum of Florence).** Closed Saturday. *Same hours as the synagogue.*

Entertainment

Teatro Comunale. Corso Italia 12, tel. 27791. This is the most important classical concert hall in Florence. The winter season features symphonic concerts, ballets, and opera. In particular, this is the central point of the Maggio Musicale Fiorentino, between May and June.

Teatro dell'Oriuolo. Via dell'Oriuolo 31, tel. 2340507. Performances often held in local dialect. Season October-April.

Teatro della Pergola. Via della Pergola 12/32, tel. 2479651. This is the most "classic" dramatic theater in Florence. Season October-April.

Teatro Niccolini. Via Ricasoli 5, tel. 213282. One of the oldest theaters in the city. The season runs from October to May, chiefly with dramatic performances.

Teatro Verdi. Via Ghibellina 99/101, tel. 212320. Performers and singers of international renown; musicals, variety shows, operettas, ballet, and modern dance.

Sports

C.A.I. Club Alpino Italiano (mountain climbing). Via dello Studio 5, tel. 211731.

Canottieri Firenze (sculling). Lungarno de' Medici 8, tel. 282130.

Shops, crafts, and fine art

Antica Libreria Baccani. Via Porta Rossa 99/r, tel. 215448. This bookshop has an ample array of books and magazines.

Antico Setificio Fiorentino. Via Bartolini 4, tel. 213861. This old silk manufactory features looms and original designs, from the 16th to the 19th c., for fine silk, used in upholstery and in high fashion.

Antiquariato Mirella Piselli. Via Maggio 23/r, tel. 2398029. Antique furniture, especially from the Tuscan Seicento, paintings, ceramics; refined antique fabrics, for collectors.

Armani. Via della Vigna Nuova 51/r, tel. 219041. High-fashion boutique.

Balatresi. Lungarno Acciaioli 22/r, tel. 287851. Fine craftsmanship. Of particular interest are the unique alabaster creations, and the exclusive artistic ceramics by Gianni Trapani.

Banchi Lamberto. Via dei Serragli 10/r, tel. 294694. This craftsman creates unique items in hand-tooled bronze and brass, with etching and fretwork.

Bartolozzi e Maioli. Via Maggio 13/r, tel. 2398633. This crafts workshop carves ("intaglio") and restores wood; creative and unusual sculpture, home furnishings, and picture frames.

Bianchi Antonella. Via dei Servi 84/r, tel. 217027. Retail outlet and workshop (on commission) for silver and gold jewelry, studded with semiprecious stones. Selection of personalized stones.

Bizzarri. Via della Condotta 32/r, tel. 211580. A venerable old shop dealing in fine essences, spices, chemical products, and material for restoration.

Bottega delle Stampe di Delia Maraschin Magri. Borgo S. Jacopo 56/r, tel. 295396. Original prints dating from the 16th c. to the early 20th c., including Art Nouveau and Art Deco. Geographic maps dating back to the 17th c. and etchings and prints for collectors. Antique-style picture frames, only handmade.

Buccellati Mario. Via Tornabuoni 71/r, tel. 2396579. Famous jewelry and silverwork; classical and modern models, with various techniques, etching, fretwork.

Caponi. Piazza Antinori 4/r, tel. 213668. Embroideries, lingerie, household linen.

Casa d'Aste Pitti. Via Maggio 15, tel. 287138. Objets d'art and antiques; fine objects on consignment.

Centro d'Arte Spaziotempo. Piazza Peruzzi 15/r, tel. 218678. This meeting point in the Florentine world of contemporary art holds exhibitions of non-figurative painting and sculpture, by major Florentine artists. The adjoining **Libreria del Centro d'Arte** (entrance also from Via dei Benci 41/r) sells publications on the visual arts.

Cirri. Via Por S. Maria 38-40/r, tel. 2396593. Embroideries, lingerie.

Corsellini. Via Ghibellina 132/r, tel. 2345665. For three generations this shop has sold its own handmade brier-wood pipes.

Emporio Armani. Piazza Strozzi 16/r, tel. 284315. Apparel for men and women.

Fallani Libreria Antiquaria. Via della Pergola 21/a, tel. 2478886. Old books, especially on art and literature; it is also possible to order by mail from their catalogue.

Farmacia del Cinghiale. Piazza Mercato Nuovo 4/r, tel. 282128. This "antica spezieria," or old pharmacy, is famous for its natural and original prescriptions and preparations; extracts, vegetal remedies, essences, oils, and scents.

Ferragamo. Via Tornabuoni 14/r, tel. 292123. Shoes and footwear; ready-to-wear.

G. Ugolini. Lungarno Acciaioli 66-70/r, tel. 290742. Traditional shop selling mosaics and inlays of semiprecious stones. Large array of objects with floral motifs, depictions of animals, landscapes, and modern subjects.

Galleria Machiavelli. Via Por S. Maria 39/r, tel. 2398586. Artistic ceramics: Guido Passeri still makes ceramics in accordance with the great Tuscan crafts tradition; while Innocenti makes them with a more modern approach to color, linked to folk art.

Galleria Mentana Arte Moderna e Contemporanea. Piazza Mentana 2/r, tel. 211985. Painting and sculpture by artists of the Italian Novecento (20th c.), fine graphic work, and promotion of contemporary artists. Collections of work by Guttuso, Sassu, Morlotti, Fiume, Crippa, and Veronesi.

Galleria Parronchi. Via dei Fossi 18/r, tel. 215109. Paintings from the 19th c. and the early-20th c., with emphasis on the Macchiaioli schools and the "post-Macchiaioli."

Giancarlo Giachetti. Via Toscanella 5/r, tel. 218567. A craftsman of wrought iron; he makes fine objects for furnishing, as well as original creations of his own.

Giannini Giulio & Figlio. Piazza Pitti 37/r, tel. 212621. This crafts shop has been in operation for over a century, making leather book binding, of great quality. Stationery, desk sets, and original marbled paper.

Gucci. Via Tornabuoni 73/r, tel. 264011. Fine leather goods; accessories; apparel for men and women.

Il Bisonte. Via del Parione 31/r, tel. 215722. Crafts workshop making bags, suitcases, travelbags, and various other leather objects in the 19th-c. style.

Jaime Marie Lazzara. Via dei Leoni 4/r, tel. 280573. In a tiny workshop just off the Piazza della Signoria, this craftsman carves, on commission, violins and violas. Restoration of antique and modern musical instruments.

La Botteghina del Ceramista. Via Guelfa 5/r, tel. 287367. Fine selection of elegant ceramic objects, featuring work from Deruta and Montelupo.

La Bottteghina. Via del Parione 17/r, tel. 2396236. A large selection of period jewelry, in gold, dating from the 19th c. up to the 1940s.

Libreria Antiquaria Gonnelli. Via Ricasoli 14/r, tel. 216835. A vast array of manuscripts, illuminated codices, incunabula, and rare books. In the adjoining hall, cultural events and temporary exhibitions are held.

Libreria F.M.R. Via delle Belle Donne 41/r, tel. 283312. Boutique selling art books and the "ex libris" of the publisher Franco Maria Ricci. Curiosities of all sorts concerning the applied arts and minor antiquary.

Libreria Salimbeni. Via M. Palmieri 14-16/r, tel. 2340904. This shop features illustrated books and exhibition catalogues from Italy and elsewhere; new, out of print, hard to find.

Loretta Caponi. Borgo Ognissanti 12/r (will change address in 1994), tel. 213668. Exquisite handmade embroideries of all sorts. A noteworthy collection of old lace and fabrics.

Officina Profumo-Farmaceutica di S. Maria Novella. Via della Scala 16, tel. 216276. One of the earliest convent pharmacies, it has been producing perfumes and pharmaceutical products in accordance with ancient prescriptions. The herbal liqueurs are renowned: "Elisir," the "Liquore dei Medici," and "Alkermes."

Paci Fiorenzo. Via S. Monaca 13, tel. 282240. Fine craftsman specializing in mosaics and inlay with semiprecious stones, producing artworks, tables, objects for interior decoration, and miniatures for jewelry.

Pineider. Piazza della Signoria 14/r, tel. 284655. Watermarked paper, prints, handmade etchings, on paper and parchment, stationery and leather desk sets, personalized desk diaries and pens.

Pucci. Via Pucci 6, tel. 287622; Via Vigna Nuova 97/r, tel. 294028. High-fashion boutique.

Quaglia & Forte. Via Guicciardini 12 r, tel. 294534. Fine workmanship of artistic coral and cameo. Interesting reproduction of Etruscan jewelry.

Riccardo Bianchi. Via Cecioni 54/56, tel. 714421. This shop does perfect reproductions of paintings from the 13th to the 19th c., entirely hand-painted on panel or canvas.

Sartoria Teatrale Fiorentina. Piazza del Duomo 2, tel. 292312. In this worshop – more than a century old – exquisite costumes are made and rented out, for processions, historical reenactments, and drama and opera, as well as for Carnevale.

Schindler Bettina. Via Maffia 51/r, tel. 240165. Restoration of antiques in ivory, tortoise-shell, and mother of pearl; specializing in fans.

Taddei. Via S. Margherita 11, tel. 2398960. Directly adjoining the Casa di Dante, this shop sells fine Florentine leather objects, for interior decoration, picture frames, jewelry boxes, and desk sets – all made by hand.

TAF (Tovagliati Artistici Fiorentini). Via Por S. Maria 17/r e 22/r, tel. 2396037. This store sells fabrics for the table: lace and embroidered tablecloths, linen sets, camisoles, children's clothing.

Traversari Giorgio. Via Guicciardini 120/r, tel. 287747. Silver jewelry in accordance with the venerable old Florentine technique of the "madrevitato"; modern silverwork and picture frames.

Folk events and traditional festivals

Scoppio del Carro. Piazza del Duomo, Easter Sunday. During the Easter mass, the flight of the "colombina"{EXPL} is the subject of omen-reading for the coming year.

Festa del Corpus Domini. Sunday of Corpus Domini. Impressive historic procession through the streets of the center of Florence.

Calcio Storico Fiorentino. Piazza S. Croce, June. This is an early version of soccer, played in Renaissance clothing, in matches between the various historic quarters of the city. There is an historic procession before the game. The final match is played 24 June.

Festa di S. Giovanni. 24 June. Patron saint (St. John) of the city. Procession in costume through the streets of the center of town, championship match of historic soccer ("calcio storico") and in the evening fireworks show.

Rificolona. On the Arno, 7 September. All Florence is decorated with colored paper lanterns and there is a procession of boats along the river in the evening.

Special markets

Mercato di S. Lorenzo. Via dell'Ariento and Piazza del Mercato Centrale. Closed Sunday and Monday. Lively and colorful, this market offers an ample array of clothing, leather products, and other things.

Mercato del Porcellino. Piazza del Mercato Nuovo. Closed Sunday and Monday morning. Note the remarkable market of Florentine straw creations, purses of all sorts, gift objects, and souvenirs. The real attraction for tourists is the "Porcellino," a handsome bronze sculpture of a warthog believed to bring good luck.

Mercato delle Pulci. Piazza dei Ciompi. Closed Sunday (except for the last Sunday of every month) and Monday. Literally, the "market of fleas," with minor art and antique objects.

Fairs and other events

Pitti Uomo, Bimbo, Casa, Filati. Fortezza da Basso, January-February/June-July. Fashion shows and trade fairs in the fields of apparel and accessories.

Mostra-Mercato Internazionale dell'Artigianato. Fortezza da Basso, April-May. Crafts trade fair.

Diplo Art Book. Fortezza da Basso, April-May. A fair of art and illustrated books.

Biennale Internazionale dell'Antiquariato. Palazzo Strozzi, October. Antiques.

The outlying quarters and the low-lying hills

Hotels

★★★ G.H. Villa Cora. Viale Machiavelli 18, tel. 2298451, fax 229086. Number of rooms: 48. Handicap-friendly. Air conditioning, elevator; parking area, garden, pool (11, C-D4, **aj**).

★★★ Villa la Massa. At Candeli, Via La Massa 6, tel. 6510101, fax 6510109. Number of rooms: 38. Air conditioning, elevator; parking area, garden, pool, tennis courts (12, A6, *off map*).

★★★ Holiday Inn Garden Court. Near the highway interchange of Firenze Sud, Viale Europa 205, tel. 6531841, fax 6531806. Number of rooms: 92. Air conditioning, elevator; parking area, pool (12, D6, *off map*).

★★★ Raffaello. Viale Morgagni 19, tel. 4224141, fax 434374. Number of rooms: 141. Handicap-friendly. Air conditioning, elevator; parking area, parking garage, garden (7, A3, **bj**).

★★★ Relais Certosa. at Galluzzo, Via Colle Ramole 2, tel. 2047171, fax 268575. Number of rooms: 69. Handicap-friendly. Air conditioning; parking area, garden, tennis courts (9, F6, *off map*).

★★★ Sheraton Firenze Hotel. Near the highway exchange of Firenze Sud, Via G. Agnelli 33, tel. 64901, fax 680747. Number of rooms: 321. Handicap-friendly. Air conditioning, elevator; parking area, parking garage, pool, tennis courts (12, F5, *off map*).

★★★ Starhotel Monginevro. Via di Novoli 59, tel. 431441, fax 4378257. Number of rooms: 127. Air conditioning; parking area, special parking garage for guests (6, D5-6, **cb**).

★★★ Villa Belvedere. Via B. Castelli 3, tel. 222501, fax 223163. Number of rooms: 26. Lodging only; no board. Air conditioning, elevator; parking area, garden, pool, tennis courts (9, F6, *off map*).

★★★ Villa Carlotta. Via Michele di Lando 3, tel. 2336134, fax 2336147. Number of rooms: 27. Air conditioning, elevator; parking area, garden (9, F6, *off map*).

★★★ Villa le Rondini. at Trespiano, Via Bolognese Vecchia 224, tel. 400081, fax 268212. Number of rooms: 42. Parking area, garden, pool, tennis courts (8, A2, *off map*).

★★★ Auto Park Hotel. at Nòvoli, Via Valdegola 1, tel. 431771, fax 4221557. Number of rooms: 114. Lodging only; no board. Handicap-friendly. Air conditioning, elevator; parking area, special parking garage for guests, garden (6, B5, **m**).

★★★ Capitol. Viale Amendola 34, tel. 2343201, fax 2345925. Number of rooms: 92. Air conditioning, elevator; special parking garage for guests (10, D1, **t**).

★★★ David. Viale Michelangiolo 1, tel. 6811695, fax 680602. Number of rooms: 26. Lodging only; no board. Air conditioning, elevator; parking area, garden (12, B3, **z**).

★★★ Fleming. at Nòvoli, Viale Guidoni 87, tel. 4376773, fax 435894. Number of rooms: 120. Lodging only; no board. Air conditioning, elevator; parking area (6, B5, **ae**).

★★★ Grifone. Via Pilati 22, tel. 661367, fax 677628. Number of rooms: 64. Lodging only; no board. Handicap-friendly. Air conditioning, elevator; parking area, special parking garage for guests, garden (12, A5, **an**).

★★★ Jane. Via Orcagna 56, tel. 677382, fax 677383. Number of rooms: 24. Lodging only; no board. Air conditioning, elevator; special parking garage for guests, garden (10, D2, **as**).

★★★ Select. Via G. Galliano 24, tel. 330342, fax 351506. Number of rooms: 38. Lodging only; no board. Air conditioning, elevator; parking area (7, F2, **bq**).

★★★ Villa Liberty. Viale Michelangiolo 40, tel. 6810581, fax 6812595. Number of rooms: 16. Lodging only; no board. Elevator; parking area, garden (12, B3, **bt**).

★★ Orcagna. Via Orcagna 57, tel. 669959, fax 677269. Number of rooms: 18. Lodging only; no board. Elevator (10, D2, **bc**).

Restaurants

Loggia. Piazzale Michelangelo 1, tel. 2342832, fax 2345288. Closed Wednesday. Air conditioning, parking area. Tuscan and classical cuisine (12, B2, **ru**).

Centanni. at Bagno a Rìpoli, Via Centanni 7, tel. 630122, fax 633123. Closed Saturday at midday and Sunday, August. Air conditioning, parking area, garden. Tuscan cuisine (12, B6, *off map*).

Capannina di Sante. Piazza Ravenna, tel. 688345. Closed Sunday, for a certain period in August. Air conditioning, garden. Classical cuisine – fish (12, B5, **rh**).

Omero. at Arcetri, Via Pian de' Giullari 11/r, tel. 220053. Closed Tuesday, August. Air conditioning. Tuscan cuisine (11, F6, **ry**).

Strettoio. At Serpiolle, Via di Serpiolle 7, tel. 4250044. Closed Sunday and Monday, August. Parking area, garden. Tuscan cuisine (7, A3, *off map*).

Camping areas

Parco Comunale. Viale Michelangiolo 80, tel. 6811977. Seasonal.

Villa Camerata. Viale Righi 2/4, tel. 601451, fax 610300. Year round.

Youth hostels

Ostello della Gioventù Europa Villa Camerata IYHF. Viale Righi 2/4, tel. 601451. A large building with a loggia and garden on the hillside to the north of the city. Reception open everyday 2 pm-11:30 pm. Accommodates 320. Open year round. Reservations required from April to October.

Ecotourism

at Galluzzo-Certosa, km. 5 ☒ 50124

"La Fattoressa." For information: Angiolina Fusi, tel. 2048418. Accommodations in individual rooms in a large fruit-orchard and farm. Archery. Wine, oil, fruit, poultry, and rabbits.

Museums, cultural institutions, and monumental churches

Archivio di Stato. Viale della Giovine Italia, tel. 241549.

Orthodox Russian church. Via Leone X 8, tel. 490148-578015. *Tours by request.*

Church of S. Miniato al Monte. Via Monte Croci 34, tel. 2342422. *Weekdays, weekends and holidays: summer 8-12, 2-7; winter 8-12, 2:30-6.*

Giardino dell'Orticoltura, a horticultural garden. Via Vittorio Emanuele II 1, tel. 483698. *Winter 8-5; summer 8-8.*

Istituto Olandese Universitario di Storia dell'Arte, Dutch art institute. Viale E. Torricelli 5, tel. 221612.

Museo del Cenacolo di Andrea del Sarto. Via di S. Salvi 16, tel. 2388603. Closed Monday. *Weekdays, weekends, and holidays 9-2.*

Museo Stibbert. Via Federico Stibbert 26, tel. 475520. Closed Thursday. *Weekdays 9-1, weekends and holidays 9-12:30.*

Pinacoteca della Fondazione Roberto Longhi. Via Fortini 30, tel. 6580794. *Tours by appointment.*

Stagni della Piana Fiorentina, an array of ponds. Village of Osmannoro and townships of Campi Bisenzio, Sesto Fiorentino, Signa. Of particular interest to naturalists are the numerous species of birds, including the handsome Black-Winged Stilt (Cavaliere d'Italia), in its seasonal migration. For guided tours, contact the WWF, Delegazione Toscana, Via Canto dei Nelli 8, tel. 2302675-216582.

at Careggi

Villa Medicea di Careggi. Viale Gaetano Pieraccini 21, tel. 4277501. It is possible to tour this Medici Villa, upon written request to USL 10/D, Viale Pieraccini 21, tel. 42771.

Convento delle Suore Oblate. Piazza di Careggi 2, tel. 411641. To tour this nunnery, contact the USL 10/D di Careggi, tel. 42771.

at Castello

Villa Medicea di Castello. Via di Castello 47, tel. 454791. *Access to the garden: Weekdays, weekends, and holidays 9-4:30; in summer, longer hours.* Inside is the **Accademia della Crusca**, tel. 454277. *Tours by appointment.*

Villa Medicea della Petraia. Via della Petraia 40, tel. 451208. Closed Monday. *November-February 9-4:30; April, May, September 9-6:30; March, October 9-5:30; June-August 9-7:30.* It is possible to tour this Medici Villa as well as the garden, which closes one hour earlier.

at Galluzzo-Certosa, km. 5 ☒ 50124

Certosa del Galluzzo, tel. 2049226. Closed Monday. *Weekdays, weekends, and holidays 9-12, 3-5.*

at San Felice a Ema

Villa del Poggio Imperiale. Piazzale del Poggio Imperiale 1, tel. 220151. Closed August. *Tours by appointment.*

at Settignano

Villa Gamberaia. Via del Rossellino 72, tel. 697205. Closed Saturday and weekends and holidays. *Monday-Friday 8-12 and 1-5.*

Entertainment and other events

Auditorium FLOG. Via Michele Mercati 24/b, tel. 490437. Debut of many young musicians. Each year, in the months of November and December, there are performances of world music, linked to the Festival dei Popoli. This is also one of the few places in Florence to hear rock and jazz, by Tuscan, Italian, and international performers.

Festa del Grillo. In the Parco delle Cascine on the day of the Feast of the Ascension, tens of thousands of crickets, enclosed in wooden cages, embellish this country celebration.

Teatro di Rifredi. Via Vittorio Emanuele II 303, tel. 4220361. A major venue for performances of contemporary theater.

Teatro Puccini. Viale delle Cascine 41 (corner of Piazza Puccini), tel. 362067. This theater, founded recently, has an array of unconventional productions, as well as comic and satirical theater.

Teatro Variety. Via del Madonnone 47, tel. 577937. Performances for the public at large, with special concentration on operetta.

Sports

Assi Giglio Rosso. Viale Michelangiolo 64, tel. 587858. Tennis courts, running track, and skating.

Associazione Polisportiva Flog Il Poggetto. Via Mercati 24/b, tel. 481285. Open pool, tennis courts, gymnasium, and lawn bowling.

Centro Ippico Toscano "Le Cascine." Horseback riding. Via Vespucci 5/a , tel. 315621.

Centro Squash Firenze. Via Empoli 16, tel. 7323055.

Circolo del Tennis Firenze. Viale del Visarno 1, tel. 353959. Tennis and an open-air pool.

Ippodromo delle Cascine. Viale del Visarno, tel. 4226076. Gallop racing.

Piscina Costoli. Viale Paoli, tel. 669744-678012. Open-air Olympic pool, diving tank, wading pool, water slide, and shaded athletic park. June-September.

Piscina di Bellariva. Lungarno Moro 6, tel. 677521. Olympic pool, partly covered, wading pool, athletic park.

Stadio Comunale "Franchi." Viale Fanti 4, tel. 574648.

at Coverciano

Centro Tecnico della FGCI. Via Gabriele D'Annunzio 138, tel. 613271. Training facilities.

The Provincial Territory

Bagno a Rìpoli   ✉ 50012 ☎ 055

Page 135

Entertainment and other events

at Gràssina, km. 4   [✉ 50015

Historical reenactment of Good Friday. Beginning at 9:30 there is a procession of hundreds of people in historical costumes. A tradition that dates back to the 17th c.

Farming

Mondeggi Lappeggi. Via di Mondeggi 7, tel. 6499068. Production and sale of extra-virgin olive oil, Chianti DOCG wine, and "vinsanto."

Barberino di Mugello   ✉ 50031 ☎ 055

Hotels, restaurants, camping, and resort villages

★★★ **Motel Barberino.** At Cavallina, Viale Don Minzoni 55, tel. 8420051, fax 8420432. Number of rooms: 78. Lodging only; no board. Elevator; parking area, garden, tennis courts.

¶ **Cavallo.** Via della Repubblica 7, tel. 8418144. Closed Wednesday except in summer. Parking area, garden. Tuscan cuisine.

¶ **Cosimo de' Medici.** At Cavallina, Viale Don Minzoni 57, tel. 8420370. Closed Monday, for a certain period in August. Parking area. Tuscan cuisine.

at Santa Lucìa, km. 9   ✉ 50030

⚠ **Il Sergente.** Village of Monte di Fo', tel. ★★ 8423018. Year round.

Museums and cultural institutions

at Cafaggiolo, km. 7   ✉ 50030

Villa di Cafaggiolo, tel. 8458793 (for the Associazione Ambiente e Turismo). Guided tours, only for groups.

Barberino Val d'Elsa   ✉ 50021 ☎ 055

Page 145

Hotels, restaurants, camping, and resort villages

★★ **Primavera.** At San Filippo a Ponzano, Via della Repubblica 27, tel. 8059223, fax 8059223. Number of rooms: 27. Lodging only; no board. Handicap-friendly. Elevator; parking area.

¶ **Il Paese dei Campanelli.** At Petrognano, tel. 8075318. Closed Monday, November. Parking area. Tuscan cuisine.

⚠ **Semifonte.** Via Foscolo 4, tel. 8075454. Sea-★★ sonal.

Ecotourism

Fattoria S. Appiano. Via S. Appiano 11, tel. and fax 8075541. Apartments in restored farmhouses. Pool, lake fishing. Production and sale of wine, oil, "vinsanto," and grappa.

at Cortine, km. 8

Fattoria Casa Sola. For information: Giuseppe Gambaro, tel. 8075028-010/308771. Accommodations in apartments in a vineyard, with garden and woods; dining. Pool. Wine, oil, "vinsanto."

at Marcialla, km. 5   ✉ 50020

Fattoria Giannozzi. For information: Simone Giannozzi, tel. 8076602. Stay in apartments in an old farmhouse and a restored silo. Farming; pool, tennis courts. Wine, oil, "vinsanto."

at Vico d'Elsa, km. 8   ✉ 50050

Azienda Agricola "La Volpaia." For information: Andrea Taliaco, tel. 8073063, fax 8073170. Stay in rooms in old farmhouses; horses. Horseback riding and long-distance rides, pool. Wine and oil.

Museums and cultural institutions

At the Pieve di S. Appiano, km. 4

Museo Etrusco Antiquarium, tel. 8075297. *Sat-*

urday and Sunday 3:30-6. In case it is closed, contact the parish priest.

Borgo San Lorenzo   ☒ 50032 ☎ 055

Page 131

Hotels, restaurants, camping, and resort villages

¶¶   **Feriolo.** At Polcanto, Via Faentina 32, tel. 8409928. Closed Tuesday, for a certain period in January and in August. Parking area, garden. Tuscan cuisine.

Museums and cultural institutions

at Grezzano, km. 8   ☒ 50030

Parco della Colla. Historic and naturalistic trail with adjoining **Museo della Civiltà Contadina**, tel. 8457197 (Town library of Borgo San Lorenzo). *Weekends and holidays 3-7.* For groups, also on other days, by appointment.

Calenzano   ☒ 50041 ☎ 055

Page 127

Hotels, restaurants, camping, and resort villages

★★★   **Delta Florence.** Via Vittorio Emanuele 3, tel. 8876302, fax 8874606. Number of rooms: 241. Air conditioning, elevator; parking area, pool.

★★★   **Valmarina.** At Settimello, Via Baldanzese 146, tel. 8825336, fax 8825250. Number of rooms: 34. Lodging only; no board. Handicap-friendly. Air conditioning, elevator; parking garage.

¶¶   **Carmagnini del '500.** At Croci di Calenzano, Via di Barberino 242, tel. 8819930. Closed Monday, for a certain period in August. Parking area, garden. Fine Tuscan cuisine.

¶¶   **Terrazza.** Via del Castello 25, tel. 8873302. Closed Sunday and Monday, Christmas-New Year's Day and August. Parking area. Tuscan cuisine.

Museums and cultural institutions

Museo del Soldatino e delle Figurine Storiche. Via Giotto 5, tel. 8879441. *Monday, Tuesday, Wednesday, Friday 3-7; Thursday, Saturday, and weekends and holidays 9:30-12:30, 3:30-6:30.*

Entertainment and other events

Carnevale Medievale. Historical costumes, in the historical center of Calenzano Alto. Last Sunday of Carnevale.

Farming concerns

at San Donato, km. 1

Fattoria Morrocchi Pancrazi. Viale dei Cipressi 8, tel. 8879457. In a medieval village; this farm

sells wines, fresh-pressed extra-virgin olive oil, and pecorino cheese.

Campi Bisenzio   ☒ 50013 ☎ 055

Page 136

Museums and cultural institutions

Villa Il Palagio. Via Saffi 1. Renaissance villa, open to public by request at the Misericordia, tel. 891113. Site of exhibitions and cultural events.

Entertainment and other events

Estate a Campi. Festival of music, theater, dance, and film, in the garden of Villa Montalvo and in the squares of the historical center. June-September.

Carmignano   ☒ 50042 ☎ 055

Page 137

Hotels, restaurants, camping, and resort villages

¶   **San Giusto.** Via Montalbano 7, tel. 8712022. Closed Tuesday. Tuscan cuisine.

at Bacchereto, km. 8   ☒ 50040

¶¶¶   **Cantina di Toia.** Via Toia 12, tel. 8717135. Closed Monday and Tuesday, November. Parking area, garden. Fine Tuscan cuisine.

at Artimino, km. 6

★★★   **Paggeria Medicea.** Viale Papa Giovanni XXIII 3, tel. 8718081, fax 8718080. Number of rooms: 37. Air conditioning; parking area, garden, pool.

¶¶¶   **Biagio Pignatta.** Viale Papa Giovanni XXIII 5, tel. 8718086. Closed Wednesday and at midday on Thursday. Tuscan cuisine.

Ecotourism

at Bacchereto, km. 8   ☒ 50040

Fattoria di Bacchereto. Via Fontemorana 179. For information: Carlo Bencini Tesi, tel. 8717191-245975, fax 8717191. Apartments and rooms in farmhouses on a large olive farm, with bee-keeping; conference rooms, dining by request. Pool, lawn-bowling, ping-pong, trekking; pottery courses, yoga, fine food. Retail sale of extra-virgin olive oil from the press, DOCG wines, "vinsanto," honey.

Museums and cultural institutions

Rocca di Carmignano. Via di Castello. *Wednesday-Thursday-Saturday and weekends and holidays 3-7.*

at Artimino, km. 6   ☒ 50042

Museo Archeologico Comunale. Viale Giovanni XXIII 5, tel. 8718124. This archeological museum is located in the Medici Villa La Ferdinanda. Closed Wednesday. *Hours: 9-1; Saturday also 3-7.*

at Comeana, km. 5   ✉ 50040

Etruscan tomb of Montefortini. Via Montefortini 43. Closed Monday. *Hours: 9-2.*

Farming concerns

at Seano, km. 3   ✉ 50040

Tenuta di Capezzana. Via di Capezzana 100, tel. 8706005. Sale of fresh-pressed extra-virgin olive oil, wines (some of them DOCG), "vinsanto," and grappa.

Castelfiorentino   ✉ 50051 ☎ 0571

Page 146

ℹ️ *Ufficio Turismo del Comune.* Piazza del Popolo, tel. 61996 e 62351.

Museums and cultural institutions

Pinacoteca di S. Verdiana. Church of S. Verdiana. Being installed.

Raccolta Comunale d'Arte, or town art collection. Via Tilli 41/43, tel. 64019. *Tuesday-Thursday-Saturday 4-7; weekends and holidays 10-12, 4-7.*

Entertainment and other events

Festival of Choral Song. November.

Teatro del Popolo. Until the 19th-c. structure can be renovated, the Sala del Ridotto is in use. Piazza Gramsci 42/r.

at Castelnuovo d'Elsa, km. 5   ✉ 50050

Rassegna del Teatro Popolare. Second half of June.

Farming concerns

at Oliveto, km. 5

Fattoria Oliveto. Via Monte Oliveto 6, tel. 64322. By request, tour of the castle and the wine cellars. Tasting and sale of DOCG wines, spumante, "vinsanto," and extra-virgin olive oil.

Cerreto Guidi   ✉ 50050 ☎ 0571

Page 137

ℹ️ *Associazione Turistica Pro Loco.* Villa Medicea, tel. 55671.

Museums and cultural institutions

Villa Medicea. Ponti Medici 7, tel. 55707. *Weekdays, weekends, and holidays 9-2.*

Certaldo   ✉ 50052 ☎ 0571

Plan, page 147

Hotels, restaurants, camping, and resort villages

🍴   **Osteria del Vicario.** At Certaldo Alta, Via Rivellino 3, tel. 668228. Seasonal, closed

Wednesday, and for a certain period in January. Garden. Tuscan cuisine (A3, **r**).

Museums and cultural institutions

Casa del Boccaccio, Library, and Research Center. Via Boccaccio, tel. 664208 or else 661252 (Town library). Sunday closed. *Monday and Thursday 4-7:30; Wednesday 9-1; all other days tours by request.*

Palazzo Pretorio. Piazzetta del Vicariato, tel. 661219. Closed Monday. *Winter 10-12, 3:30-6; summer 10-12:30, 4:30-7:30.*

Entertainment and other events

"Mercantia," Teatralfestivalmercato. Compagnie del Teatro di Strada, crafts festivals. Historical center, third week in July.

Premio Letterario Boccaccio and Boccaccio-Europa, two literary prizes. Third Saturday in September.

Farming concerns

at Fiano, km. 9   ✉ 50050

Castello di S. Maria Novella. Via. S. Maria Novella 121, tel. 669050. By request, you can tour the 11th-c. castle, the medieval village, and the old park. They sell extra-virgin olive oil, wines (some DOCG), "vinsanto," honey.

Dicomano   ✉ 50062 ☎ 055

Page 132

Shops, crafts, and fine art

Merlini Costante. Piazza Buonamici 34, tel. 838007. Oil lamps, lanterns, funnels, and copper objects with the appearance of bygone times.

Émpoli   ✉ 50053 ☎ 0571

Page 138

ℹ️ *Associazione Turistica Pro Empoli.* Piazza Farinata degli Uberti 8/9, tel. 76115.

Hotels, restaurants, camping, and resort villages

★★★   **Tazza d'Oro.** Via G. del Papa 46, tel. 72129, fax 77370. Number of rooms: 51. Handicap-friendly. Elevator; special parking garage for guests.

🍴   **Bianconi.** Via Tosco Romagnola 96/98, tel. 590558. Closed Wednesday, for a certain period in July. Air conditioning, parking area, garden. Tuscan cuisine.

🍴   **Galeone.** Via Curtatone e Montanara 67, tel. 72826. Closed Sunday, for a certain period of time in August. Classical cuisine-fish.

Museums and cultural institutions

Antiquarium. Piazza Farinata degli Uberti 11, tel. 78961-78711. *Saturday-Sunday and weekends and holidays 5:30-8.*

Museo Casa "F. Busoni," con annesso **Centro Studi Musicali.** Piazza della Vittoria, tel. 711122. Tours by request.

Museo Civico di Paleontologia (environmental reconstruction of the Valdarno Inferiore). Piazza Farinata degli Uberti 7, tel. 707817. Closed Monday. *Weekdays, weekends, and holidays 5-7:30. Mornings by appointment.*

Museo della Collegiata di S. Andrea. Piazza della Propositura 3, tel. 76284. Closed Monday. *Sunday-Tuesday-Wednesday 9-12; Thursday-Friday-Saturday 9-12, 4-7.*

Entertainment and other events

Teatro Excelsior. Via Ridolfi 75, tel. 72023. Opera season from November to April.

Teatro Shalom. Via Busoni 24, tel. 77528. From October to December "Giornate Busoniane"; from March to May "Concerti di Primavera." A theater season in the old tradition.

Fièsole   ✉ 50014 ☎ 055

Plan, page 117

ℹ️ *Ufficio Informazioni of the APT of Florence.* Piazza Mino da Fiesole 37, tel. 598720.

Hotels, restaurants, camping, and resort villages

⁎⁎⁎   **Villa Aurora.** Piazza Mino 39, tel. 59100, fax 59587. Number of rooms: 27. Air conditioning; parking area, garden (A2, **b**).

⁎⁎⁎   **Villa San Michele.** Via Doccia 4, tel. 59451, fax 598734. Seasonal. Number of rooms: 28. Air conditioning; parking area, garden, pool (B3, **a**).

⁎⁎⁎   **Bencistà.** Via B. da Maiano 4, tel. 59163, fax 59163. Number of rooms: 42, of which 30 have a bath or shower. Parking area, garden (B3, *off map*).

⁎⁎⁎   **Villa Bonelli.** Via F. Poeti 1, tel. 59513, fax 598942. Number of rooms: 20. Elevator; parking garage, garden (A3, **c**).

🍴   **Cave di Maiano.** At Maiano, Via delle Cave 16, tel. 59133. Closed Thursday and Sunday evening, for a certain period in August and Christmas. Parking area, garden. Tuscan cuisine (B3, *off map*).

🍴   **Dino.** At Olmo, Via Faentina 329, tel. 548932. Closed Wednesday, for a certain period between January and February. Parking area, garden. Tuscan cuisine (A3, *off map*).

⚑⁎⁎⁎   **Panoramico.** Via Peramonda 1, tel. 599069, fax 59186. Year round.

Ecotourism

at Maiano, km. 2   ✉ 50016

Fattoria di Maiano. For information: Francesco Miari Fulcis, tel. 599600-597089. Accommodations in apartments in a renovated former convent. Hiking, trekking, horseback riding, fishing.

Retail sales of wine, oil (Laudemio), meat, and other delicacies.

Museums and cultural institutions

Fondazione Museo Primo Conti. Via Duprè 18, tel. 597095. Closed Monday and weekends and holidays. *Weekdays 9-3:30, Saturday 9-1:30.*

Museo Bandini. Via Duprè 1, tel. 59477. Closed Tuesday. *Weekdays, weekends, and holidays 10-1, 3-6; summer 9:30-1, 3-7.*

Museo Civico, Archeological Area, Antiquarium Costantini. Via Portigiani 1, tel. 59477. In winter, closed Tuesday. *Weekdays, weekends, and holidays 9-6; summer 9-7.*

Museo G. Duprè. Via Duprè 19, tel. 59171-598745. Tours by request, preferably from March to October.

Museo Etnografico Missionario. Via S. Francesco 13, tel. 59175. *Weekdays, weekends, and holidays 9:30-12:30, 3-6; summer 9-7.*

Art gallery and library of the Fondazione Berenson. Villa I Tatti, Via di Vincigliata 26, tel. 608909. Headquarters of the Centro di Studi di Storia del Rinascimento of **Harvard University (center for the study of Renaissance history).**

at San Domenico, km. 1   ✉ 50016

Fondazione Scuola di Musica di Fiesole. Via delle Fontanelle 24, tel. 59571. Concerts on Sunday Mornings; seminars in the fall, spring, and summer.

Istituto Universitario Europeo. Via Badia dei Roccettini 9, tel. 46851.

Entertainment and other events

Estate Fiesolana. Festival of dance, theater, music, and film, in the Roman theater (Teatro Romano). July and August.

Shops, crafts, and fine art

at Caldine, km. 4   ✉ 50010

Bottega del Ferro Forgiato. Via Faentina 169/7, tel. 5040311. Crafts production of wrought-iron objects, including garden furniture.

Figline Valdarno   ✉ 50063 ☎ 055

Page 134

Hotels, restaurants, camping, and resort villages

⁎⁎⁎   **Torricelli.** Via S. Biagio 2, tel. 958139, fax 958481. Number of rooms: 39. Elevator; parking area.

🍴   **Antica Taverna Casagrande.** Via Castel Guinelli 84, tel. 952403. Closed Monday, for a certain period in January. Parking area, garden. Tuscan cuisine.

⚑⁎⁎⁎   **Norcenni Girasole Club.** Via Norcenni 7, tel. 959666, fax 959337. Year round.

Museums and cultural institutions

Antica Farmacia dell'Ospedale Serristori. Piazza XXV Aprile 10, tel. 95081. *Tours by request.*

Collegiata di S. Maria. Piazza Marsilio Ficino 43, tel. 958518. Adjoining Museo della Collegiata, a museum. *Tours by request.*

at Gaville, km. 6

Museo della Civiltà Contadina. Pieve di S. Romolo. *Saturday 3-6, Sunday 3-7*

Entertainment and other events

Teatro Comunale Garibaldi, tel. 953531 (Ufficio Cultura del Comune). From November to March an opera season, and concerts of classical music throughout the year.

Firenzuola   ⊠ 50033 ☎ 055

Page 131

[*i*]   *Pro Loco,* tel. 819366.

Shops, crafts, and fine art

Carli. Via Brenzone 91, tel. 816036. Monumental copies of great quality, by a master of shaping and carving "pietra serena."

Fucecchio   ⊠ 50054 ☎ 0571

Page 139

Hotels, restaurants, camping, and resort villages

Renato. Via Trento 13, tel. 20209. Closed Saturday, for a certain period in August. Air conditioning. Tuscan and classical cuisine.

at Le Vedute, km. 7

Vedute. Via Romana Lucchese 121, tel. 297498. Closed Monday, and for a certain period in August. Parking area. Classical cuisine.

Museums and cultural institutions

Museo Civico. Piazza Vittorio Veneto 27, tel. 20349. Closed for restoration.

Entertainment and other events

Infiorata del Corpus Domini. Sunday of Corpus Domini.

Palio delle Contrade. Last Sunday in May. Procession in costume, in the morning; bareback horse races, in the afternoon.

Sport

Tiro a Segno Nazionale (target shooting). Via Pistoiese-Botteghe 22, tel. 260678.

Farming concerns

"Fattoria Montellori" di Nieri Giuseppe. Via Pistoiese 5, tel. 260641. They also sell DOCG wines and spumante.

Gambassi Terme   ⊠ 50050 ☎ 0571

Page 148

Hot springs spas

Stabilimento Termale Comunale. Acqua di Pillo, salso-bicarbonate-sodic-sulphate-alkalino-ferrous. For digestive cures, Piazza G. Di Vittorio 1, tel. 638141 (*April-October*). For breathing cures, Via Volterrana 30, tel. 638579 (*all year round*).

Greve in Chianti   ⊠ 50022 ☎ 055

Page 142

[*i*]   *Ufficio del Turismo.* Piazza Matteotti 83, tel. 8545243.

Hotels, restaurants, camping, and resort villages

★★★   **Del Chianti.** Piazza Matteotti 86, tel. 853763, fax 853763. Number of rooms: 16. Air conditioning, elevator; garden, pool.

★★★   **Giovanni da Verrazzano.** Piazza Matteotti 28, tel. 853189, fax 853648. Number of rooms: 11, of which 10 have a bath or shower.

★★★   **Villa Le Barone.** At Panzano, via S. Leolino, tel. 852621, fax 852277. Number of rooms: 27. Parking area, garden, pool.

★★★   **Villa Sangiovese.** At Panzano, piazza Bucciarelli 5, tel. 852461, fax 852463. Number of rooms: 19. Garden, pool.

¶¶   **Omero Casprini.** At Passo dei Pecorari, Via G. Falcone 70, tel. 850715. Closed Wednesday, for a certain period between July and August. Parking area, garden. Tuscan cuisine.

¶¶   **Trattoria del Montagliari.** At Panzano, Via Montagliari 29, tel. 852184. Closed Monday, for a certain period in August. Parking area, garden. Tuscan cuisine.

Entertainment and other events

Mostra Mercato del Chianti Classico. Tasting and sale of Chianti Classico DOCG wines. September.

Shops, crafts, and fine art

Antica Macelleria Falorni. Piazza Matteotti 69/71, tel. 853029. Production of Tuscan salamis, in the traditional way.

Il Ferrone. Via Chiantigiana 36, tel. 850782. Manufacture of fine Florentine terracotta tiles.

Farming concerns and wine cellars

Castello di Uzzano. Via Uzzano 5, tel. 854032. Tasting and sale of Chianti Classico and extra-virgin olive oil. Breeding of pure blood Arabian and Friesian horses.

Enoteca del Gallo Nero. Piazza Santa Croce 8, tel. 853297. Permanent exhibition and sale of DOCG Chianti Classico wine and other local products.

Impruneta ⊠ 50023 ☎ 055

Page 120

Hotels, restaurants, camping, and resort villages

🍴 **Cavallacci.** Viale A. Moro 3, tel. 2313863. Closed Monday and midday on Tuesday. Parking area, garden. Fine Tuscan cuisine.

🏨 **Internazionale Firenze.** At Bottai, Via San ⋆⋆⋆ Cristofaro 2, tel. 2374704, fax 2373412. Seasonal.

Stabilimenti Termali

at Tavarnuzze, 5 km. ⊠ 50029

Terme di Firenze. Via Cassia 217 (S.S. 2), tel. 2020151. Salso-bromo-iodic and moderately sulphuric waters for drinking, bathing, and fumes (*from mid-May until late December*).

Museums and cultural institutions

Museo del tesoro di S. Maria all'Impruneta. Basilica di S. Maria all'Impruneta, Piazza Buondelmonti, tel. 2011700 (Biblioteca Comunale, or town library). *Summer Thursday, Friday 10-1; Saturday, Sunday 10-1, 3:30-7; winter Friday 10-1; Saturday 3-6:30; Sunday 10-1, 3-6:30.*

Entertainment and other events

Rassegna internazionale di canto corale. International Festival of Choral Singing. June.

Festa dell'Uva. Procession of allegorical floats from the four quarters of the town. Last Sunday in September.

Fiera di S. Luca. Festival of the patron saint, with a market, horse races, stalls, and various events. 18 October.

Shops, crafts, and fine art

Poggi Ugo. Via Imprunetana 16, tel. 2011677. Gardening vases and floor tiles from the Impruneta area.

Incisa in Val d'Arno ⊠ 50064 ☎ 055

Page 134

Hotels, restaurants, camping, and resort villages

⋆⋆⋆ **Galileo.** At Prulli, tel. 863341, fax 863238. Number of rooms: 63. Handicap-friendly. Air conditioning, elevator; parking area, parking garage, garden, pool, tennis courts.

Lastra a Signa ⊠ 50055 ☎ 055

Page 138

Hotels, restaurants, camping, and resort villages

🍴 **Cupoli.** Via L. da Vinci 32, tel. 8721028, fax 8721028. Closed Monday, November. Parking area, garden. Tuscan cuisine.

🍴 **Antica Trattoria Sanesi.** Via Arione 33, tel. 8720234. Closed Sunday evening and Monday, and for a certain period between July and August. Air conditioning. Tuscan cuisine.

Museums and cultural institutions

Museo Vicariale. Pieve di S. Martino a Gangalandi. *Tours by request.*

Shops, crafts, and fine art

Ceramica "La Lastra." Via Livornese 287, tel. 8720264. Objects for interior decoration and artistic ceramic vases, made by hand.

Farming concerns

at Malmantile, km. 4 ⊠ 50050

Tenuta S. Vito in Fior di Selva. Via S. Vito 32, tel. 51411. They also sell DOCG wines, "vinsanto," grappa, and organic honey.

Marradi ⊠ 50034 ☎ 055

Page 131

ℹ️ *Ufficio Informazioni Turistiche (tourist information offices).* Via Umberto I 3, tel. 8045170.

Hotels, restaurants, camping, and resort villages

🍴 **Camino.** Viale Baccarini 38, tel. 8045069. Closed Wednesday, for a certain period between August and September. Tuscan cuisine and the cuisine of Romagna.

Museums and cultural institutions

Centro Studi Campaniani "E. Consolini" and the Town Library (Biblioteca Comunale). Piazza Le Scalelle 5, tel. 8045943.

Entertainment and other events

Premio Internazionale di Poesia Dino Campana, an international poetry prize. Every two years, at the end of the summer.

Teatro degli Animosi. An 18th-c. building, recently restored. Season November-April.

Shops, crafts, and fine art

at Sant'Adriano, km. 5

Cappelli. Via Faentina 52, tel. 8044049. Wrought-copper and embossed dishes and vases, unique items of remarkable quality.

Montaione ⊠ 50050 ☎ 0571

Page 148

Hotels, restaurants, camping, and resort villages

⋆⋆⋆ **Vecchio Mulino.** Viale Italia 10, tel. 697966,

fax 697966. Number of rooms: 19. Lodging only; no board. Parking area, garden.

Ecotourism

Azienda Agricola Pievelinghe. Loc. La Pieve 181. For information: Anna and Dieter Pildner, tel. 69502. Rooms and apartments in farmhouse and small villa; manmade lake. Guide to farming; pool, barbecue. Chianti wine, extra-virgin olive oil.

Pistolese Ranch. Via Sanminiatese 117, village Le Mura. For information: Riccardo Battigelli, tel. and fax 69196. Accommodations for those interested in horseback riding, trekking, "equiarcheology" – or archeology on horseback. Horseback tours. Fine natural food.

at Sùghera, km. 7

Azienda Agricola "Il Poggio." For information: Massimo Sbrana, tel. 677071-050/85564. Numerous apartments in farmhouses; dining. Basketball, volley ball, pool, game reserve, horseback riding, tennis courts. Wine, oil, vegetables, poultry.

Museums and cultural institutions

Sacro Monte di S. Vivaldo. Convento di S. Vivaldo, tel. 699252.

Museo Comunale Mineralogico and Paleontologico della Val d'Elsa. Palazzo Pretorio, Via Cresci 15, tel. 699252. *Tours by request.*

Entertainment and other events

Classica. Musical afternoons at S. Vivaldo. July.

Estate Montaionese. Festival of music, theater, film, and exhibitions. June-September.

Shops, crafts, and fine art

Ticciati Tosco. Via Buozzi 38, tel. 69261. Artistic objects for interior decoration and jewelry, in onyx and in semiprecious stones, entirely made by hand.

Farming concerns

at Castelfalfi, km. 11

Tenuta di Castelfalfi, tel. 698093-4. Medieval fortress and old village. Sold here: DOCG wines, extra-virgin olive oil, freshly pressed in a stone mill, honey.

at Orzale, km. 2.5

Azienda Agricola Orzale. In a 13th-c. fortress. In the old chapel, they sell DOCG wines and extra-virgin olive oil.

Montelupo Fiorentino   ⊠ 50056 ☎ 0571

Page 138

Hotels, restaurants, camping, and resort villages

★★★ **Baccio da Montelupo.** Via Don Minzoni 3, tel. 51215, fax 51171. Number of rooms: 22.

Lodging only; no board. Air conditioning, elevator; parking area.

Museums and cultural institutions

Museo Archeologico e della Ceramica. Via Sinibaldi 45, tel. 51352. Closed Monday. *Weekdays 9-12, 2:30-7; Sunday 2:30-7.*

Entertainment and other events

Festa Internazionale della Ceramica. Exhibition and events in the historical center. Second half of June-first half of July.

Mercato Antiquario di Oggetti in Vetro e Maiolica. In the historical center, market of glass and majolica, third Sunday of April and October.

Shops, crafts, and fine art

Of particular note is the ceramic production of Montelupo: decorative dishes, goblets, vases, and various other types of item. For detailed information on the ceramic production of the area and for retail outlets, contact: **Consorzio della Ceramica.** Palazzo Comunale, Via Cento Fiori 12, tel. 917516.

Montespèrtoli   ⊠ 50025 ☎ 0571

Page 146

Museums and cultural institutions

Museo di Arte Sacra Locale. Canonica della Pieve di S. Pietro in Mercato. (Museum of religious art; scheduled to open by 1995). For information, Ufficio Turismo del Comune, tel. 609412.

Entertainment and other events

Mostra del Chianti. Last Sunday in May-first Sunday in June.

Farming concerns

Fattoria Sonnino. Via Volterrana Nord 10, tel. 609198. In an 18th-c. villa. They sell wines, some DOCG, "vinsanto," grappa, extra-virgin olive oil.

at Poppiano, km. 4

Fattoria Castello Guicciardini, tel. 82315. Tasting and sale of DOCG wines, "vinsanto," spumante, grappa, extra-virgin olive oil.

Palazzuolo sul Senio   ⊠ 50035 ☎ 055

Page 131

[i] *Ufficio Turistico* (open in the summer). Piazza Alpi, tel. 8046125. In other periods, c/o Comune, tel. 8046008.

Hotels, restaurants, camping, and resort villages

¶¶ **Locanda Senio.** Borgo dell'Ore 1, tel. 8046019. Closed Tuesday evening and Wednesday in the off season, Epiphany (6

January)/mid-February. Garden. Tuscan cuisine.

 Visano. At Visano, S.P. della Faggiola, tel. 8046106. Seasonal.

Museums and cultural institutions

Museo Archeologico. Palazzo dei Capitani, tel. 8046154. *From May to October weekends and holidays 3:30-6:30.* Guided tours for groups, in other periods as well.

Museo della Civiltà Contadina e Artigiana. Palazzo dei Capitani, tel. 8046008-114. *From July to August every day 4-7; closed January-February; in the other months, holidays 3-6.* Guided tours for groups, in other periods as well.

Entertainment and other events

Ottobre Palazzuolese. On the second, third, and fourth Sunday in October is the fair of the very fine Florentine chestnut; it is also possible to buy mushrooms, truffles, marmalade and preserves, and other products of the forest and the underbrush.

Shops, crafts, and fine art

La Bottega dei Portici. Piazza Garibaldi 3, tel. 8046019. Excellent distillates of raspberry, blueberry, juniper berry, and so on; excellent marmalades, honey, salames, and cheese.

at Lozzole, km. 7

Fattoria Lozzole, tel. 8046505. In this farm retail outlet, you can purchase excellent goat's-milk cheeses.

Poggio a Caiano ✉ 50046 ☎ 055

Page 137

Hotels, restaurants, camping, and resort villages

★★★ **Hermitage.** At Bonistallo, Via Ginepraia 112, tel. 877040, fax 8797057. Number of rooms: 61. Air conditioning, elevator; parking area, pool.

Museums and cultural institutions

Villa Medicea. Piazza dei Medici 14, tel. 877012. *Everyday 9-1:30.*

Entertainment and other events

"Festival delle Colline." Music festival in the park of the Medici villa. June-July.

Pontassieve ✉ 50065 ☎ 055

Page 134

Hotels, restaurants, camping, and resort villages

★★★ **Moderno.** Via Londra 5, tel. 8315541, fax 8315542. Number of rooms: 120. Lodging

only; no board. Handicap-friendly. Air conditioning, elevator; parking garage.

¶¶ **Girarrosto.** Via Garibaldi 27, tel. 8368048. Closed Monday, August. Parking area, garden. Tuscan and classical cuisine.

Ecotourism

Tenuta di Bossi. Via dello Stracchino 32. For information: Donatella Gondi, tel. 8317830, fax 8364008. Accommodations in apartments in old farmhouses on a large estate; dining. Wine and oil (Laudemio).

Entertainment and other events

Toscanello d'Oro. From Wednesday to the Sunday of the third week in May. Fair and market of wine, with tasting and sale. Display of farm equipment.

Farming concerns and wine cellars

Chianti Ruffino. Via Aretina 42/44, tel. 83605. Production of wine Chianti Ruffino DOCG.

at Santa Brigida, km. 14 ✉ 50060

Fattoria Castello del Trebbio of Baj Macario e c., the village of Trebbio, tel. 8300051. Chianti DOCG, extra-virgin olive oil, horses and equitation.

at Sieci, km. 5 ✉ 50069

Cantine Frescobaldi. Via Aretina, tel. 830902. Production and sale of Chianti Rufina DOCG from the cellars of the estate of the Marchesi Frescobaldi.

Reggello ✉ 50066 ☎ 055

at Saltino, km. 11

ℹ️ *APT Vallombrosa,* tel. 862003 (seasonal).

Hotels, restaurants, camping, and resort villages

★★★ **Villa Rigacci.** At Vaggio, Via Manzoni 76, tel. 8656562, fax 8656537. Number of rooms: 18. Air conditioning; parking area, garden, pool.

★★★ **Archimede.** At Pietrapiana, Via di Vallombrosa, tel. 869055, fax 868584. Number of rooms: 18. Parking area, garden.

¶¶ **Archimede.** At Pietrapiana, Via di Vallombrosa, tel. 869055. Closed Tuesday except July-September. Parking area, garden. Tuscan cuisine.

Museums and cultural institutions

at Vallombrosa, km. 12 ✉ 50060

Abbazia di Vallombrosa, tel. 862029. *Tours upon request, by calling ahead.*

Shops, crafts, and fine art

at Tosi, km. 13 ✉ 50060

Bertini Paolo. Via Berenson 31, tel. 864624. Production and sale of fine furniture.

Rignano sull'Arno   ✉ 50067 ☎ 055

Ecotourism

Azienda Agricola "Il Castiglionchio." Loc. Castiglionchio. For information: Emilio Terenzi, tel. 8303063-8303471, fax 8303063-8303472. Numerous apartments in a complex with an 18th-c. villa and farmhouses. Billiards, game room, conference room, stereo hall; pool, tennis courts, horseback riding, mountain-biking. Fruit, wine, oil.

Rùfina   ✉ 50068 ☎ 055

Page 134

Hotels, restaurants, camping, and resort villages

★★★ **La Speranza-da Grazzini.** Via Piave 14, tel. 8397027, fax 8397028. Number of rooms: 29. Parking area, parking garage, garden.

Ecotourism

Fattoria di Petrognano. Loc. Petrognano. For information: Cecilia Galeotti Ottieri, tel. 8318812-8317830. Apartaments in the villa and in renovated farmhouses; rooms in the tavern. Fishing, pool, tennis courts, hiking. Wine, oil, honey.

Museums and cultural institutions

Museo della Vite e del Vino. Villa di Poggio Reale, Viale Duca della Vittoria 125, tel. 8397932. Undergoing restoration.

Farming concerns and wine cellars
at Pomino, km. 9   ✉ 50060

Fattoria Pomino, tel. 8318810. Built in the 16th c., this farm has large and excellent wine cellars owned by the Marchesi Frescobaldi, and a production of "vinsanto."

San Casciano in Val di Pesa
Page 143   ✉ 50026 ☎ 055

Hotels, restaurants, camping, and resort villages
at Mercatale, km. 5

🍴 **Fedino.** Via Borromeo 9, tel. 828612. Closed Monday. Parking area, garden. Tuscan cuisine.

🍴 **Il Salotto del Chianti.** Via Sonnino 92, tel. 8218016. Closed Wednesday, for a certain period in January; open only in the evening. Garden. Fine Tuscan cuisine.

Ecotourism

Azienda Agricola "Il Molinaccio." Village Falciani, Via Castelbonsi 25. For information: Elisabetta Partini, tel. 8228080, tel. and fax 06/8083439. Accommodations in apartments in an 18th-c. villa, with period furniture, and in farmhouses. Poultry, rabbits, eggs.

at Mercatale, km. 5   ✉ 50024

Azienda Agricola Salvadonica. For information: Francesca and Beatrice Baccetti, tel. 8218039, fax 8218043. Apartments and rooms in a farm complex dating back to the 15th c. Pool, soccer field, tennis courts, mountain-biking. Chianti wine, extra-virgin olive oil, fruit, vegetables.

at Montefiridolfi, km. 7   ✉ 50020

Fattoria La Loggia. Via Collina 40. For information: Giulio Baruffaldi, tel. 8244288, fax 8244283. Numerous apartment in a restored Renaissance village; restaurant. Pool, horseback riding, barbecue, volleyball, bicycling, ping-pong. Chianti wine, spumante, oil, grappa, fruit, vegetables, home-made bread.

Museums and cultural institutions

Museo Vicariale di Arte sacra. Church of S. Maria del Gesù, Via Roma 3/1, tel. 8228220-8229444. *Saturday 4-7, weekends and holidays 10-12, 4-7.*

Museo della Misericordia. Via Morrocchesi 72. *Tours by request.*

Farming concerns and wine cellars
at Ponte di Gabbiano, km. 7

Frantoio del Grevepesa, tel. 821353. Production and sale of extra-virgin olive oil.

San Piero a Sieve   ✉ 50037 ☎ 055

Page 129

Hotels, restaurants, camping, and resort villages

🍴 **La Felicina.** Piazza Colonna 14, tel. 8498181. Closed Saturday, for a certain period between February and March, and in August. Garden. Tuscan cuisine.

★★★ **Mugello Verde.** Via Massorondinaio 39, tel. 848511, fax 8486910. Year round.

Museums and cultural institutions

Castello di Trebbio. Information from the Associazione Ambiente e Turismo, tel. 8458793. *Guided tours, only for groups.*

Fortezza di S. Martino. Information from the Associazione Ambiente e Turismo, tel. 8458793. *Guided tours, only for groups.*

at Bosco ai Frati, km. 3,5

Museo del Convento del Bosco ai Frati, tel. 848111. *Hours: 8-12, 3-7.*

Scandicci   ✉ 50018 ☎ 055

Page 138

Hotels, restaurants, camping, and resort villages

★★★ **Touring.** At Casellina, Via B. da Montelupo 16, tel. 753938, fax 755556. Number of rooms: 27. Lodging only; no board. Elevator; parking area.

Entertainment and other events

Teatro Studio. Via Donizetti 58, tel. 757348. This is one of the chief centers of experimental theater in Tuscany.

Farming concerns

at San Martino alla Palma, km. 4 ⊠ 50010

Azienda Agricola Pio Del Torricino. Village of Vigliano. Via di Valimorta 10, tel. 768615. Medieval comples and Romanesque villa belonging to the Pulci-Antinori family. They also sell DOCG wines, "vinsanto," grappa, fruit preserves, pickled vegetables, honey.

Fattoria S. Martino. Via S. Martino alla Palma 41, tel. 768748. In the 14th-c. Villa Torrigiani. They sell DOCG wines, extra-virgin olive oil, freshly pressed in a stone mill, "vinsanto," grappa, and vinegar.

Scarperìa ⊠ 50038 ☎ 055

Page 130

Museums and cultural institutions

Palazzo dei Vicari, tel. 8430671 (Town library).

Museo dei Ferri Taglienti. Via Solferino, (For information Biblioteca Comunale, tel. 8430671). *Saturday and Sunday 3-7:30.* On other days, group tours by calling ahead.

at Sant'Agata, km. 3 ⊠ 50030

Mostra di Vita Artigiana e Contadina, or exhibition of crafts and peasant tradition, tel. 8406750. *Weekends and holidays, winter 3:30-6, summer 3:30-6:30.*

Sport

at Senni, km. 2.5

Autodromo Internazionale del Mugello, SAIM, car racing, tel. 8495800.

Shops, crafts, and fine art

Berti Severino e C. Via della Resistenza 12 and Via Matteotti 64, tel. 8469903. Crafts production and sale of knives and other cutting tools, as well as collector's items.

Sesto Fiorentino ⊠ 50019 ☎ 055

Page 127

Hotels, restaurants, camping, and resort villages

★★★ **Forte Agip.** Near the highway interchange of Firenze Nord, tel. 4205081, fax 4219015. Number of rooms: 163. Handicap-friendly. Air conditioning, elevator; parking area.

★★★ **Villa Villoresi.** Via Ciampi 2, tel. 443692, fax 442063. Number of rooms: 28. Parking area, garden, pool.

Museums and cultural institutions

Museo delle Porcellane di Doccia. Via Pratese 31, tel. 4210451. *Tuesday-Thursday-Saturday 9:30-1; 3:30-6:30.*

Etruscan tomb "La Montagnola." Via Fratelli Rosselli 95, tel. 4489941. *Summer, Tuesday and Thursday 10-1; Saturday and Sunday 10-1, 5-7. Winter, Saturday, and Sunday 10-1.*

Etruscan tomb "La Mula." Via della Mula 2, tel. 4492144. *Summer, Tuesday 10-12; Saturday 10-12, 5-6:30. Winter: Saturday 10-12.*

Entertainment and other events

Teatro della Limonaia. Villa Corsi Salviati, Via Gramsci 426, tel. 440852. A festival of international new theater is held here, known as "Intercity." Second half of September-first half of October.

Signa ⊠ 50058 ☎ 055

Page 138

Hotels, restaurants, camping, and resort villages

★★★ **Europa.** Piazza Stazione 10, tel. 8734345, fax 8734041. Number of rooms: 124. Handicap-friendly. Air conditioning, elevator; parking area, pool.

Tavarnelle Val di Pesa ⊠ 50028 ☎ 055

Page 145

Hotels, restaurants, camping, and resort villages

★★★ **Park Hotel Chianti.** At Pontenuovo, Via Cassia, tel. 8070106, fax 8070121. Number of rooms: 43. Lodging only; no board. Air conditioning, elevator; parking area, garden, pool.

❙❙ **Toppa.** At San Donato in Pòggio, Via del Giglio 43, tel. 8072900. Closed Monday, for a certain period in November. Garden. Tuscan cuisine and the cuisine of Romagna.

❙ **La Gromola.** Tel. 8050321. Closed Tuesday, and for a certain period in January. Open only in the evening (except holydays).

Youth hostels

🏠 **Ostello della Gioventù del Chianti.** Via Roma 137, tel. 8077009. Sleeps 54. Open March-October.

Museums and cultural institutions

Museo d'Arte Sacra. Pieve di S. Pietro in Bòssolo. *Saturday 4-7; weekends and holidays 9-1, 4-7.*

at Passignano, km. 8

Badia di Passignano. *Guided tours, on Sunday afternoon.*

Vaglia   ✉ 50030 ☎ 055

Museums and cultural institutions

at Monte Senario, km. 8
Convento di Monte Senario. Via Montesenario 1, tel. 406441. *Weekdays, weekends, and holidays 7-12:30, 3-6.*

at Pratolino, km. 6   ✉ 50036
Park of the Villa Medici-Demidoff. Via Fiorentina 6, tel. 2760538 (Assessorato alla Cultura della Provincia). *From May to September Friday, Saturday, Sunday 10-8.* In summer concerts, performances for children, exhibitions, and conferences.

Vicchio   ✉ 50039 ☎ 055
Page 132

Hotels, restaurants, camping, and resort villages

★★★ **Villa Campestri**. At Campestri, Via di Campestri 19/22, tel. 8490107, fax 8490108. Seasonal. Number of rooms: 20. Handicap-friendly. Parking area, garden, pool.

Museums and cultural institutions

Museo Civico "Beato Angelico." Tours by request, tel. 8497026 (Town library).

at Vespignano, km. 6
Casa Natale di Giotto (birthplace), tel. 844782. *Thursday, Saturday, and Sunday 3-7.*

Vinci   ✉ 50059 ☎ 0571
Page 137

Hotels, restaurants, camping, and resort villages

★★★ **Alexandra**. Via dei Martiri 38/40, tel. 56224, fax 567972. Number of rooms: 37. Air conditioning: parking area, garden.

🍴 **Torretta.** Via della Torre 19, tel. 56100. Closed Monday, for a certain period in August. Air conditioning. Tuscan cuisine.

Museums and cultural institutions

Biblioteca Leonardiana. Via La Pira 1, tel. 56590.

Museo Ideale Leonardo da Vinci (Arte, Utopia, Cultura della Terra). Via Montalbano 2/4/6, tel. 56296. *Weekdays, weekends, and holidays 10-1, 3-7.*

Museo Leonardiano. Castello dei Conti Guidi, tel. 56055. *Winter 9:30-6; summer 9:30-7.*

at Anchiano, km. 2.5
Casa Natale di Leonardo (birthplace). *Winter 9:30-1, 2:30-5; summer 9:30-1, 3:30-6.* Closed Wednesday.

Entertainment and other events

Celebrazioni Leonardiane. "Letture Vinciane," lectures by world-renowned scholars. In the month of April.

Fiera di Vinci. Historic procession and the traditional reenactment of the flight of Cecco Santi from the tower of the castle. Last week in July.

Index of Places and Things

Florence Atlas

City key map

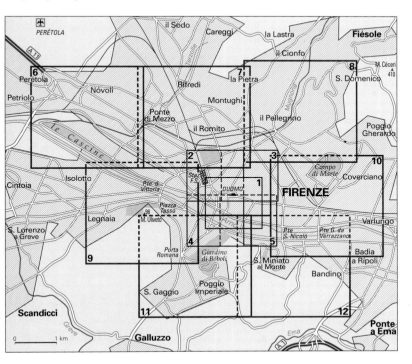

Conventional signs

▮ Palazzi, Museums		▒ Gardens	
▮ Hospitals		▦ Cemeteries	
▯ Buildings		▬ Main roads	
✚ Churches		— Railroads	
Hotels; Restaurants		Pedestrian zones	
Walls		**1-5** ▯ 1:6,000 (1 cm = 60 m)	
City limits		**6-12** ▯ 1:12,000 (1 cm = 125 m)	

Greater Florence area
1:100.000 (1cm = 1km)

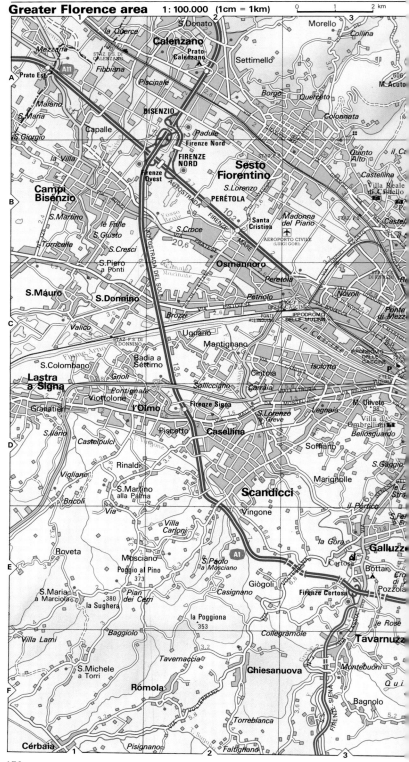

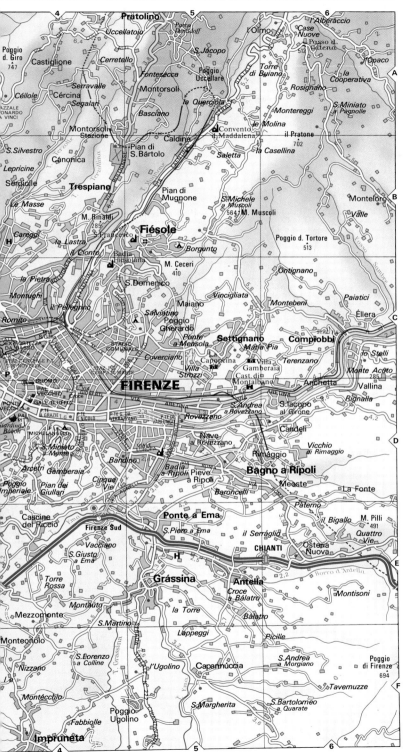

177

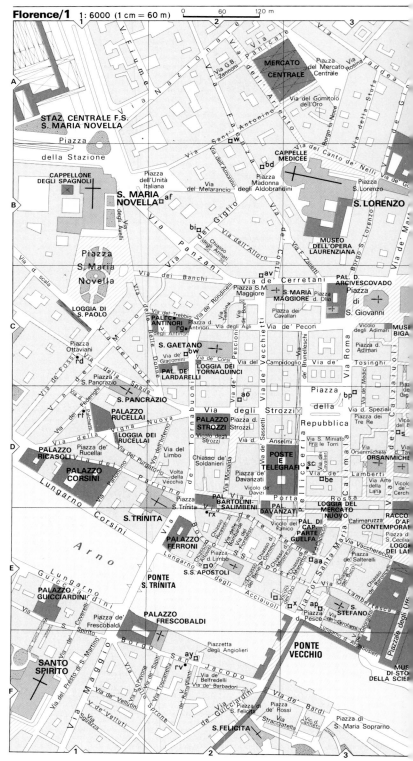

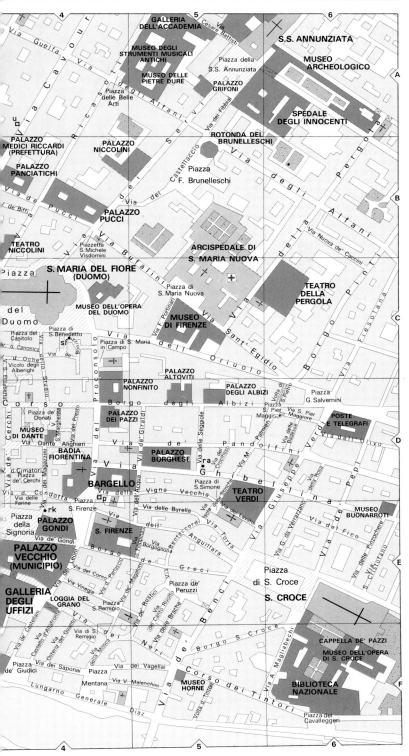

GALLERIA
DELL'ACCADEMIA

MUSEO DEGLI
STRUMENTI MUSICALI
ANTICHI

Via Cesare Battisti

Via Guelfa

Via Cavour

Via Ricasoli

Via degli Alfani

MUSEO DELLE
PIETRE DURE

Piazza della
S.S. Annunziata

S.S. ANNUNZIATA

MUSEO
ARCHEOLOGICO

PALAZZO
GRIFONI

Via dei Fibbiai

Via della Pergola

A

PALAZZO
MEDICI RICCARDI
(PREFETTURA)

PALAZZO
NICCOLINI

PALAZZO
PANCIATICHI

Via de' Pucci

Via del Castellaccio

Via dei Servi

ROTONDA DEL
BRUNELLESCHI

Piazza
F. Brunelleschi

SPEDALE
DEGLI INNOCENTI

Via degli Alfani

Via Nuova de' Caccini

B

de' Biffi

Via

PALAZZO
PUCCI

Via de' Servi

Piazzetta
S. Michele
Visdomini

Via de' Pucci

Via Bufalini

TEATRO
NICCOLINI

Piazza

S. MARIA DEL FIORE
(DUOMO)

del
Duomo

Piazza del
Capitolo

Piazza di
S. Benedetto

V. d. Canonica

Via d. Oche
Vicolo degli
Alberighi

ARCISPEDALE DI
S. MARIA NUOVA

Piazza di
S. Maria Nuova

MUSEO DELL'OPERA
DEL DUOMO

Via F. Portinari

Via Sant'Egidio

MUSEO
DI FIRENZE

Via dell' Oriuolo

TEATRO
DELLA
PERGOLA

Borgo Pinti

Via Fiesolana

C

Via dello Studio

Via de' Bonizzi

Piazza di S. Maria
in Campo

PALAZZO
ALTOVITI

PALAZZO
NONFINITO

Via del Proconsolo

Borgo degli Albizi

PALAZZO
DEGLI ALBIZI

Via S. Pier Maggiore

Piazza
S. Pier
Maggiore

Piazza
G. Salvemini

Via delle Badesse

Via di S. Pier Maggiore

Via dei Pepi

Via Verdi

POSTE
E TELEGRAFI

Via dell' Olivo

D

Corso

Via de' Cerchi

Piazza de'
Donati

MUSEO
DI DANTE

Via Dante Alighieri

Via S. Margherita

BADIA
FIORENTINA

V. d. Cimatori
Piazza
de' Cerchi

Via d. Condotta

Via delle
Farine

PALAZZO
DEI PAZZI

Via de' Giraldi

Via

PALAZZO
BORGHESE

Via de' Pandolfini

Via del Crocifisso

Via M. Palmieri

Via delle Seggiole

Via del Proconsolo

Via della Rosa

Via Giuseppe Verdi

Via de' Pepi

MUSEO
BUONARROTI

BARGELLO

Via della Vigna Vecchia

Piazza di
S. Simone

TEATRO
VERDI

Via dell' Acqua

park

S. Firenze

Piazza
della
Signoria

PALAZZO
GONDI

Via de' Gondi

PALAZZO
VECCHIO
(MUNICIPIO)

Via dei Leoni

Via de' Magazzini

Via delle Burella

Via dell'Anguillara

Via della Vigna Vecchia

Via delle Stinche

Via Isole delle Stinche

Via G. da Verrazzano

Via de' Fico

Via delle Pinzochere

Via dei Lavatoi

Via de' Pepi

Via Torta

S. FIRENZE

Via de' Neri

Piazza de'
Peruzzi

Piazza
di S. Croce

S. CROCE

Via delle Conce

Via M. Buonarroti

Via dei Macci

E

GALLERIA
DEGLI
UFFIZI

Via de' Castellani

LOGGIA DEL
GRANO

Via de' Guanto

Via di S.
Remigio

Via Vinegia

Piazza
S. Remigio

Via del Corno

Borgo de' Greci

Via de' Rustici

Via del Carlo Braghe

Via de' Benci

CAPPELLA DE' PAZZI

MUSEO DELL'OPERA
DI S. CROCE

Via A. Magliabechi

Via Castello d'Altafronte

Via Osteria del Guanto

Via della Mosca

Piazza
Mentana

Via V. Malenchini

Via di S.
Remigio

Via dei Saponai

Piazza
de' Giudici

Via dei Vagellai

MUSEO
HORNE

Corso dei Tintori

Via de' Bardi

Via A. Magliabechi

BIBLIOTECA
NAZIONALE

Lungarno Generale Diaz

Volta di Tinaio

Piazza dei
Cavalleggeri

F

4   5   6

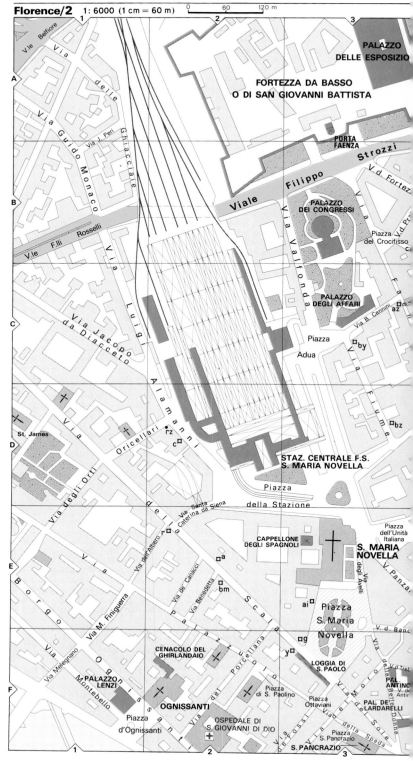

Florence/2

1:6000 (1 cm = 60 m)

0   60   120 m

PALAZZO
DELLE ESPOSIZIO

FORTEZZA DA BASSO
O DI SAN GIOVANNI BATTISTA

V.le   Belfiore

Via   delle

Via   Guido   Monaco

Via   J. Peri

Via   Ghiacciaie

PORTA
FAENZA

Strozzi

V. d. Fortez

Viale   Filippo

PALAZZO
DEI CONGRESSI

Via   Valfonda

Piazza
del Crocifisso

V. d. Pra

ca

V.le F.lli   Rosselli

Via   Luigi

Via   Jacopo
da Diacceto

PALAZZO
DEGLI AFFARI

Via B. Cennini

az

Piazza
Adua

by

Via   Fiume

Via   Alamanni

St. James

Via   degli   Orti   Oricellari

rz

c

bz

STAZ. CENTRALE F.S.
S. MARIA NOVELLA

Piazza
della   Stazione

Piazza
dell'Unità
Italiana

Via Santa
Caterina da Siena

CAPPELLONE
DEGLI SPAGNOLI

S. MARIA
NOVELLA

V. Panzan

Via
degli   Avelli

Via   Borgo

Via   M. Finiguerra

Via dell'Albero

Via de' Cavallacci

Via Benedetta

a

bm

Scala

ai

Piazza
S. Maria
Novella

V. d. Banc

Via   Meleghano

Ognissanti

Via   Montebello

PALAZZO
LENZI

CENACOLO DEL
GHIRLANDAIO

Via del   Porcellana

g

y

LOGGIA DI
S. PAOLO

Via   Moro

V. d. Tret

PAL.
ANTINO

PAL. DE'
LARDARELLI

V. d.
Antir

OGNISSANTI

Piazza
di S. Paolino

Piazza
Ottaviani

Via   della   Sale

Via   de' Fossi

Donne

Piazza
d'Ognissanti

OSPEDALE DI
S. GIOVANNI DI DIO

Piazza
S. Pancrazio

Piazza
della   Spada

S. PANCRAZIO

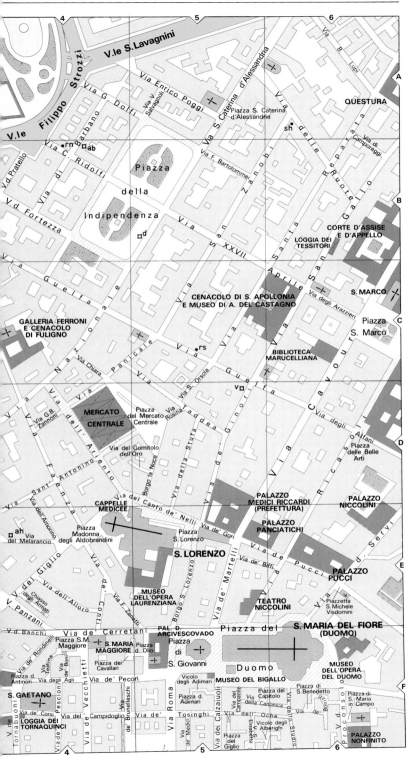

181

Florence/3 1:6000 (1 cm = 60 m)

V.le S. Lavagnini

QUESTURA

PALAZZO
PANDOLFINI

Via Enrico Poggi

V G
Dolfi

Via S. Caterina d'Alessandria

Piazza S. Caterina
d'Alessandria

Via di
Camporeggi

Piazza

della

Indipendenza

Via F. Bartolommei

Via XXVII

Aprile

Via Nazionale

Via delle Ruote

Via Santa Reparata

br

CHIOSTRO
DELLO SCALZO

LOGGIA DEI
TESSITORI

CORTE D'ASSISE
E D'APPELLO

Via
della Dogana

CENACOLO DI S. APOLLONIA
E MUSEO DI A. DEL CASTAGNO

Via degli Arazzieri

S. MARCO

MUSEO
DI S. MARCO

Piazza
S. Marco

UNIVERSITÀ

Via Panicale

Via S. Orsola

Via Guelfa

Via Cavour

Via Cesare Battisti

BIBLIOTECA
MARUCELLIANA

GALLERIA
DELL'ACCADEMIA

MERCATO
CENTRALE

Piazza
del Mercato
Centrale

Via Rosina

Via Taddea

Via della Stufa

Via Ginori

aq

Via de' Ricasoli

Via degli Alfani

MUSEO DEGLI
STRUMENTI MUSICALI
ANTICHI

MUSEO DELLE
PIETRE DURE

ax Piazza
S.S. Annunzia

PALAZ.
GRIFON

Via del Gomitolo
dell'Oro

Borgo la Noce

Piazza
delle Belle
Arti

ROTONDA DE
BRUNELLESC

Ariento

Via del Canto de' Nelli

Via de' Conti

Via F. Zanetti

Via B. S. Lorenzo

Via de' Gori

CAPPELLE
MEDICEE

Piazza
S. Lorenzo

PALAZZO
MEDICI RICCARDI
(PREFETTURA)

PALAZZO
PANCIATICHI

PALAZZO
NICCOLINI

Via degli Alfani

Castellaccio

del

Piazza
F. Brunelleschi

S. LORENZO

Via de' Martelli

Via de' Biffi

MUSEO
DELL'OPERA
LAURENZIANA

PALAZZO
PUCCI

Via de' Pucci

Via Bufalini

ARCISPEDALE D
S. MARIA NUOV

TEATRO
NICCOLINI

Piazzetta
S. Michele
Visdomini

S. MARIA
MAGGIORE

PAL. D.
ARCIVESCOVADO

Piazza
d. Olio

Piazza
di
S. Giovanni

Piazza del

Duomo

S. MARIA DEL FIORE
(DUOMO)

Piazza di
S. Maria Nuova

Via V. S. Egidi

MUSEO
DI FIRENZE

V. de' Pecori

Via Roma

Vicolo
degli Adimari

MUSEO DEL BIGALLO

Piazza d.
Adimari

Via Tosinghi

Via de'

Via de' Medici

Via de' Brunelleschi

Piazza del
Capitolo
Via
della Canonica

Via dello

Via del Campanile

Via dell' Oche

Vicolo degli
<Alberighi

Piazza
del
Giglio

MUSEO DELL'OPERA
DEL DUOMO

Piazza di
S.Benedetto

Via del
Proconsolo

Via dell'Oriuolo

Piazza di S. Maria
in Campo

PALAZZO
ALTOVITI

PALAZZO
NONFINITO

PALAZZO
DEGLI ALBI

182

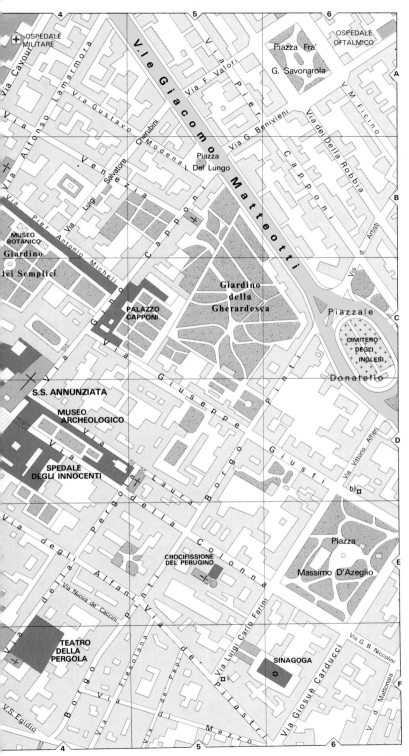

OSPEDALE MILITARE

Via Cavour

Via Alfonso Lamarmora

Via Gustavo

OSPEDALE OFTALMICO

Piazza Fra'
G. Savonarola

V. M. Ficino

V.le Giacomo Matteotti

Via F. Valori

Pier

Via G. Benivieni

Cherubini

Modena

Via Venezia

Luigi Salvatore

Via Pier Antonio Michelli

Piazza
I. Del Lungo

Capponi

Via dei Della Robbia

Via d. Artisti

MUSEO BOTANICO

Giardino
dei Semplici

PALAZZO CAPPONI

Via

Giardino
della
Gherardesca

Capponi

Piazzale

CIMITERO
DEGLI
INGLESI

Via

S.S. ANNUNZIATA

MUSEO ARCHEOLOGICO

Via Laura

Via Giuseppe

Borgo

Giusti

Pinti

Donatello

Via Vittorio Alfieri

SPEDALE DEGLI INNOCENTI

Pergola

della

bl

Via degli

Alfani

Via Nuova de' Caccini

Colonna

CROCIFISSIONE DEL PERUGINO

Piazza

Massimo D'Azeglio

Via

de'

Via Pinti

Via

Fiesolana

Via de' papi

de'

Pilastri

Via Luigi Carlo Farini

Via G. B. Niccolini

TEATRO DELLA PERGOLA

Borgo

SINAGOGA

Via Giosuè Carducci

V. d. Mattonaia

V.S. Egidio

Via di

Mezzo

i

183

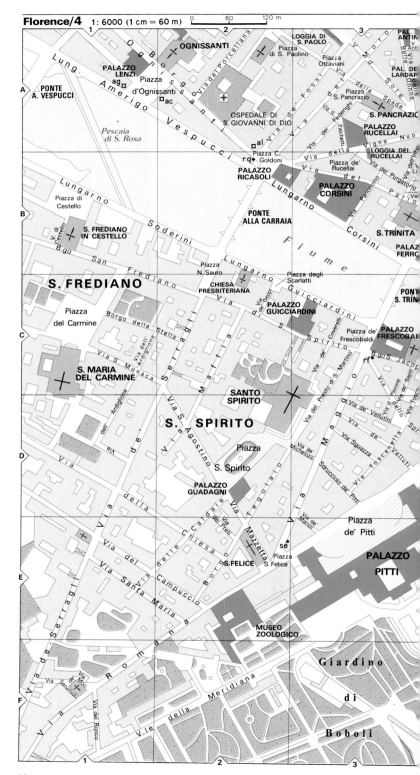

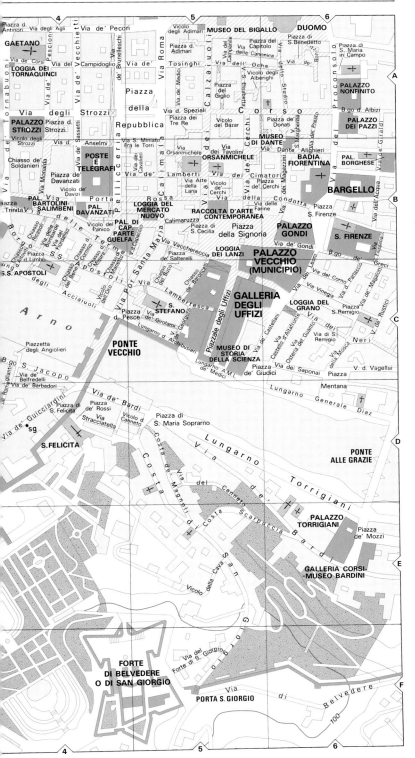

185

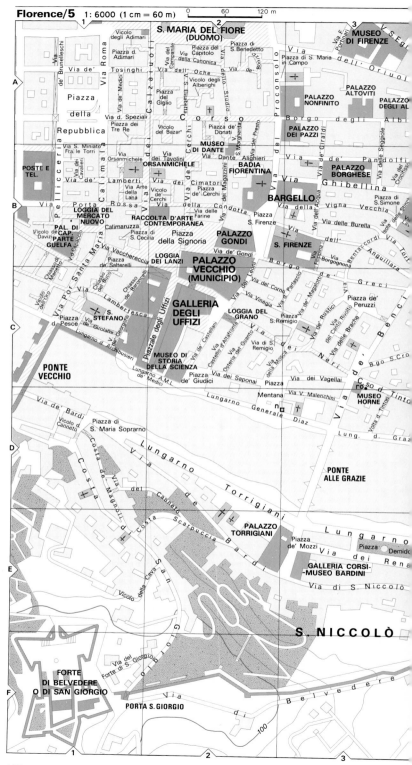

Florence/5 1:6000 (1 cm = 60 m)

186

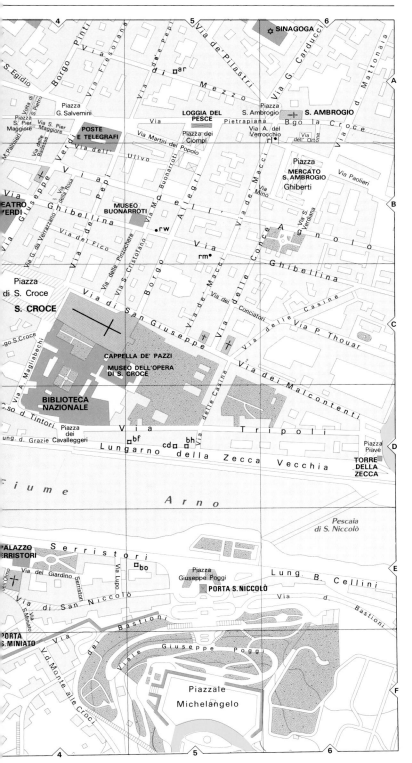

SINAGOGA

Via G. Carducci

Via de-Pilastri

Via di Mezzo

d. Pepi

Borgo Pintu

Via Fiesolana

S. Egidio

Piazza
G. Salvemini

Piazza
S. Ambrogio

S. AMBROGIO

Bgo la Croce

Volta di S. Pietri
Piazza
S. Pier
Maggiore
Via S. Pier
Maggiore
M.Palmieri
Via delle
Badesse

POSTE
E TELEGRAFI

LOGGIA DEL
PESCE

Via

Pietrapiana

Via A. del
Verrocchio

Via
dell' Orto

Via d'Mattonaia

Via Martiri del Popolo

Piazza dei
Ciompi

Via de' Macci

Piazza
MERCATO
S. AMBROGIO

Via Paolieri

Via dell'Ulivo

Ghiberti

Via Giuseppe Verdi

TEATRO
VERDI

Via Ghibellina

Via de' Pepi

Via della Rosa

Via Buonarroti

Via de' Macci

Via Mino

Via S. Verdolana

MUSEO
BUONARROTI

Via del Fico

Via G. da Verrazzano

Via delle Pinzochere

Via S. Cristofano

Borgo Allegri

Via de' Macci

Via delle Conce

Via delle Casine

Ghibellina

A g n o l o

Piazza
di S. Croce

S. CROCE

Bgo S.Croce

Via di San Giuseppe

Via dei Conciatori

Via P. Thouar

Via A. Magliabechi

CAPPELLA DE' PAZZI

MUSEO DELL'OPERA
DI S. CROCE

Via delle Casine

Via dei Malcontenti

Via de' Benci

BIBLIOTECA
NAZIONALE

C.so d. Tintori

Piazza
dei
Cavalleggeri

Via

Tripoli

Lung. d. Grazie

Lungarno della Zecca Vecchia

Piazza
Piave

TORRE
DELLA
ZECCA

F i u m e

A r n o

Pescaia
di S. Niccolò

PALAZZO
SERRISTORI

Serristori

Via del Giardino

Via Lupo

Via Serristori

Piazza
Giuseppe Poggi

Lung. B. Cellini

Via dell'Olmo

Via di San Niccolò

Via S.Minato

PORTA S. NICCOLÒ

Via d. Bastioni

PORTA
S. MINIATO

Via dei Bastioni

V.d. Monte alle Croci

Viale Giuseppe Poggi

Piazzale
Michelangelo

187

Florence/6 1:12 500 (1 cm = 125 m)

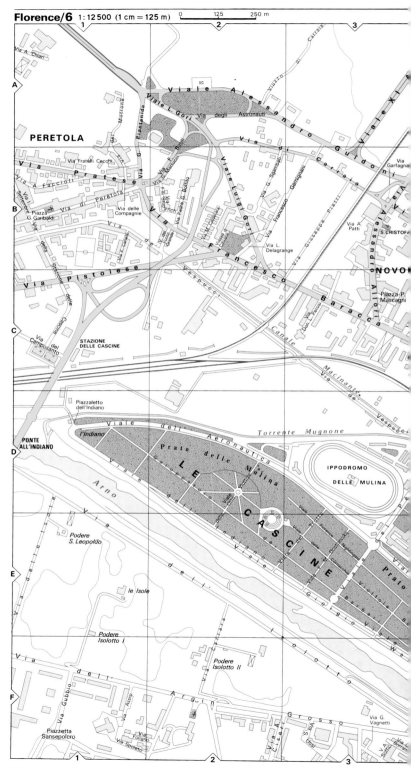

PERETOLA

STAZIONE
DELLE CASCINE

PONTE
ALL'INDIANO

Piazzaletto
dell'Indiano

l'Indiano

Torrente Mugnone

IPPODROMO
DELLE MULINA

Prato delle Mulina

LE CASCINE

Arno

Podere
S. Leopoldo

le Isole

Podere
Isolotto I

Podere
Isolotto II

Piazzetta
Sansepolcro

NOVO

Piazza P.
Mascagni

S. CRISTOFA

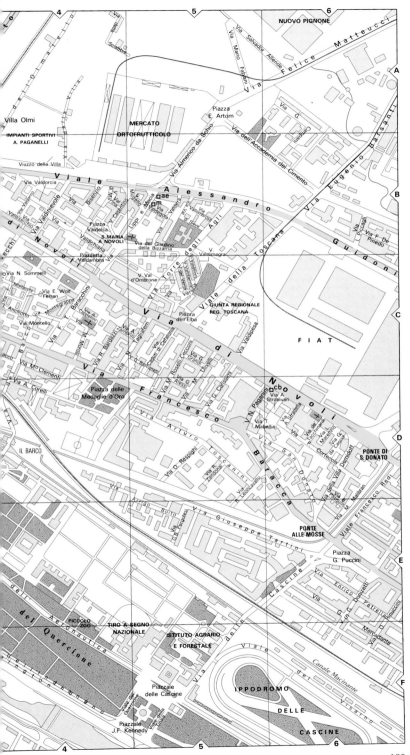

NUOVO PIGNONE

Villa Olmi

IMPIANTI SPORTIVI
A. PAGANELLI

MERCATO
ORTOFRUTTICOLO

Piazza
E. Artom

Via dell'Accademia del Cimento

Viuzzo della Villa

Viale Alessandro

Via Valdorcia

Piazza
Valdelsa

S. MARIA
A NOVOLI

Via del Giardino
della Bizzarria

Piazzetta
Valdambra

V. Val
d'Ombrone

Via N. Sommelli

Via E. Wolf
Ferrari

GIUNTA REGIONALE
REG. TOSCANA

Piazza
dell'Elba

Via di Novoli

F I A T

Via Montello

IL BARCO

Piazza delle
Medaglie d'Oro

Via Francesco Baracca

Novoli

Via A.
Stradivari

Via T.
Mabellini

PONTE DI
S. DONATO

PONTE
ALLE MOSSE

Via Arrigo Boito

Via Giuseppe Tartini

Piazza
G. Puccini

PICCOLO
ZOO

del Quercione

TIRO A SEGNO
NAZIONALE

ISTITUTO AGRARIO
E FORESTALE

Canale Macinante

IPPODROMO

Piazzale
delle Cascine

DELLE

Piazzale
J.F. Kennedy

CASCINE

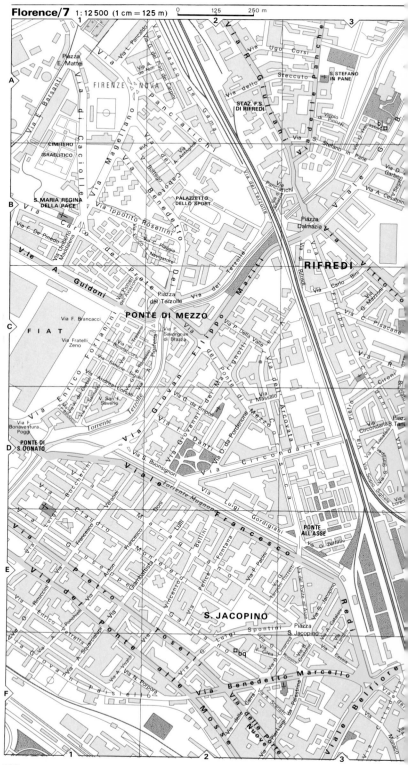

Florence/7 1:12 500 (1 cm = 125 m)

0   125   250 m

FIRENZE NOVA

Piazza E. Mattei

Via F. Basilati

Via di Caciolle

Via Pancialichi

Via de' Noli

Via VC dei Carpini

Via Vasco De Gama

Via Ugo Corsi

Via Reginald delle Bianche

Steccuto

S. STEFANO IN PANE

STAZ. F.S. DI RIFREDI

Via dello Steccuto

Vicolo d'Cinema

castello

Via D. Garbo

Via A. Cesalpin

Via Stefano in Pane

CIMITERO ISRAELITICO

Via Magliano

Via Borgo Carignani

Via dei Campi

Via Antognini

Via dei Pancialichi

Via dei Terzolle

Via del Terzolle

S. MARIA REGINA DELLA PACE

Via Carlo del Prete

Via F. De Pinedo

Via Umberto Maddalena

Via Ippolito Rosellini

Via Enrico

PALAZZETTO DELLO SPORT

Piaggia Navigatori

Piazza Dalmazia

RIFREDI

Via Vittorio

Via Carlo Bini

Via dei Martiri

V.le A. Guidoni

Piazza del Terzolle

PONTE DI MEZZO

Via dei Pratoni d'Aviazione

Via dei Terzolle

Via G. Mazzoni

Via Pisacana

FIAT

Via F. Brancacci

Via Fratelli Zeno

Via Enrico Fortanini

Via Simone Buck

Via Andrea Corsali

Via A. Boncecorsi

Via G. da Empoli

Via Filippo Ponte di Mezzo

Via P. della Valle

Via II Massaio

Via dell'Alcoviata

Via Circondaria

Cironi

Via Brigidia

N. San F. Saverio

Via Bonaventura Poggi

Torrente Terzolle

PONTE DI S. DONATO

Via Dante

Via G. da Pordenone

Via Giovanni del

Piazza Circondaria B. Tani

Via Scano Sighele

Via Giovan Filippo

Viale Torrente Mugnone

Via S. Buonsignon

Via Torrente Mugnone

Via Luigi Gordigiani

Via Francesco

PONTE ALL'ASSE

Via G. Zeffirini

Via Bocchirre

Via Ponte alle Mosse

Via Claudio

Via Francesco Montanelli

Via Giuseppe Giambottista

Via Vincenzo

Via Litti

Via Bellini

Via Fontana

Via F. Petrini

Via del Ponte alle Mosse

S. JACOPINO

Via Pietro

Via O. Rinuccini

Via Enrico Petrella

Via Toselli

Via Luigi

Spontini

Piazza S. Jacopino

Via Redi

Via S. Jacopino

Via A. Squarcialupi

Via G. Via A. Vivaldi

Via N. Porpora

Via Paisiello

Via Clea

Via Rossini

Via A. Scarlatti da Palestrina

Viale Belfiore

Benedetto Marcello

Via delle Porte Nuove

Via Pier Luigi da Palestrina

Via Monaco

1:12 500 (1 cm = 125 m)

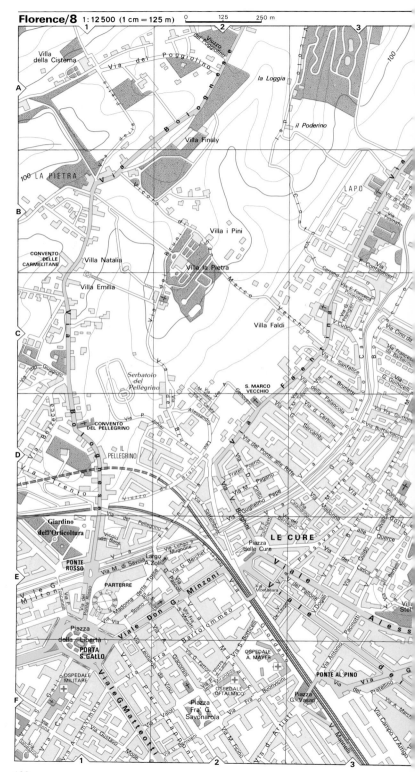

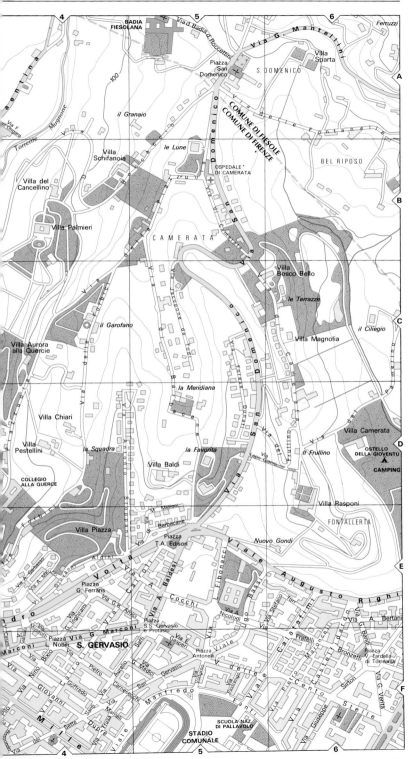

193

Florence/9 1:12 500 (1 cm = 125 m)

0 125 250 m

IPPODROMO
DELLE
CASCINE

Piazzale J.F. Kennedy

LE CASCINE

Viale delle Piramide
Viale dei Lecci

PISCINA "LE PAVONIERE"

Viale degli Abramo

Fium

Piazza dell'Isolotto
Viale dei Bambini

Piazzetta del Salice
Piazza dei Tigli

Piazzetta F. De Pisis

Via del Sansovino

Piazza P. Batoni

Viale Francesco Talenti

Antonio del Pollaiolo

Piazza Pier della Francesca

MONTICELLI

il Boschetto

OLIVUZZO

Via Maso di Banco

Via Gherardo Starnina

Villa Chiocchin

Via Duccio di Buoninsegna

Coppo di Marcovaldo

Villa Papini

Villa Bigazzi

BIGAZZI

CIMITERO DELLA MISERICORDIA

Villa dei Cipressi

Villa Venturini

Villa Martelli

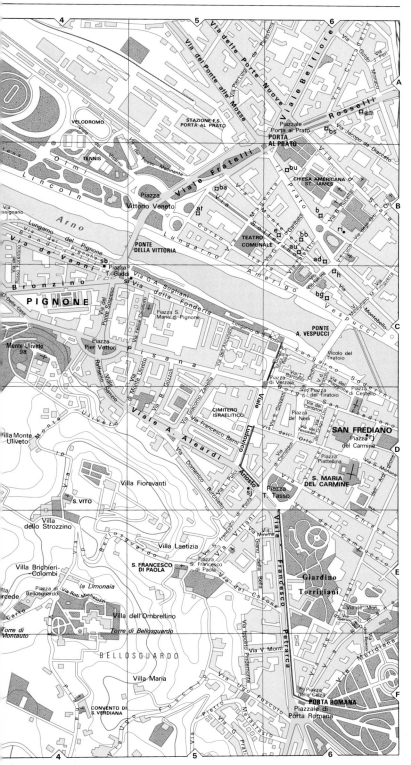

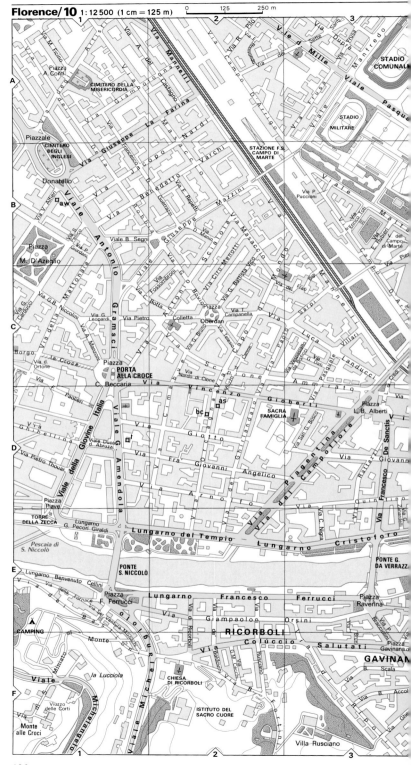

Florence/10 1:12 500 (1 cm = 125 m)

0   125   250 m

STADIO COMUNALE

STADIO MILITARE

CIMITERO DELLA MISERICORDIA

Piazza A. Conti

Piazzale

CIMITERO DEGLI INGLESI

Donatello

STAZIONE F.S. CAMPO DI MARTE

Piazza M. D'Azeglio

Via P. Puccioni

Piazza Colletta

Piazza Oberdan

Via I. Campanella

Piazza PORTA ALLA CROCE

Borgo la Croce

Via d. Ortone

Via C. Beccaria

SACRA FAMIGLIA

Piazza L. B. Alberti

Piazza Piave

Piazza Giotto

TORRE DELLA ZECCA

Lungarno G. Pecori Giraldi

Pescaia di S. Niccolò

Lungarno del Tempio

Lungarno Cristoforo

PONTE S. NICCOLÒ

PONTE G. DA VERRAZZ.

Lungarno Benvenuto Cellini

Piazza F. Ferrucci

Lungarno Francesco Ferrucci

Piazza Ravenina

CAMPING

Via Giampaolo Orsini

RICORBOLI

Via Colúccio Salutati

Piazza Gavinana

GAVINAN

Monte

la Lucciola

CHIESA DI RICORBOLI

Viale Michelangelo

ISTITUTO DEL SACRO CUORE

Monte alle Croci

Viuzzo delle Corti

Villa Rusciano

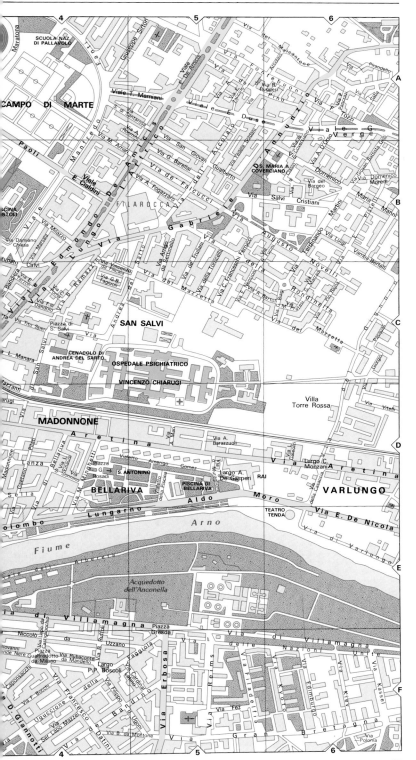

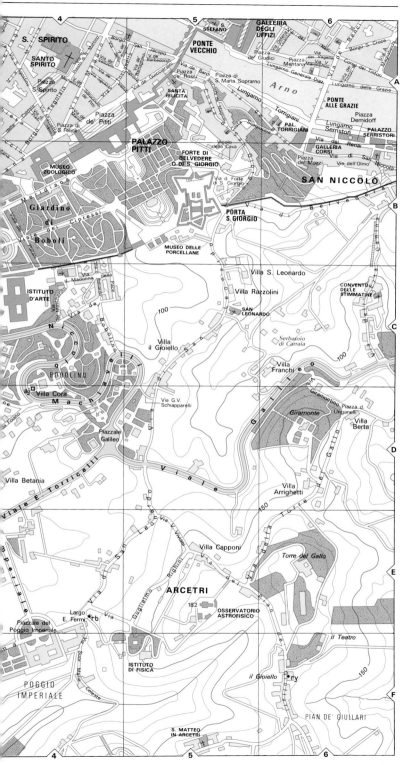

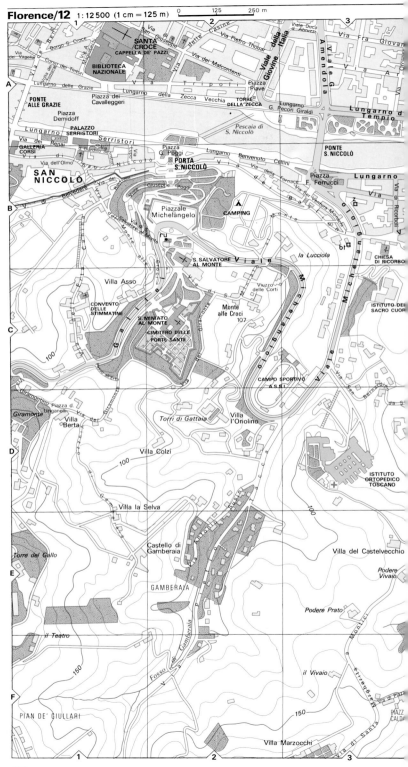

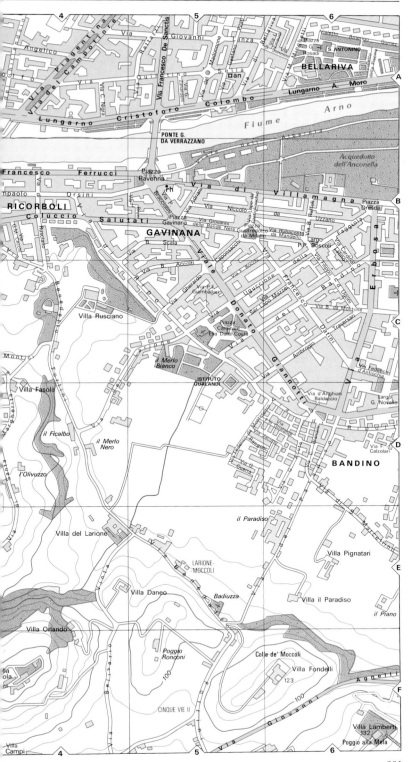

201

"Easy Italy" Coupons

This guidebook comes with a number of coupons that will give the reader excellent services at low prices.

Hertz
The voucher will give the reader a discount of 15 dollars on any car rental in Italy (minimum five days).

Hotel Forte Agip
This coupon gives a 10 percent discount on room prices in all Forte Agip hotels, the latest addition to Forte's collection of international hotels, present in 17 cities in Italy.

Accor Hotels
The hotels in the four chains - Ibis (economy class); Mercure (first class); Novotel (first class); Sofitel (up-scale), with a total of 19 hotels in the largest cities of Italy - offer a discount of 30 percent to those who spend a weekend in any hotel in the chain. Special welcome for families: accommodations and breakfast are free for children under 16 sharing parents' room (except Ibis).

Autogrill
The largest chain of self-service restaurants on the Italian highway system offers a discount of 20 percent on a maximum of three meals, to be eaten together.

- Call your local Hertz office for reservations.

- This coupon should be delivered to Hertz staff prior to the commencement of your rental.

- This coupon is not exchangeable for cash, it is not transferable and cannot be combined with any other promotional offer.

Hertz rents Ford and other fine cars.

SAVE 10%

On hotel accommodation in Italy

VALID 1/1/97 - 31/12/97

FORTE
Agip
HOTELS

- This voucher entitles you to 15 dollars (or equivalent in Italian currency) off your next rental in Italy.

- This offer is available when booking at Hertz leisure tariffs (except prepaid), for a minimum rental of 5 days, in Italy.

- Advance reservation is required.

- Offer expires: *Dec. 31, 1997*

COUPON FOR $ 15 (US) OFF

 our first choice in Italy

Forte Agip Hotels are the latest addition to Forte's collection of international hotels; they provide good quality accommodation at exceptional value for money. Conveniently located on the major access roads to the principal cities, Forte Agip Hotels are easy to find and ideal for both the business and leisure traveller.

 erms and conditions

This coupon entitles you to a 10% discount off the published room rate in the Forte Agip Hotels in Italy; every day of the week including weekends. The period of validity is 1st January 1997 - 31 December 1997.
The discount is for one room only per total stay, it is subject to availability and is exclusive of any other offer or discount.

 ow to book

For further information and reservations when travelling in Italy call toll free 167-820088

Forte Agip Hotels are present in 16 locations:
Bologna, Cagliari, Catania, Florence, Livorno, Milan Assago, Modena, Palermo, Rome, Sarzana, Siracusa, Turin, Trieste, Venice, Verona, Vicenza.

ECONOMY CLASS HOTELS   FIRST CLASS HOTELS   FIRST CLASS HOTELS   UP SCALE HOTELS

Try one of the Accor Hotels in Italy for a Week-End at

DISCOUNT

VALID 31/12/1997

Special welcome for families...

the accomodation and breakfast are free
for children under 16 years sharing parent's room
(except for Ibis Hotels)

MORE THAN 2400 HOTELS IN THE WORLD *L'esprit* **ACCOR**

20% DISCOUNT COUPON
FOR THE SELF SERVICE RESTAURANTS
ON THE ITALIAN HIGHWAY SYSTEM

OF **▲ AUTOGRILL**®

BUONO SCONTO 20%

NEI RISTORANTI SELF SERVICE AUTOSTRADALI IN ITALIA

DI **▲ AUTOGRILL**®

he Ambrosiana Foundation for Art and Culture
s a non-profit organization whose purpose is to
xhibit superb collections of the most important
0th Century artists throughout Italy:

Salvador Dalí - Pablo Picasso - Marc Chagall

"Dalí Sculptor
Dalí Illustrator"

Permanent Exhibition
Piazza Santa Croce, 12
Florence

Daily : 10 a.m. to 7 p.m.
Closed Mondays
Entrance fee: L. 10.000
Reduced fee: L. 6.000

Dalí sculpture
" Alice in Wonderland"

Toros y Toreros
Goya, Picasso, Dalí"

0 March - 3 November
stituto degli Innocenti
?iazza SS. Annunziata - Florence
)aily from 10 a.m. to 7 p.m.
:losed Mondays
ntrance fee: L. 10.000
?educed fee: L. 6.000

Pablo Picasso "Tauromaquia"

"Chagall e les Livres"
6 July - 3 November

Piazza Santa Croce, 8 - Florence

Daily from 10 a.m. to 7 p.m.
Closed Mondays
Entrance fee: L. 10.000
Reduced fee: L. 6.000

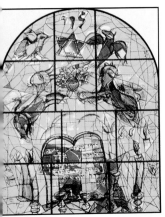

Marc Chagall
The Jerusalem stained glass windows

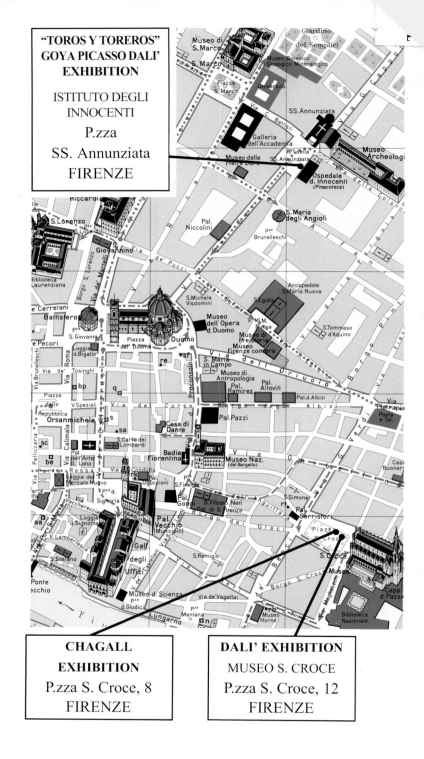

"TOROS Y TOREROS"
GOYA PICASSO DALI'
EXHIBITION

ISTITUTO DEGLI
INNOCENTI

P.zza

SS. Annunziata

FIRENZE

CHAGALL

EXHIBITION

P.zza S. Croce, 8
FIRENZE

DALI' EXHIBITION

MUSEO S. CROCE

P.zza S. Croce, 12

FIRENZE

Fondazione Ambrosiana Arte & Cultura
20147 Milano - Italy - Via G. Canella , 4 - Tel: (39 2) 483251 Fax (39 2) 41231